DOCTOR SPOCK
Biography
of a
Conservative
Radical

Lynn Z. Bloom

DOCTOR
SPOCK
Biography
of a
Conservative
Radical

The Bobbs–Merrill Company, Inc.
Indianapolis/New York

The Bobbs-Merrill Company, Inc.
Indianapolis • New York

Copyright © 1972 by Lynn Z. Bloom
All rights reserved
Library of Congress Catalogue Card Number: 78-173209
Designed by Nancy Dale Muldoon
Manufactured in the United States of America
Second printing

To MARTIN BARD LAIRD
who made
" trust yourself "
a reality

ACKNOWLEDGMENTS

MY deepest thanks go to Dr. Benjamin Spock; the members of his immediate family, Jane, Michael, John, and Judy; his mother, the late Mrs. Mildred Spock; three sisters, Marjorie Spock, Elizabeth Spock Brucker (Mrs. Herbert), Sarah Spock Jordy (Mrs. William); two cousins, Gertrude Hooper and Olivia Ross; and a second cousin, James T. Evans, Jr. Dr. Spock's brother, Robert, was also accessible for consultation, but because of his geographical remoteness I was unable to see him. With kindness and courtesy the family provided countless letters, documents, photographs, home movies, and memorabilia, much of it never before used for publication. They were available for interviews not once but many times, as often as was necessary; they explained, clarified, amplified whatever I needed to know. Dr. Spock's cordial hospitality, and willingness to discuss the trivial as well as the significant, the evanescent as well as the permanent, to fill in gaps, to communicate as honestly and fully as he could, during five years of his own incessantly demanding schedule, have been a biographer's delight.

The numerous, extensive interviews with persons other than the Spock family are also highly significant throughout the biography. I am greatly indebted to the following people for sharing their information, expertise, perspectives; for re-creating the past with depth and feeling; for providing good will and cooperation throughout the writing of this book: Donna Allen, Ann Andrews, Marian Barnes, M.S.W., Mary Bergen, M.S.W., Hiram Bingham, Sylvia Bingham (Mrs. Alfred), Douglas Bond, M.D., Kay Peabody Brewster, Phyllis Brody, M.S.W. (Mrs. Ralph), Henry Brosin, M.D., Sey Chassler, Jane Clark (Mrs. Robert), the Reverend William Sloane Coffin, Jr., Henry Cooper, Elizabeth Cramer (Mrs. C. H.), Joseph Cramer, M.D., Natalie and James Diener, Alta Dietz, R.N., Charles Duell, George Dyer, Ph.D., Emily Ebert (Mrs. Robert), W. Caldwell Esselstyn, M.D., Michael Ferber, Rennie Ferber (Mrs. Kelvin), Patricia Foote (Mrs. Harry), William Foote, Robert Frymier, M.D., Pearl and David Goldthwait, M.D., Mitchell Goodman, Sanford Gottlieb, Bruce Gould, T. Hale Ham, M.D., Joyce Hartman (Mrs. Daniel), Mildred Hathaway, Ph.D., William Heroy, M.D., H. Stuart Hughes, Ph.D., Frances L. Ilg, M.D., Rose Jackson (Mrs. John Day), Jane Jenkins, R.N., Anny Katan, M.D. (Mrs. Mauritz), John Kennell, M.D., Jane Kessler, Ph.D. (Mrs. Morris), Donald Keys, Rosi Kuerti, Ph.D. (Mrs. Gustav), Douglas Lenkoski, M.D., Joan and Theodore Lettvin, Mary and the late William Lescaze, Denise Levertov (Mrs. Mitchell Goodman), Freeman Lewis, Jerome Liebman, M.D., Margaret and Vernon Lippard, M.D., Florence Marcus, M.D., Katie Marshall (Mrs. Edward), Margarita and Ake Mattsson, M.D., Mary McCaw, Julia McDill (Mrs. John), Margaret McFarland, Ph.D., I. Arthur Mirsky, M.D., Elizabeth and Dan T. Moore, mothers of nursery school children at Arsenal Family and Children's Center, Pittsburgh, Norma Nero (Mrs. Richard), Paul Olynyk, Ph.D., parents of children in the Child Rearing Study, Case Western Reserve University, Sidney Peck, Ph.D., Ann Carolyn and Hector Prud'homme, Barbara and Marcus Raskin, John Reinhart, M.D., Janet Rosenberg, M.S.W. and Marvin Rosenberg, Ph.D., Edwin Roth, M.D., Marie Runyon, Janet Sax, M.D., Susan Scherer (Mrs. Robert), Bayard Schieffelin, Milton J. E. Senn, M.D., Grace G. Smith, M.A. and Randolph Smith,

Ph.D., William Spaulding, Samuel Spector, M.D., Claire Staples, Robert Stein, Brigita Streeter, M.D., Henrietta Thacher, the late Norman Thomas, Mrs. Paul Twichell, the late William Wallace, M.D., Cynthia Weir, M.S.W. and William Weir, M.D., Israel Weisberg, M.D., Eleanor Weisberger, M.S.W. (Mrs. Austin), Jane and Jerry Weiss, Mrs. Freddie Williams, Fefa and Alfred Wilson, Dagmar Wilson, Lois Woodyatt.

The following people and institutions have most graciously supplied professional advice, documents, photographs, or tours of houses or facilities where Dr. Spock lived, worked, or vacationed: American Society for Metals, Elliott Arnold, Gregory Bateson, Rose Bloom (Mrs. Edward), Leonard Boudin, Brearley School, Kingman Brewster, Jr., Butler University Library, Case Western Reserve University Libraries, Jo Ann Chittick (Mrs. S. W.), Cleveland Heights Public Library, Cleveland Public Library, Helen Cowley, R.N., M. Cronin family, F. E. Erlandson family, Joseph Flora, Ph.D., Irja Friend, Paul Goodman, Jerry Gordon, Hamden Hall, Fenno Heath family, Hubert H. Humphrey, Indianapolis Public Library, David Lyle, Darlis Martin, Mayo Clinic Library, New Haven Colony Historical Society, Quisset Harbor House, Lee Reidy, R.N,, Irving Rosenbaum, M.D., Sohi Sabet-Sharghi (Mrs. Zabih), SANE, Joseph Sax, Peter Schwed, Anson Smith, Parker Snead, I. F. Stone, Edmund Trent family, Thomas Wittenberg, John Wood, Yale University Libraries, Mildred and O. T. Zimmerman, Mitchell Zimmerman. Bob Stalcup generously contributed publicity photographs.

The nurturing of this book, like the rearing of a young child, has been largely a private matter, absorbing the biographer's energies and time, points of view, sense of values, and qualities of mind. Yet, as a child should not be raised in virtual isolation, so the manuscript has, in its several drafts, been aided immeasurably in its progress toward maturity by the perspicacious reading and careful attention to accuracy, organization, and style of: Shirl Ann Matthysse (Mrs. William), Fifi and James Norton, Ph.D., Richard Teleky, Ph.D., Helen and Howard Webber. To William H. Y. Hackett, Bobbs-Merrill vice president, editor Elizabeth Kelly, and Mary Judge I am grateful for unfailing enthusiasm, astute suggestions, and various courtesies extended while the book was being edited and published. I have been blessed with the liberation, and the liberty, that come of being married to Martin Bloom, not only agreeable to subsidizing such an extensive undertaking financially, but wholeheartedly willing to share his professional expertise (social psychology), literary and philosophical acumen, and our domestic responsibilities. To him, my most profound appreciation for this life.

L.Z.B.
Indianapolis, Indiana
March 1972

PERMISSIONS

xi

CONTENTS

FOREWORD

"**O**UR lives are made up of selected fictions," says the cynically philosophical Pursewarden in Lawrence Durrell's *Balthazar,* and as I researched and wrote my doctoral dissertation on literary biography[1] I had regretfully concluded that so, indeed, were many biographies. My major conviction was then, as it is now, that biography must first and foremost represent the truth.

But what is the "truth" about a human being? Himself as he appears to himself? To his close friends or relatives? To his fellow professionals or associates in the community? To his enemies? To a dispassionate—or biased—observer or analyst who through biography provides an interpretation (which by definition is "selective")?

Does the "truth" about a person emerge through his writings, works, and deeds, consciously or unintentionally? Does fidelity to fact always capture the truth of the heart, the essence of the spirit, which may be the ultimate reality? Is the "truth" altered by the distance of geography,

time, or imagination; the change of philosophies or shift of interests; or the alteration of cultures or other milieus? (Lord Byron,
for instance, blackguard libertine to Victorian Harriet Beecher
Stowe, in more recent times is seen as an engagingly unconventional
political libertarian.)

Ultimately, one man's truth is another man's fiction—and vice
versa. The prism of memory filters the cold light of reality, breaks
it up into its component colors, distorts and beautifies as it sends
out flashing rays—essential, felt "truths" which may well be
"selected fictions"—to illuminate the darkness that is past, the
darkness that will come.

It was with these considerations in mind and the conviction that
a critic of biography (or any medium) ought to gain the humility of
understanding through practicing what he preaches that I decided
to learn through firsthand experience whether it was possible to
capture the truth of a man through biography. Aware of biographer
Mark Schorer's observation that "a prominent man is in many
ways a mythological man," in the fall of 1966 I asked Dr. Spock,
then on the verge of retirement, if I might write his biography. He
seemed, from my viewpoint, a natural and congenial choice of subject: both of us were on the faculty of Case Western Reserve University (I in the English Department); we lived about a mile apart
in Cleveland Heights and knew many of the same people, though at
the outset, each other not at all; and, importantly, my husband and
I, like eighteen million other American families, were enthusiastically rearing our two sons, then four and two, according to *Baby and
Child Care*. Other affinities later became apparent. Both Dr. Spock
and I, the oldest children of several in professional middle class
families, are New Englanders and bring independence of mind and
a strongly moralistic heritage to bear on many facets of our professional and personal lives. Both of us are conservatives in behavior, dress, mode of living; and liberals in thought, though Dr.
Spock is more radical in political advocacy and action than I. I believe that this closeness has permitted a greater latitude and depth
of understanding than would have otherwise been possible, but
I do not think it has produced a sympathetic distortion of perspective to blot out objectivity and the very truth which I have sought.

I have tried throughout to act upon my belief that the biographer
of a living subject must be ever sympathetic, but never a sycophant.

The significant dissimilarities between myself and my subject have helped to make this possible. One of the crucial differences helps to explain why Dr. Spock, an accomplished writer himself, would willingly cooperate with a biographer instead of writing his own full-length autobiography. As we will see, Dr. Spock's professional style is pragmatic, impressionistic, anecdotal. He was not eager to undertake the time-consuming, painstaking labor over mountains of documents, masses of research details needed to shore up the mansion of memory that is obligatory for the writer of a full-length, multidimensional biography. I was.

Furthermore, in 1966 Dr. Spock was immersed in the third draft of his spiritual autobiography, *Decent and Indecent,* and committed to revising *Baby and Child Care* and to writing a book of advice for teenagers, in addition to his monthly *Redbook* column. These undertakings, on top of his medical school duties and efforts in the peace movement that at times have exhausted this biographer in trying to keep up with them, left him no time for additional projects. So he good-naturedly agreed to cooperate.

My previous research in biography had made me skeptical of the secondhand, the hearsay, the speculations of which so many biographies are constructed, and I resolved to derive as much as possible from primary sources. In fact, it was a necessity, for there were no other biographies of Spock. I therefore sought the "solidity of specification" through interviews; letters, Spock's writings, and other original documents; visits to where he lived, worked, vacationed; absorption in his medical, intellectual, political, personal milieus. Throughout 1966–67 I spent one afternoon a week with either Jane or Ben, tape-recording the interviews, perusing family photographs. Donning a white coat, I followed the physician about the hospital, to lectures and clinics. The ubiquitous tape recorder, notebook, and I were present at cocktail parties, peace rallies, the Child Rearing Study playgroup, the skating rink, testimonial dinners.

The biographer's bane is the telephone, for conversations are gone with the wind. I was fortunate to have a letter-writer for a subject, and spent long hours, many evenings and weekends, in Dr. Spock's office reading all the documents, recording many. Not knowing what I might find, I examined everything—not only letters, but books, pamphlets, lecture notes, contracts, canceled checks, boat blueprints. Only about 2 percent of these are visible in the biography, though the other 98 percent have formed a solid substructure which I am convinced is a necessity in any biography which attempts to convey the essence of the subject in his milieus. Such is this biographer's compulsivity that even if I had known in advance which 2 percent I would use, I probably would have studied everything anyway; once, over lunch, Dr. Spock asked, "Well, have you had enough?" (meaning "to eat?") and I replied, automatically, "No biographer *ever* has enough!" The mosaic pieces that were to become the man began to emerge; the myth of Spock the Superman, the Superdoctor, to recede.

When Dr. Spock left Cleveland in June '67 I quit teaching in order to devote full time[2] to the biography—and to my family. After all, as a devotee of *Baby and Child Care* I could scarcely say to my small sons, "Go away, don't bother me, I'm busy writing about Dr. Spock." I learned to work accommodating carpools, nursery school schedules, and other aspects of middle class maternity, often with my children and their friends and their toys literally underfoot, in our booklined bedroom that doubled as a study.

Much of the work—fun, really—went on in the "outer world" as I gathered auxiliary material. Perhaps fitting for a pediatrician, certainly indicative of his interests, Dr. Spock's own recollections focus most amply on his childhood and early adolescence. For the remainder of his life corollary materials, particularly many interviews, were necessary to flesh out the skeleton subject and place it in its appropriate contexts. Dr. Spock supplied me with a letter of introduction to anyone I wished to interview, friend and foe alike. Only one person, a close relative, refused to see me, claiming that the memories of her childhood were too painful to re-create for publication. The other interviewees received me with the same gracious cordiality that characterized my subject: in doctors' and publishers' offices; in schools, homes, and restaurants; on planes; behind the scenes at peace meetings and the trial; by motorboat at Honnedaga Lake; even in Sally Spock Jordy's swimming pool! From albums emerged photographs; from strongboxes and heirloom chests, letters, genealogies, receipts, and other documents; from memories, vital anecdotes, impressions, details, interpretations; from professionals, expert knowledge and assessments of Spock's works and accomplishments. These points of view have been invaluable. Only a few persons were less than wholly candid in an effort to protect what they considered the sanctity of the Spocks' private life; a very few lied to protect their own images.

Then came the actual writing, which posed a number of issues relevant to the art of biography in general, in particular to the matters dealing with a living, highly active subject. For Spock's life, though its major outlines seem to be determined, is still in the process of change and flux. The Spock of 1961 (before SANE) is not entirely the Spock of 1967 (the year that led to his indictment) nor the Spock of today.

A true, total portrait of Dr. Spock was my goal, yet whose truth, what truths, had to be defined in the process of the writing. Ultimately I decided that "whose truth" had to be my truth, the biographer's, for I was the only person to whom all the information, all the points of view (some kept confidential from Spock for decades) had been available. Dr. Spock, at his request, has read and commented on the manuscript, but the final decisions, interpretations, and responsibilities have been mine.

If conflicting information was obtained from equally reliable informants, then how could I decide who was right? Corroborative evidence often helped; when it was not available I chose to take the word of the most objective informant, the person with the fewest vested interests. When I still could not decide, or when divergent interpretations or points of view seemed equally valid and significant, I have included the alternatives.

From the moment I started writing I had to choose between the literal truth and the artistic representation of truth. My doctoral training had left me with an abhorrence of the conjecture on one page that metamorphoses into an assertion of indubitable fact on the next, the invented dialogue, the imaginary scene, the sneering or salacious innuendo in the rhetorical question. The biography could contain no lie, no invention; everything had to be capable of documentation. Even the fictions of memory can become "truth" if documented.

Yet a biography of Dr. Spock, much of whose works and impact rested on his advice and appeal to a general audience, had to be written for many of that same audience, readers more likely to be interested in a zestful, interpretive narrative than in a plodding, day-by-day account replete with every available fact and figure; readers impatient with the scholar's paraphernalia of footnotes and fine print. So, although I have tried to quote faithfully from printed documents and letters (except, for the correspondents' protection, to alter names and some revealing information in letters and conversations discussing serious personal problems), I have generally omitted footnotes.

In the interests of speeding the narrative pace, from the myriads of redundant or overlapping documents I have tried to select the typical, the relevant, the significant, the bizarre, the colorful. For instance, using these criteria, over four thousand letters from people with personal problems were represented in but six pages of the typescript. I have tried to maintain the appropriate balance and proportion of each item, each fact, in relation to its ultimate significance in the subject's life. Sometimes, therefore, a single, small detail ("With evening clothes Dr. Spock wears celluloid collars") may count as much as twenty repetitive anecdotes or a hundred letters on a given subject. At other times, as with the trial, a month of a lifetime warrants an entire chapter.

In accommodating the many hundreds of hours of interviews, artistry has also taken precedence over literal truth. It has had to, in order to attain the truthful essence. The bulk of conversation, even among highly educated people accustomed to lecturing publicly, is extraordinarily redundant. Yet, paradoxically, it is highly discursive. To reach a given conversational destination is like following a dog's trail through the snow; it proceeds randomly, circles around, doubles back on itself, heads off in a variety of directions—and may or may not end up where it intended to go. Though the side jaunts may be serendipitous, such conversations are chaotic, repetitive, and virtually unintelligible when transcribed verbatim. In many instances, therefore, I have reorganized the interviews logically and topically and have drastically pruned the conversational underbrush to enable a vigorous, well-shaped subject to emerge. Except in the case of a few previously printed interviews, I have not used ellipses to indicate these alterations for . . . frequent ellipses give the impression either of halting . . . stuttering speech or of significant . . . innuendoes. Both impressions would have been false; my informants were, to a man, highly articulate, and I was sometimes startled by their candor.

A perplexing problem for the conscientious biographer in pursuit of the truth of a living subject is how to treat his private life. This is not necessarily a matter of how many family skeletons to rattle or which keyholes to peep through, but often simply of whether to emphasize the public or the private side of the subject's existence. No uniform answer can be given, so varied are people's lives. In Spock's case, I decided to focus on those aspects of his life for which he is best known and in which popular interest has been the greatest —those related to *Baby and Child Care* and to his involvement in the peace movement. Except for his childhood, his public life has been far more significant, unusual, interesting—and controversial—than has his personal, private life. His humanness comes out as fully in the humanity of his profession and his avocation as it might in another subject's boudoir.

Furthermore, both Ben and Jane are very reticent about personal matters, either physical or psychic, and they are protective of their sons' privacy, though Mike and John are themselves much less reserved. Because my relationship with the Spocks has always been that of biographer to subject, cordial but professional, they may understandably be guarded in my presence, for they know that what I know may well appear in print. Yet a professional relationship with one's biographical subject permits as its compensation attendant latitude for objectivity and for enabling the total portrait to emerge from the minutiae. This is in most cases preferable to too intimate an association ("God save us from the biographies of widows and children," one critic has lamented) which promotes vested interests or in which protectiveness or fond adoration, like plastic surgery, removes the subject's warts and wrinkles—and character—and instead presents to the world a bland, unblemished mask.

But when, to the reader, it seems as if the true man has been revealed, rather than a mask depicted, the biography is given what is deemed the highest praise. It is called "definitive," as if to imply that the biographer's interpretations and artistic re-creations— "selected fictions," if you will—have conveyed all that is worth saying and that no other definition will ever be needed. In that sense no biography is ever definitive. Yet every biography is a definition. The influence and life of a person, whether significant for his accomplishments or simply because he existed, warrant assessment by various contemporaries, cultures, nationalities; and reassessment, redefinition by succeeding generations, each according to their own biases, orientations. It is the sum of these definitions—a continuing process, a changing calculus—that forms the living truth, the "selected fiction" of the subject of biography.

PROLOGUE

WHEN Dr. Spock was in his office at Western Reserve University the door was always open, from hospitality and from, he says, "a slightly claustrophobic dislike of being closed into one small, silent, stuffy room." To be sure, he was shielded from traffic in the hospital corridor by a filing cabinet and a partly folded screen, but the barrier was only visual. Anybody could come in, and many did: professional colleagues, medical students, visiting doctors from around the world, occasional troubled parents and children, secretaries, maintenance men, interviewers, peace people.

At the approach of a visitor, Dr. Spock would thrust himself forward, beaming, from behind his large, slightly battered walnut desk piled with letters, peace pamphlets, the *New York Times*, and boat blueprints. "Why, hel-loo," he'd exclaim, laughing, conveying by his delighted manner and firm handshake the impression that the caller, no matter who he was, was the very person Dr. Spock had been hoping to see. This routine was repeated so many times each day that Spock rarely accomplished any writing or class preparation at his office. Yet except for people trying to exploit him for commercial gain, Dr. Spock was genuinely receptive to most visitors.

He'd offer the caller a chair, even his own high-backed swivel chair if one needed to write at the desk. His six-foot-four-inch height shrank the twelve- by twenty-foot office lined with bookshelves, two whole rows filled with foreign translations of *Baby and Child Care*. Invariably clad in an impeccably tailored, carefully pressed dark suit with a buttoned vest and high starched collar held in place by collar pin and collar button, he looks the very model of the genteel turn-of-the-century Ivy League aristocrat, which by birth and background he is. But when he speaks, in his colorful, emphatic Connecticut-Yankee twang, the old-fashioned starchiness of his appearance vanishes because of his animation.

For Dr. Spock speaks not only with his voice, but with his hands, his body, his feelings. As he discusses babies, beneath the grandfather's ruddy, faintly mottled skin emerges the disgusted pout of an infant refusing another spoonful of spinach. Spock has become the baby, the very child anatomized in *Baby and Child Care*.

As he demonstrates a crew stroke, leaning in his chair as far forward as he can, then as far back, forward and back, gritting his teeth and straining his still muscular 184-pound frame, he becomes again the twenty-year-old Yale junior whose team rowed to an Olympic victory. He completes the performance with a characteristically hearty laugh—of fondness for the pleasure the sport once gave him, of recognition of his ludicrously uncomfortable posture in "the only sport played sitting down and going backwards."

Or, as he illustrates an address given by former Secretary of State Dean Rusk to a meeting of the National Advisory Council of the Office of Economic Opportunity in 1964 when Spock was a member, the officious, somewhat threatened demeanor of Rusk reappears memorably, pounding the lectern and hissing, "Communist nations have *ap*-petite. They have *appetite!*"

Only when Dr. Spock talks about the Indochina war, world peace and, most recently, national as well as international ills (like many a crusader, he cannot bear to be away from his cause for more than ten consecutive sentences) does his manner change. Gone are the easy affability, the frame-shaking laugh that punctuates his other remarks, particularly when they are self-critical. Gone is the relaxed demeanor that puts visitors so at ease they soon forget they are in the presence of a famous man. Instead there emerges Dr. Spock, the self-styled moralist of a nation that accepted his morality as it pertained to the rearing of generations of infants, but tried and convicted him (for a time) as a criminal when he attempted to apply that morality to international politics. Dr. Spock the moralist is earnest, sober, uncompromising; Dr. Spock the moralist is worried; Dr. Spock the moralist is radical—but conservatively. As his voice drops in despair, rises in anger, the youthfulness that permeates his being when he talks about children or relives his own youth is replaced by the old age he assumed when he undertook the role of patriarch. For his cause he has given much: money, reputation, a fair measure of his unquenchable energy, the repose to which retirement from a career as teacher and parental advisor might have entitled him were it not for his conscience. But though he has given, he has not given up—neither the cause nor the enjoyments of life which made it possible for him to espouse the cause so wholeheartedly.

Said Virginia Woolf, novelist and character analyst par excellence, "A biography is considered complete if it merely accounts for six or seven selves, whereas a person may well have as many thousand." Dr. Spock has revealed several of his selves in the narrative that follows; his voice, his laugh, his animation provide an obbligato to the written words. Yet the several selves of the public person are only some of the multiple selves that make up the complex character and personality of the man Benjamin Spock. Other selves are represented through the perspectives of Spock's wife, his two sons, his close friends, his sisters, his publishers, his colleagues in medicine and in the peace movement, his students, his antagonists. But who can know another wholly? Do these selves, in sum, make up the whole man? It is the task of biography to undertake this reconstruction.

**DOCTOR
SPOCK**
Biography
of a
Conservative
Radical

one

THE BABY- AND CHILDHOOD OF DR. SPOCK

BENJAMIN McLane Spock was indeed a Spock baby—and then again, he wasn't. Some of his mother's firm ideas on child rearing so strongly affected his character that he incorporated them without change into *Baby and Child Care,* while he rejected others entirely.

When the book was published, Dr. Spock showed it with some trepidation to his mother, nearing seventy, and was much relieved when she finally pronounced, "Why, Benny, it's really quite sensible." During her many years of mothering she would never have needed his famous opening dictum: "Trust yourself. You know more than you think you do." For she did trust herself, absolutely.

She assumed she knew as much about child rearing as anyone else who might have offered advice on the care and feeding of her six children; she was dubious of doctors and preferred to rely on her own medical judgment. On one occasion she compared her children's symptoms with those described in her favorite home doctor book, concluded that the children had malaria, took them to the local doctor in New Haven, and demanded treatment. The physician skeptically pointed out that malaria was by then a tropical disease, for it had been virtually eliminated in such temperate climates as Connecticut's. Undaunted, Mrs. Spock marched her brood to a lab for a blood test and found her diagnosis confirmed. When her eldest son graduated from medical school, she gave him her "malaria book," with congratulations.

The motto of many of Dr. Spock's ancestors might well have been "Trust Yourself," whether uttered in Old English, Elizabethan dialect, or Boston twang. For generations during the Middle Ages and early Renaissance, his mother's family had been solid English citizens, yeomen, and landed gentry. But a number of them eventually became religious or political dissidents and defended their views forthrightly. Some protested; at least one was martyred for his outspokenness. John Hooper of Somersetshire, a religious reformer, was burned at the stake in 1555 after refusing to retract his statements (unspecified in the family chronicles) about the English Reformation. Others emigrated to preserve the integrity of their principles, arriving in the Massachusetts Bay Colony only fifteen years after the first settlers. One, Samuel Wardwell, became the victim of the Puritan rule he had sought to establish and was executed for witchcraft in 1692. At least four others defended their beliefs by force of arms as colonial officers in the Revolutionary War, and another defiant spirit, William Hooper of North Carolina, signed the Declaration of Independence.

Dr. Spock's New England forebears have been described, in words that characterize the physician himself, as "ambitious, strong-minded, and self-reliant . . . possessed of keen mental faculty and initiative." Among the most independent was Spock's maternal great-grandfather, Robert Chamblett Hooper. He entered Harvard at thirteen, dropped out at fifteen to go to sea, and had traveled the world as a merchant captain before he was twenty-one. Hooper eventually returned to Boston, bought and managed several wharves and marine businesses there, and married Adeline Ripley, daughter of General James Wolfe Ripley (labeled as "truth and duty incarnate") of Springfield. He died in 1869, at sixty-four, popular and prosperous.

Captain Hooper's daughter, Ada Ripley Hooper, began the stern matriarchal dynasty into which Benjamin Spock was born. Throughout her long life she was graceful and erect and her dress was elegant. But whereas the conventional Victorian beauty was dimpled, slightly pudgy, demure, and dependent, Ada was angularly handsome, outspoken, and independent. In 1869, when she was twenty-two, she married Charles Bradley Stoughton, a match which should have been auspicious. Stoughton was a Civil War hero who at twenty-four had been the youngest Brigadier General ever appointed in the Vermont Brigade of the Sixth Army Corps. His family was socially and politically prominent; his uncle, Edwin Stoughton, later became Minister to Russia, and his father, Henry, was a successful New York patent attorney. Stoughton was attractive—a suave, moustached, flirtatious man of the world whose dandyish garb habitually included a gay bowler and a rakish black eyepatch which concealed a Civil War wound. Charles took his wife to New York, where they lived for ten years while he practiced law in his father's firm. Five of their six children were born there: Ada (1870), Laura (1872), Leila (1875), Mildred, Spock's mother (1876), and their only son, Bradley (1873). Bradley later became a renowned metallurgical engineer and wrote a classic college textbook on the subject.

As time went on, Charles began to take frequent out-of-town trips, and to drink too much. He finally broke away from his father and moved his practice of admiralty law to New Haven, Connecticut. Its population was 80,000 and growing, as immigrants came from Ireland, Germany, Italy, and eastern Europe to work in the factories producing hardware, guns, clocks, corsets, and rubber goods. Yet New Haven's most notable enterprise was then, as it is today, Yale University, which provided the focal point of the city's geography, its intellectual life, and to an extent, its economy. Though town and campus blended architecturally, arched by elms, supported by Grecian columns and Georgian brickwork on old colonial underpinnings, they did not always blend temperamentally, and did battle at intervals.

The Stoughtons settled within walking distance of Yale, at 129

Whitney Avenue. Then Charles sought independence from his wife. In pursuit of women and wine he disappeared for periods of time which became longer and longer, though he did return and father a last child, Isabelle (born 1881). Ada continued to adore her husband long after he had ceased to play any role in his family except that of a shadowy, peripatetic figure, but even her devotion had its limits. Though the children endowed their father with a certain romance, Ada eventually came to despise him so much that she refused to see him even when he was dying.

With Charles gone, Ada's hair turned prematurely white. She moved her family to a gloomy, gingerbread-encrusted house at the top of socially elite Prospect Hill, where she lived a life of not-quite-shabby gentility amidst heirlooms and castoffs of three and four generations. Ada provided for her family largely through discreet doles from her Boston relatives and the earnings of daughters Ada and Leila, who conducted classes in dancing and gymnastics. Yet she always managed to afford two Irish maids, paid at the going rate of three dollars a week, who lived in the attic, cooked in the cellar, cleaned all the rooms in between, and did the voluminous laundry.

Some outsiders saw Ada Stoughton as "formal, correct, elegant, and charming." Others found her "lively and entertaining," with a delightful sense of humor. Still another remembers her as an "indefatigable jam and jelly maker." All agree on her complete moral integrity.

But for her children she had no charm and little humor; they found her cold, harsh, and rigid. Complaining that she had never wanted children, she encouraged in her six offspring her own independent, self-reliant spirit by obliging them to put on their coats and high-buttoned boots without help and by making them read to themselves as soon as they could.

Nevertheless, she tried to subdue their independence when it was directed against her own authority. If the children ever dared to question her request she snapped, "I want it. Don't ask why." If they were impolite, as when one daughter asked a guest how long he was going to stay, she sent them to bed for the day. For other infractions, said her daughter Mildred, she "beat them with a rawhide whip, or locked them in little closets."

Even by the standards of an era in which harsh punishment of children was common, Ada Stoughton's discipline was severe. On one occasion she locked an erring daughter in a closet, went to Hartford for the day, and returned to find the child babbling, temporarily crazed from her ordeal. (These disciplinary methods were such a part of the heritage of Ada's children that Dr. Spock's sister Sally remembers being the victim of an identical punishment when their own mother, Ada's daughter, locked her in a dark closet and went away for the day—in the definitely un-Victorian year of 1925.)

Dr. Spock himself views his grandmother's repressiveness with tolerance born of psychological and historical hindsight: "A child psychologist would be certain that the children, since they turned out well, not only felt their father's affection but must have recognized their mother's devotion and even love under her harsh exterior. If she had been basically cold and unloving they would have turned delinquent. She and others at that time had no hesitation in releasing their angry feelings on their children. It's the style, not the substance, which has changed greatly." Yet through *Baby and Child Care* Dr. Spock has been more influential in changing both the style and the substance of child discipline than any other American parent educator in the twentieth century. Among other things, his book stands as a most vigorous rebuttal to Grandmother Stoughton.

Even Ada, who insisted on absolute control, couldn't control everything. Her eldest child died at twenty-one of typhoid fever. The most vivacious, Laura, bore an illegitimate child, which her brother raised until she married some years later. Bradley and Mildred, against their mother's wishes, visited their father in an old soldiers' home in Brattleboro, Vermont shortly before his death from tuberculosis in January 1898. And Mildred, in flashing-eyed beauty and temperament most like her mother, decided to marry a tall, slender, soft-spoken lawyer, Benjamin Ives Spock.

Ada objected to the engagement because she felt Spock's family wasn't good enough for her daughter. His father, William Henry Harrison Spock, was an unsuccessful carriage maker, and later circulation manager of the *New Haven Register*. His grandfather, Stephen Spock of Newark, New Jersey, had worked for a hat manufacturer and had served his employer's tour of duty in the War of 1812. His great-grandfather, John Spock, and great-great-grandfather, James Spock, had been flour millers in VanCourtlandtville, New York. Although James had fought for the colonists in the Revolutionary War, he had not been an officer, only a private. Earlier family records were lost in Holland, from where the Spocks had come (perhaps the still small fishing village of Spaakenburg?), so who could tell what kind of people they were?

Ada tried to discourage young Mr. Spock, but he persisted in the courting. He had gained in self-assurance when he was an undergraduate at Yale (class of 1885), where, by the social standards of the day, his accomplishments had been most prestigious. He had sung in the Glee Club; joined Delta Kappa Epsilon, one of the "best" junior fraternities; and had been tapped for Wolf's Head, one of the four much-sought senior secret societies. With these qualifications and a law degree, also from Yale (1898), he felt good enough to marry anyone, even a girl as beautiful and as brilliant as he deemed Mildred. Though Mr. Spock was too polite to argue with Ada, he was too enamored to disappear, particularly when Mildred was adoringly encouraging him in open defiance of her mother. So Ada sent for help from her proper Bostonian brother. Will came to New Haven, pink-faced, bald-headed, and fashionably dressed, to discourage Spock—and ended up liking him immensely. Ada capitulated.

Benjamin Ives Spock and Mildred Louisa Stoughton were married on June 30, 1900 and settled at 165 Cold Spring Street, New Haven—just seven blocks from Ada. Their plain, pleasant frame house had a porch across the front, four cherry trees in the backyard, three little bedrooms to accommodate the profusion of children anticipated by proper couples of the time, and a maid's room in the attic. The Spocks had six children in rapid succession, and another later. Their first child, a boy, died at birth. For practical purposes then, Benjamin (after his father) McLane (after his father's wealthy best friend from undergraduate days, Guy McLane), born May 2, 1903, was considered the oldest. Sixteen months later Marjorie ("Hiddy") was born, followed by Betty (1907), Anne (1908), Bob (1912), and Sally (1917).

Mr. Spock was as eager to succeed in his profession as he had been to succeed at college and in winning his bride. But as he matured success no longer meant popularity, parties, or social prestige, but rather professional prestige and a substantial position with a substantial firm. As the new century began, America's future seemed to be riding the rails, and Mr. Spock banked his professional future on the railroads. Since the end of the Civil War the New Haven Railroad had been expanding and incorporating rival lines; the local symbol of its success was the Union Depot, built in 1875, a hybrid of cathedral and music hall architecture. For the New Haven Railroad Mr. Spock worked the standard forty-eight-hour week—nine hours on weekdays and half-days on Saturdays—and eventually attained the position of general counsel. Between 1900 and 1925 his salary rose from $5,000 to $30,000 a year, the latter equivalent in buying power to $125,000 today. Mr. Spock's income and the length of his tenure—nearly his entire professional life—are particularly remarkable because in an industry dominated by robber barons, price fixing, watered stock, forced mergers, and other corrupt business practices, he and his work for the New Haven remained rigorously honest. Yet for all his prominence in the company, Mr. Spock retained throughout his life the modest warmth of his young manhood. So he was beloved not only by his wife, daughters, and friends. but by all who knew him on the railroad, from conductors to the company president. In 1970 Dr. Spock was still getting letters of fond reminiscence from regulars on the New Haven who had known his father forty-five years earlier.

√ Mr. Spock's serene temperament doubtless contributed to the harmony of the household, which his wife ruled with fire, brimstone, and little opposition. "Father was," says his eldest son, "very quiet, like some men are, especially in America. He wasn't namby-pamby, but he very discreetly kept out of a lot of things. However, there was never a cleavage between my parents. I can't imagine my father undermining my mother's discipline."

Betty recalls her father as "someone we had fun with and could relax with. He was the leavening influence on Mother's sternness. We were absolutely certain that Father loved us and that Mother hated us." Sally agrees: "Father always treated me as someone nice; Mother treated me as someone disgusting. Mother was violent and impulsive, throwing scenes and hurting people because even with her tremendous I.Q. she never showed any insight. Father was fair, decent, and devoted. He would come into my bedroom at night and cover me with his bathrobe if it was cold." Hiddy amplifies: "Mother was more persuasive than Father but we liked Father better. He impressed us with his moral standards in such a gentle, kind, warm way that we adored him. I would never have hesitated to lie to my mother, because in an argument she forced us into a corner. But I never lied to my father. Once, when Mother had locked me into my room for lying, Father came in and hugged me, exclaiming sadly, 'Oh, my child, if only I could convince you that the entire world is founded on trust.' "

Mr. Spock read bedtime stories to the children, such as *The Man Without a Country*, and narratives of patriotic heroes for the children to emulate, such as "Peter of Haarlem: The Boy Who Saved His Country," or "David Farragut: The Boy Admiral." His daughters remember him as a sympathetic listener, but his sons found him, "though absolutely just, reserved and often silently disapproving."

Because of Mr. Spock's working hours and the fact that the children had to eat 5:30 supper and be in bed for the night by 6:45, they saw relatively little of their father. But their mother was ever present. Though the family always had a live-in maid (paid fifteen dollars a month) and a laundress, they never had a nurse or a babysitter, for Mrs. Spock entrusted the children to no one but herself. She devoted her entire life to caring for them until the last one was grown, over a span of thirty-three years. With a concern that seems excessive even by the standards of her own time, Mrs. Spock devoted nearly every waking moment to making sure that her children grew up to be wholesome, responsible people who placed the welfare of others before their own.

To attain these goals she herself practiced constantly what she preached. When the other mothers sipped sherry on the front porch while watching their youngsters, Mrs. Spock drank tomato juice. Although she was a crafty bridge player and loved the game, she refused to play cards as long as her children were still living at home. (After they were grown she relaxed and enjoyed regular afternoons of bridge and even an occasional cocktail.) The Spocks rarely went out in the evenings, for Mrs. Spock thought they belonged at home. She never accompanied her husband to New York to attend the opera, which he loved, even though they could have traveled free on a railroad pass. Four times a year they dined at friends' houses, and once every five years they repaid their social obligations with a dinner party for which they prepared months in advance.

Having been convinced by her mother and the example of her unchaste sister Laura that sex was sinful, Mrs. Spock took measures to repress all manifestations of sexuality in herself and in her children. She believed that short hair was much too provocative, so she wore her long, prematurely white hair in a severe bun, rather than in the coquettish curls and ringlets of the prevailing fashion. She wore properly matronly clothes in somber colors; nightgowns which were loose cocoons of thick flannel; and, at the beach, the customary enveloping bathing costume— tank suit, middy blouse, bloomers, and long black stockings. Says Sally, "She never let anyone see her naked in her whole life, including her husband."

Mrs. Spock's constant surveillance of her children was as much to ensure their moral purity as their physical safety. She was ever vigilant against masturbation. After an earnest lecture to Ben on the necessity for not only a clean life but clean thoughts, she would end, "You want to have normal children, don't you?"—a warning only vaguely comprehended by his young mind. Hiddy remembers, "If we departed in the least from the standards she imposed, we felt as if the devil had us by the throat." The success of Mrs. Spock's domestic Comstock campaign may be indicated by the fact that as adults four of her children have had psychiatric help. A fifth, Hiddy, received comparably maturing experience through her anthroposophical training under Rudolf Steiner, which encouraged expanded consciousness. Moreover, three never married—Hiddy, Anne, and Bob; of the three who did, Betty and Sally were divorced, and made happier second marriages.

But even the most assiduous caretakers need a bit of relief, and when Mrs. Spock was out of sight, Benny, as the oldest, was expected to tend the smaller children. On one occasion in early childhood, after their bath, he suggested to Hiddy that they meet their father at the trolley. So off they went, hand in hand, naked down Cold Spring Street to Whitney Avenue, one of New Haven's most elegant thoroughfares. When Mr. Spock got off the train, they were astonished to see his pleased look of anticipation replaced by an anguished blush. He marched them quickly home.

As a small boy, Benny's effectiveness as a baby tender was limited by the fact that he was a long time in learning to talk (he spoke very little until he was over three), and when he did say anything he spoke with maddening slowness. Mrs. Spock was out of the room one day when Benny and Hiddy were playing happily in the bathtub. Several long seconds after Hiddy had fallen over backwards, Mrs. Spock rushed to the rescue, then berated Benny for not telling her that Hiddy's head was submerged. He replied stolidly, "I . . . was . . . calling . . . you . . . and . . . calling . . . you . . . and . . . you . . . didn't . . . come."

Mrs. Spock paid obeisance to her regal mother five or six afternoons a week by carting the children to tea at "Nannie's" house atop Prospect Hill. Originally she trundled them up Canner Street by baby carriage or coaster wagon. Later she had one of the first electric automobiles in New Haven, and one day when it was traveling up the steep street at the astonishing speed of twelve miles an hour, Betty tumbled out over the back. Benny, still slow of speech, failed again. He murmured, "Betty's . . . gone."

Mrs. Spock didn't hear him, even when he repeated, "Betty's . . . gone." Only when she reached the top of the hill did Mrs. Spock realize that Betty, screaming and kicking, was lying in the street several hundred yards away.

"What happened, Benny?" she snapped.

"She . . . fell . . . out," was all he could muster.

They made it to Nannie's that day and, as usual, Benny found her, he says in retrospect, "a terribly severe, awesome sort of person. She always wore a black dress with a high lace collar held up by whalebone. We had to tiptoe into her parlor where she served tea in cups of such thin china that we could see right through them. In a formidable voice she would say, 'McLane, would you like a cooky?'

"I would say, 'Yes, Nannie.' Then she would hold out the dish of cookies and I would take one, never *two*. Except for saying 'Thank you,' I was never supposed to say anything else or ask anything else. Then I would turn and get out of the room."

But the tea parties had some compensations for the youngsters.

The young Spocks and their cousins explored the "secret passages" connecting the closets of various attic bedrooms, made the wicked-seeming discovery of old bedpans there, and climbed a perilously tall pine tree in the yard.

At home, the Spock children enjoyed other pastimes as well. Hiddy reminisces, "Ben and I were as thick as thieves. If there was ever a boy who made you think little sisters were to treasure, it was he. We practically read through all the bookshelves, lying on the floor on our stomachs and laughing over *Tom Sawyer* and *Huckleberry Finn*." Dr. Spock remembers particular juvenile favorites, *Ivanhoe, Black Arrow, Westward Ho,* and *Treasure Island,* with more enjoyment than any he ever read as an adult, though he attributes significant influence to only one volume (read as he was about to enter medical school): "Cushing's *Life of Osler* almost discouraged me from studying medicine because I didn't seem to have any of the qualities that made Osler such a good doctor." In a secret code brother and sister wrote mysterious messages telling where gold was hidden, and put them in bottles which they buried in the backyard for the neighbor children to find.

The bottles were bound to be discovered, for in the two houses adjacent to the Spocks' on Cold Spring Street (dubbed "Offspring Street" by Yale President Hadley) were thirteen children—six Bennetts (heirs to the Winchester Repeating Arms Company) and seven Jacksons (whose father owned the *New Haven Register*). Favorite neighborhood activities included stamp collecting, butterfly and polliwog catching, roller skating, hoop rolling, fort building, jumping up and down on the joggledy board, swinging, bicycling, and playing tunes on the Spocks' popular pianola.

Summer activities were solitary, for every summer Mrs. Spock packed her children off to an isolated, rockbound coastal town or island in Maine: Cushing's Island, Pemaquid Point, Vinalhaven, New Harbor, MacMahan Island. Dr. Spock remembers the journey as "the most exciting event of the year. A large carriage from the livery stable would take us to the railroad station in New Haven. The carriage's unique smell was compounded by mildewed upholstery and horse. The amiable driver, if I got close enough, had a smell which I later learned was booze. To while away the four-hour train trip to Boston we each were given a new ten-cent-store toy. For several years I received a set of tiny railroad cars and a locomotive, each about an inch long, molded out of light metal, small enough to be played with very satisfactorily on the parlor-car windowsill. In Boston we transferred to another carriage for the bumpy ride over cobblestones to the dock of one of the imposing white steamships bound for Portland or Rockland. It's exciting still to picture the small cabin that each two of us would occupy, with double-decker bunks and in the corner stand a washbowl with a pitcher. My father would disappear for an hour to be sure that the crates of hammocks on which we'd sleep all summer on the porch of the small cottage were brought from the train and put aboard the boat. . . . I remember how one [servant] girl rushed us to the rail of the boat to see a dead cat undulating in the filthy harbor water and how disapproving my mother was when she found out. Though we yearned to, we were never allowed to have dinner in the brightly lighted dining saloon. We ate safe sandwiches brought from home."

When they finally reached their destination, there weren't many other children around, and Mrs. Spock seldom approved of those who were. Since the Spock children weren't allowed to associate with people of moral standards less high than their mother's, they usually had to play exclusively with one another. Though they fought a lot (which Mrs. Spock later indignantly denied, saying "Thank goodness, *none* of my children ever showed the *slightest* spark of jealousy!"), the children remember with nostalgia the enchanting pastimes Benny invented to triumph over tedium. Dr. Spock explains: "Each of us would appropriate one of the pools of rain water on the cliffs for playing endlessly with tiny tugboats, barges, sailboats, that we had made from pieces of shingle. In the woods we built miniature houses on the needle-carpeted ground by sticking pieces of shingling into the ground, and equipped them with fences, barns, wells, and even well houses in which buckets would be hoisted on thread spools. We lay on our bellies for days on end living the lives of our imaginary householders. In the woods we also discovered 'secret' paths that led to climbable trees, sunlit clearings, soft patches of moss, and spots where wood thrushes and ovenbirds could be watched."

Mrs. Spock loved lobsters as a cat loves catnip, but she hated to kill them. (When she was ninety and in a nursing home in Hartford, Connecticut shortly before she died, a visitor, seeing that Hiddy had sent her a fresh Maine lobster, asked in what way she liked them. Mrs. Spock, piercing blue eyes flashing, rose up in her wheelchair and shouted, "Dead!") Dr. Spock remembers, "Whoever supplied her with lobsters had to boil them also. All six summers we were at New Harbor I had to walk, every Saturday, four miles to Pemaquid Point and four miles back, alone, to bring back the lobsters, baked beans, and brown bread from Minnie Martin's little candy-grocery store there. I used to go along the rocks by the coast, like a mountain goat leaping from huge cliff to huge cliff. This feels lonely when you're a ten, twelve-year-old boy. Eight miles took about three hours altogether. But I was interested in birds at that time, so I listened and watched for them."

The routine of Christmas was as unvarying during Benny's childhood as were the summers. Dr. Spock enthusiastically recollects the holiday: "Early on Christmas morning, in front of a fire in the den, there was the opening of the smaller-sized and immediate-family presents that were in the stockings (my mother's black cotton stockings). . . . Later in the morning our austere maternal grandmother, 'Nannie,' would arrive, by means of an elegant cube-shaped electric automobile, and we would open her presents and the larger packages that had been piled under the tree. (Generally her presents were well chosen, but when I was about ten she got a mistaken message, somehow, that I wanted an encyclopedia. The package felt heavy enough, but what a disappointment!) After dinner came the usual nap—no exceptions for Spocks! (We got plenty of rest: naps till eight years of age if school hours permitted. . . .)" Then came a ceremonial visit to Mr. Spock's family, either to see grandfather William Spock, a jolly person with a big black beard; grandmother, wrinkled and quiet; or Aunt Jessamine, a plump lady addicted to baroque, beruffled dresses and enormous, flowered hats. Grins Dr. Spock: "Part of the problem of Christmas afternoon for a small child was being kissed by Aunt Jessamine and being scratched by her whiskers. She was married to a jocose physician, Charles Vishno. If someone asked him, 'How are you, Charlie?' he'd always say, 'Able to sit up and take nourishment!' "

The Spocks visited the Vishnos only once a year because Mrs. Spock looked down upon her husband's hearty, relaxed relatives. The Vishno parlor was always blue with cigar smoke by mid-afternoon. The teetotaling Spocks ate Christmas dinner at noon;

the Vishnos ate their way through the afternoon, accompanied by suitable liquid refreshment. To Benny, already cast in the puritanical mold, it seemed inconceivable and fascinatingly wicked for people to eat for hours at a time and smoke and drink—and to enjoy doing these things—without being punished.

Though Benny's childhood had idyllic aspects, he led a far more Spartan existence than his peers because of his mother's conception of what constituted a wholesome upbringing. Mrs. Spock wanted her children to be hardy, so they slept, year-round, in an unheated canvas tent erected on the roof of the front porch. Although the chamber pot iced up in the winter, the children survived. Mrs. Spock agreed with the precepts of the Dr. Spock of her generation, Dr. Luther Emmett Holt's *The Care and Feeding of Children: A Catechism for the Use of Mothers and Children's Nurses* (1895), and she imposed vegetarianism on her children until they were twelve. Dr. Holt also recommended that children abstain from raw vegetables, salads, ready-to-serve cereals, hot breads, griddle cakes, pastry, nuts, candy, dried fruits, cherries, berries, bananas, pineapple, lemonade, cider, soda-water, tea, coffee, and alcoholic beverages. So the Spock youngsters lived largely on milk, stewed fruit, oatmeal, and eggs—and the eggs were always runny and poorly done. Until he was twelve, Ben was obliged to have nursery supper at 5:30 with the younger children.

Dull though the menu was, it must have been nutritious, for all the children developed robust constitutions and grew taller than average. Ben reached six feet four, surpassing his father's height by five inches. All the girls were taller than their mother's five feet six inches. Hiddy, five feet eight and one-half inches, once built a log cabin, unassisted, out of abandoned telephone poles which she floated out to an island in Lake Millinocket, Maine.

Though people of the Spocks' income level customarily sent their children to private schools, Mrs. Spock chose to do so not from custom but because she sought both quality education and good companions for her youngsters. Yet the early years of Benny's schooling were nevertheless unconventional. Mrs. Spock didn't believe children should go to school until they were seven; unmoved by the regulations of the school officials, she kept her six-year-olds at home. In preparation for her oldest son's entrance into school, the summer that he was seven she must have felt a touch of guilt, for she decided to teach him to read. She expected instant mastery of the subject; he proved to be as slow in learning to read as he had been in learning to speak. After fifteen minutes of instruction, in exasperation she grabbed him by the hair and shook him, yelling, "How can you be so stupid?" "Mother was really too impatient to be a teacher," he now says, gently.

At seven and eight years, Benny was tutored in a class of five or six children in a friend's home by a prim governess, Miss Ogden. "At that time I was scared of a lot of things," says Dr. Spock, "fire engines, lions that I thought inhabited the thicket near our house, the dinosaur which my friend Mansfield Horner said lived at the bottom of his cellar stairs, and fat Italian immigrant women who came down the street in the spring digging dandelions. Some child probably told me they'd take me home in the huge bags they wore dangling from their waists. I'd rush into the vestibule with palpitating heart when I saw them a block away, slam the door and peek at them through the little window in the door as they passed. I was afraid to go to school by the most direct route because it would take me past a barking, charging dog and a bully. On my way to gym one Saturday I was stopped by a gang of tough boys, one of whom started to take off his coat because he said I wanted to fight him. But while he was doing this I fled so fast that my feet barely touched the ground for a full mile."

Miss Ogden, who'd probably had no teacher training, was scarcely soothing to Benny: "She came to long division when I was eight, and told us about the trial divisor. This was just too much for my brain. I broke down and cried each day, thinking, 'I'll never catch on to this.' "

As if in unwitting defiance of his mother's special plans, Benny enjoyed the few months in the only public school he ever attended, third grade at Worthington Hooker, far more than he did the rest of his private elementary education. Dr. Spock remarks, "Psychologically, most school-age children love to conform to the class, and love routine tasks. At Worthington Hooker the monitors would pass out oak leaves and each of us would trace an oak leaf. Then they would pass out readers and everybody would open his reader to page fourteen and take turns reading a couple of sentences. Then the readers would all be called in and they'd pass out the arithmetic books. I *loved* it. I *loved* being a cog in a machine in a regular class."

This utopia didn't last long. Many of Mr. and Mrs. Spock's friends were Yale faculty members, and inspired by Mrs. Hocking, the wife of a philosophy professor, they decided to start a fresh-air school for their children. At the time, fresh air was thought to cure a variety of physical and spiritual afflictions, from tuberculosis to loss of appetite to mental depression. If a little fresh air was good, reasoned the parents, a lot of fresh air would be even better. So, throughout the severe Connecticut winter, in a tent built on a wooden platform in the Hockings' backyard, ten-year-old Benny, Hiddy, and twenty faculty children clustered like bees for warmth. In addition to wearing sweaters, coats, caps, mittens, and sheep-skin-lined boots, the children were encased from feet to armpits in thick felt bags. Whenever they became numb the teacher, middle-aged Miss Jocelyn, led them in faltering folk dances on the open end of the platform.

The class bad boy was Bob McFarland, scarcely a delinquent by today's standards, but deemed an underdisciplined nonconformist by his refined overseers. He was grumpy. He made gunpowder in his cellar. He teased the Hockings' goat and pushed the girls into butting range. When he disobeyed, Miss Jocelyn sent him into exile in a little red toolshed on the back of the property, where through the dusty window he thumbed his nose and made faces at the other children. Ben relished his friendship with the naughty boy, but was discomfited by his own goodness and his powerlessness to alter himself for the worse.

Benny's unwelcome feeling of goodness was intensified during his eleventh year, when the school moved from its genteel setting to the rear of the Edwards Street public school, in a comparatively tough neighborhood. Perhaps because their mother's "higher standards," rigidly applied, had made the Spock children feel so different from others, they seem to have been more uncomfortable than most people when removed from their accustomed, sheltered milieu. Until they reached maturity, if then, they never felt fully accepted by unfamiliar contemporaries. (This feeling, says Sally, led both herself and Betty into unhappy first marriages.) Environments clashed in the Edwards Street schoolyard, as the local youths hurled "hot air kids" and more profane epithets at the folk dancers. Though Benny already towered above his classmates, he was too timid to defend them. Even if he had felt able to, he would never have dared to use those few four-letter words he understood.

Ben was bewildered by the way his character seemed to change as he associated with different kinds of people. Dr. Sanford, a surgeon and amateur naturalist whose high-strung son Bill was a classmate of Ben's, approved of Spock's slow, stolid manner and encouraged the youngsters' friendship. Bill was one of the few children in town reared even more protectively than the Spocks, and with him Ben sometimes had the strange and fascinating feeling that he was "a tough, dirty-minded kid." This occurred not when he was collecting moths, a hobby to which Dr. Sanford introduced him, nor during their ordinary pastimes, but on at least one occasion when he recognized his own budding sexual interest. One summer day the boys went sailing on Weekapaug Pond in Rhode Island with Bill's governess (Miss Ogden) and her friend. The friend's skirt was pulled up high—way above her ankles. Eleven-year-old Benny watched, fascinated. Miss Ogden saw him and signaled to her friend "that an oaf was ogling her legs." The signal itself was sufficient punishment: Benny felt guilty for the rest of the afternoon, "as if I'd been labeled a sex fiend."

By this time war had broken out in Europe, and as the German armies marched toward Paris, war orders from England and France poured into the New Haven munitions factories. Immigrants poured into the city to work in these factories (fifteen thousand employed by Winchester alone), and by late 1916 the city was nervously fearful of German spies and saboteurs. After Congress declared war on Germany, April 6, 1917, ten thousand New Haven men were mobilized, hundreds more over forty-five signed up for the Home Guard, and most of the Yale students enrolled in ROTC or the Yale Naval Training Unit. The Second Connecticut Regiment camped in the shadow of the Yale Bowl, where the soldiers drilled. Yale's great dining hall was turned over to the Red Cross. To allay the citizens' fears that the munitions plants might be attacked by German planes or zeppelins (how such craft would have the power or fuel to reach New Haven was never realistically considered) an anti-aircraft gun and six soldiers were planted on East Rock, a three-hundred-foot cliff visible from the Spocks' house.

Ben collected recruiting posters and plotted the Western Front on a map of Europe; he and his classmates wrote encouraging letters to a former teacher who was an ambulance driver in France. But the Great War had little effect on Ben's life, for he was too young to fight or to be aware of its manifold implications. In 1915 to have predicted his antiwar leadership fifty years later would have been equivalent to predicting a man on the moon in the same decade—incredible and impossible.

From 1915 to 1921 Ben's world was the sheltering world of preparatory schools in New Haven and Andover. Within their walls was a privileged group of boys; without, the rest of the universe accessible to Ben primarily through the magazine articles on world affairs which he occasionally read. Within, the idyll that Ben's earlier schooling had aimed for but had not created; without, medical, social, and political problems that he was to become involved in decades later.

In 1915, when he was twelve, after a year at deteriorated Hopkins Grammar School, Ben was finally placed in exactly the right educational setting for him, Hamden Hall, a small, proper, country day school on the outskirts of New Haven.

He was finally allowed to eat meat and to dine with the grownups. According to the custom of the time, he was given his first long-trousered suit. Dr. Spock explains: "Trousers in the World War I period were very tight, and until you were accustomed to them you'd kneel down the way you used to when you wore short pants and pretty soon, with the cheap kind of suit a father would buy a growing boy, you'd go through the knees. My parents thought that to conserve wool for the war effort, and to save money, it would be a good idea to give me a suit that my father had never been able to wear out. It was made of iron-like worsted, and was utterly the wrong cut for a young man. In the style of a fifty-year-old professor or banker, the jacket had two buttons instead of four, and the pants had no cuffs. I don't think I've ever suffered in my life as much as I did with that suit. My mother's favorite advice, 'If you know you're right, it doesn't matter *what* other people think. You should be *proud* to be different,' didn't help at all. It only emphasized the fact that I felt like a queer kind of a guy who is not accepted easily."

Ben did fit easily into Hamden Hall. With fifty other wholesome lads eleven to fifteen, he was very happy: "There were no choices and there was nobody different to make fun of me." For Hamden Hall's Golden Anniversary yearbook in 1963 he described the school as it was then: "There was an assembly-study hall which held us all . . . [and] two small recitation rooms. Once a week there was an art class in an upstairs room. . . . The gallery at the back of the assembly hall was used only once, to isolate Frank Minor, who had eaten a peck of small raw onions from his garden and was surrounded by an aroma having a radius of twenty feet.

"Dr. [John P.] Cushing, the headmaster, with iron-gray hair and moustache, seemed gruff to us then and we felt daring to call him 'Doc' behind his back. Now I realize how kindly he was. His sternest reprimand was, 'Boys, boys, stop that foolish prattle.' Mr. Twichell and Mr. Babcock, the two other masters, were splendid teachers and models for boys. They gave us a clear sense of what was right and wrong but with great friendliness, and they were good athletes too. How I envied the easy way they ran for high batted balls, looking over their shoulders, and always seemed to catch them. Mr. Twichell blushed easily and those were very prim days. A picture of the statue of the she wolf suckling Romulus and Remus in our ancient history class book convulsed the class with snickers and turned Mr. Twichell crimson to the tips of his prominent ears. Mr. Babcock always looked immaculate and elegant in his blue suit with chalk stripes, and I've tried to have one of the same kind ever since. . . .

"By the age of fifteen I was six feet four inches tall and weighed about one hundred pounds. One afternoon while I was standing on a bench in the locker room climbing into a suit of long wool underwear, the type we all wore then, one of the masters couldn't help mentioning the poem 'The Skeleton in Armor.' Glad to follow any road to popularity, I learned to suck in my abdomen until I looked even more like a skeleton."

His first patriotic efforts were devoted to playing the bugle in the Hamden Hall drum and bugle corps which was organized to accompany the Yale Navy trainees on parades. Dr. Spock confessed in the Anniversary yearbook: "We practiced noisily for months under two Marines. On Memorial Day we proudly marched all over New Haven in front of the Yale Navy, but it wounded our pride when the news leaked back that our short, quick, boyish steps had exhausted and infuriated them. We paraded once more the next fall, all over Hamden this time and all by ourselves, when word came that an Armistice had been signed [on November 7, 1918], but it proved to be a false alarm. When the real Armistice came a few days later we were kept at our desks.

"On the last day of school," Dr. Spock wrote, "there would be a play. I remember *Everyboy,* patterned loosely after *Everyman.* The high point . . . was when Bill Hammond came rattling down a ramp onto the stage in an express wagon declaiming, 'My name is Slang. I own a gang of ugly words. . . . ' Another year I was assigned the role of a British officer in *Mrs. Murray's Dinner Party.* I joined one of my speeches in the second act to a speech in the third act, thus neatly eliminating one-third of the play. No one noticed but the master who coached us."

In the ninth grade Ben was a "Form Leader" in academic achievement; he won prizes for English composition and drawing, and a silver cup for "Excellence in Athletics." At his graduation from tenth grade in May, 1919, towering like a flagpole above his classmates, he again received the former two awards, and a prize for "General Information." Impressive though these honors were, the leaves fall from the laurel when one remembers that the class numbered fewer than ten.

In the estimation of Mrs. Twichell, widow of Ben's former master, the prizes retained full glory. At eighty-nine she asserted that she had always known Ben would be a great man because he had been an outstanding youth. The wisdom of hindsight confers great prognostic powers on us all. The youthful Ben made a lifelong impression on her. After not having glimpsed Benjamin Spock for forty-eight years, she finally saw the mature Dr. Spock on television. Leaping from her chair, she waved wildly in her lonely apartment, "Hi, Ben Spock. Hi!"

About the time Ben entered Andover, in the fall of 1919, the Spocks moved from Cold Spring Street to a handsome, ten-year-old house at 67 Edgehill Road. The new home (sold at Mrs. Spock's

death for $60,000) was emblematic of the Spocks' moderate afflu-
ence. They had exchanged a modest, vaguely Victorian frame house
for an impressive, graciously Georgian one of red brick; a shingle
roof for slate; a canvas sleeping porch for a widow's walk; gas-
light for both gas *and* electricity; and many small rooms for more
large ones—even the new kitchen seated twelve. Like his quarters
at home, Ben's rooms in 2 Day Hall at Andover, a single bedroom
and a study shared with a roommate, were spacious, comfortable,
and ornamented by yards of dark woodwork.

The Spocks sent Ben to Andover, then as now among the nation's
best college preparatory schools, because Mrs. Spock thought that
an all-male environment would be more wholesome than the atmosphere at the academically excellent but dangerously co-educational
New Haven High School. Andover was intentionally wholesome.
Founded in 1778 in the bucolic town of Andover, Massachusetts,
Phillips Academy was committed to teach, said its constitution,
not only "English and Latin Grammar, Writing, Arithmetic, and
[the] Sciences . . . but more especially . . . the great and real
business of living. . . . The Master's attention to the disposition of
the *minds* and *morals* of the youth under his charge [was to]
exceed every other care . . . both united form the noblest character,
and lay the surest foundation of usefulness to mankind. . . ." Sunday and Wednesday chapel services—and an 8 p.m. curfew—were
compulsory in 1919 as in 1778, but by the twentieth century, secular
as well as sectarian speakers were scheduled.

In 1919 Andover's enrollment was five hundred boys, many with
social and economic backgrounds similar to Ben's, but with some
Jews, a few Negroes on scholarships, and one American Indian.
There were also three refugee Georgian princes, the M'Divani
brothers, who worked their way from the Andover scullery to
Hollywood fame within two decades, as each married a wealthy
movie actress.

During his first year Ben roomed alone in a rooming house. In
his second year, Mrs. Spock saw to it that Ben had a wholesome
roommate. She selected William Foote (later an editor of the
Hartford Courant), son of her good friends Yale professor
"Uncle Harry" Foote and his wife, "Aunt Patty." It didn't matter
to Mrs. Spock, says Editor Foote, that her choice was only a lower-
middler (sophomore) when Ben was a senior; that William, as a

new student, was unaffiliated while Ben was in a fraternity, Alpha Gamma Chi; or that William was really Hiddy's special friend, rather than Ben's. William and Ben roomed together and Ben accepted William's inevitability with cheerful grace. Ben accepted being away from home with even greater cheer. "No Spock was ever homesick," Dr. Spock grins. "Not that we didn't love each other, but we realized how fond we were of each other particularly when we were away."

Andover, then under the distinguished headmaster Dr. Alfred E. Stearns, had far higher academic standards than Hamden Hall. Though Ben needed remedial tutoring in algebra, he was less bothered by his difficulties with mathematics than he had been by the trial divisor when he was eight, and in general enjoyed his studies and his teachers. Dr. Spock feels that "At the time most boarding schools floated on their traditions and didn't have to bother to keep up-to-date. Andover took its reputation seriously, and had very good teachers. I went in heavily for Latin and Greek, partly from academic snobbery, I realize now. Everybody took Latin, but it was unnecessary to add Greek. I also took physics and chemistry, though I didn't have to; I had no idea then of becoming a doctor."

In his senior year he was elected to Cum Laude, the honor society of the top 5 percent of all the boarding schools in the country, and graduated with B averages in the sciences and A's in the humanities. His college entrance examination averages were a predictable improvement over his exams at Hamden Hall: English, 78; algebra, 73; plane geometry, 70; Latin, 75; Greek, 83; chemistry, 80; and physics, 98.

Andover encouraged a sound mind in a sound body. So Ben went out for soccer, played a mediocre game on a club team, and eventually abandoned it for high jumping. His long legs and his height gave him sufficient advantage to make the varsity track team, win third place in a track meet, earn a school letter, and give him the illusion that he was an athlete. The Andover yearbook, *Pot Pourri,* claimed pompously that, win or lose, "the distinction of [playing for] Andover is eminence enough." But Ben felt the distinction was a personal triumph.

He also went out for the glee club, as he had the track team, not so much from a love of the activity as, Dr. Spock acknowledges, "from a tremendous ambitiousness to be accepted and to be a success. In the background was always the fact that I felt different and unacceptable." His damaging self-assessment is typical of adolescents who have yet to find an acceptable self-definition and to live comfortably with it. It is also quite unrealistic. Like his peers in those days, he regarded the proper clothes as symbols of his acceptability: "At Andover the elegant thing was a tweed Norfolk jacket and white flannel trousers that you wore all year. You never had the trousers cleaned, so they were sort of a gray-tan color. You got people's signatures on them. I finally persuaded my parents to buy me a pair, but they were outraged when I got the signatures. Button-down shirt collars were just coming in then but I didn't have any until I got to Yale." Yet Ben's yearbook pictures show him dressed like everyone else and, hair carefully parted on the left, looking much like everyone else except that he was a head taller than most of his classmates.

He wasn't left out. Though he wasn't voted anything at all in the senior class poll, either complimentary or otherwise, his friends remember him as "graceful," "congenial," and "tremendously popular at Andover, in spite of a dreadful plague of boils." Spock thinks of himself as having been far less appealing.

But by the end of his senior year Ben got up enough courage to go on one group date, something he knew would make his mother uneasy. "I always loved dancing and I always loved girls, but I was hopelessly shy," Dr. Spock recalls with a grin. Mrs. Spock hadn't allowed him to attend Miss Chadbourne's prim dancing class at Hamden Hall, though he yearned to go. Upon returning from soccer practice in a muddy, sweaty uniform, he would spy his schoolmates scowlingly propelling girls in white dimity dresses around the floor of the assembly hall. Even the patent leather slippers the boys and girls had to wear appealed to Ben, who thought the dancers incredibly romantic. He was finally permitted to go to a small, private dancing class when he was fifteen.

When he reached Andover in his sixteenth year, Ben might have been the prototype of the gangling hero in Booth Tarkington's *Seventeen*, a best seller published only three years earlier. In the years from twelve to sixteen he had attended Sunday School enthusiastically, not from piety but because he could sit several rows behind Marta Schneelok, a pretty girl he believed to be an orphan, and admire her happily from afar. From sixteen to twenty Ben was smitten with Peggy Ramsey, a beautiful, quiet girl whose father had died. He invited her to football games and proms at Andover and Yale, but could rarely think of anything to say to her. (It was not until his psychoanalysis, begun at age thirty, that Ben realized that the third girl he adored—and eventually married—was also fatherless. This pattern was interpreted as indicating an unusually deep fear of competing with his own father.) Young Ben at boarding school listened with fascinated incredulity to his classmates' tales of taking girls dining and dancing. He would never have dared include such an expense in the accounting he made to his parents on requesting another ten dollars, and he assumed that no proper girl would be allowed to accept such an invitation.

Though he felt foredoomed to associate with nice girls, Ben, like many of his fellows, was fascinated—from a distance—with those who weren't so nice. One Sunday afternoon in his last spring at Andover, Ben went with several other seniors to call on two Andover girls whom he himself had never met—a daring act in itself. Though from perfectly proper families, the girls were clearly more tolerant and flirtatious than those he knew in New Haven. Eager to become a man of the world at last, Ben urged himself to make a mild advance, but could not surmount the barriers of his rigorous training. In an act of unacknowledged teasing retaliation, in the next of his obligatory biweekly letters home, he quoted one of the girl's mildly provocative compliments. He received by return mail a blistering indictment of the girl's morality and his own, and a warning that he would have to renew his ideals by living at home when he went to Yale.

Until he went away to school Ben had been sufficiently subdued by his mother so that he gave in to her demands without a struggle, but with a great deal of concealed resentment. Arguing only risked further restrictions. Only once does Ben remember disobeying his mother—with disastrous results for himself. On arriving one Christmas vacation from Andover, happily anticipating a full schedule of parties, he found that the first was banned because of the host's reputation for serving liquor to underage guests. Ben and Hiddy defiantly but secretly met their friends in the front yard of the forbidden house. A neighbor told Mrs. Spock, who decreed with outraged indignation, "No more parties for the rest of the vacation." In vain her children pleaded; in vain they ground their teeth and silently cursed; in vain even Mrs. Spock's dowager friends protested the penalty. Though Ben eventually learned the trick of circumventing some of his mother's moral barbed wire by following his own dictates away from home and keeping quiet, he never learned how to best her in direct confrontation. Having been early forced to subdue his wrath, throughout his adult life he felt it necessary to rein in his anger, even his assertiveness, in public, until the Indochina war raised his indignation to the boiling point and he could express moral outrage to the public at large.

Dr. Spock comments on his moral coming-of-age: "My mother disapproved of the girls that obviously intrigued me. She'd say, 'Benny, why can't you like *wholesome* girls?' The word 'wholesome' is *anathema* [laughing] to me even now, and it always has been. [Nevertheless, he uses it frequently.] It was one of the most distressing things to realize as I grew older that I liked wholesome people and that I belonged to the wholesome group." Speaking about his involvement in the peace movement he remarked, "This is where all the fragments of my past, after being jumbled up, come together again in a strange way. I realize now that I haven't changed myself at all, much as I've tried. I've worn snappier clothes, and I've gone with people who were more fun than my family's friends. But I end up being a moralist, like the family I grew up in, having something very important to be moralistic about."

two

BOOLA BOOLA

EXCEPT to enjoy the fruits of the boom years of the twenties, Ben Spock as an undergraduate between 1921 and 1925 was indifferent to his country's economic situation and completely apolitical. The focus of his typically classical education was on the past; he took no sociology, government, or political science. He thought little about the attempt to partition the vanquished European nations after World War I or about the formation of the League of Nations. That the strong, idealistic President, Democrat Woodrow Wilson, was broken in health and spirit by the Senate's failure to ratify his cherished League of Nations Treaty didn't seem to matter much to Ben or his friends. In 1921 Wilson was succeeded by Republican Warren Harding, *Main Street* mentality incarnate, coiner of the ungrammatical concept "back to normalcy" and dedicated to its preservation. Mr. Spock voted for Harding, but his son, too young to vote, was indifferent to the election.

After World War I U.S. Attorney General A. Mitchell Palmer and his agents undertook to rid the country of subversive foreigners believed to be Communists and labor agitators. Palmer summarily jailed six thousand men—and sometimes their visitors—for days or weeks without due process of law, without making the charges clear. The Sacco-Vanzetti case, in some ways similar to the Spock conspiracy trial of the sixties for its political overtones, carried the spirit of the Palmer raids on through the twenties. Young Spock was hardly aware of these cases.

Throughout the decade the generation gap appeared and widened in "respectable" circles. Flapper girls shortened their skirts—from instep to kneecap in seven years—and cast aside layers of confining undergarments. They strove to look like men and to drink bootleg liquor like men; they took up smoking in public and petting in private.

Though Ben was far more interested in the flapper girls than in most of the crucial issues of the day, he was even more interested in personal success. At the age of eighteen he thought that "to go to Yale, of course, was the only thing that a person with a Yale father could do. I'd absorbed from my father this feeling of the importance of doing well at Yale; there was nothing *casual* about the way I went there. My ambition wasn't scholastic. I wanted to be a successful Yale man as I felt my father had been, to triumph socially or in a sport or in some extracurricular activity. But I had little confidence that I would be accepted by the most dashing, successful types. I later learned in psychoanalysis that, most of all, I also wanted to surpass my father. Yale College was the field of combat."

Success, as defined by Yale undergraduates from the Reconstruction Era to the Second World War, was signified by election to one of the four secret senior societies at the end of one's junior year. Skull and Bones was the most prestigious, followed by Scroll and Key, Wolf's Head, and Elihu Club. During the time Ben was an undergraduate, 1921–25, Yale's secret societies were somewhat like undergraduate honorary fraternities on other campuses, only more elaborately ritualistic. Their manifest purposes were to honor extracurricular accomplishment, to promote camaraderie among the members, and to foster intellectual and oratorical facility by requiring each member to address his peers on various subjects. On two evenings a week they provided (in private dining rooms) better food than the quadrangles did, and good cigars. In the ingrown, self-conscious, white Anglo-Saxon Protestant social system that was Yale's before World War II, the latent effects of the senior societies were extremely potent, with a force scarcely comprehensible to today's collegians who scorn the former status symbols of ancestry, dress, athletic prowess, and social affiliation. Their exclusiveness and secrecy encouraged the members' sense of superiority—and the non-members' sense of ostracism: if the societies' names were mentioned in public, and thereby profaned, a member was obliged to rise in umbrage and leave the room.

This emphasis made the curriculum seem secondary. Ben took a conventional liberal arts program. Without much effort he maintained four years of a gentlemanly C average that in those days was good enough for just about anything—including admission to medical school. Somewhat surprisingly he majored in English, considering that the grades in his first three courses were 65, 60, and 55. However, by senior year his English grades had improved to 80, 83, 88, and the highest grade he ever received in college, 92. Dr. Spock remembers, "The fascinating courses then at Yale were English. Chauncey Tinker on The Age of Johnson. Johnny Berdan on The Age of Pope. Robert French on The Age of Chaucer. William Lyon Phelps on nineteenth-century poetry. The more literary or intellectual student thought that aside from the extracurricular and social life you came to Yale to hear these delightful scholars tell you about literature." Ben began a collection of old, leather-bound volumes of English poetry and novels, and imagined himself as a tweedy English don reading and musing in a dusty library. Once he entered medical school the collection languished, as did this dream.

In addition to minoring in history, Ben took four semesters of French, two math courses, and the minimum number of science courses compatible with medical school entrance requirements—two semesters of sophomore biology and five semesters of chemistry. Despite his later psychiatric orientation as a physician, he found undergraduate psychology incredibly dull, and his performance in the two-semester sequence was predictably uninspired, 76 and 70. In June 1925 he graduated with an unimpressive average grade of 77.

Although academic performance was a matter of some indifference, excellence in extracurricular activities was important in
those days for the seeker of social recognition. Crew, football,
hockey, and swimming were the prestigious sports. But Ben
assumed that his only athletic asset was his long legs in the high
jump. His Andover record of five feet six inches was good enough
to get him onto the freshman track team at Yale, but it proved
his absolute ceiling, inadequate for the varsity.

One late winter day, as a thin-necked, timid freshman, he was
in the gymnasium on his way to jumping practice when he stopped
to watch the varsity crews working out on the rowing machines.
He happened to stand behind a handsome man with huge shoulders,
a noble Roman head, and a regal carriage, Langhorn Gibson,
varsity crew captain (and son of Virginia artist Charles Dana
Gibson, creator of the dignified, wasp-waisted beauties of the
1890's). Gibson turned around, noticed Ben's height, and asked
condescendingly, "What sport do *you* go out for?"

Ben replied, "High jumping." He almost added, "sir."

Gibson said scornfully, "Why don't you go out for a *man's*
sport?"

Ben was not offended by the insult, but delighted with the
invitation, which he took so seriously that he signed up immediately. Over a hundred other freshmen went out for rowing that
spring and were assigned to eight-oared crews lettered in de-
scending order of ability, A through M. Ben, never having been
in a shell before, was happy enough to be on Freshman M. He
decided to keep his third place on the freshman high jump squad,
which required only three hours of practice a week, and to devote
most of his afternoons to crew.

Alfred Wilson, captain of the 1925 crew (later executive vice
president of Honeywell, Inc.) and friend of Spock's since Andover
days, observes: "Rowing is an intimate sport, even though it's
non-contact. You live long hours together." Another former crew
member says, "Rowing takes eight months' practice a year to
reduce an abnormal motion to a reflex." And Dr. Spock emphasizes: "Rowing was the most genteel of all the sports. It only
appealed to polite people, and my God, we were restrained, protected boys. Nobody even cursed—and I doubt if most had gone
beyond hand-holding with girls."

Although there were only three or four races each spring, the crews started practicing in September and continued until June, every day of the week except Sunday, on the Housatonic River at Derby, a half-hour bus ride from New Haven. In winter they worked out at rowing machines—oar handles attached to pedestals bolted to the floor. The varsity crews practiced blade work in the rowing tank, using full-length oars which pushed water around a course. Though the exercise was inherently repetitive and monotonous, it never seemed so to Spock, eager for success.

Luckily for Yale—and for Spock—in the fall of his sophomore year, 1922, the crew got a new coach, Ed Leader, who immediately changed the old order. Before he arrived, generations of Yale crews had been rowing an English style, which depended on an extreme body angle. The rower was obliged to reach forward as far as he could. At the end of the stroke he was bent way over, head down, back up. To get himself out of bow he had to lean equally far backward—an inefficient and exhausting procedure which had resulted in consistent losses for Yale.

Leader's much easier western American stroke depended instead on a long track for the sliding seat, and an oarsman had to be at least six feet tall to have legs long enough to move the seat the desired distance. Ben as a novice had the enormous advantage of not having to unlearn the English stroke. On the first day of fall practice Ben, splendidly tall, splendidly ignorant of rowing, and splendidly eager to learn, was promoted in one leap from Freshman M to fourth varsity. He was elated; his acquaintances who had been oarsmen at prep school and in their freshman year were incredulous: "What the hell is Spock doing on a varsity crew?"

This elysium lasted only a few days. When Coach Leader got around to inspecting the fourth varsity he saw how little Ben knew, and demoted him to Sophomore F crew. Ben, characteristically, kept at it and worked back up, step by step, from Sophomore F to junior varsity, where he stayed for the rest of the year. The crew lost its first two races, but it did defeat its arch rival, Harvard.

In those days the Yale-Harvard boat race was the most splendid collegiate social event of the spring. New London was jammed with students in white flannel trousers and "boater" straw hats, girls in their fanciest clothes and cartwheel hats, alumni with their families. Open railroad cars with parallel tiered bleachers under canvas canopies trundled the spectators slowly along the race course so they could see every stroke. The Thames River held an enormous fleet of yachts "dressed" in banners and signal flags, overloaded with guests. Visitors also crowded every summer house for miles around, eating, dancing, and drinking with indiscreet enthusiasm.

By the end of his sophomore year Ben had gained a measure of independence from home. Dr. Spock smiles, "I had sold my father a bill of goods that I'd have to eat at the training table or I wouldn't be strong enough to row." And that meant living in a dormitory. He had just joined Zeta Psi, the most humble of the five junior fraternities and the only one that had invited him, and was scheduled to room in Harkness Quadrangle the following year.

After the boat race Hiram "Harry" Bingham, Jr., Ben's future roommate and son of a prominent political figure, took Ben to a large private dance at Black Point held annually after the boat race. Harry, a local resident, introduced Ben to several girls, among them Cynthia Cheney, whose long eyelashes and blond hair in short ringlets enhanced her prettiness. Ben was attracted as much by her mysterious taciturnity as by her appearance, and concluded from her amused silence that she was "an older woman of twenty-seven."

Even when he eventually learned that Cynnie was really fifteen and that her laconic speech was caused by shyness, he was sufficiently intrigued to accept her invitation for a weekend visit at the Cheney family home later that summer. He arrived just in time to join the college and debutante set at a dance at the Oswegatchie House near Black Point, where he met Cynnie's seventeen-year-old sister Jane, a slight girl with a curly brown bob and soft brown eyes. Ben invited Jane to dance the fox trot, a popular step at which he felt quite expert. He found that although Jane, five feet six inches tall, was nearly a foot shorter than he, she could follow his lead perfectly, but when a waltz struck up, he had to confess that he didn't know how to dance it. Jane offered to teach him, and tactfully suggested that they adjourn to a gazebo on the lawn where he could learn in private. He learned, they waltzed again and again and again, and Cynnie was forgotten in the long moonlit evening.

Not only was Jane a good dancer; she was not exactly the kind of girl that Mrs. Spock would approve of, which made her even more appealing. Dr. Spock says, "Though Mother pretended that she had no snobbery to her at all, she was a fraud in this regard. To meet her exacting standards, a person had to have a respectable social background—not money, but a good family—and a very fine character," which implied wholesomeness as well as honesty and all the other virtues. Mrs. Spock approved of the "wholesome, fine" Cheney family—of respectable, enterprising colonial stock on both sides. Jane's father, John Davenport Cheney (Yale '92) and his many brothers and cousins had owned the Cheney Silk Mills in Manchester, Connecticut. Mr. Cheney, an engineer, had also supervised the public works in the town of Manchester; the Cheneys ran their company town with benign paternalism. After Mr. Cheney's death when Jane was thirteen, Jane, her mother (Mary Russell Cheney), and sister continued to live in South Manchester in considerable comfort on income from the mills, but the shift to rayon and the depression of the thirties eventually cut this to a fraction.

Virtuous Jane was. But wholesome, in Mrs. Spock's rigid construction of the term, she was not. She was pretty. She was feminine, and spoke slowly in a low, throaty voice. She was discreetly coquettish. Her mother, described by Jane as "approachable, very pretty, easygoing-seeming but not really, underneath, and wonderful with young people," had taught Jane's best friend how to flirt. Jane herself says she hadn't needed any lessons. Jane wore flesh-colored stockings and high heels, instead of the gunmetal gray hose and Ground Gripper shoes Mrs. Spock imposed on her daughters. She later incurred Mrs. Spock's disapproval by wearing to a Yale dance a Spanish shawl over her gown and leaving one shoulder bare. Worst of all, Jane used lipstick; Mrs. Spock had been known to throw more than one lipstick into the fire upon finding it in her home after the dates of Ben's friends had stayed there, exclaiming righteously, "Oh, this can't belong to one of *my* girls!"

Ben, who had had his first single date scarcely two years before, was enchanted. As the girl, the weekend, the music, the moonlight, and his own idealism blended, it seem to Ben perfectly natural to ask Jane to make a commitment to marry him someday. It seemed to Jane just as natural to say "No." Jane remembers emphatically, "I never said 'Yes.' I immediately said 'No.' I had been engaged the winter before and I wasn't going to get engaged again and not have it work out. I was barely seventeen. I said, 'I'm very fond of you,' but I didn't really know how I felt about him twenty-four hours after I met him. I went on seeing everybody and had lots of fun. Ben couldn't understand this at all."

By the standards of the time, Jane was prudent to remain unengaged. In 1923 no self-respecting man married unless he could support his wife. Ben had two more years of college to finish— and at least four more after that if he studied medicine, as he'd begun to contemplate. He had no income at all. Jane was just beginning college, and marriage as an undergraduate was unheard-of. (In many colleges, including Yale, undergraduates who married were expelled.) Monastic bachelorhood was expected of medical students as well, says the former Dean of the Yale Medical School. Dr. Vernon Lippard. Even interns and residents who married had to get permission from their chiefs.

After the weekend they parted. Jane stayed home and Ben returned, smitten, to the second of his three summers as recreation counselor at the Newington Crippled Children's Home. The handicapped boys remained at their permanent base, near Hartford, for the first month of the summer, and moved the second month to a cottage at Woodmount, on Long Island Sound. Because the boys were cared for by matrons during the school year, male counselors in the summer were thought to provide a beneficial change, and Ben had been hired readily even the preceding year, when he had no training, no experience, and no knowledge of what he was supposed to do. For working from 7 a.m. to 9 p.m. seven days a week, a counselor's typical schedule, Ben was paid the going rate of one hundred dollars a summer.

His employers relied on Ben's intuition as well as on his love of children, and so did he. He was initially unsure of his discipline, though he felt it was essential when twenty crippled boys swam together in the tides of Long Island Sound. Early in his first summer one of his charges refused to come in from the water when the swimming period was over. In this first known instance of Spockian firmness applied, Ben deliberately lost his temper, plunged into the water with all his clothes on, grabbed the boy by the arms, shook him, and told him that when he said "Come in" he meant it. From then on he had little difficulty.

"Looking back on it," says Dr. Spock, "I think I also probably played favorites. I paid most attention to some relatively pathetic, woebegone, younger boys. The bigger ones didn't seem to need as much care. Perhaps I went at it more as a mother than as a father. It's the motherly in a person that makes him go into pediatrics, which I had decided to do partly as a result of my counseling job. So unconsciously, I was playing mother or competing with mother all the way along."

Ben liked children in particular, as well as in the abstract. He was compassionate without being sentimental. His mother's idealistic training had given him a feeling of being morally obligated to serve humanity. (Mrs. Spock's influence was pervasive. Not by chance did five of her six youngsters devote their professional lives to helping children, though only Ben and Betty had children of their own. Hiddy and Betty were elementary school teachers. After years of teaching in boys' preparatory schools, Bob is now headmaster of a private school in Seattle. In middle life Anne quit a career in personnel work in the State Department to earn a doctorate in clinical psychology, and now directs a guidance clinic. The only maverick is Sally, a researcher for the Rutgers Center for Studies on Alcoholism.) Ben assumed that as a physician he could earn an income comparable to his father's, though he prefers to think of doctors, especially in academic medicine, as "relatively low paid."

Ben's decision to become a doctor was made with only somewhat more conscious thought than was his proposal to Jane. For Spock, like most who are not Machiavellian in their calculations, bases his major decisions on a mixture of facts, thoughts, desires, half-reasons half-realized, and unrecognized or unacknowledged feelings. Most of the decisions he has made in this manner have been right for him, for he has been able to live comfortably with them, heart, mind, and soul.

As a result of his first summer's work at Newington, and more specifically from seeing an orthopedic surgeon perform operations there, the idea of being a children's physician (but not a pediatric surgeon) first consciously occurred to Ben. So he began during his sophomore year to take courses in chemistry "just in case" he should later make a definite decision. He kept on working at Newington and taking chemistry. At the end of his junior year he applied to Yale Medical School, again "just in case." He doesn't remember ever having to make the final decision; he just turned up at medical school in the fall of 1925.

From the vantage point of his later psychoanalytic training, Dr. Spock acknowledged that he was probably "first steered toward pediatrics by taking care of younger brothers and sisters. The first child is very likely to be drawn into a parental attitude toward the other children in the family, and not just because the parent needs help. This is the way to avoid some of the pangs of jealousy, by pretending that you're not the baby's competitor, but that you're, you might say, a third parent."

Although as a younger child Ben had occasionally tended Hiddy, Betty, or Anne, his parental responsibilities increased when he was nine and his brother Bobby was born. Mr. Spock was away on the sole excursion of his married life without his family—a summer's trip to Europe with Ben's well-traveled godfather. So Ben served as a junior parent, rocking Bobby to sleep in the carriage, keeping the flies and the sun off, and looking out for the infant's general well-being. Ben remembers enjoying both the duties and the acknowledgment of his responsibility.

But by the time he was in college, Ben's parental attitude toward his siblings had been replaced—in their eyes—by suave, worldly big-brotherliness. His sisters, handsome but maternally wholesome, needed all the help he could give them to counteract their mother's insistence that they be more demure than they wanted to be. As they matured, like their mother they had to wear their hair long and in buns; Mrs. Spock banished Betty from the household for a time after she defiantly cut her hair. The only cosmetic the girls could use was cold cream. Mrs. Spock made her teenage daughters wear undershirts. "If you don't," she scolded, "it will give horrid thoughts to boys." Over these went Ferriss waists, which flattened the girls from armpits to hips, topped by shapelessly decorous dresses. Adorned thus, the Spock sisters were expected to go to dances, which they hated, for they thought that all their friends were less awkward, better dressed, and much more seductive—and they were right.

Ben advised, "Look gay." But his advice didn't seem to work very well. The girls would have loved to have attractive boyfriends, but the boys who did come on their own were singularly unpopular, defeated souls looking for comfortable girls who wouldn't scorn them. The Spock sisters treated them with kindness. But Mrs. Spock judged her children's guests by a paradoxical double standard which was equally damning no matter which way it was applied. She ridiculed her daughters' awkward callers for their lack of savoir-faire, while simultaneously condemning the girls of Ben and his friends for their worldliness.

On one occasion, however, Ben and Betty collaborated in a delicious triumph over Mrs. Spock. Betty, the family beauty, had been invited by Harry Bingham, at Yale preparatory to a career in the diplomatic service, to the inaugural ball of his father as Connecticut's governor. Mrs. Spock refused to buy Betty a new dress, even for this most brilliant of social events. When Betty, dismayed, asked Ben what to do he replied simply, "Why, make one. I'll help you."

Although Ben was experienced in the manly arts of wood chopping, water pumping, and carpentry, and though he knew how to make beds, dry dishes, and wash clothes, Mrs. Spock had never required him to sew. Betty, who knew only slightly more about sewing than he, bought nine yards of orange satin and went to work, running between the second floor sewing room and the cellar, where Ben was doing carpentry. Together they concocted the dress, with a flounce and a train made out of a piece of old lace. Ben's big fingers left big smudges on the satin where he held it during the fittings. Betty felt elegant, danced superlatively, and to this day gives Ben credit for her newfound composure, though she admits that in any eyes but their own, the dress must have looked horrible. On this occasion, Mrs. Spock remained tactfully silent.

Nor was Mrs. Spock outwardly critical of Ben's girl, just cool in her presence. In the fall of 1923, after their meeting the previous June, Ben invited Jane to Yale's most important autumn social event, the football game with Harvard. She said she couldn't go with him—because she already had a date with one of his best friends. So Ben invited Peggy Ramsey to the game and to the dance the night before. But when he learned that Jane's plans had changed he performed a rare act of ungracious self-serving. He arranged for someone else to take Peggy to the dance and escorted Jane himself. She stayed at the Spocks' house until Sunday afternoon, and left elated and far more interested in Ben than she had been the preceding spring. From then on they saw each other more often, mostly for the major athletic events and proms.

During the time Ben was in college his family rose early on Sunday morning and went to services at Yale's Battelle Chapel. Mr. and Mrs. Spock, although nominal Episcopalians, were not formally religious. Only Ben and Hiddy had been christened; Mrs. Spock claimed she didn't have time to baptize the rest.

Mrs. Spock did not compel her children to attend Sunday school and scrupulously allowed them religious freedom. All the neighborhood children went to the Center (Congregational) Church Sunday school, so the young Spocks went too, and loved it for the conviviality, if not for the doctrine. (Mrs. Spock refused to let her adolescent daughters join the church even though their friends did. She insisted they wait until they were mature enough to know what they were doing.) Ben never joined the church, though when he was living on campus he often met his family at Battelle Chapel, for daily and Sunday chapel attendance was compulsory for Yale students then. Sometimes he invited his Yale friends to join the family, for he realized that his mother wanted college men to see wholesome girls—and he wanted his sisters to see college men.

After church, Ben sometimes bought his little sister Sally a nickel package of Chiclets. "The great symbol of love," she now says with ironic humor. "I still think of Chiclets when I think of Ben. Ben was the glamor chick." Often, Ben's friends would then come to the Spocks' for Sunday dinner. Mrs. Spock was indifferent to good food, and the caliber of the cuisine depended on the imagination and skill of the current cook. The food usually ranged from average to dull, though Sunday dinner was the focal point of the week's menus, with roast chicken, mashed potatoes, creamed onions, cranberries, and a mousse ice cream. Conversation was awkward and painful for the girls, for Mrs. Spock's rapier wit and her husband's easy discourse only intensified the sisters' stiff, inarticulate self-consciousness when visitors were present.

Ben's friends were similar in many ways, though their paths diverged considerably after graduation. All of them, Harry Bingham, Geo (pronounced "Joe") Dyer (political scientist, author, military intelligence specialist in two wars), Al Wilson, Gayer Dominick (in investment banking while he was married to Betty Spock), Bayard Schieffelin (first in banking, then financial officer of the New York Public Library), Ed Richards (attorney), and Hector Prud'homme (World Bank and finally assistant to the Chancellor at the University of Hartford), among others, were carefully brought up sons from conservative, professional families. Although by today's standards they could not have been considered zealous students, they were proud of going to Yale because it had a distinguished faculty and encouraged extracurricular ambition. They made quite a point of scorning what they called Princeton's "houseparty atmosphere," though a visitor from another country might not have detected any differences. And, also defensively, they valued Yale's "democracy"; they said proudly that family background by itself did not confer distinction, as they claimed it did at Harvard. "Send your son to Groton and then to Harvard—and then shoot him" was a popular motto.

Their politics were as conservative as their four-button suits, and as conformist. In Ben's senior year a Liberal Club was started, recalls the doctor, "by ten earnest intellectuals, the single manifestation of political interest in our four years on campus. My friends and I thought it a strange, unnecessary thing to do. When a labor organizer came to Waterbury to organize the brass company workers, my father (who for several years was counsel to the Chase Brass Company), the chief of police, and the company officials promptly put the man in jail, where they felt a troublemaker belonged. When the Yale Liberal Club protested, my father remarked indignantly, 'On what basis do these whippersnappers think they're entitled to go up there and stick their noses into something they know even *less* about than the organizer?' I saw no reason to disagree with my father." Politically consistent, Ben and his classmates rose as one raccoon to name Calvin Coolidge "the biggest world figure of today" in their senior class poll. Rightly so, Ben felt, since on his father's recommendation of Coolidge as "the greatest President the United States ever had" Ben had voted straight Republican in 1924—his first political act.

Like generations of college students, Ben and his friends enjoyed lengthy bull sessions, particularly around midnight. A perennial subject was girls, what they should be like and how to win them. Ben's problem was the latter. His friends offered advice and, on at least one occasion, a poem:

> I think you smile
> As tenderly on other men.
> I know you do; but oh, the thought cuts deep.
> Somehow I would so like to have you keep
> A greater meaning for when you are with me
> And then, ah, show it then. . . .
> I am oppressed with [doubt] and fear.
> Ah, do you care for me, my dear?

Ben offered to buy the poem to entreat Jane with, but the poet, Geo Dyer, gave it to him in a burst of romantic magnanimity. Both Dr. Spock and his wife have forgotten whether he ever used it; such is the fate of immortal verse.

Other than wooing Jane, which Ben could do only at intervals or by letter (long distance phone calls were a luxury reserved only for emergencies then), the main endeavor of his junior and senior years was still crew. He made the varsity his junior year, along with Captain James Rockefeller, Alfred Lindley, Howard Kingsbury, Lester Miller, Alfred Wilson, Frederick Sheffield, and Leonard Carpenter. After winning two major races in the spring of 1924, the crew impressed many as the team that should represent the United States in the Olympics to be held in Paris that summer. Crew coach Joe Wright of the University of Pennsylvania called the Yale varsity the best crew he'd ever seen: "It has more than the physical attributes of weight, power and speed. It also possesses sagacity, the right mental poise, cool confidence, initiative, and a sort of sixth sense that makes it instinctively a dangerous, forbidding opponent in any situation."

But even as late as mid-May, Coach Leader had decided against entering Yale in the Olympics because it was too hard to train the crew for the two-thousand-meter sprints required for the Olympic trials in early June and then the four-mile endurance race against Harvard a week later. The crew was devastated and pleaded with Leader, whose skill and fairness they admired, to reconsider. Leader changed his mind. Yale beat Navy in the last twenty strokes by a narrow margin in the finals of the Olympic trials, managed in a sloppily rowed four miles to defeat Harvard a week later, and left for Paris June 21 aboard the S. S. *Homeric* to the tumultuous farewell of the brass band and cheering students.

On Tap Day in May Ben had been elected to membership in coveted Scroll and Key. No longer did he have to look up to the "dashing, successful" leaders, for he was institutionally recognized as one of them. While the crew was on the high seas, this accolade appeared in the *Boston Post* of June 24: "Out of the season's rowing in the East, the best individual performer is B. M. Spock . . . a general choice. . . . In all the races which were rowed by Yale in 1924, he passed the stroke down his side of the shell with such smoothness and accuracy that he kept all forward of him in line, and between him and the stroke there was a touch of imperceptible sympathy that had as much to do with rendering Yale crews perfect as any other cause cultivated by Leader."

Coach Leader was in some respects as puritanical as Ben's mother, and as indifferent to the prestige of his charges. He enforced training rules vigorously, restricting the crew to plain roast meats and boiled vegetables despite the ship's elaborate menu. Twice daily, amidst the clicking of spectators' cameras, he required the crew to do calisthenics and work out on rowing machines on deck.

Although there was dancing aboard the ship well into the evening, the anxious coach ordered his crew to bed every night at 9:30. During one evening's entertainment the ship's most illustrious passenger, Hollywood superstar Gloria Swanson (voted favorite, along with John Barrymore, of the Yale class of 1925), emerged from the regal seclusion of her suite to dance with each crew member in turn. Ben was introduced to her by a teammate so overawed that he could exclaim only, "Big Ben!" The petite star, detecting Ben's even greater bashfulness, replied, "Big Ben

—but no alarm!" This totally undermined his aplomb, and he was grateful to be cut in on after one silent, dizzy circuit of the dance floor. (In contrast, Coach Leader deliberately refused to be impressed. After his dance with Miss Swanson he grumbled, "I didn't get no kick out of her!")

At another evening's dance on board Ben, elegant in the first tuxedo of his own, found himself stuck with a girl whom no one else seemed interested in cutting in on—the only approved method of changing partners in those days. As the fateful hour of 9:30 approached, a more self-assured person might have explained his situation or have simply returned the girl to her nearby parents. But these solutions didn't occur to guileless Ben, who kept on dancing as he watched his crewmates depart. At 9:40 he was still guiding her apprehensively about the floor. Suddenly, at 9:45, Coach Leader strode onto the floor, shouldered aside startled couples, and bellowed, "Spock! Get to your cabin." Ben fled.

Though Ben was one of the boys, the rest of the crew, figuring he would be under surveillance, dared not invite him to join their unprecedented rebellion planned for the same night. As Ben lay in bed worrying about the consequences of his transgression, his mates secretly drank great quantities of champagne and wandered happily over the ship for hours.

The next morning Coach Leader was in a thunderous mood. After the workout he angrily reported Spock's shameful disloyalty to the rest of the crew and roared, "Spock, I'll send you home on the next boat if you ever do it again!" The other oarsmen stared at the culprit reproachfully and Ben, accustomed to disapproval at home but not in the outer world, felt criminally guilty. His feelings were dissipated by a mixture of relief and indignation when he later learned how the rest of the squad spent the night. Whether Leader ever found out is still unknown.

They arrived in Paris June 28 and found the official "huts" and the food at the enormous Olympic Village in Colombes scarcely up to their standards. So the Yale managers, well-endowed by alumni, transferred the crew to a large house in the elegant suburb of Saint Germain-en-Lai and arranged for their meals at a gourmet restaurant next door. The assiduous managers combed the city for American shredded wheat and rolled oats, which the waiter insisted on calling *potage,* and the crew happily settled into their scheduled activities for the seventeen days preceding the race.

They practiced on the Seine twice a day, guided in their estimate of the current and wind direction by the large number of wine bottle corks that a Paris sewer deposited into the race course. The bath-conscious Americans were amazed that there was no shower in the boathouse loaned them by a French rowing club; French oarsmen were accustomed to dabbing themselves with toilet water instead. However, the managers installed a shower and, shades of Mrs. Spock, the crew kept to their long naps after lunch, ate wholesome dinners, and went to bed at the predictable 9:30. Their protective coach allowed them only one excursion during this time. In the city famed for the Louvre, L'Opera, and Notre Dame, they went to a horse race at Longchamps—though Leader warned his charges to avoid sitting on any cold masonry there for fear of piles!

The crew gradually realized that they were the youngest, tallest, and heaviest among the competitors, and that no one was betting against them. During the trial heat of the two-thousand-meter race the American and Dutch crews tried to row without shirts, but an offended judge recalled them. Shirts on, the Americans won in record-breaking time, 5:51. On July 17 they met Great Britain, Canada, and Italy for the final heat. Says the 1925 Yale yearbook, "In the grandstand shortly prior to the start the Americans, particularly the large Yale contingent, became silently emotional. It was neither the time nor the place to become emotional, but we will freely admit it was impossible not to be emotional under such circumstances. Too much was at stake."

"The start was on time at 6:30 o'clock."

Boasts the yearbook chauvinistically, "It is a mistake to have the two-syllable French word *'Partez'* uttered by a Frenchman, in place of a pistol shot or the English word 'Go.' You can see *'Partez'* coming out of his brain and up through his throat, so we were away on the first letter, 'P,' to a perfect start. In just twenty strokes, or thirty seconds, we had a lead of fifteen feet." At the halfway mark the United States crew had increased its lead to seventy-five feet. At the finish, in 6:33 2/5, it was nearly three hundred feet ahead of its nearest rival, Canada, a fanstastic margin for such a brief sprint.

The victorious crew was presented with enormous gold-wash (over bronze) medals, ornate glass vases, and poster-sized inscribed scrolls showing Grecian gods and goddesses in various states of classical undress, strumming lyres and twining ivy around columns.

Armed with their scrolls and the keys to the kingdom, most of the crew members remained for sightseeing, but Ben had to return to the United States to resume his regular summer job (at fifty dollars for what remained of the summer). Three of Ben's best friends, Geo Dyer, Gayer Dominick, and Ed Richards, had planned to bicycle in France that summer and had invited Ben to go with them. Because he had agreed to be a counselor again at the crippled children's camp, he told Geo he'd have to ask his parents, and later reported that they'd said "No."

So Geo tried. He talked first with Mr. Spock, telling him that it would be possible to arrange for someone else to substitute for Ben at camp. Mr. Spock, reserved but polite, said he felt that Ben should honor his obligations.

Then Geo approached Mrs. Spock, who reacted as if he were Satan tempting Ben to an eternity of decadence. Wrathfully she proclaimed, "Benny made that commitment and he's going to carry it out." That was that.

But Ben did have time for one brief adventure before he left. Naïve newcomers to Paris head straight for the Eiffel Tower, and Ben and Al Wilson, in their Ivy League summer outfits of blue blazers and white flannels, were no exception. As the immediately recognizable tourists were entering their cage-like elevator car at each of the elevator changes, they became aware of an unusually beautiful, refined-looking girl whose elevator was always leaving ahead of theirs. Giaconda-like, she seemed to be smiling mysteriously at them as she ascended out of sight. They finally caught up with her at the top, but their protected upbringing made them hesitate to speak to her. However, she was still smiling, so they took a chance.

From her purse she pulled a Folies Bergere program which displayed on its cover a photograph of "Mimi"—a most beautiful, refined-looking girl—naked to the waist. *"Je suis 'Mimi,'"* she said, and invited them to her next performance.

They went, and were delighted when she sent them a note at

intermission asking them to meet her after the show. She introduced them to an agreeable-looking companion, Gigi, and suggested that they all visit Fontainebleau together—an overnight excursion.

"*Mais, nous sommes vierges,*" stammered Al, feeling that honesty was the only reliable defense.

"*Justement,* we'll take separate rooms," Mimi said. But even that was too much for the youths, so they compromised by going dancing at Zelli's, a favorite nightclub of young Americans in Paris.

For a youth who had yearned for acceptance, Ben in his junior year had been a success beyond his most fantastic imaginings. In his sixties Dr. Spock recalled, "After that I was able to worry less about what people thought of me. But those desperate, singleminded efforts of my first three years at Yale have made my ambitious strivings ever since seem relatively moderate, though professional success was also difficult to achieve. So I relaxed and enjoyed my senior year very much, though looking back I do see traces of a mild letdown. In Scroll and Key I gave a slightly cynical talk on 'What Is Life For?' in which I said that when you've made the promised land it may not prove to be that great. But still it was fun."

Part of the fun was being elected to the Academic Class Day Committee and the Triennial (reunion) Committee, testaments to his popularity. Part of the fun was taking fascinating English courses and earning an 80 average for the first time. Part of the fun, as an acceptable Yale man, was being invited to debutante parties in New York—sometimes as many as three a night.

And part of the fun was to contemplate what would happen after graduation. Although Ben would enter medical school in the fall of 1925, with the sophisticated detachment of the college senior he unemotionally professed to regard a career in medicine as simply the most acceptable of possible alternatives. Yet that same year he confessed to a friend in a moment of enthusiasm that he wanted to become a pediatrician, for, he said, "Why not work with children, who have their whole lives ahead of them?"

three

THE MAKING OF
A DOCTOR

THE slight disenchantment that Ben experienced during his senior year intensified as he settled into medical school. To a small extent this reflected the disillusionment of the more intellectual and worldly members of his generation who scorned their bourgeois heritage, the Babbitts, Rotarians, and Main Streeters of America. They read *Vanity Fair* and hooted with pleasure at H. L. Mencken's derisive attacks on "the booboisie," at debunking biographies, and at a new, sophisticated magazine, *The New Yorker,* with its motto "Not for the old lady from Dubuque." They cynically recognized the side effects of Prohibition—bootleg liquor, hijacking, racketeering, organized mobs, gang warfare, and mass murders —matter-of-factly went on drinking, and became suspicious of reform movements and reformers. They viewed the Scopes "Monkey Trial" being conducted that hot summer in Dayton, Tennessee, to the accompaniment of ballyhoo and revival meetings, with the superior detachment of those

47

for whom, if God wasn't dead, the issue of religion was nevertheless buried. They believed in freedom—from convention, from restraint, from Victorian sexual mores—but for what?

Though Ben was intrigued by wordliness, he rejected such freedoms because of both his background and his choice of profession. After graduation he spent a pleasant, lucrative, and thoroughly unchallenging summer as a tutor-companion to four children, one of whom, S. Winston Childs, later became his brother-in-law by marrying Jane Cheney's sister, Cynthia. The end of the summer was enlivened by Jane's capitulation. She finally agreed to marry Ben some day, but marriage seemed so far in the future that they didn't think of telling anyone. Three days afterward his new fiancée, her mother, Cynnie, and the family housekeeper departed for a long-planned year on the Continent, a new experience for them all. As intended, Jane had studied only two years at Bryn Mawr, an abbreviation quite in keeping with the expectation of the time. A year abroad was deemed a suitable complement to the Cheney sisters' education.

When the summer ended, Ben went to Yale Medical School and found it an enormous letdown. Its buildings were a mile away from the college campus; the "fascinating" English courses were over; his "dashing friends" were gone; Jane was out of reach; his membership in Scroll and Key was irrelevant. He had traded in his crew shirt with the varsity Y for the ascetic lab coat of the medical student, and he was again living at home, which wasn't much fun either.

The first and second years of the curriculum consisted of lecture after lecture, laboratory after laboratory, fact after fact to memorize. From eight in the morning until five in the afternoon, physiology, biochemistry, but mostly anatomy—skeletal anatomy, cardiovascular anatomy, muscular anatomy, neurological anatomy, histological anatomy. The human being, the sick patient with sensitivities, desires, fears, and family, disappeared, dissected into atoms which the student was allowed to assemble, if he could or cared to, only after two years of dehumanizing preclinical work.

The beginning medical student's first patient was a cadaver (Ben's was so fat it was known familiarly as "Oily") which he laboriously dissected to bits for a year. His first smells were of formaldehyde, preserver of the dead rather than insurer of life; his first sights were of a dismembered, mutilated corpse instead of a living, healthy body. His first thoughts were not how to preserve health and life, but instead how to memorize an infinite number of minute details—often with the aid of mnemonic devices in the form of dirty jokes passed down from previous generations of disenchanted and desperate students. The curiosity and compassion which had inspired him to undertake a career in pediatrics had to be subordinated to the exigencies of mastering a mountain of necessary molehills.

The prospective Dr. Spock was depressed. This was not what he wanted to learn, and this was not the way he liked to learn it. He has always preferred the human to the impersonal, the overview to the minutiae. He has always loved to interpret, analyze, prescribe; he has always hated to memorize. So he found that "Anatomy, in particular, was dull, overwhelming. After supper with my family I'd go upstairs to study and would just sit there with the anatomy book open. I couldn't make myself learn the description of the clavicle, which includes the two ends, the anterior surface, the posterior surface, the superior surface, and the inferior surface; and where the muscles attach to it; and where the blood vessels go into it and come out of it. It's as meaningless as this, and I just couldn't make myself do it."

"Unfortunately for me," continues Dr. Spock, "the Yale Medical School had just adopted a new system in which the student was completely on his own instead of being oppressed by constant examinations, which most medical schools still have. That's how they make the students learn the damn stuff—by giving them a test on every subject every two weeks; you have to cram and cram. But Yale had a great dean, Dr. Milton Winternits, with an inspired idea, and there were no tests at all. After two years, or longer if you wanted, you took comprehensive preclinical examinations, which were to show you knew enough to go on to the clinical work.

"In the depressed state I was in I took advantage of the fact that nobody was testing me. I got the general idea from lectures but didn't learn any of the details; I would have been better off with a test every two weeks." Nevertheless, Ben did manage to pass the tests—fortunately, the only grades were pass and fail.

The summer that intervened between the first two years of medical school was as difficult as the studies, but it was a decided contrast. With life at home as "plain, repressed, and strict" as ever, Ben yearned for the "glamorous" existence he had led as an undergraduate. When the Yale Bureau of Appointments found him a summer job as a "tutor companion" at five hundred dollars (a high figure for those days) in the fashionable resort of Southampton, Long Island, with much time off and a car at his disposal, Ben was jubilant. But he hadn't counted on his mother's infuriated reaction, "Aren't you ashamed of yourself to be looking forward to that disgusting kind of life?"

The next day Ben strode back to the Bureau of Appointments and groaned, "Give me something really difficult," taking out on himself the anger he felt toward his mother. The amazed counselor looked through the files and finally said, "Here's something nobody's interested in—Frontier College." Ben took it.

Frontier College was in some respects Canada's precursor to the Peace Corps. It was founded in the early twentieth century by two retired clergymen to help the floods of immigrants become assimilated into Canadian culture. During the daytime the "College's" faculty, college students on summer vacation, were to work along with the immigrants to win their confidence. Observes Spock, "That's a hard way to win people's confidence." Then, after supper, they were to teach the immigrants Canadian ways and the English language.

So Ben, the son of the general counsel of the New Haven Railroad, was assigned to the Canadian Pacific Railroad extra gang number two working out of Winnipeg. He earned thirty cents an hour for a ten-hour working day, out of which he had to pay a dollar a day for food and wooden boards to sleep on.

Railroad tracks were ordinarily taken care of by a section gang of six to ten men, but for big jobs the extra gang of forty or so men, seasonal laborers, was sent out. In the boggy muskeg country of western Ontario, the ties and track were laid on a bed of sand mixed with rocks. The intermittent pressure of the train wheels caused the track to bounce and wobble, eventually to lose its straightness, and the shoulders of the roadbed to slide down into the muskeg. In the summer the extra gang had to reshape the roadbed and straighten out the track.

Dr. Spock recalls that this "was the hardest physical labor I've ever done, especially since most of it was bent over double. The men would begin shoveling at seven a.m. with three-foot shovels, scarcely suited to a six-footer. We'd stand in the swamp all day, scraping up shovelsful of rock and sand and tossing them up around the tracks. This was awful at first. After I'd been bent over for an hour I couldn't stand up straight. It was painful to be bent and more painful to straighten up. Eventually I acquired a magnificent physique—and a long red moustache."

The Italian foreman, his Italian assistant, and the English paymaster, retired from His Majesty's Army in India, were conscious of their status and declined to associate with the rest of the men, who were Galicians. These Galicians worked in lumber camps in the winter, in the spring on railroad extra gangs. In August they left the railroad, where they had netted two dollars a day, for several weeks of the wheat harvest at five dollars a day as long as it didn't rain. Then they went back to the lumber camps for the winter. In between jobs they saw their families for a few days, perhaps to father another child or to view the last baby, born in their absence.

Though Ben was separated from them by an almost impenetrable barrier of language, he learned to appreciate their honor, simple dignity, and cheerful accommodation to a rigorous life in the wilderness. Though church was inaccessible, on Sundays they dressed up in suits, pongee silk shirts without collars, and felt hats. Then arm in arm, two by two, they promenaded with stateliness up and down the track as if they were back on the main street of their village in the old country.

Ben for the first time got a glimpse of the deprivations and defenselessness of unskilled labor, not only of their low wages but of their primitive living conditions. (During an epidemic of intestinal flu the absence of toilet facilities struck him as particularly inconvenient and undignified.) He wrote to his father, who had an executive's skepticism about the motives of workmen, righteously pointing out their need for unionization in order to bargain for some rights and benefits, though at the time Ben was unaware of such amenities of employment as workmen's compensation, retirement pay, and other fringe benefits. His father did not argue back, and though Ben himself abandoned the crusade when he returned to medical school, he had made a minute start toward social activism.

After supper, or after the two hours overtime that most of the gang put in when it was available, Ben was supposed to teach English to his fellow laborers. With high hopes and aching back, he held his first English class, on the most elementary level, for fifteen men. The second night he held his second English class—for five men. The third night he waited with some apprehension, and only one man showed up—a Cockney named Alf who could already speak English. Dr. Spock remembers, "After that the evenings were just social between Alf and me. Alf was not very interesting, though he talked all the time and clung to me like a leech, for we were the only English-speaking laborers. I was discouraged to find that the Galicians weren't interested in learning Canadian ways— or the English language, though actually they had no great need of either. Or else I just wasn't an inspiring teacher. Of course, the twelve-hour working day also held the school attendance down."

As the other laborers left for the wheat harvest, Ben acquired seniority and was eventually promoted to flagman, a sinecure. That didn't last long because Ben almost caused the demolition of the entire gang. When the gang was working on a track, the flagman had to go up the track a couple of miles ahead to attach two torpedoes to one of the rails to warn any oncoming trains. The flagman himself was an additional warning for the engineer to cut down the speed of the train and proceed cautiously to the site of the track repairs.

Every day the boss told Ben to pick up the torpedoes at 11:45 and start walking back to the gang, for otherwise the track would be impassable during the lunch hour. One day he forgot to give Ben any instructions. The cattle train, more important than passenger trains because cattle had to be brought in on time, was due to come through at 11 o'clock sharp. It hadn't come by 11:15 or by 11:30. When it failed to arrive by 11:45 Ben decided to do as he had been customarily instructed. He had just finished picking up the torpedoes when he heard the cattle train tooting in the distance. He held to the assumption that the boss wouldn't want him to detain the cattle train unnecessarily, and he allowed it to rush by. But as he walked back, worrying about his decision, his foreboding was justified. The gang had started back for lunch on their hand cars and were rounding a blind curve when they heard the cattle train thundering toward them on the same track. They barely had time to get off, and were pale and angry when Ben reached them. Ben requested different duties and was made "Bull Cook" (caretaker of the cars the men lived in) for the rest of what Spock remembers as "a long and strange summer."

It is characteristic that Spock, when challenged, would take on a difficult job and then obstinately stick with it. His compulsion to fulfill any obligation he undertakes, major or minor, pleasant or unpleasant, has often frustrated his wife and children. But he himself enjoys this means of satisfying his stern conscience and he takes much pride in performing difficult chores.

The gloom of Ben's second year of medical studies was relieved considerably by his determination to get away from home and home town. He would transfer to Columbia's College of Physicians and Surgeons in New York, and he would marry Jane. Their separation for twelve months and, Jane says, the "great, thick, wonderful letters" that they wrote so regularly made them sure that they could no longer live without each other. After Jane returned from Europe they spent every weekend together, either in Manchester or New Haven, and eventually rebelled against the seven-year wait they would have had if they had delayed marriage until Ben could support them. So they set out to get their parents' permission and, more crucially, their financial cooperation.

Explains Ben, "To father, who had put himself through college and law school and who still had five more children to educate in private schools and colleges, I finally found the courage to say, 'I want to get married.' Father looked dumbfounded and asked in all sincerity, 'On what?' It was embarrassing to have to answer, in effect, 'On you, father.' My actual words were, 'I hoped you would give me an allowance.' "

Ben and Jane speculated that Ben's robust mother was unconsciously jealous of their romance, for she manifested "heart symptoms" during two different weekends that they spent at Jane's home during their engagement. She summoned him home in alarm each time, but recovered promptly when he got there. Surprisingly, Mrs. Spock, whose philosophy, like St. Paul's, may have been "Better to marry than to burn," persuaded her husband to give the couple $1,000 a year for Ben's remaining two years of medical school, of which $600 was designated for tuition at P. and S. That didn't leave much to live on.

Jane's mother, affectionately known to the family as "Boody," was less agreeable than Mrs. Spock at first, for, says Jane, "She didn't want me to marry anybody who wasn't able to support me. She had always said, 'You should marry a well-established man, like a diplomat or a statesman.' She was just worried that I couldn't manage, but she was a dear and gave me what she would have spent on me anyway—$200 a month." The couple were afraid they might need more than $2,800 a year for living, so Jane said she'd go to work, a decision almost as startling in their milieu then as was their plan to marry while Ben was still in school.

Ben and Jane arranged the wedding for June 25, 1927, the day after all their friends would be attending the Yale-Harvard boat race, an event much more significant to them all than Lindbergh's solo transatlantic flight the month before or the execution of Sacco and Vanzetti, scheduled for two months after. Geo Dyer came from San Francisco to be the best man, most of the dozen ushers were Ben's friends from the Yale crew and Scroll and Key, and one of the six bridesmaids was Jane's Bryn Mawr roommate, Mary Hand, daughter of famed Judge Learned Hand. As the attendants arrived Jane's Uncle Les assured each of them in a hoarse voice, "Don't worry. Everything's under control. I have my men around everywhere." Since no one except the wedding party was visible, they didn't know how to answer until Jane whispered, "He's not all there. He thinks he's the head of the United States Secret Service. Don't pay any attention to him."

The ceremony took place under an apple tree in the elongated oval garden of Jane's Aunt Polly, in Manchester. Though Ben thought little about religion, while Jane was, says her husband, "rather strenuously anti-religious, feeling there was no really scientific basis for religion," they were married in a modified Episcopal ceremony, to vows they had memorized. Jane, a modern bride, did not promise to obey her husband, though she recited her vows sweetly, with a butterfly hovering over her head.

The 350 guests went back to the Cheney yard for punch with liquor in it, Prohibition notwithstanding, punch without, and an enormous tiered fruit cake with white frosting. While the bride and groom were still in formal attire, the members of Scroll and Key of various generations, and their wives, withdrew to an upstairs room in the Cheney house. Barricading the door with some massive, ornately carved chairs, one of the older Scroll and Key members conducted a second ceremony—the traditional Scroll and Key wedding, in which the new bride was formally initiated into her husband's secret society and given a secret name to complement his. (Jane's was "Calliope.") There, they drank champagne and sang the traditional songs. Unfortunately, the solemnity of the ritual was hampered by the room's stifling air and the piles of wedding presents that crowded to the windowsills, though Ben and Jane had brazenly asked for checks wherever possible. They collected nearly $8,000, mostly from friends of Jane's mother.

Jane's mother had donated her car and a relative's chauffeur to take the newlyweds to a borrowed cottage in Barnard, Vermont, where they were to stay for the summer. Its location, just two mountain peaks removed from the Green Mountain National Forest, might have been considered a good omen for honeymooners: seven miles north of Prosper, ten miles southeast of Gaysville, at the foot of Delectable Mountain, on Silver Lake.

They intended to spend their wedding night in an old colonial inn at South Deerfield, Massachusetts. When they arrived, the inn was totally dark, for its electric wires had been damaged in the storm that had begun shortly after their departure from Manchester. However, it was romantic to be lighted up the stairs and into the best front room by candlelight, and to bathe amidst flickering shadows. They had just blown out the candles and got into bed—when the room was illuminated by a blinding glare. The power had come back on, as would have been all too evident to the occupants of the adjacent house, a scant twenty feet away.

The next day the rain kept up. Among the mountains the car almost skidded over a cliff and Jane developed a severe toothache, but their spirits remained high. The chauffeur eventually deposited them in the century-old shingled cottage and departed, taking the car with him. They self-consciously signed their names in the guest book and were touched to find that their hosts had left a cooked chicken and fresh strawberries in the icebox.

So they began housekeeping in the first of the many isolated areas they chose to vacation in throughout their married life. It was a quiet contrast to Ben's previous summer on the railroad gang. Jane's toothache disappeared, but she soon developed an infection which she remembers as having caused incessant, severe pain, though her husband retrospectively labels it "a minor but persistent illness." Ben, with the medical student's typical limited knowledge and the exaggerated anxiety of both the student and new husband, lost confidence in the local practitioner and requested a consultation. An instrumental examination was performed without anesthesia; Jane squeezed Ben's hand for comfort as the pain mounted. Before long he began to tremble and turn pale, and would have fainted out of sympathy for his wife's suffering— another sign of insufficient professionalism—if the nurse hadn't made him sit down. Although as a doctor he was always responsive to his patients' problems, he never again identified quite so personally with their pain.

For the month of July, a time of flagpole sitting and marathon dance contests elsewhere in the country, Jane recuperated and her husband did all the housework. Her old-fashioned treatment required six hot sitz baths a day, taken in a big tin washtub, for which Ben heated the water on a wood-burning stove, after he'd chopped the wood, made the fire, and pumped the water. He also did the cooking and the laundry, and together they read aloud Thomas Mann's *The Magic Mountain.*

Later they hiked, and three times a week walked together for a mile down the dirt road to the general store, pulling an express wagon to carry home their groceries. Jane, totally inexperienced in cooking and housekeeping, asked for "A pound of onions, please."

The clerk put one big onion on the scale. As the dial registered a pound Jane said, "I guess I'd like six pounds of onions."

"Jest settin' up housekeeping?" asked the storekeeper.

When the anticipated answer followed, he cannily offered to bring the couple meat from Rutland twice a week and, recalls Jane ruefully, sold his captive customers a variety of tough, fatty cuts he wouldn't have dared to offer his regular patrons.

The Spocks had a surprising number of visitors for honeymooners, including Father Riggs (the Yale Catholic chaplain), college friends, the Learned Hand family, Mrs. Spock, and Sally. Surprisingly, Mrs. Spock as a mother-in-law and as a parent to her grown children was quite different from the mother who dominated the household when the children were young. Jane found her " 'Hands off when they are married' policy simply marvelous. The only time she couldn't resist interfering with us was to have lunch alone with Ben once and say to him, 'Benny, I hope you're not using birth control because that's not right.'

"He replied, 'Mother, that's none of your business—and I am.' "

Jane continues, with an affection and courtesy that seems to her sisters-in-law more of a reflection of Jane's own good breeding than Mrs. Spock's due, "When we were living in New York she used to come down alone and sleep on our living room sofa. She'd take us to the theater. After Mike was born she'd go to the park with me and the baby. She was just great. She was very fond of me, and I was very fond of her, though she was a difficult person. We had respect for each other, and we got along beautifully because we were so tactful with each other. I'd talk to her about Ben, but when we came to a difficult subject we just left it alone."

The summer cost the Spocks $236.13, mostly for food and transportation. But two items are entered cryptically in their account book (Ben has kept meticulous financial records from that day to this) as "Pleasure," which cost $1.00 for the summer, and "Beauty" —60 cents.

The came the search for truth, or at least for medical knowledge. The newlyweds moved to 19 West Eighth Street in Greenwich Village, which with its bohemian charm seemed a romantic place to begin married life. For $75 a month they rented an apartment in, Ben wrote to Geo Dyer, "a bourgeois apartment house which forever smells of onions and coal gas, and where the garbage can and wastebasket are set outside each door at night for the early morning janitor. But our apartment is a gem, I should guess an emerald, painted green with beautiful old furniture and loads of books and an orthophonic victrola and lots of red seal records."

Jane got a job, for about $20 a week, in the Constitution Laboratory at Presbyterian Hospital on a research project directed by Dr. George Draper, which was studying the relationship of body build and temperamental makeup to susceptibility to various diseases—a precursor to William Sheldon's somatotyping. Jane's first assignment was to take psychological and family histories on patients with inguinal hernia.

And Ben began his third year of medical school, at Columbia College of Physicians and Surgeons. He was still examining his values, and sounded like a typically disenchanted member of his generation. He wrote: "I say that life is simply physical and physiological and psychological (the two latter merely complications of the first) and that any man is foolish who starts out trying to make it philosophical or religious, thereby voluntarily obligating him to act this way and not that way and to do everything because he ought. I came about as the result of the interplay of physical laws and I owe nothing to anyone or any idea (though I am as a matter of fact a slave of heredity and environment). But insofar as I have volition and a certain range of freedom I will not sign it away by obligating myself to ideas. . . . I say I am protoplasm that is here but will only last a certain length of time (after that nothing)." Characteristically, his idealism prevailed and he concluded, "I have capacities for satisfaction which is good. How can I satisfy myself? Sensuality has been proved the bunk too often before. It is not complicated enough nor permanent enough to satisfy the protoplasm of *homo sapiens*. What has served to satisfy me *always* before? 1) Living close to men, working with them and 2) Progressing (enriching by experiences and developing into a more complete individual by fighting each day to keep out of that rut and keep training and acquiring). My God, this isn't what I *do*—this is what I want."

Ben told a friend he thought the only really interesting people in his class were Jews; he found the rest of the medical students "not any more impressive" than those at Yale Medical School. As an example, he cited with scorn a student who was enjoying the very things that Ben himself had loved three years before—deb parties and an honorary fraternity. But with a mixture of hope and defiance he decided, "Medicine is much bigger than any of these aspirants and you don't get discouraged by them. It gives you lots of stuff to think about and resolve against."

At Columbia he was learning to think about actual medical treatment of real people with real problems, physical and psychological, in hospitals and clinics. He found he could now study with enthusiasm, for the personal contact made meaningful what at Yale had been only dry particulars in abstruse textbooks. His grades improved phenomenally, though, ironically, in light of his later fascination with psychiatry, he found that subject "just a series of dry lectures. . . . (We never saw a psychiatrist in the ordinary medical ward or clinic.)" Though he nearly failed that course, he graduated with the highest average in his class. He was elected to Alpha Omega Alpha, the equivalent in medical schools to Phi Beta Kappa among undergraduates. He was pleased, but decided not to join because he said he didn't want to spend the money for the initiation fee, though this was more likely an expression of superciliousness. Even more pleasing was the reaction of one of his classmates, who had been placed next to him for two years because of the alphabetical seating arrangements. When the class standings were announced, Ben's seat-mate blurted, "Spock, of all people! Why, I thought you were stupid!" He had been misled by Spock's frequent querying of classmates when he was uncertain about a lecturer's points.

As important as clinical experience in the education, medical and otherwise, of the prospective Doctor Spock were his long conversations with other students on the subway while they traveled to clinics at hospitals throughout the city. He listened to and talked and argued with students from the slums and ghettos, as well as from the suburbs; with Jews and Italians and even a few theoretical Socialists and Communists, whose views on such matters as Mussolini's dictatorship in Italy, Hitler's release from prison and rising ascendancy in Germany, and Chiang Kai-shek's break with the Chinese Communists opened new vistas on the conservative Republican perspective that was his heritage. Jane herself had been a Socialist in college, and throughout their marriage she was active in many liberal political and social causes years before her husband was. Along with the *New York Times* they subscribed to the liberal *New Republic* and the Marxist *New Masses,* and as early as 1928 Ben had been convinced by Jane and his new friends that "to be a Republican was not the ultimate wisdom." For President that year he voted for Democrat Alfred E. Smith, administrator extraordinary, opponent of Prohibition, Roman Catholic. (Spock's father, a staunch supporter of Herbert Hoover and the establishment, thought Smith's shoddiness was typified by the fact that he cleaned his fingernails in public.)

Ben describes the process of his political metamorphosis: "For several years, as I tried to make up my own mind, I argued during the daytimes as a conservative against my new liberal and radical friends, and then turned around in the evenings and argued as a radical against my conservative Yale friends. People commonly behave this way when they remain in doubt about important issues. Yale at that time could not have tolerated a nonconformist, whereas in New York you could be a radical and still have a social life as long as you were a good conversationalist. Whenever anyone mentioned anything *near* economics or politics I would pounce on them. I never realized that I was the one provoking all the arguments; I thought that suddenly all of my friends were passionately debating politics. That whole period really shook me up. Eventually I settled down as a New Dealer. But I find it amazing now that I had any friends left at all in those days."

Ben accommodated to married life more easily than to political changes. After six months of marriage he noted approvingly the passage in Kahlil Gibran's *The Prophet*, "But let there be spaces in your togetherness. . . . Love one another, but make not a bond of love." Ben wrote: "This is absolutely true and should be the law of marriage—it's hard to practice—it's the means of preserving the lover & mistress relation instead of shifting to ball and chain."

He told a friend, "Jane works all day and I work all day and then we come home and make supper and sit by a fire and study and read.

"All the disciplinary atmosphere of New Haven is gone and it sets free lots more energy for other things.

"We are honestly having a grand time. There is so much to do that there's no time to worry and the work is interesting and compelling and the vista is unlimited."

But Jane, though immensely proud of her husband then as now, found marriage more difficult. Jane's mother visited the couple for Sunday lunch and when Ben was out of the room whispered worriedly to Jane, "What's the matter with you? You never talk." Jane explains, "This was because I was overcome with everything in married life. I'd never had a full-time paying job before. I had to take a long trip on the subway every day. I was learning how to cook and run a house. And I was married. All this at once! I had never boiled an egg before, not anything!"

She continues, "I did all the laundry at night, and smoothed Ben's wet shirts along the edge of the bathtub to get out the wrinkles. But he was wonderful—he only expected me to iron the parts that showed. We put his pants under the mattress to get the crease back in. In those days I mended everything—even stockings. And there were no frozen foods. I had to go to market every day and prepare all the vegetables. I was busy every minute. I was exhausted."

Ben helped his wife when he could, but studying took precedence. He spent their first Thanksgiving cooking the dinner, cleaning all his suits with evil-smelling fluid, and pressing them when they were dry. (He had become an expert at pressing creases in the knees, a technique—learned from his father—he willingly demonstrates to visitors to this day.)

Once one is above subsistence economic level, poverty is relative. Ben and Jane honestly thought of themselves as "really as poor as church mice." So did their better-off friends, who believed them quite courageous, as they themselves felt, to start out married life on what the Spocks invariably recall as an annual budget of $2,400. (Even that figure approximated the average income for an American family of four in 1927; 40 percent of American families had incomes of less than $1,500.)

Perhaps in retrospect from the vantage point of the annual income of $50,000 to $100,000 they have enjoyed since 1951, the Spocks' income during their early married years *seems* like half the amount it really was. At any rate, Jane's earnings of around $1,200 a year (1927–30), when added to the $2,400 contributed yearly by Mrs. Cheney, plus the medical school allowance from Ben's father, made the Spocks' income in 1927–28 $4,600. It rose somewhat during the subsequent years of Ben's medical training because of income from the sale or dividends of their 5,000 shares of stock and bank interest on their wedding present money, and on the $5,000 nest egg bequeathed by Ben's godfather. This capital reserve, including a legacy from Jane's mother who died in 1931, made it possible for Ben to continue his advanced medical training until 1935 without earning money, which medical trainees were unable to do then.

The couple spent about $5,500 a year during this time, for life in New York was not cheap even during the Depression. The Spocks have always tried to economize, partly from Jane's continual concern about financial security, partly from Ben's intermittent Yankee thriftiness, and have pointedly avoided ostentation and waste. They have generally purchased only what was, to them, justified by utility or psychological necessity, though their felt needs have sometimes exceeded those implied by a more modest standard of living. Even when Dr. Spock reached the height of his income he bought a house under $40,000. They have never owned new houses; they sometimes bought secondhand cars even in the 1960's. (To carry out her first job Jane bought a twelve-year-old Chevrolet roadster with a top but no windows or door latches, which stopped dead during rainy weather.) Yet the Spocks have always enjoyed domestic comforts. During their first year together they bought a $69 washing machine, $73 worth of blankets (for a $15 bed), a hundred-dollar rug, and a splendid refrigerator for $295. And, following parental custom, after their first six months of marriage they have always had at least a part-time maid—at $30 a month full-time during the Depression.

They have also enjoyed dressing well. During the thirties they spent about ten percent of their income on clothing, though this percentage has decreased considerably as their income has risen. Because of his height, long neck, and broad yet slightly rounded shoulders, Ben has insisted that his clothes had to be custom tailored to fit, often by the cheapest tailor he could find, though occasionally at Brooks Brothers. He knows exactly what he wants, and gives explicit, practical instructions to his clothiers, as the letter he wrote to Witty Brothers in 1966 reveals: "Past experience [indicates] that we will not solve the problem [of fitting the suit across the shoulders] merely by pinching out more and more of a hollow in the middle of both shoulders. . . . Not only the shoulder seam but the attachment of the sleeve and the collar need to be opened so that the front and back panels that meet at the shoulder seam can be really freed, then laid on the shoulder so that they really fit it, then pinned together; finally the collar and sleeve can be pinned on."

Despite the vicissitudes of fashion over the years and his recent radicalization, Ben has consistently worn a pin-stripe or other conservative business suit, size 46 long, with a buttoned-up vest spanned by a gold-plated watch chain. ("I bought him the chain for $22," says Jane. "He's always giving it to children to play with, and I was afraid he'd lose a more expensive one. Since Uncle Guy's watch wore out years ago, he's worn it just for decoration.") With this he has always worn a pale blue or white shirt with a white, high, rounded collar held down by a collar pin; somber wool tie; black or brown oxfords; and black stockings.

In the spring of 1929 the Spocks spent $260 for a twelve-foot, secondhand sailboat, a psychic indulgence charged to the wedding present account. The care of the boat, burning and sanding off seven coats of paint to the wood and then repainting it, made Ben's and Jane's off-duty time even more exhausting than the working days. But the labor helped to justify his puritanical contention at the time that "pleasure is an incidental accompaniment of certain activities and cannot be purposefully indulged in." Recalls Dr. Spock with satisfaction, "The boat turned out gorgeous—but there was no point to it. It was a typically perfectionist project." It was characteristic of him to have gone at it so doggedly—and typical of Jane to have stuck with him for the whole project, even though at the time she didn't like sailing much, especially in the rough or windy weather her husband relished. They sailed the boat for two summers, sold it for $100 as the Depression settled in, and didn't buy another until after they moved to Rochester, Minnesota seventeen years later.

By July 1929 gang murders, including the sensational St. Valentine's Day Massacre, and racketeering had prompted the new President Hoover to appoint the Wickersham Commission to investigate law enforcement and Prohibition. Yet spirits were high, for still the stock market spiraled upward. Spock, not yet fully accustomed to being called by his newly earned title, "Doctor," was optimistic, too, as he began a two-year internship in medicine at New York's Presbyterian Hospital. Internship there was much sought after because of the Hospital's excellent staff and careful supervision. The two years were subdivided among a variety of three-month services: laboratory, pathology, emergency ward, surgical and medical ward, private patient, house physician. The hours were long, as they still are for any intern. Up at 7 a.m. (the habit of rising early persists in Dr. Spock's retirement), to the ward for blood samples and rounds by 8:00, followed by examinations of patients, and treatments. The intern also had to find time to take medical histories and examine new patients, to write up records, to read professional journals. The day was supposed to end at 5 p.m. if all the work was done, on the alternate nights off duty; during on-duty nights, the interns had to spend all night at the hospital, snatching sleep in between routine crises. But because the Depression came soon after Spock's internship began, many people could no longer afford private medical care. They crowded the emergency rooms and clinics, needing immediate attention, and the staff worked long hours overtime to accommodate them. Whatever glamor the interns had was invented by the general public; the interns themselves thought of their jobs as hard work but valuable training.

Dr. Spock's growing interest in the psychological and whole-patient approach began to appear in his patient histories. The customary medical history consists of information noted under several headings: family history, past medical history, and personal history; a "review of systems"; and a sequential discussion of the patient's current illness. In this format the information is unavoidably fragmented. But Dr. Spock was intensely interested in the patient as a whole human being, particularly in his emotional makeup, and was inclined to run the parts of the history together. He also insisted, rebelliously, on putting the story in ordinary language rather than in the traditional stereotypes.

By the time her husband was an intern, Jane had accustomed herself, she says, "to this new life, and I was talking by then. I wasn't so overcome with it. We had lots of friends and if Ben was on duty that night they'd say, 'Well, you come anyway for dinner.' So I went out by myself all the time. There wasn't anything improper about it. We lived then at 168th Street, and I never would let anybody take me all the way home because it was a long trip for them and an expensive one in a taxi. I'd just say, 'I'll go home on the subway.' If people had thought they had to take me home and then go home again afterwards, the man who was there for dinner as my escort wouldn't have wanted to come. So it was very smart of me to be independent. People loved it, and I had a wonderful time."

Jane was talking in public as well as in private to promote the causes she believed in. *Vogue* noted her streetcorner speeches against Prohibition: "Jane Cheney Spock drew crowds and astonished everyone who knew her by the power with which she did it, leaning earnestly forward and saying, 'You must listen to what I have to say about Prohibition.'" Jane laughs, "We had no microphones and were bellowing out, one day outside Bloomingdale's, against the noise of the trolleycars going by. I just had a five- or ten-minute speech and then I'd tell the crowds to ask questions. I had boned up on all the answers. I had Gene Tunney's wife and all sorts of fancy people shaking little boxes to get money for our cause. I had no idea I could do this. In front of the Public Library and on Wall Street, too. They had one truck with a microphone and eventually sent me with that because I was so good. They wanted to send me all over the state but then I found I was pregnant so I refused to go."

Jane also quit work, in anticipation of the baby to be born in the spring of 1931. But her pregnancy didn't inhibit the Spocks' energetic social life. Their enthusiasm for dancing—fox trots, rumbas, but especially waltzes—and the need for economy led them to organize "The Dancing Academy" among their friends and friends' friends. For $40 a night they rented the Mayo Hall, a tin-ceilinged ballroom frequented by the Irish in Yorkville on their day out; for $400 they hired a twelve-piece orchestra. Their admission fee was $1.50 per person. Their motto was "Don't Tread on Me." Their rules were: No introductions necessary. No cutting in. No two consecutive dances with the same person.

Dr. Spock was among the most elegantly dressed of dancers, if slightly on the anachronistic side. He preferred tails to a tuxedo, and with his dress shirt wore then, as now, a high, custom-made celluloid collar—an item as common today as a buggy whip. He has been willing to tolerate the collar's sharp edge (later claiming, in a letter of sartorial advice to choral conductor Robert Shaw, that "the neck gradually adapts to this, probably with an invisible callus") because the celluloid doesn't wilt during even the most strenuous dancing.

Every woman who ever danced with Dr. Spock, which means, in effect, nearly every woman who ever met him socially until the last decade when fund-raising tours supplanted many of his evenings of dancing, remembers the experience of being whirled about by a lithe, masterful dancer with tremendous savoir-faire and a booming laugh. Typically, a matron recalls wistfully, "Ben was the most popular dancer on the floor. During Leap Year dances the girls stood in line to dance with him. He was marvelous." To this day Dr. Spock gets letters that begin, "I'm the girl in the yellow organdy that you danced with twice at the Shamrock Ball in 1930. Do you remember?" The men who saw him dance are more reserved in their recollections, like the friend who remarks, slightly acidly, "Ben and Jane fancy themselves the best waltzers in the world," though even he adds that "The cover charge in some nightclubs was waived for the Spocks because they were so attractive."

Perhaps the Spocks' frenetic life made them more susceptible to physical afflictions than they might otherwise have been. Early in 1931 Dr. Spock developed spontaneous pneumothorax, a condition in which, he explains, "a blister on the outside of the lung breaks, air escapes through that hole from the lung into the pleural cavity, a potential space between the lung and the chest wall, like the potential space between the football bladder and the leather outside. If air leaks out, the elastic lung shrinks to a small, solid mass." Whenever Spock ran up the subway stairs, he could feel his lung bouncing around in his chest.

Like many doctors whose continual exposure to illness and death makes them unwilling to acknowledge their own afflictions or those of their families, Dr. Spock observes, "I'm uncomfortable about taking my own illness seriously unless it's damn severe. I'm afraid of being a hypochondriac; to pay attention to small things seems submissive, unmanly. But by the time I know I'm really sick I'm willing to go to a doctor." He did tell a fellow intern he suspected pneumothorax, in those days considered tuberculosis. The intern confirmed his diagnosis and Spock was put to bed for two months and forced to miss the last four months of his internship.

Jane was hospitalized at the same time, because their first baby, born two months prematurely, weighed only 3¼ pounds and lived just a day. They decided that others might be able to gain hope from their despair, and donated his body to the hospital for research. Though they didn't talk about it much, one of their friends says, "Their example gave us the courage to do the same when our baby died."

Saddened and shaken—the doctors warned Ben that because of the danger of tuberculosis, a disease of which a cousin and a grandfather had died, he would have to watch his health for many months—Ben and Jane emerged from the hospital together at the end of March. Their mood matched the deepening economic and political gloom that appeared to be settling over all Europe as well as the United States, but it was relieved somewhat by Mrs. Spock and friends of Mrs. Cheney's, who gave the couple enough money to go to the Riviera to recuperate. They sailed aboard the *Bremen*, a German ship where the tourist class abounded in beer, Gemutlichkeit, and impecunious young American intellectuals, some of whom figured they might as well expatriate because they couldn't get jobs at home. The somber circumstances of their departure were in marked contrast to Ben's exuberant voyage to the Paris Olympics seven years before.

Nevertheless, the trip over was pleasant enough, but the French Riviera turned out to be something of a fiasco. The Spocks had envisioned themselves lolling on the sand in the sun, but it was so cold they donned overcoats for their walks on the beach. Their hotel near Nice was a partial compensation for the weather. Attached to the side of the cliffs, it was built like a little upside-down skyscraper, bigger at the top than at the bottom. The living room was on the top floor near the entrance from the road, and all the bedrooms were below that. The couple enjoyed going to their room downstairs instead of upstairs, and felt cozily isolated there. Barred from the water by the cold, and barred from activity by their convalescence, they read constantly, bundled up on their balcony facing the Mediterranean. Jane has always read voraciously—fiction, history, biography, anthropology, world affairs—but Ben remembers that trip in 1931 as the last time he read novels or short stories, a strong indication of his shift of interests and of his conception of the relevance of fiction since his undergraduate days as a major in English literature.

Just as they had finally begun to relax, word came that Ben's father, fifty-nine, had died suddenly of a coronary occlusion while on a vacation in Bermuda. The grief-stricken Mrs. Spock was, on this rare occasion, able to relent in her stern expectation of duty, and delayed sending the cablegram until after the funeral and cremation so Ben and Jane would not feel compelled to rush back to the States. They stayed on, uneasily.

Jane remembers, "About a month after we had been there, Ben

developed what was known medically as night sweats and felt feverish. Because these were possible symptoms of tuberculosis, he was very nervous about himself and went to a French doctor in Cannes, whose efforts at reassurance took the form of dismissing the possibility of disease before conducting the examination. He even doubted the necessity of an X ray. Ben had no confidence in him, so we went to Paris by train and saw a doctor there who also said he was healthy. We stayed at an inexpensive hotel and had a wonderful time for two more weeks before we came home; we saw our friends the Prud'hommes and used to go out to eat and dance with them."

But by the time they docked in New York, Jane was having severe abdominal pains, which necessitated immediate removal of her gall bladder. They had to wait eighteen months for another baby.

In the summer of 1931 Dr. Spock began a one-year pediatric internship at a small obstetric and pediatric hospital connected with Cornell Medical College, New York Nursery and Child's Hospital in upper Hell's Kitchen at West 61st Street and Tenth Avenue. The hospital was a neighborhood necessity. Its obstetrical service delivered babies not only on the wards but in the homes of nearby mothers; its "boarding-out" department kept orphans and abandoned children until they could be placed with foster families. Its clinic was crowded with children, primarily from poor families, together with their mothers—and sometimes well brothers and sisters if there was no one to leave them with—on narrow wooden benches waiting their turn.

These children and the children Dr. Spock saw from 1933 to 1947 in the Pediatric Clinic at the New York Hospital (of the Cornell Medical Center, opened in 1932) suffered from the usual variety of illnesses common before the advent of effective antibiotics, mandatory milk pasteurization, and the more recent immunizations. So Dr. Spock treated tuberculosis, pneumonia, emphysema, mastoiditis, rheumatic fever, urinary tract infections, peritonitis, polio (there was a severe polio epidemic in 1931). In addition, the Depression—on top of the hard times many families were already suffering—produced other problems that the clinic pediatricians tried to relieve. Some were physical: rat bites, worms, lice, infantile diarrhea, rickets and other effects of malnutrition. Others involved family or community difficulties as manifested in physical neglect, family despair, and behavior problems.

Devastating though these ills were for the afflicted, they provided an extraordinarily broad and far-reaching education for the new doctors who were dealing with them, Dr. Spock included. Many physicians grow quickly bored with routine ailments and find their interest kindled only by a rare disease or complicated surgical problem. It was the opposite with Dr. Spock. He found the commonplace fascinating and, he says, "almost unconsciously made mental note of thousands of details of child development." He became absorbed in each patient's life history and in the daily problems the mothers encountered.

Not all the children regarded him with the same enthusiasm. One-year-olds were particularly terrorized by the sight of a white coat. Even if the baby was screaming, Dr. Spock would shout pleasantly to the mother over the din, as one clinic nurse recalls, "sincerely making each mother feel as if she were the *one* mother he wanted to see, with the *one* baby he wanted to see." Which, for the moment, was true. Another clinic colleague says, "Nothing was ever too much trouble for Ben. Once I saw him spend twenty minutes teaching a nervous young mother how to read a thermometer. There was another woman who came to the clinic who drove the rest of us crazy because she yak-yakked on and on about her child. But Ben would sit patiently and let her spill out everything on her mind. He said, 'I *like* them to talk. It helps both of us.'" With at least some of the mothers the rapport was tremendous. One of them, now living in the Bronx, still writes regularly to Dr. Spock about notable occasions in the life of her son, now nearing forty, whom the physician had seen as a youngster.

Dr. Spock would take an unusually thorough hour's history about each new patient, including information on his infant feeding pattern, weaning, toilet training, fears, and nightmares. "I drove the nurses crazy with mȳ slow pace," he says. To conduct the physical examination Dr. Spock, like most pediatricians, mastered the technique of pinning down a screaming, thrashing infant in much the same way one would subdue an opponent in wrestling. He would lean his body gently over the child's, parallel to the table, not actually squashing the child's body and wildly kicking legs, but allowing them very little space to move. (Dr. Spock's torso is nearly as long as most pediatric examining tables.) He'd first examine the infant's chest, abdomen, and extremities. Then, with his hands free, he'd examine the baby's eyes, nose, and throat, for pediatricians, unlike physicians of adults, always leave the head till last, because that examination provokes the greatest fear and protest. Babies invariably urinate on their captors, perhaps as a form of self-defense, and for this Dr. Spock was never able to devise a preventive. He had little remedy except to mop up and reassure the embarrassed mother.

Dr. Spock fared better with juvenile patients who could more easily discriminate among the faces atop the white coats. No child, from the seven-pound infant he could pick up in one huge hand to the most sophisticated grammar schooler, was ever awed by his size, or, in later life, by his reputation. (Some modern moppets confuse him with the pointed-eared Spock of *Star Trek*, and others with Dr. Seuss, the nonmedical author of bouncy children's stories.) Children can quickly spot indifference, insensitivity, and false affection—and in their reactions to Dr. Spock, generations of them have seemed to know, simply, that he liked them, and that his interest in them and their problems was genuine.

Dr. Spock got down to his patients' level, literally, by crouching. Though he played and kidded with small patients, he was invariably gentle. As he treated them he was developing the ability to see children's problems clearly from their point of view, as well as from the perspective of the doctor and the parents, that was to prove so valuable when he wrote *Baby and Child Care* a decade later. Yet he had no illusions of infallibility. With characteristic self-effacement Dr. Spock once told a friend that he couldn't claim much credit for the recovery of one child "full of pus" which the parents had considered nearly miraculous: "I'm glad I'm working with children because no matter how many mistakes I make, children have wonderful recuperative powers."

During the year of his pediatric internship Dr. Spock decided to take a year's residency in psychiatry and, eventually (by 1937), to devote his career "to figuring out the application of psychiatric and psychoanalytic principles, in a preventive way, within the practice of ordinary pediatrics. This was a field that realistically needed exploration." In *Redbook* in 1967 he clarified his motives somewhat critically: "I suspect now that it appealed to me for two additional unconscious reasons: to find ways to bring up children without quite as many kinds of uneasiness as I had experienced, and to shy away from direct competition in traditional ways with other local pediatricians and explore a new field by myself. In football terms: Go around end instead of bucking the line."

So he wrote to a number of pediatric leaders around the country who were interested in the emotional aspects of child development, inquiring where a pediatrician could get some training in applied psychiatry. Since such training didn't exist, he took a year's residency in adult and child psychiatry at the Payne Whitney Clinic of New York Hospital, 1932–33. Child patients were slow to appear, so Spock spent most of his time caring for manic depressive and schizophrenic adults.

Although he felt he learned almost nothing directly applicable to pediatrics, he did discover two important things that year, he says: "First, that my own pet theories about human nature were ridiculous. When Jane had told me, seven years before, that it was believed that a child's personality was already fairly well established by two years of age, I declared emphatically that this was nonsense. Actually I didn't know beans about it, because child development was not included in my college psychology course and I'd done no reading. I suppose I was resisting the idea of determinism, fighting for free will. Second, I realized that on the psychiatric staff of the Payne Whitney Clinic, the people who made sense of the cases were psychoanalytically trained. So I decided that I needed such training. This consisted, at that time, of being analyzed myself, participating in many seminars over a five-year period, and analyzing satisfactorily, under close supervision, an adult patient with neurotic problems. (Today analytic candidates must analyze several patients, and usually for a longer period than in the thirties.)"

Dr. Spock's own analysis was conducted in 1933–34 by Dr. Bertram Lewin, a disciple of Freud's who was highly respected in the New York Psychoanalytic Society. Dr. Spock explains, "The purpose and method of the psychoanalysis of a trainee is no different from that of a patient. It is, schematically speaking, to eliminate neurotic ways of thinking and acting by exposing their childhood roots, buried deep in the unconscious, to the light of reason. In the case of the trainee it is particularly important that he understand the true meaning of his own emotional difficulties great or small; otherwise his picture of the problems of his future patients will be distorted by his own distorted lens."

Then it was Dr. Spock's turn to be analyst. His first patient, who started at a fee of one dollar an hour (but who later, because of the Depression, was able to pay only twenty-five cents), proved to be paranoid, and unanalyzable. The second, an obsessive-compulsive with authority problems, quarreled his way out of his job and out of the city after a month of treatment. The third, an intensely feministic woman, argued fiercely against every interpretation for over two years, which resulted in little therapeutic benefit for the patient, but considerable education of a painful sort for the doctor. These experiences helped Spock decide to stay in pediatrics and try to work out the preventive psychiatric principles of that field, rather than to move into straight child psychiatry.

Twenty years later, when he was Professor of Child Development at Western Reserve University Medical School, he tried again, under supervision, to analyze two more patients, children this time, in order to deepen his insight as a teacher. He confesses, "I was not successful in either case—partly because they were relatively difficult, but essentially because I'm not a skilled therapist at a deep level. Part of the trouble, I assume, is that my feelings are over-controlled; as a result, my awareness of other people's deeply unconscious feelings is restricted. Of course, my preoccupation with the more general and theoretical aspects of psychiatry made it possible for me to write the many pages of generalizations in *Baby and Child Care*. But the effective psychoanalyst shies away from generalizations, knowing they will interfere with his close attention to what one particular patient is saying and feeling. I functioned satisfactorily at a more conscious level as a psychiatric consultant at the Mayo Clinic and as counselor in the pediatrician's office."

The supervisor of his efforts at child analysis, Dr. Anny Katan, then in the Department of Psychiatry at the Western Reserve Medical School, is less critical of Dr. Spock's lack of success than he himself is. She says, with admiration, "He came to Western Reserve eager to learn something new even in his older age. With youthful keenness, he went to psychiatric seminars and meetings of the psychiatric nursery school staff just as a trainee would. Whereas analysts might draw on their deep knowledge of several children, Ben contributed valuably the great breadth of his experience with hundreds of mothers and thousands of children."

She continues gently, "But Ben simply hadn't the training to expect to be successful as a child analyst. This takes five or six years; lots of courses, intensive seminars, a personal analysis over several years, and close supervision of one's training analyses. When we have a patient one year in analysis, we feel we haven't even scratched the surface. All a person can get in this time is a certain intellectual grasp on problems, but not an understanding in depth. Ben didn't have this background, so why should he expect to succeed with shortcut training?"

Nevertheless, in Dr. Spock's limited failure has been humanity's unlimited gain, for as a pediatrician in practice and in print Dr. Spock has been able to apply his psychoanalytic knowledge to entire generations, rather than to merely the few hundred patients he might have seen in a professional lifetime as a child analyst.

four

PEDIATRIC PRACTICE, PSYCHIATRY, AND PARENTHOOD

BY the spring of 1933 the Depression had reached alarming depths. That Hitler had burned the German Reichstag in February seemed to Americans less important than the grave problems at home. Thirteen million were unemployed, salaries had plummeted forty percent and wages sixty percent from the peak of prosperity in 1929. A million transients (including 200,000 children) drifted about the country seeking jobs, apple sellers and panhandlers crowded the sidewalks, breadlines stretched for blocks. With Franklin D. Roosevelt's landslide victory in 1932 and the confidence generated by his inaugural address, "the only thing we have to fear is fear itself," the American people were able to weather the bank holiday in March with the confidence epitomized in the Walt Disney ditty of the hour, "Who's Afraid of the Big Bad Wolf?" Roosevelt launched an alphabetical onslaught on the ills of the American economy—the T.V.A., the N.R.A., the A.A.A., the C.C.C., the P.W.A., to name only a few. Though there was some immediate relief and much hope, times were harder than they had ever been since Spock was born.

In September of this highly inauspicious year for new business ventures, at the age of thirty, Dr. Spock opened a private pediatric practice which he continued for eleven years. He began with high hopes, no patients, and a mind receptive to the newest—and most radical—theories of child rearing. His fees were moderate for medical charges but high in relation to wages—three to five dollars for office visits, five to ten dollars for house calls, depending on income. For the first three years of practice he scarcely made expenses, and he and Jane continued to live on the legacies of Mrs. Cheney and Ben's godfather. Dr. Spock recalls, "I certainly practiced a slow style of pediatrics that kept me from making much money, even when, years later, I had all the patients I could cope with. My office visits would be twice as long as the average pediatrician's because I was ready and willing to discuss in detail any psychological problems, which can be very time-consuming. My psychoanalyst once pointed out that I was scared of making money because that seemed aggressive, in the unconscious, like robbing somebody. (It's not admirable to be afraid of money.) I could tell myself that I wasn't practicing pediatrics—or later writing *Baby and Child Care*—primarily to make money, but because I thought children and parents were entitled to the fruits of the newest medical and psychodynamic principles."

Spock received few patients from referrals; most obstetricians thought he was a psychiatrist; psychiatrists knew he wasn't; and most established pediatricians, their clientele reduced by the Depression, had no patients to spare. Spock observes, "Before I started practice I used to say in a somewhat lofty manner, 'I don't think it is wise to have friends as patients,' meaning that it might be difficult to keep the two roles separate and that one role might destroy the other. It was lucky that many of my friends did not have the same idea because the largest part of my practice at first came from friends and friends of friends. Some mothers came because they had met and liked Jane. Some met me as patients in the pediatric clinic at New York Hospital and decided to be private patients." According to Dr. Milton J. E. Senn, who was (among other eminent positions) Arnold Gesell's successor as Director of the Yale University Child Center, Dr. Spock was known as a

"Freudian, psychoanalytically oriented pediatrician, who was competent, painstaking, sympathetic, understanding, gay, and full of fun."

However, some of Spock's closest friends, who knew him well enough to be invited to his home, selected other pediatricians. In the Spocks' well-mannered, upper middle class social milieu, children were strictly regulated according to precise schedules of feeding, sleeping, and toileting, and according to equally demanding codes of etiquette and custom. Although some of Spock's best friends found him personally, as one mother says, "highly complicated, highly attractive, and highly interesting," and though they trusted his medical judgment and professional discretion, they thought him unduly permissive with his own child—Mike was born just before his father went into practice—and feared he would preach to patients what he practiced at home. A few expressed uneasiness that Jane might give advice too, and so stayed away.

Dr. Spock's integration of psychoanalytic concepts with pediatric advice came about gradually, as he learned more in practice and studied more in seminars. In 1963 he explained to *Redbook* readers that until the 1940s "a rigid attitude permeated pediatric care. Babies had to be fed exactly at six, ten, two, six, ten, not earlier, not later. It was believed that if a baby discovered that he might be fed whenever he cried, he would demand to be fed more and more often and so would ruin both his digestion and his character. Most physicians prescribed the exact quantity of formula to be given . . . [with] no leeway. . . . It was believed that even occasionally to pick up and comfort a small baby would spoil him. . . . Toilet training was usually begun not on the basis of the baby's readiness but at a certain arbitrary age—often early in the first year."

He continued, "It seems strange to us now that this kind of unsympathetic rigidity could be practiced on infants at the very same time that newer concepts, such as the importance of love, the avoidance of excessive hostility and deprivation, the awareness of individual differences, were being recognized. The main reason was simple. Up into the first quarter of the twentieth century, the principal physical danger to babies had been the severe diarrheal diseases that killed hundreds of thousands of bottle-fed infants each year, particularly in summertime. No one knew for sure what the cause was. One theory blamed overfeeding, irregular feeding, improper formulas. It turned out that the real culprit was the bacterial contamination of milk, which was finally controlled by the universal use of pasteurized or evaporated milk. But it took until the mid-1940's for doctors to be reassured that irregularities in the amounts and hours of feeding were not harmful."

During his first few years in practice Spock didn't know how to resolve the various conflicting theories, and knew of no authoritative advisor. He says, "For instance, some psychoanalysts believed . . . on evidence from neurotic adult patients, that too early or too hurried a weaning from breast or bottle might cause lasting resentment in the child's unconscious feelings. But psychoanalysts couldn't give positive, practical advice to a pediatrician like myself about what *was* the right method or the right age for weaning. . . . My own psychiatric residency training had taught me that an individual who has irrational fears needs psychiatric help. Yet I found in pediatric practice that a majority of young children have irrational fears at one time or another. Did they all need to go to psychiatrists? I had no idea at first."

So initially, beginning practitioner Spock "worried a lot, gave the safest middle-of-the-road advice I could conceive of and anxiously assessed the results. With increasing experience and observation I came to some conclusions of my own, and I gradually acquired more assurance in counseling."

With this greater assurance came advice that was prognostic of the recommendations Dr. Spock was to make eight years later in *Baby and Child Care*. He gradually began to advocate far greater flexibility in feeding schedules and developed a much more casual attitude toward toilet training than most of his contemporaries. For by the late thirties experience had led him to believe that it wasn't the earliness or lateness of toilet training that was crucial, but the "mutual relationship of mother and child in the second year." He encouraged breast feeding, which at the time was unfashionable with most pediatricians and mothers because it was considered animal-like and thought to spoil the mother's figure; even the few mothers who wanted to try worried about not knowing how much the baby was receiving and assumed that success was rare because of the tensions of urban life. He even encouraged the use of the pacifier, then regarded as a disgusting and unsanitary anachronism, to provide the infant with some sucking in addition

to nursing. In his desire to make family living easier and more
enjoyable for both parents and children, Dr. Spock urged that
babies be cradled, hugged, and handled. Some pediatricians considered these recommendations dangerously permissive.

But the parents who consulted him relished the advice, and
their children even enjoyed going to the doctor. For Dr. Spock's
waiting room was a playroom filled with wondrous toys, including
a dollhouse or parking garage (whichever the child wished to pretend) with an elevator; and a child could take home a miniature
toy. After climbing the little staircase and going through the
trapdoor to the examining table, the children reached the doctor
relaxed and happy. He kept them that way, treating each child and
each parent with the same deference, courtesy, and intense interest
that he showed his clinic patients, and talking over their problems
at length. Says an office mate, "Ben spent so much time discussing
psychological aspects with the parents that he always ran late on
appointments. But even under pressure, he never lost his humor.
One patient came in with a rambunctious three-year-old, and she
was expecting another child. I heard Spock tell the nurse, 'Be
especially kind to her. She has a touch of pregnancy.'"

Dr. Spock denies that he was as relaxed as he appeared to others:
"I was asked to join a club of young doctors from various specialties
that met once a month, when each in turn would read a paper.
There I was intensely conscious of my tension, my relative lack of
success, and of trying to make the right impression on my peers."
One of Dr. Spock's unusually frank patients informed him that she,
too, sensed his tension, and complained that he appeared to be
rushing her. Though he assured her he had not meant to, he felt
that "there are continual tensions in private practice. You have a
terrific responsibility for every case. You have to keep everything
in mind and remember how many telephone calls still have to be
made. You keep thinking, 'Don't fall behind; keep your speed
up.'"

Yet many other mothers who consulted Dr. Spock during the
thirties found him relaxed, painstaking, and reassuring. One who
saw him for over a decade about her four youngsters raves: "I
think as a pediatrician Dr. Spock was a great teacher of mothers.
I apologized once for calling him up about something in connection

with our first baby. He said, 'You must always call me about anything that bothers you. I don't care how trivial it is.' Well, you do it for a while and then you begin to get embarrassed because you know he's got a lot of other things to do. So I apologized, but he said, 'Don't apologize. You don't realize it, but the more help I can give you on this first child the less I'll have to do on the second. You'll learn to distinguish between the serious and the non-serious.' And he was right."

Because of his psychoanalytic emphasis, over the decade of 1933–43, Dr. Spock gradually developed a clientele among psychologists, psychiatrists, psychoanalysts, psychiatric and medical social workers, progressive educators, and anthropologists, including Dr. Margaret Mead. Other doctors referred young children with severe feeding or toileting problems, anxieties, and other difficulties, and Spock advised the parents, though he didn't treat the children directly.

Many mothers found his advice revolutionary but satisfying. One recalls, "I was brought up in a family with three brothers where the grownups were always peering to see whether the boys were handling themselves. At least before this began with my own children I had enough confidence in Dr. Spock's judgment so that I wouldn't have made a comment on something like that without taking it up with him. So when our oldest boy was about two and began fondling his penis I asked Spock what to do. He looked me in the eye and said, 'Look, it's his penis. He's exploring, finding out about it. You don't have to worry at this age, though you might if he were a lot older. Just make sure his pants aren't too tight.' Well, this was good stuff."

Dr. Spock not only exuded confidence in his radical convictions, he also had the much-appreciated talent of giving parents confidence in their own common sense. A grateful mother remembers, "Dr. Spock gave you the feeling that 'Look, your baby is a human being. He has feelings. He isn't just a person that you feed three times a day and keep in a cellophane package in between times. He's a child whom you nourish—and nourish in all senses.' Because Dr. Spock was a very responsive person and enjoyed children himself, he was again reassuring. He gave you the feeling that you could really be a human being with your child and enjoy it; that you weren't going to make all the mistakes you were afraid you were going to; that you were really going to get along all right and you could do well."

Dr. Spock's booming laugh and cheerful voice gave him the manner of a lanky pediatric Santa Claus and buoyed parents up immensely. Typically, they remember with admiration, "In he'd come charging with those big long legs and you just knew everything was going to be all right." However, a few patients and colleagues were offended by what they considered his raucous, inappropriate laughter in serious medical situations. They were unaware that Dr. Spock's frequent laughter, though genuinely hearty, is not always genuinely mirthful. It is often a sign of stress or uneasiness, and invariably occurs when he recounts an embarrassing incident or criticizes himself or another.

A few parents left his practice for more traditional pediatricians who were less permissive, less forgiving, more punitive. But those who remained appreciated his recommendations which, laced with practical ingenuity, usually managed to accomplish their aims while still accommodating the psyches and personalities of their youngsters. Thus Spock advised the weary mother of an infant who persisted in flinging off the covers and standing up in his crib even after he had been tucked in for the hundredth time, "Put a snowsuit on him and let him fall asleep standing up. When he lets go he'll still be warm, and you won't have to wake him by coming in to cover him up."

Dr. Spock as a pediatrician also possessed the ability he later demonstrated so meaningfully in *Baby and Child Care* to see children and their problems from the viewpoints of the child and the parent, as well as from his own medical perspective. The mother of one timid tot was afraid her daughter would be in agony by being hospitalized for a tonsillectomy. She remembers Dr. Spock trying hard to find a surgeon who would give the girl anesthesia in her own bed, whisk her to the nearby hospital, remove the tonsils, and then rush her home again. But alas, this proposal was too radical —or too bothersome—for the medical establishment. After much searching, Dr. Spock did manage to find a hospital where the mother could spend the night with her daughter—even more difficult to locate in the thirties than it is now. Both mother and daughter were much relieved.

Mothers also appreciated Dr. Spock's immediate accessibility.

If he was out of the office, he could always be reached through his answering service, even on vacations. One delighted father re-members, "He gave us his summer address and phone number and told us to call him long distance if we ever needed to. We did write him once, and got back a long, detailed letter which included such advice as 'And put a little honey in the baby's milk.' "

A number of doctors, particularly like-minded pediatricians such as Milton Senn and Vernon Lippard, and psychiatrists such as John Reinhart (now Director of the Psychiatric Clinic at the Children's Hospital of Pittsburgh), have high praise for Dr. Spock as a pediatrician. "He represented a change in pediatric thinking," says Dr. Reinhart. "Before the influence of C. Anderson Aldrich and Joseph Brennemann in the thirties, pediatrics was essentially concerned with infectious diseases, nutrition, and biology. Under their influence, Spock and Senn added psychiatry to these concerns." Western Reserve University Professor of Pediatrics John Kennell adds, "In both his practice and his writings for parents, Dr. Spock was able to translate psychiatric concepts into lay terms. This was his most important contribution to pediatrics." Dr. Lippard agrees: "His great contribution has been in making child care less mys-terious." Dr. Frances Ilg, Director of the Gesell Institute of Child Development, glowingly adds, "He was one of the really great pediatricians. He had a miraculous way of handling children."

Other New York physicians of the thirties objected to the way Dr. Spock practiced medicine for the very reasons that the above physicians praised him, though even the critics began modeling their waiting rooms after Spock's playroom. Many thought that he was too psychoanalytically oriented, and that he overemphasized the psychological aspects of child care at the expense of the physi-cal. Some believed him too intuitive, claiming he trusted his own feelings and judgments but that he was not scientific enough. Still others felt that his interests and abilities lay in treating normal, well children, but that "he was not a good sick child doctor."

Dr. Spock himself had many misgivings about his handling of mentally handicapped children, though he learned from experience. In 1964 he confessed to the Ohio Council of Exceptional Children in a speech, "Difficulties in Caring for Exceptional Children": "When I would walk into the examining room and see a child of two or three years who was not able to do anything more advanced than lie on his back and play with his toes, my heart would sink. I felt bad about the problems the parents and child faced. But worst of all I dreaded being the one who would have to tell them that their fears were justified. I felt guilty in giving them the diagnosis, almost as if I were the creator of the defect. So I would put on my severest professional face and drag out the history and physical examination as long as possible, to put off the painful moment. When I sensed that the parents were searching my face for signs of my conclusions, I bent lower over my desk. Finally when I had told them the diagnosis I would go on to give them the talk which I knew was theoretically right; that though there was no cure for the retardation, this child like all children would need cheerful, loving parents who would appreciate his good qualities (rather than dwell on his limitations) and who would provide him with companionship and suitable playthings and training. But how hollow this talk must have sounded coming out of my grim face. I must have been convincing them, by my manner, of how tragic I thought their problem was. This could only have the effect of making them more uncomfortable with their child, rather than reconciling them to him.

"When I made the diagnosis of mongolism on a newborn baby I (like most pediatricians of that time) believed that I was giving the best possible help to the parents by advising them, if they could afford it, to place him at once in a nursing home, preferably without ever seeing him. This was on the theory that then they would not become painfully attached to him, and would be better able to provide a cheerful atmosphere and plenty of attention to their subsequent children. As if anguish and guilt could be solved by trying to forget."

He added, "It was years later before I realized that though having one's child live somewhere else than at home might be the better solution in one case (after much thought and discussion and perhaps after a trial at home), it certainly would not be better in another."

During the mid-1930s the political situation in Europe was becoming more and more ominous, from an American point of view. In 1935 Mussolini stormed into Ethiopia, without hindrance from the League of Nations, Britain, France, or isolationist America. In early 1936 Hitler marched on the Rhineland, again without effective opposition. The Spanish Civil War broke out, with the Republicans (supported by Socialists and Communists) opposing Franco's forces (the army, the capitalists, the upper hierarchy of the Church) supported by the Fascist governments of Germany and Italy. Again the neutral nations refused to take sides. ("A nightmare," laments Spock, staunch partisan to this day.) The abdication of England's Edward VIII to marry an American divorcee, Wallis Simpson, appeared merely a diversion, albeit a sensational one, to the more menacing events on the Continent. One of the few positive effects of the rending of Europe was the impetus to the training in psychoanalysis in America, as many brilliant disciples of Freud, Jewish and otherwise, fled before Hitler's bullying Brown Shirts.

During this time, as his wife was volunteering hours of effort to alleviate the plight of the children in Republican Spain, Dr. Spock was benefiting from the extraordinarily vigorous psychoanalytic climate in New York, which was becoming to psychiatry what Vienna had been a decade earlier. As part of his psychoanalytic training, Dr. Spock took two seminars a week for four or five years at the New York Psychoanalytic Institute. "Here," Spock says, "I was learning, among other matters, about Freud's concepts of emotional development in children, the phases in their attachment to parents and in their rivalry with parents, the effects of the excessive repression of hostility and sexuality. I was particularly interested, as a pediatrician, in the significance attached to breast feeding, thumb-sucking, toilet training, children's fears."

Although Dr. Spock found the seminars immensely stimulating, by the time they were concluded, in the spring of 1938, he regretfully decided that he would stay in pediatrics rather than move across to child psychiatry and analysis. Without having analyzed any patients successfully, he could not qualify as an analyst, though he could have persevered by attempting to analyze additional patients. He comments, "Consciously, I realized by then that there was a lifetime career in pediatrics in working out the preventive applications of psychoanalytic concepts. But probably just as important was the fact that I failed in the analysis of that feminist girl. I think if I had had the experience of helping her to change from a very unhappy person into a happy, well-adjusted one I might have chosen psychoanalysis because that seems more creative than the formulas and nose drops of pediatrics."

Although not formally a psychiatrist, Dr. Spock united the fields of psychiatry and pediatrics in his professional papers, as well as in his writings for parents. With Dr. Mabel Huschka of New York Hospital he wrote "The Psychological Aspects of Pediatric Practice," which appeared as a chapter in the *Practitioners Library of Medicine and Surgery*, XIII (D. Appleton-Century, 1938) and was reprinted by the thousands for students and parents. The process of writing it forced him to think through a number of the seeming contradictions between psychoanalytic concepts and what he was seeing in pediatric practice.

The fifty-page "Psychological Aspects of Pediatric Practice" applies Freudian theory to feeding, weaning, toilet training, discipline, and various behavior problems and nervous symptoms. It anticipates, in brief, much of the psychological essence of Dr. Spock's pediatric advice in *Baby and Child Care*, which was to follow eight years later. Drs. Spock and Huschka ask, for example, "What then is the harm in strict training? The answer is that few children can stand the constant interference with their wishes, the steady domination, and remain psychically healthy. They either surrender their spirits and become submissive, or they rebel. . . . [The child's] rebelliousness is usually a slow smoldering that brings him no gain but impairs his own character. The inadmissible hatred arouses anxiety, he turns the resentment against himself and finds ways to hurt himself in the real world or in neurotic symptoms." On these grounds the authors, radical for the time, encourage the "psychologically . . . natural and sound pattern of letting the child at all times (except under extreme circumstances) take the responsibility of deciding the quantity of food it wants" and of indicating its own readiness for toilet training.

Drs. Spock and Huschka were also innovative in introducing in their article subjects hitherto considered beyond the realm of pediatrics, such as the Oedipus complex. Dr. Huschka recollects, "[Ben] wanted to include a discussion on the Oedipus complex, and I said no, pediatricians weren't ready for that, but he went ahead and did it anyway, and did it so simply and well. We were pleased because a doctor who read the article said, 'It's fine—it's earthy.' "

From 1942 to 1944 and 1946 to 1947 Dr. Spock also combined pediatrics and psychiatry as a consultant in Pediatric Psychiatry to the New York City Health Department, and as a member of the Advisory Committee on Mental Hygiene of the Bureau of Child Hygiene. Three times a week he visited one or another of New York's sixty-eight child health stations, leading discussions of staff physicians and nurses concerning the prevention, detection, and handling of everyday psychological problems. He had also begun to lecture to various groups of parents, teachers, and nurses, who responded enthusiastically to his relaxed, chatty manner, if not always to his psychiatrically oriented subject matter.

In the Psychoanalytic Institute seminars Dr. Spock met a fellow student, Caroline Zachry, whose breadth of perspective and keenness of insight affected him most profoundly. Her experience included elementary school teaching, a Ph.D. in educational psychology earned under noted progressive educator William Kilpatrick, and psychoanalytic training. In 1938 she founded the Institute of Personality Development, affiliated with New York University and the Progressive Education Association, of which she was a leader. This was a training institute for professionals concerned with child care—physicians, teachers, social workers, nurses, and others. Among her disciples, in addition to Dr. Spock, were anthropologist Margaret Mead and foundation director Lawrence Frank.

Dr. Zachry asked Dr. Spock to share in leading the weekly discussions relating to the handling of children's physical, emotional, social, and scholastic development. He explains, "This was sound progressive teaching. When you want to influence a person, you make him a staff member and then he has to learn a lot. Caroline presided at the sessions, which were enormously educational for me. She was the best teacher I had ever known, teaching about what children are made of and how you understand and help them. Her teachings were partly based on psychoanalytic concepts but filled in with all kinds of knowledge that pediatricians and psychoanalysts don't have, such as how a seven-year-old typically differs in behavior from a six-year-old; what sorts of school subjects interest what sorts of children; how you motivate children who have become discouraged; how you use the curriculum to draw an asocial child into the group. When you've had psychiatric and psychoanalytic training, the answer to all problems in behavior tends to be, 'We'll get him into a psychiatric clinic or into psychoanalysis.' That *is* one answer, but it leaves out an enormous amount of what can be done in the school or pediatrician's office to cope with children with different kinds of academic and emotional problems."

He continues, "From Caroline and other educators I was gaining entirely new ideas about how children learn. Francis Parker, John Dewey, and Kilpatrick (among others) had recognized the importance of giving children opportunities to experiment and experience and feel as well as just to learn by rote, enlisting their interest and participation through real life projects appropriate to their age, using each child's strong points to arouse his enthusiasm and thus to overcome his weak points, seeking the reasons, when any student was doing poorly in school, keeping in mind the crucial influence of the teacher-pupil relationship in all learning."

Dr. Spock adds, "It would have been amusing for an observer to see me first learning from Caroline Zachry. I, of course, thought Andover and Yale were the cream of the cream in American education. But Caroline, grounded in the progressive concepts, thought of my schools as rather quaint anachronisms from medieval England. She never spoke bluntly; but very patiently she explained the fundamentals to me."

So to Dr. Spock's education in Freudian psychodynamics were added the most influential theories in contemporary education. In significant ways Dewey's philosophy differed from Freud's. Dewey emphasized the rational aspects of human mentality and claimed that one's basic personality was malleable through education. Freud was concerned with the irrational, unconscious, instinctive forces which determined human behavior. Freud focused on an individual's retrospective experience in order to shed light on his current problems; he interpreted the past verbally, symbolically. Dewey concentrated on actual experience in the present and on its implications for the future; for him "behavior" encompassed the entire range of human endeavor, which he dealt with literally, actively. Freudian theory emphasized the individual's solitary self as molded by unvarying psychosexual stages of development and responsive essentially to itself and to a small group of immediate family members, father, mother, siblings, or surrogates for these, in relationships that were inevitable. Deweyan theory stressed the individual in relation to a vast number of interactions and relationships with people, institutions, and environments which were capable of infinite variation and great power. Freud's goal was to enable the individual to know himself in order to maintain psychic equilibrium in the face of inevitable conflicts between his instincts and the demands of society. Freud's tool was psychotherapy; his mode was autocratic. Dewey's goal was to enable the individual to know his world, of which he himself was but one part, in order to control and refashion it and himself. Dewey's tool was pragmatic education; his mode was democratic.

Dr. Spock was not at all disturbed by the different approaches of Freud and Dewey. The theories of both excited him. So in his own thinking and later writing he chose what he needed from each, adding to psychodynamics the leavening of common sense pragmatism which lent theoretical validity to his own intuitive reactions.

At this time Dr. Spock was also learning much about schoolchildren firsthand—at least, about upper class schoolgirls. For, in addition to his other activities, in 1936 he became physician for the Brearley School, an excellent private school for girls five through eighteen. During his daily hour-long visits he not only examined the noses and throats of those returning after illness, but learned a great deal in conferences with the teachers about what a good school could do to help children emotionally and socially as well as academically. He realized that the perceptive teachers could see each child in the context of the whole class and so understand her in a way the pediatrician never could. The perspective he gained at Brearley, too, was to be drawn upon at length in his later writings for parents.

But Dr. Spock learned less about children from his own fatherhood than might be expected, especially as a novice father of a new baby. He explains that in the year Mike was born, during the internship in psychiatry, 1933, "I was beginning to get some idea that pediatrics shouldn't be rigid, but I had no positive philosophy and no great confidence, so there was no real theory to raise Mike on." There was no "Doctor Spock" to raise him on, either.

So the Spocks, as nervous as most new parents, began by rearing

Mike according to the standards they were accustomed to—with modifications. Following his father's new psychoanalytic knowledge (and immemorial custom), Mike was breast-fed at first. But, like most new parents, the Spocks had much to learn. Jane sighs, "I had a tremendous amount of milk for Mike at first. Then I came home with a practical nurse and it began to vanish. Ben didn't know anything about feeding the baby more often to stimulate the milk production, and he didn't know supplementary feedings would hinder the nursing. It was all handled just the wrong way so my milk went. When John was born, eleven years later, we had both learned a lot, and I didn't have this problem." She adds, rather grimly, "Mike was fed every four hours and if he screamed for an hour before feeding, he screamed"—sometimes causing the neighbors in adjacent apartments to bellow, "Keep that damn baby quiet!"

"Anyway," Jane continues, "I had a very good time bringing up Mike. He was a very cute baby. Our only real problem when he was an infant was caused when my mother died suddenly of a heart attack. This upset me very much. Mike, who by the age of six months had been eating potatoes, vegetables, and all kinds of things, refused to eat anything but meat, orange juice, and milk. It was nearly killing me to see him getting thinner and thinner. If Ben saw me handing him any food more than once after Mike had turned his head away, he'd snap, 'Stop, stop, no more!' But as soon as I got over my depression, in about two months, Mike went right back on his regular diet. We were all relieved."

By the time he was two, Mike was expected to behave in a more mature manner than parents raising their children according to *Baby and Child Care* expect today of their toddlers—or than the Spocks later required of John at the same age. His parents made Mike share his toys with other children in the park, "whereas with John," Jane says, "we knew enough not to make him share at two." In accord with the latest theories of the day, Mike was sent to nursery school, Jane says, "too young—at two. He had his lunch and nap there, and was gone all day, from nine to three. That caused some problems. We had trouble with Mike getting loose from me." (In spite of the problems, in the first edition of *Baby and Child Care* Dr. Spock recommended nursery school for mature two-year-olds. Eleven years later he raised the age to three; theories had changed.)

Speaking as an adult with children of his own, Mike felt that his childhood had been governed by "clear rules and clear limits." Dr. Spock was never an absolutist in his pediatric writings, but as Mike's parent (and later, as a peace advocate) he "always dealt in absolutes," said Mike in an interview with the *Ladies' Home Journal* of May 1969. "Something was either right or wrong. Having communicated those limits to me, I'd know the areas in which I could operate. The limits? Don't be disruptive, don't butt in, don't be slow dressing, don't forget to write thank-you notes to Grandma."

The limits were rarely enforced by spankings, though the Spocks had occasionally slapped Mike's hand as a reprimand when he was between one and two. Before long he outwitted them by putting out his hand immediately after he was slapped so they could slap him again. "So we stopped that," Jane says. Thereafter, the limits were enforced more by raised voices and eyebrows than by raised hands. Mike says, "I had more freedom than my friends—but within the limits of my strongly developed superego," which derived from the strongly developed standards of his parents. "Even when Ben wrote the baby book he was much less permissive than the book sounded," Mike explains.

In general the Spocks impressed on their sons the rules of civilized living as much by example as by lecture. Dr. Spock says, "I knew Jane and I were highly moral people and assumed that this was seeping across. Like other parents who considered themselves sophisticated, I thought at the time it was corny to preach too much about values and ethics. Now, thirty years later, I'm writing in a different vein, saying I think parents ought to teach their children specific ideals like world service, service to the country, generosity to friends. But we were certainly fussy about immediate, personal things like being polite to people. My general aims for my children were the ones that had been taught me as a child—high aspirations, honesty, loyalty, politeness. I deviated somewhat, partly because of my own rationality and partly because of the doctrines I'd learned—no need to make an issue about eating everything on your plate; better not scare children about sex."

In a matter-of-fact way the Spocks did try to dispel the mysteries surrounding Santa Claus and sex. Jane was most emphatic about this, she says, "partly because my boy cousins teased me about

Santa Claus unmercifully, and they said, 'That's not true about the stork bringing babies. The man rips open the woman's stomach with a knife and hauls the baby out.' I was determined never to put my own children through the agony I experienced—not just that I had lost faith in my parents, but that I was made to feel so ashamed because I believed after I was too old. If my children told other children the truth which their own families hadn't told them, then the other parents could just suffer. I thought it was right for our children to know the truth, though when they were older I did ask them not to tell other younger children the facts of life."

Jane concludes, "We used to read them 'The Night Before Christmas.' I'd tell them this was a wonderful story that people used to believe. I built it up as a story and they loved it just as much, though when we'd go to see Santa Claus they never asked him if he was going to come down the chimney." (By 1959 Dr. Spock recommended that young children not be taken at all to see the department store Santa Clauses, whose noisy, intrusive behavior and strange costume he thought might upset small believers. This advice drew the wrath of some columnists and was headlined in newspapers, "DOCTOR SPOCK KILLS SANTA CLAUS.")

The Spocks thought of themselves as affectionate parents; Jane a doting mother, Spock a loving father. Both Mike and John remember their mother as quite demonstrative, but their father as distinctly reserved. Mike says, "I can't imagine my behaving [as my own children do] when I was a boy. My kids are free with physical affection. We kiss good-night and when we say good-by. My father enjoys this with them too, because they are spontaneous with him. I never kissed my father." Yet though the children felt repressed in this and other respects, the Spocks believed they were encouraging them to be spontaneous—as well as interesting, successful, and polite: "Neither of us wanted bratty children," says Dr. Spock when accused of overpermissiveness.

Yet a number of the people who knew Mike as a child remember him as unpleasantly bratty. One Boston dowager claims that when Mike was of grammar school age at the summer colony of Honnedaga Lake in the Adirondacks he was "a pain in the jaw, a pest. He was weaned on beer. He would climb the fire escape and watch people dress. But he got along well with the other children—and I understand he's turned out very well as an adult. It's amazing."

The comments of another friend, whose children were Spock's patients and who "adored him because he was an absolutely wonderful pediatrician," corroborate this view: "We felt that Ben went way beyond his book in bringing up his own children. Where we'd normally say 'don't' to our children, they didn't." Still another friend felt that the Spocks should have been less indulgent of Mike: "When we'd stay overnight with them in New York, Jane would tell us, 'You're going to have to sleep in the living room. We asked Mike if you could sleep in his bedroom and he said 'No.'" It is possible that envy of the success of Dr. Spock's book would breed anecdotes calculated to undermine his efficacy as a parent. Yet Mike himself remembers being allowed to wander, pajama-clad, among his parents' cocktail parties, taking a sip of a forgotten drink or a puff on an abandoned cigarette. (As an adult he smokes not at all, drinks sparingly.)

But Mike's Aunt Hiddy thinks he was raised just right. From her perspectives, both as a devoted aunt and as an elementary school teacher convinced of the rightness of progressive education, "Mike was an absolute sunbeam, so welcoming and so friendly, so interested in other people. He was enormously loved, and would stop the other children at school from being mean. He'd make them take the tacks off the teacher's chair." Indeed, Mike looked as cherubic as Hiddy says he acted—fair-haired, round-faced, and boyishly engaging. As a grown man he still looks appealingly boyish.

Were the Spocks too permissive as parents? Or too strict? (Mike underwent nine years of psychoanalysis after he went away to college.) Or middle-of-the-road? The widely varying commentary of father and son, relatives, friends, and acquaintances makes the answer difficult to determine. If the test of successful parenthood is whether or not the child grows up to be happy, productive, self-fulfilled, then the Spocks did a good job. If the test is whether or not the child had a tranquil, problem-free childhood and adolescence, then the Spocks were less successful.

Mike's troubles as a toddler disappeared from three to six, after he got used to being separated from his mother when he went to nursery school. But other, more severe, problems arose when he entered first grade. He started off gaily. By the end of the first month he was beginning to get confused—he couldn't distinguish 'b' from 'd,' 'p' from 'q,' 'E' from 'B,' didn't recognize what the trouble was, and couldn't explain his problem to the teacher. During the second month he began to hate school, and by the third month he hated everybody. He was suffering from dyslexia, and sometimes read words from right to left instead of from left to right. So the word "was" often looked like "saw," "pot" looked like "top," and most of the words looked like nonsense.

Medical consensus today is that dyslexia is an inborn disorder or a result of "minimal brain damage," but Spock feels that his relationship with Mike may have intensified the problem: "I imposed a lot of strain on him—my inexperience, the fact that I was a tense person when he was young, my severity with him. When Mike was three and four years old I would get deeply bothered when he cried or was a sissy. I'd hiss, 'Don't be a booby.' I'm sure that my scorn was very painful. I acted this way because I was a sissy in childhood and felt ashamed of myself.

"I was hard on Mike in another way," Dr. Spock says. "As a reaction against my distance from and awe of my own father, I was trying to be pals with Mike in inappropriate (as well as appropriate) ways. I thought then that it was sensible to take off the tension by getting down on the floor with him and playing bear and lion, or doing pretend wrestling or pretend boxing. Now it's believed that this isn't a good outlet for the unconscious rivalry and hostility between father and son. In the boy's unconscious his father is too threatening a person and shouldn't reinforce his awesomeness with such play."

The pediatrician appears here, as in other instances, to be assuming too much of the blame. He overlooks the many pleasant things he and Mike did, which on any psychological balance sheet might have more than counteracted the activities which produced tension. And he ignores the physical basis of the problem.

Although the shoemaker's child didn't really go unshod, father and son didn't have very much time together. Dr. Spock was at the hospital, at Brearley School, or in his office from 8 a.m. often until 7 p.m. (though his office hours theoretically ended at 5 p.m.), and was attending seminars, giving lectures, or out with Jane on many evenings. When he was home, he was "forever on the telephone to mothers," Mike remembers. But the time they did spend together was intensive. Jane says, "On Sunday mornings I usually took Mike in the car with roller skates or a bicycle or a toy and we went on Ben's house calls so that he could be with his father from door to door. When Ben was inside, Mike would skate on the sidewalk in front of the house in Brooklyn, the Bronx. . . . Ben would take patients from anywhere. We needed the money."

Mike explains, "When father was available I had as much contact with him as anyone. Times of intimacy and companionship were mainly in the morning and in the bathroom. We'd get up about seven. I'd sit in the bathtub, while he'd shave and help me with my multiplication tables or tell me about a movie he'd seen.

"To stop my dawdling he devised a race against me over a period of months. When I beat him he bought me a silver-plated loving cup with my name on it, which years later turned black and peeled.

"A fuss was made over losing a tooth. If I discovered a loose one, I'd make it really wiggly before going to my father to help me pull it out. It never hurt because he did it quickly. He didn't pull, but gently punched it and poked it out with his thumb. Later, when I was asleep with it under the pillow, he'd slip in a quarter. I never thought there was a tooth fairy any more than I thought there was a Santa Claus.

"My parents were very generous at Christmas. My father loved to shop, and we'd go together for Mother's presents. When we went into the lingerie departments I found it embarrassing, but Father, with complete assurance, took a long time selecting nightgowns."

To this day Spock gives Jane presents of lingerie and accompanies her on clothes-shopping expeditions with great enthusiasm. He sometimes buys more expensive clothes than she would—including once a Geoffrey Beene dress for $180—and hats that, he beams, "Only Jane could carry off." He even enjoys looking through the racks at Macy's while Jane tries on sports clothes (during their third year of marriage she clerked briefly in Macy's Little Shop), finding the right sizes and holding onto the clothes she's chosen. Jane, who appreciates his patience and his interest, says proudly, "He's so well dressed himself, too. He is vain. He only likes women who are vain, too. You have to be feminine and attractive to please him, though since he's gone into the peace movement he's much more tolerant of plain women than he used to be."

Among Mike's more memorable presents was a toy fire engine that really pumped water. Home movies show Dr. Spock igniting a homemade cardboard skyscraper while Mike, resplendent in another gift, a Canadian Mountie uniform, manned the pump. Another favorite was the electric train that ran on tracks along a raised platform that father and son built around Mike's bedroom walls and even over the bed. A less successful endeavor was stamp collecting. When Mike seemed interested in stamps, Dr. Spock transferred his own boyhood stamp collection to a special album for his son, whose ardor was immediately quenched. Sunday afternoons at the circus and hockey games in Madison Square Garden proved more enjoyable, as did family rollerskating and sledding in Central Park. Cramming his long frame onto a child-size sled, Dr. Spock belly-flopped with gusto.

But Jane, like most American mothers, spent much more time with her son than his father did. Though Jane was deeply involved in the New York chapter of what later evolved into the politically liberal Americans for Democratic Action (she is currently a member of the national executive board) as well as in the Spanish child welfare effort, and they had a live-in maid, she made a point of being home when Mike arrived after school. She took him with her to "all sorts of cultural things because I enjoyed these and I thought he would." He did, so much so that he has made a career of museum work. When he was eight, on his own initiative he asked to become a Junior Member of the Museum of Modern Art. The director found this without precedent, but Mike was duly enrolled, and written up in *Harper's Bazaar*—"a whole story *and* a picture"—as the first Junior Member.

Because of his reading difficulties Mike was enrolled from second grade on in a special program at progressive Fieldston School in the Bronx, an hour's ride from the Spocks' Manhattan apartment. No school friends lived near him, so Mike was raised primarily in adult company. His childhood was pleasant but quiet in a well-bred, Eton-suit-and-cap way. Mike was quiet too, and admits to never being very outgoing or playful.

Both of Mike's parents were tense during the tense thirties, and it was inevitable that they transmitted some of it to him. Ben was tense mainly because the evidence that he could succeed in medical practice was so slow in coming.

Jane was tense partly from a series of miscarriages after Mike was born. She generates some tensions of her own. As a very thoughtful person who feels great responsibility for those she loves and whose life is as meticulously organized as she can make it, Jane has always worried about matters big, intermediate, and small: where to get leeks for the vichyssoise; whether her guests are comfortable; the inadequacy of the family income; and the state of her own health or her children's or her husband's. " 'He's doing too much.' We've all heard that a lot," observes one lifelong friend. Jane's anxiety about her husband's health was particularly justified during the period preceding World War II. Despite excellent general health over the years, in addition to the spontaneous pneumothorax in 1931, Dr. Spock suffered from appendicitis in 1935, pneumonia in 1937 and 1942, hay fever from 1938 to 1942, and back strain intermittently from 1940 on.

Jane also has the problem of living with an energetic, ambitious, dominating and critical husband. Dr. Spock himself says, "I think in many ways both of us are extremely critical and controlling people and I'm sure we're mildly irritating to some who like affability." Jane agrees, but adds, "Ben doesn't give this impression to the outside world. He comes across as a lovely, sweet, easygoing, natural kind of person and this isn't what he is at all. He's highly critical of others and himself, drives himself hard, and sets terrific standards for me and unconsciously did for the children, although he tried not to say it. But they felt it."

Everyone who knew Spock well in the thirties agrees with this description. He does, himself, though the consensus is that in the last twenty years he's mellowed considerably; "In my old age I'm becoming more tolerant and can get along comfortably with all kinds of people. I've accomplished enough so that if I do nothing more my conscience will admit that I did my job. I'm also relaxed because nothing could be better calculated to placate my harsh, chronically dissatisfied conscience than to be in the peace movement where I'm gaining nothing for myself but presumably working for the survival of humanity."

During the thirties both were psychoanalyzed. Jane's initial period of analysis had been recommended by her first employer as professional background, to facilitate her taking of psychological histories and discussing these with staff members who were psychoanalytically oriented. Ben's original year of analysis (in the thirties a year was considered sufficient for training purposes) had the predictable results both of benefiting his personal adjustment and of making him more aware of other problems as they arose. "Analysis," he explains, "is not like the baking of a cake or a piece of pottery which is suddenly 'done.' It is all relative. You have some analysis and then see how it works. Probably most psychiatrists and lay people who have been analyzed go back at least once again for problems." With this orientation, Ben later had another year of analysis with the famed Dr. Sandor Rado "because of the tensions involved in relationships with peers and other adults," and Jane, too, was further analyzed. She credits the analyses with giving them insights which strengthened their marriage immeasurably. Ben observes, "On a lifelong average I don't think Jane and I are much more tense than the average couple. Because we turned, on occasion, to psychoanalysts did not mean that we had greater tensions than most people but that it was natural, with our professional associations and experience, to get help for ourselves and our children whenever we felt the need, just the way college-educated middle class people turn to physicians for advice about mild physical symptoms, not waiting until they are at death's door."

One aspect of life which involved far more joy than tension for the couple was their remarkably active social life. By the time Ben was finished with internships and nights on duty the Spocks were dining out three nights a week and having six guests at home on another night. Spock says, "We didn't just go out on Friday or Saturday. We and our friends entertained on Monday, Tuesday, Wednesday, Thursday as well. We had to invite people two or three weeks ahead in order to get people who would be interesting to each other but wouldn't know everyone else. Jane is a marvelous hostess in every way—food, service, watching the guests to make sure they are not stuck with the wrong person. We both enjoy entertaining. We both like the same kinds of people, sparkly and mildly flirtatious; those interested in ideas and causes and the arts, whether they are conservative or radical, conventional or eccentric, as long as they can present their views in a way that's interesting to others and that invites response—no monologists. We had hundreds of delightful friends in New York and were always finding more."

Their guests over the past forty-five years enthusiastically confirm the Spocks' success at entertaining. Says one, "They were wonderful hosts, unbelievably giving of themselves." Says another, "Their parties were fun, exciting. Unusual for the thirties, the Spocks *loved* to have political after-dinner conversation. Their eyes would sparkle if they had a pronounced fascist type at their table."

But beyond the dinner table politics were the real national and international crises. As the dust settled over millions of farm acres in the west and midwest, hundreds of thousands of "Okies" joined the nomads made jobless by the Depression and became "fruit tramps" on the West Coast. The proliferation of alphabetical Government bureaus under Roosevelt was matched by the expansion of the alphabetical labor unions—A.F. of L., C.I.O., U.A.W., U.M.W.—and a wave of sit-down strikes in heavy industry. In spite of the great social changes that had been made during Roosevelt's first term, he acknowledged in 1937 that one-third of the nation was still "ill-housed, ill-clad, ill-nourished."

In 1937, too, Franco's armies attacked Madrid; the Japanese bombed Shanghai. A year later the uranium atom was split; Hitler took over Austria. Germany's preparations to engulf Czechoslovakia precipitated the Munich Crisis and led to Neville Chamberlain's ironically sanguine conclusion, "I believe it is peace for our time." The strongly isolationist mood in America began to crumble, particularly in 1939 as Hitler made a mockery of the Munich Agreement and conquered the rest of Czechoslovakia; as Barcelona—and all Spain—fell to Franco; as Mussolini seized Albania. In response to the German invasion of Poland, England declared war on Germany. Still the German armies swept on, in 1940 through Denmark, Norway, Holland, Belgium, and France.

The Spocks, like millions of other Americans, were dismayed about the European situation. Jane felt "The world was in a turmoil, and I didn't want to get into an elaborate apartment," but her husband, at last earning a comfortable living of twenty thousand dollars a year, was eager to move from the rather cramped and dingy railroad flat in an old building at 112 East 81st Street where they had lived for six years. So in 1940 they rented a large new three-bedroom apartment at Park Avenue and 95th Street "for only two thousand dollars a year. It wasn't expensive for those times or any times," claims Jane. "Ben wanted to put on a good appearance, and insisted on having the place done up with carpeting and all new furniture." (They were still using much of it thirty years later, after a number of reupholsterings.) "Twenty thousand dollars! I had all the curtains made at home so it would be cheaper—a terrific job."

Two years later, when the United States entered the war, Dr. Spock, like other physicians, was notified to "volunteer" for military service, and did so willingly. The Army promptly rejected him because of his back trouble and lung disorders. However, anticipating that he might be drafted later as Army standards became less rigorous, he wanted to move to a smaller, less expensive apartment which Jane could manage by herself if necessary. So they moved again.

During the first two summers of the war years, the Spocks spent a month at Honnedaga Lake, where Dr. Spock had been the resident physician for the Adirondack League Club summer colony since 1936. In this remote location, twenty miles from the nearest small town, Forestport, New York, the world upheaval was almost completely absent—if one chose not to read the newspapers or listen to the radio. The colonists' fifty cottages were scattered around the circumference of a lake ten miles long, and were accessible to each other only by boat. The way of life was casual; the cottage owners there amidst the thick forests of evergreens, yellow birch, and maple, were "relaxed, simple people"—and very rich. Most of them were industrialists from various cities in upper New York state. And, most of them liked the Spocks and considered Ben "a lovely, gentle, sweet, beaming person, always kind to children," and Jane "the firebrand of the outfit." Still, they thought of Dr. Spock as a servant, "living in squalor in the doctor's cottage with a closet full of old drugs"—even though he brought along his own maid to do the laundry and to give Jane a complete rest.

In return for room and board, Dr. Spock had to tend to the residents' medical problems. He averaged a patient a day, mostly executives with high blood pressure and a few loggers injured in the timber stands nearby. He also removed splinters and cemented in an occasional loose false tooth. He beams, "It was marvelous. No problems at all." So the Spocks swam, sailed when they could borrow a boat, and played a lot of tennis. By long tradition the doctor cared for the tennis courts, and Spock spent much of one summer resurfacing one of them. Jane, the family fisherman, couldn't fish in the big lake, for the water was so clear and totally devoid of algae that the fish couldn't survive in it, though she and Ben sometimes fished at outlying camps. In bad weather they chatted or joined one of the incessant bridge games.

In 1943, settled comfortably in this tranquil atmosphere, Dr. Spock began to write *Baby and Child Care*.

five

THE BIRTH OF "THE BOOK"

DR. Spock succinctly explains his facility with the written word, "All Spocks can write. They've had to." When her children were away at boarding school, visits, summer jobs, or college, Mrs. Spock demanded two letters a week; on one occasion she sent her eldest a telegram which warned, "Write or come home." Says Spock, "You had to tell just what you had done and with just what kinds of people. You couldn't spread Sunday morning out and move Sunday evening up and hope she wouldn't notice that you hadn't said anything about Sunday afternoon." If the letter wasn't detailed enough to capture the flavors of the correspondent's experiences, Mrs. Spock complained. As a result, the children developed a literary fluency which has made Dr. Spock feel that, to this day, he can speak more freely and expressively through written words than in person.

Through effective written prose he has spoken to millions. In 1938, when Dr. Spock's reputation as an *avant-garde* pediatrician was spreading, Doubleday asked him to write a child care manual for parents. He didn't think he knew enough, and declined. In 1943, Donald Porter Geddes of Pocket Books, a pioneer in paperback publishing, asked him again, claiming that his firm "could sell 'em by the hundred thousands, whether or not the book is any good."

This time Dr. Spock was willing. After eight years of medical training and ten years of pediatric practice he felt that he knew what he had set out to learn. He explains, "I had several different motives. No book existed which combined sound pediatrics and sound psychology. Most books written by pediatricians were basically physical; they gave only offhand answers to psychological questions, whereas I believed the two should be tightly integrated. I took it for granted that what I had learned about everyday problems would be as helpful to mothers reading a book as it had been to mothers in my office. I wanted it to be really complete—and there's never been before or since a child care book where a mother could find some kind of an answer to nine out of ten questions."

Dr. Spock continues, "Most books for parents—pediatric and psychological—appeared to me to be condescending, scolding, or intimidating in tone ('You are ignorant and if you don't do just as I say you'll kill your child'), which my training and experience told me was destructive of the parents' confidence and effectiveness. So my most important aim was to write a book that increased parents' comfort and independence; I wanted the book to avoid as much as possible telling parents what to do. I wanted to tell them how children develop and feel and then leave it to the parents to decide on their own course of action. My greatest joy later was to receive letters which began, 'I feel as if you are speaking to me personally and as if you think I am a sensible person.' Of course, I wasn't averse to earning money from the book, but without an advance, the initial royalty of a half a cent a copy would only add up to $1,500 a year if the book sold 200,000 copies at twenty-five cents each, and even that seemed optimistic. Yet I was glad that the book's low price would make my views available to as many people as possible."

He adds, "Several interviewers have said that I wrote a book on how to treat children gently as a reaction to having been raised with such sternness. This is a great oversimplification. I assume that the main unconscious reason for my going into pediatrics and writing a book on child care was because I identified with my parents, who devoted their whole lives to the rearing of their children. I agree with most of my parents' ideals and with half of their methods."

The customary procedure in writing such a book would be for the author to review the current literature on his subject or at least to review his notes on the care of his own patients. He might even consult volumes similar to his projected one to see how other doctors had handled the material, trying to avoid their mistakes and to benefit from their experience.

But not Dr. Spock, who claims he wrote the book entirely from his own experience: "I never looked at my records. It really all came out of my head," except for the suggestions made by other doctors, educators, Jane, and two other mothers to whom he sent the completed text. In his head were the poignantly vivid memories of his own childhood ("I myself was the basis for the description of the first child," he says) and the thousands of observations made during the course of his medical career. He explains that as a pediatrician he was informally researching thumb-sucking, weaning, feeding problems, toilet training, and the forty or so other subjects that his interest in the development of normal children had led him to focus on, none of which had been discussed adequately in pediatric literature. After discussing a child's particular problem with the parents, he would suggest a method of handling it that seemed to accommodate the child's physical and psychological needs. If he observed over time and in a number of cases that the method didn't get appropriate results or had undesirable side effects, he'd try another. And so it would go until a successful solution was worked out, when possible.

Typical of his investigations were changing recommendations on toilet training. In the mid-thirties he rejected the current vogue for training infants at six months as being psychologically unwise, and suggested that training begin at one year, when a child could better understand what was expected. But when some babies grimly balked, Spock, fearful of the neuroses that might result from intense conflict, modified his suggestion. In the late thirties he recommended that training start at eighteen months, when much of the automatic resistance would be outgrown and when some children expressed disgust at soiling. But some toddlers still objected. Spock, in the early forties, heard from several mothers that younger children of around two years, an imitative age, had trained themselves by observing the toilet habits of their older siblings. By 1943 he had arrived at the conclusion presented in the first edition of *Baby and Child Care:* "The best method of all is to leave bowel training almost entirely up to your baby," with success anticipated between eighteen months and two years "if no struggle has taken place." (However, this view, too, was modified considerably on the basis of later observations and evidence, and he began to expect more cooperation from the child at an earlier age. For Spock the printed word has never necessarily been the last word.)

With a variety of ideas on a multitude of other subjects from abscess to zwieback stored in his memory, Dr. Spock began to commit them to paper in the summer of 1943 at Honnedaga Lake. His summer practice at the lake was reduced to thirteen families because of the war, so he had abundant time to think and to write—more time, in fact, than he ever had again until he retired, twenty-five years later.

After a morning of tennis and swimming, the Spocks would take their portable typewriter out to a picnic table on the back porch of the rustic boathouse and try to compose. It was a slow process, as the beginnings of books usually are. Dr. Spock sat on the log railing, balanced precariously, dictating to his wife, who often nearly fell asleep over the typewriter during the long pauses between sentences. She had learned to type in case she needed to get a job if her husband was drafted, and welcomed the opportunity to practice—as well as to be with him. He spoke with painful slowness and she followed him easily.

As the book began to emerge, the Spocks returned to New York and Dr. Spock arrived at the method of composition which he followed for the next two years. During the next eighteen months of the writing, Dr. Spock would return home after a twelve-hour day of practice and teaching. He would play with Mike for a while, or help him with his homework. Then, by candlelight, he and Jane would dine, and after that the real work would begin. Jane recalls happily, "We found that going out socially three times a week slowed the work hopelessly, so we stopped going out altogether and

I gave up all my outside activities. I had become pregnant just about the time we started the book, I think because I was not tired and tense with all those things, and also because I was very happy working with Ben. We had gone ten years wanting more children, and were simply delighted."

Jane, petite and pregnant, sat at a large, rectangular desk which her husband had made years before for thirty dollars from two two-drawer filing cabinets bridged by a plywood top covered with linoleum which is just now beginning to peel off after forty years' use. Dr. Spock paced up and down the living room. Silence. Jane leaned her head on her hands. Silence. Dr. Spock ran his hand through his thinning hair—he had just turned forty that spring. Silence. More pacing. It took four trips up and down the living room for every sentence. Suddenly he boomed: "Some babies always vomit orange juice." Jane typed it, triple-spaced to leave room for corrections.

"No, no. Let's start over again . . . Some *young* babies always vomit orange juice."

So it went, silence four-fifths of the time, punctuated with staccato bursts from the typewriter, until 1 a.m. seven nights a week with longer sessions on weekends and vacations. "If it's easier to sterilize formula right in the bottles than to boil the bottles, nipples, and formula separately, why would anyone do it the hard way?" Dr. Spock would wonder, wearily.

"Because in the 'easy way' the milk scum clogs the nipples, and it's hard to clean the bottles inside," Jane answered. "They break, too."

"O.K. Let's put in the reasons." He dictated: "The main difficulties are from scum which clogs the nipples . . . breakage of bottles, and milk which sticks to the inside of the bottles and is hard to scrub off."

Dr. Spock himself wrote later drafts in a large, loose longhand scrawl at a draftsman's tilted-top table. He sat on a high wooden stool, an incongruity amidst the beige plush chairs and marble-topped tables, but an appropriate preventive of back trouble.

"Should avocado be mentioned for two-year-olds?" Dr. Spock wondered. "Does it make any difference? Why not just ignore the question? But California mothers will want to know. Put it in. Then the mother won't have to ask her doctor."

"But there are plenty of times when a mother ought to call her doctor. What to tell her so she doesn't call for every little stomach-ache but isn't taking chances? How to keep her from being frightened without making her too complacent?"

Gradually he hammered out the solution: "You certainly should get in touch with the doctor for any stomach-ache that lasts as long as two hours, whether it is severe or not. There are dozens of causes. A few of them are serious, most are not. A doctor is trained to distinguish between them and prescribe the right treatment. People are apt to jump to the conclusion that a stomach-ache is either due to something that has been eaten, or to appendicitis. Actually, neither of these is a common cause."

So he went from topic to topic, backtracking and going forward, clarifying, simplifying, covering all the familiar aspects of child care and the common diseases. Though the manuscript was already longer than the publishers wanted, new topics kept cropping up and being inserted.

During the second year, the process of writing was much the same as in the first, but the background had changed radically. By the spring of 1944 the Russian Army had swept from Stalingrad, where Germany had nearly defeated it in 1942, 800 miles west to territory within Poland and Rumania. Allied forces were preparing to liberate Rome, while troops under General Eisenhower were massing in southern England, preparatory to invading the Normandy coast. American bombs were raining on the Pacific islands, Guam, Kwajalein, Truk, Saipan. As the United States exerted every resource to end the war quickly, a new call for physicians was issued and this time Dr. Spock was pronounced physically qualified for active duty. Friends in the services suggested he apply for a commission in the Navy, which he received in March 1944 as Lieutenant Commander, the standard rank given to middle-aged specialists.

The Navy needed psychiatrists more than it needed pediatricians, so Dr. Spock was classified as a psychiatrist and was sent to Bethesda Naval Medical Center for a month's orientation. This consisted largely of learning how to thread his way among the miles of medical red tape without getting tripped up, learning how to practice psychiatry the Navy way. His main function during his two years in the Navy was not to treat psychiatric disorders, for Navy psychiatrists were expected to retrieve only the battle-fatigued Marines. The rest of the psychiatrically diagnosed were to be "discharged from the Navy as quickly as possible without making them full-pension claimants all the rest of their lives just because they were no damn good to start with," says Dr. Spock. He was usually in charge of a locked (prison) ward where the patients, guilty of repeated AWOL offenses, were there for only as long as it took to process their discharge papers (four to six weeks). Spock explains, "The typical patient in the prison ward was an impulsive, irresponsible person who had been deprived of love and care in early childhood. He was left back two grades in school, had a lot of truancy and finally quit school at about fifteen. He had rarely stuck to any job for more than two weeks. He left his jobs, he said, because the boss was riding him or he wasn't paid enough or because the noise made him nervous. You could write one of these discharge 'surveys' in your sleep."

The birth of the Spocks' second child began one rainy spring evening while Dr. Spock was still at Bethesda, on April 20. He had to take the milk train back to New York, and arrived just twenty minutes before baby John did. Barred from the labor room at New York Hospital, he hoped for a closer look at the baby in the nursery. As he joyfully approached the door of the room he had come to know well during his twelve-year association with the hospital, the head nurse met him, hissing, "You can't come in here! You're not Doctor Spock now, you're just a father. Get out!" So he slunk out, separated from his child by an impenetrable glass window and a century of tradition. He has since used this incident to teach medical students to be compassionate to fathers as well as to mothers.

Not long afterward, in May, Dr. Spock was able to live at home and to see his son in a more congenial environment. He was assigned to the U.S. Naval Hospital in St. Albans, Long Island, as a Ward Medical Officer in the Neuropsychiatric Service. In many ways the day's routine was much more orderly than when he had been a civilian pediatrician. He commuted to work with a congenial car pool of other doctors. He arrived at the hospital at 8 a.m., but, a pleasant change from pediatrician's hours, he could count on leaving at the Navy's sacred quitting hour of five. At night and on weekends there were no phone calls (Dr. Spock had turned his private practice over to a colleague, Dr. Clement Cobb), no house calls, no emergencies; his time off was his own—and Jane's—and the manuscript's, for *Baby and Child Care* was growing right along with baby John Spock.

The daytimes, too, differed considerably from civilian practice, but in less pleasant ways. Spock explains, "In a bad boys' ward such as mine there were two or three nurses and a dozen corpsmen on duty to care for about forty patients and to keep them from smashing the place to pieces. After 11 p.m., the nurses were off duty and only one corpsman was in charge—alone. Most of the patients were irresponsible roughnecks, and as soon as the lights went out they would throw their heavy boots at a more sensitive patient they didn't like, or dismantle his bed. The corpsman had to barricade himself in the nurses' station for fear that the patients, just for fun, would gang up on him. Because the Executive Officer disliked psychiatrists even more than he disliked psychiatric patients, he never cooperated with me in disciplining the trouble-makers.

"When I came to the ward," Spock continues, "the corpsmen were dispirited and the nurses were crying because the patients insulted them. I threw myself into the project of organizing the ward. I had staff conferences to which the corpsmen came, as well as the nurses. We went over case histories and discussed how to deal with various problems. We secured sports and recreational equipment. After a while corpsmen from other wards who had an interest in psychiatry were applying for transfer to my ward. The nurses were happy to work there and it was really clicking and humming quite well for a basically worthless purpose. Somebody has to shovel these people out, and if you're given that shovel at least you might do it well." Dr. Spock's administrative experience proved so successful that it helped give him the confidence to tackle a more complex administrative job with more complex personalities in Pittsburgh seven years later.

On went the writing, on and on and on. Jane, described by her husband as "a very practical person who knew how to do things clearly and exactly," made many utilitarian suggestions. She knew how to pin diapers and which way to lay out the equipment in the aseptic technique of sterilizing formula. She realized that a baby's sweater "should have shoulders that unbutton so you don't skin his nose putting it off and on." Yet, though as highly opinionated as her spouse, "Jane showed remarkable forbearance," Dr. Spock beams, "in never arguing with me over the way I said things for those three long years. It's all the more remarkable because in other circumstances she's quite free in telling me when I'm mistaken." He also credits his wife with extraordinary tact, for, he says, if she had expressed her opinions on his writing she might only have made him more determined not to change it, to the detriment of the book.

As the publisher's deadline approached and passed (the book was two years overdue), "it fell into order just by the necessity of getting it together," says a colleague, and the natural organization of a baby's typical day provided the pattern for organization within the sections arranged according to the child's age (infancy to one year, one to two, three to six, and six to eleven). Thus feeding came first, followed by sections on bathing, clothing, and sleeping; and the special problems were placed separately at the end of the book.

In the process of rewriting the book, Dr. Spock removed some of the rude, tactless, or overly candid remarks he had made. He says, "I knew they couldn't stay in. But if I tried to omit them at the time, I'd be obsessed and blocked, unable to go on to other points. So I wrote them in. For example, one out of three baby nurses that mothers get to go with them for a few weeks with their new baby are obnoxious women who are offensively overbearing with their small professional knowledge. As a pediatrician I'd feel sorry for the inexperienced mothers who were constantly being abused and belittled and shoved aside by these tyrants. In the book I wanted to say, 'Two out of three of them are absolutely poisonous. If you find you've got the poisonous kind, let her go.'"

He revised the passage to a more diplomatic: "[Helpful] is a practical nurse who will do part of the housework, who is willing to fit in with your way of doing things, who will let you feel that the baby is yours, and who has a relaxed, agreeable personality. If you find that you have a nurse that you can't stand, for goodness' sake get rid of her right away and take a chance on finding a better one."

He went through the manuscript again, removing from each page dozens of repetitions of the word "get" ("*get* well," "*get* new nipples," "*get* experienced") ; and another time extensively revising with an eye to clarity and safety.

By early 1945 Dr. Spock was circulating a much revised version of the book, now in mimeograph form, among various medical specialists, educators, and parents, for suggestions. Dr. Milton Senn remembers it with great excitement. He found himself quite sympathetic with the point of view on such matters as nursing, toileting, and "fears around three, four, and five" in which Dr. Spock suggested, "If your child develops a fear of the dark, try to reassure him. This is more a matter of your manner than your words. Don't make fun of him, or be impatient with him, or try to argue him out of his fear. . . . Naturally you should never threaten a child with bogiemen or policemen or the devil."

But when Dr. Spock continued, "Avoid movies [for young children] like the plague. The child is scared enough of his own mental creations," Dr. Senn objected. "What's wrong with the movies?" he wanted to know.

Dr. Spock replied, "I guess you don't go to the movies. Plenty of three-year-olds and younger do," and left in his warning. (Dr. Spock may have gained his impression of children's reactions to the movies when Nelson Rockefeller once told Jane that in 1939, after *Snow White and the Seven Dwarfs* had been showing for months at the Radio City Music Hall, all the seats had to be reupholstered, so often had they been wet by terrified moppets.)

Although Dr. Senn believed *Baby and Child Care* to be a very important book, he was more conservative than Dr. Spock in the preparation of food; he objected to the book's "unsafe short cuts" and, counter to his former colleague's advice, he recommended that all drinking water be boiled for children under a year old. Dr. Spock agreed and adopted the suggestion.

Another reader was Dr. Oscar Schloss, then Professor of Pediatrics at New York Hospital-Cornell, whose reputation for scrupulously thorough medical care and a thorough knowledge of medical literature made him one of the most sought-after consultants in New York. Paradoxically, though Dr. Schloss felt that physical diseases were treated too sketchily, he questioned whether the book might tell so much that parents would believe they could be doctors to their own children. Dr. Spock thought not, for he had carefully included many admonitions to parents, such as "consult your own doctor"; "the doctor has to judge"; "the child must be examined regularly."

Dr. Schloss was also "bothered by the [book's] excessive reassurance, particularly in the case of physical illness, feeling it might make parents too contemptuous of possible complications." For instance, Dr. Schloss found "too reassuring" such passages as: "If your child is ever found to have a positive tuberculin test . . . ("up to 50% of the children in some cities") . . . there's no need to be alarmed, since a great majority of the cases discovered throughout middle childhood have either healed already or will heal gradually with care. On the other hand, you don't want to neglect any precautions." The text then continues with a whole page of precautions.

Another consultant, Dr. Frances Ilg, made few suggestions for changes, for, she recalls, "That manuscript hit me hard. I couldn't put it down. I said, 'This is really marvelous.' He anticipated all kinds of emergencies in the life of the child, and provided tremendous security for the parents. He showed awfully good common sense. And to think that Ben got it all within this *simple* framework; his kind of simplicity is the most advanced. His book is a wonderful companion to the book Dr. Gesell and I did—*Infant and Child in the Culture of Today,* even though Ben couldn't see how we got age levels and kept saying 'I just don't understand it.' "

Among others consulted were Sidonie M. Gruenberg, Director of the Child Study Association of America, and, predictably, Dr. Caroline Zachry, whose suggestions were, says Spock, "relatively few but sensible." He also called on two "expert mothers," Mrs. Sylvia Bingham and Mrs. Mary Lescaze, both of whom felt the book was enormously helpful and "filled with Ben's great, gentle compassion toward parents and his marvelous humor. You could almost see him throwing his head back and giving a great guffaw now and then."[1] Dr. Spock incorporated most of their suggestions.

Though for a while the writing had seemed endless because of the multitude of topics to cover, Dr. Spock decided he had to stick to the most common matters and let the rarer diseases go. He devoted half the book to the first year of life, which he felt corresponded to how much help the mothers needed when they needed it. "There's nothing on pets," he acknowledges, "and when one mother asked why I didn't have anything on babies' names I wanted to say, 'Think up your own names, dammit.' "

Then came the problem of illustrating the book. Dr. Spock believed that illustrations were absolutely necessary, not for decoration or even as a relief to pages and pages of solid text, but to make practical things vivid, as in preparing formula, or to reinforce certain philosophical points made in the text, such as the need to distract babies from forbidden things rather than to always say "No."

He had seen and admired Dorothea Fox's drawings of children. When he suggested her to Donald Geddes at Pocket Books, Geddes complained that her work was expensive. "Why, we can get baby drawings at ten dollars a yard," Geddes snorted. After examining the bargain pictures, Dr. Spock still insisted on Mrs. Fox, and she was engaged.

She arrived at the Spock apartment one day, agent in tow, to discuss the illustrations. Dr. Spock found her "a very real person; warm, human, maternal, and just naturally frank." They agreed easily on many of the drawings. But then came the matter of how to explain to nursing mothers a new method of manually expressing breast milk which Spock had learned about from nurse Velma Davies. The pediatrician, with contorted hands applied to his chest and with some embarrassment, was trying to show Mrs. Fox the position of the mother's fingers on the breast. The agent looked uneasy, but Mrs. Fox said with aplomb, "I happen to be nursing my baby. Come into the bedroom, and let's see if I can understand what you mean." The agent chose to stay in the living room, but the doctor had no choice. So into the bedroom they went, and emerged a few minutes later, the problem solved.

The illustrations in the first edition were so successful that many mothers remarked on them to the author and only a few were changed during the next quarter century, primarily to accommodate new technical developments. In February 1960, when preparing to revise the directions on artificial respiration so his readers could learn the new mouth-to-mouth method, Dr. Spock requested of Mrs. Fox drawings that for the sake of young children "wouldn't make the victim look like an old corpse and make the procedure look like cannibalism or a perversion." He got what he wanted, including a picture of the victim "so appealing that she doesn't look like a victim [even after] her mother has yanked her up on her neck, bent her head back into a most unnatural position, and begun to breathe down her nose."

By this time the war was just ending in Europe. Roosevelt had died of a heart attack; Hitler had committed suicide; Mussolini had been shot. An era had ended, and a new one was beginning. The United Nations was organized, in part, "to save succeeding generations from the scourge of war" and to "develop friendly relations among nations based on respect for the principle of equal rights and self-determination of peoples"—brave hopes betrayed by later events. Yet the Cold War was beginning even while the "hot war" was still blazing. Three months later, the war in the Pacific culminated in the nuclear bombing of Hiroshima and Nagasaki. Ironically, in light of his later, vociferous opposition to nuclear testing and nuclear warfare, at the time Lieutenant Commander Spock welcomed the speedy end of the war.

Victory over Japan notwithstanding, Dr. Spock and his new base hospital unit were ordered to the Navy Personnel Depot in San Bruno, California on September 2, preparatory, he thought, to being sent to the Pacific. Pocket Books, knowing he would be away from New York, had offered to have the book indexed professionally, but Dr. Spock assumed that a professional indexer would not know under what headings mothers would look up such matters as "[Baby] carriage—letting him out" and "Nose—objects in," and decided he had to do the indexing himself. He began the job while jammed aboard a sweltering cross-continental troop train for seven days and seven nights. His section mate was a fat old warrant officer who fell asleep immediately after every meal and snored with such loud strangling sounds that it was difficult for the author to keep his mind on the indexing. In an equally incongruous scene the rest of the car's passengers, GI's scarcely older than the adolescents discussed in *Baby and Child Care,* sang, drank beer, and played poker.

While stationed for eight weeks in San Bruno, Dr. Spock spent the days writing more discharge surveys to ease more disturbed men out of the Navy. During the evenings he continued to index. This led to more rewriting on the galley proofs, for the process of indexing made the author aware not only of repetitions in the book but of slight variations in the repetitions: "If I said to use 'a mild soap' on page 50 and then on page 75 I said to use 'a soap' I knew that an anxious mother might be driven into a slight panic wondering whether I meant a *mild* soap on page 75. It's important from a literary point of view to get the repetitions out, if possible. If not, then the repetition must sound *exactly* like the first statement so the advice will be unmistakably clear." In addition, Dr. Spock was still finding ambiguities. Clarifying necessarily involved rewriting, for "you can't start changing in the middle of a sentence, so this damn sentence has got to be started over again; and some of the times you've got to go back to the sentence before that."

Following supper, Spock would head for the telephone center to put in an editorial call to Jane. After an hour's wait—there were a dozen booths to accommodate a hundred eager callers—the operator would call back to say that because of the usual heavy phone traffic there would be a two-and-a-half-hour delay in putting the call through. Dr. Spock would hurry to his dormitory to do some more indexing before returning to the telephone center. Waking Jane in New York (because of the time difference he usually reached her between 1 and 2 a.m.), he would begin "Galley page 73, line 42, presently reads . . . change to read. . . ." This went on for half an hour at a time, much to the annoyance of the operators, who kept interrupting to ask him to terminate his call for the benefit of others still waiting.

The following morning Jane would take the corrections to the publisher. The following night her husband would call again with more corrections. So it went for a month, until finally the book was printed, bound, and couldn't be changed any more—at least, not for a while. The phone bill was $150—a terrifying amount for an officer on a $5,000 salary.

The military moves in ways mysterious to civilians, and perhaps even to its own personnel, but it moves a lot. For the remainder of Dr. Spock's time in the Navy, he was to play a series of two-and three-month stands in military hospitals up and down the California coast. At the end of October, 1945, he was sent to the U.S. Naval Air Station in San Diego.

Although he went there as a psychiatrist, he was put in charge of pediatrics at the Family Hospital and Clinic, the first time in his life that he had real authority in a newborn nursery. A pediatrician in private practice goes from hospital to hospital to attend his newborn patients, but the baby is bound to the hospital's routines, not the doctor's, except under extraordinary circumstances.

Dr. Spock explains, "I had been keenly interested in breast feeding in New York but never got a chance to write the orders that would make its success likely. Unfortunately, although half of the few women in New York in the thirties who wanted to breast-feed seemed to come to me because they heard I approved, only a determined minority were able to succeed. In those days private patients stayed in the hospital twelve to fourteen days after childbirth, which was enough time to put an end to the breast feeding in most cases. It was very frustrating for the mothers and for me. But in San Diego the babies went to the mothers every four hours day and night, no formula was given, I gave talks, and the nurses were indoctrinated to be encouraging. I sent the babies home 90 percent breast-fed. Although *Baby and Child Care* hadn't come out yet, I was comforted to find that what I had written there had validity."

On December 1 Jane and the children arrived, after it seemed certain that Lieutenant Commander Spock would not be sent overseas. For three months they lived pleasantly in an ample house with oranges and roses in the backyard and furnished down to the last dishtowel, rent-controlled at $125 a month. They even found a live-in maid.

Then Dr. Spock was transferred to the U.S. Naval Hospital at San Leandro, across the bay from San Francisco—back to the psychiatric ward and more report writing. Postwar housing was scarce and, Jane grimaces, "It took him three and a half weeks to find a very cheesy stucco cottage down on the mud flats in East Oakland. There were no blankets or sheets or pots or pans. It had a toy-sized ice box with room underneath for only a small pan to catch the water. When we went away for the weekend the ice would melt all over the floor. I did all my own work and diapers and laundry except what could be sent to the Naval Hospital, and had five or six meals a day to get because John's were always different."

John, then nearly eighteen months old, had developed celiac disease, a chronic inability to digest starches and fats which resulted in a foul-smelling diarrhea, poor nutrition, and irritability. A San Diego specialist did not get positive results on the chemical tests, so John remained on a diet that intensified the problem until the family returned to New York months later. Yet despite John's affliction the Spocks enjoyed the redwood forests, Yosemite, Monterey, and panning for gold in the Mother Lode.

On May 7, 1946 Dr. Spock was released from the Navy. He received the customary citation from the President, which was to prove ironically prophetic in light of his later antiwar activities: "As one of the Nation's finest, you undertook the most severe task one can be called upon to perform. Because you demonstrated the fortitude, resourcefulness and calm judgment necessary to carry out that task, we now look to you for leadership and example in further exalting our country in peace."

The Depression was decidedly over. Federal controls were off, and for middle income families the cost of living had risen 28.4 percent between 1940 and 1945, and was to rise another 31.7 percent by 1949. But wages surpassed prices and people rushed to spend their wartime savings on synthetic stockings, real coffee, prefabricated houses, and new "used" cars. Personal controls were off as postwar optimism reigned, and the shadow of the hammer and sickle did not seem nearly as ominous as the shadow of the swastika. Men and women were returning from the service in droves, reestablishing families, starting families. The baby boom was on; the United States population grew by twenty million in the decade of the forties, an increase of eleven million over the growth in the previous decade. The time could not have been more auspicious for the publication of a baby book.

The Spocks returned to New York in May 1946, just in time for the publication of *Baby and Child Care*. The usual procedure of the time was for a book to be published in hardcover first and, after a year or two when (and if) the sales began to dwindle, for it then to be reprinted in paperback at a considerably lower price. But *Baby and Child Care* was contracted for by Pocket Books, exclusively a paperback publisher. Yet in 1946 libraries did not stock paperback books and reviewers did not review them, so to ensure the widest coverage, Dr. Spock wanted to have the book published simultaneously in hardcover and paperback—a phenomenon unique at the time.

Publisher Charles Duell, a Yale friend of Dr. Spock's and father of three of his patients, had found Spock's book as well as his pediatrics "lively and modern and interesting," and was willing to take a chance by publishing a simultaneous hardcover edition—a risk that another hardcover publisher had been unwilling to assume. So in May 1946 appeared the hardbound *Common Sense Book of Baby and Child Care,* published by Duell, Sloan, and Pearce, at $3.00 a copy, and the identical paperback *Pocket Book of Baby and Child Care,* at one-twelfth the cost.

Dr. Spock was right. During the first ten months after publication the paperback spread widely, outselling the hardcover version by a ratio of 90 to 1—541,460 to 6,478—a quantity nearly as large as the total distribution of the erstwhile best seller, Dr. Luther Holt's *The Care and Feeding of Children,* over thirty-nine years. Paradoxically, with the paperback royalty of $\frac{1}{2}\phi$ per copy for the first 150,000 and $\frac{3}{4}\phi$ (a 3 percent royalty) thereafter, Dr. Spock's income the first year from the relatively meager hardcover sales surpassed the paperback income by 20 percent—$2,609 to $2,178. As Alfred Wilson, the Spocks' great friend, and financial advisor during the thirties, observes, "Ben has been characterized by not using his talent to make money. In insisting on getting the widest readership possible, he's made about the least amount of money that anyone could have."

Within three years of publication, the paperback sales reached a million copies a year—to date, totaling over 24,000,000 copies—and making *Baby and Child Care* the world's all time best seller after Shakespeare and the Bible. The book's hardcover sales still average 10,000 copies annually. Since 1950 the book has netted its author between $25,000 and $60,000 a year.

Dr. Spock was, as a fledgling writer, dependent on his publishers' judgment. As he matured and gained in stature as an author, he began to seek greater independence—and a more equitable royalty. Because the paperback and hardcover versions of *Baby and Child Care* had been published simultaneously, Pocket Books hadn't had to pay the customary 3 percent reprint royalty to the hardcover publisher. Dr. Spock thought that the extra 3 percent should be his, on the basis of the sacrifice he made in simultaneous publication, and as early as November 1947 began to nag the editors of Pocket Books for it. At that time Robert DeGraf of Pocket Books replied to the pediatrician's request: "Frankly, we believe that your book will continue to sell for years, but . . . nothing is certain. We have seen too many books of excellent sales, year in and year out, suddenly . . . stop selling." In 1949 the reply was the same, but the reasons were different. *Baby and Child Care* was a much larger book than the ordinary 35¢ paperback (502 pages) and required a number of revisions not customary with paperback reprints. Both factors made the book more costly to produce than the ordinary paperback, so Pocket Books couldn't afford to pay the author more money.

By 1957, with a revised edition in the offing, the editors had yielded, and Dr. Spock's royalty had been raised to 6 percent. But a new problem occurred. Dr. Spock's new editor, Freeman Lewis, told him that in order for Pocket Books even to be able to sell such an unusually large book (by then 627 pages) for such an unusually low price (50¢), they would have to insert advertising in it. But, Lewis soothed his author, who was already beginning to bristle, this wasn't to be unique, but the start of a general trend. Many paperback books, to be called "book-a-zines," would soon be carrying ads appropriate to their subject matter. Baby books would advertise baby products, cookbooks would advertise foods and housewares, and so on. Advertising, Lewis said, had been common in nineteenth-century books, and control of it was the publisher's prerogative.

Dr. Spock's lawyer, Henry Cooper of the Pittsburgh firm of Houston, Cooper, Speer, and German, did not see a legal basis for objection. So Dr. Spock, though he thought ads would "cheapen" the book, grudgingly said he'd permit advertising, provided that, he wrote Cooper, "1) Other books besides mine carry advertising; 2) It is made clear that these are advertisements and that there is no connection between . . . me . . . and the products advertised; 3) I have no medical objections to the product; 4) The advertising claims are not exaggerated, competitive, undignified, I to be the judge; 5) There is a contract between Pocket Books and me establishing the above rights." Over the objections of Freeman Lewis, who believed that such a contract would undermine both the author's and the publisher's rights, a contract amendment was eventually drawn according to Dr. Spock's specifications—as it later turned out, a serious mistake on Spock's part.

As a result, Dr. Spock scrutinized the copy of each ad for each printing to make sure it fitted his criteria and was in accord with medical ethics. He objected to superlatives, to mysterious and miracle ingredients, and to unsubstantiated or exaggerated claims.

Thus on a sample ad for Johnson's "unique, no-tears formula" baby shampoo he penciled to the publisher, "Is this one *really* 'no tears'? . . . I'll try a drop in my eye if they'll send me some." On one occasion he was seen in his office at the Western Reserve Medical School, erect and proper, sucking on a baby bottle nipple in an attempt to test a manufacturer's claim. He has never let dignity inhibit honesty.

The existence of the advertising continued to rankle. Dr. Spock was spending many hours examining the ads, but he refused to accept the fat fee offered by the publisher for his efforts because medical ethics forbade a commercial nexus, as did his personal revulsion against commercialization. He objected to Pocket Books's "ill gotten" gains; in 1964, typically, they made between $6,500 and $7,500 a page for every 500,000 copies, or about $260,000 extra income annually. Spock continued to complain, but to no avail. By 1962 advertising in other books had proven economically unfeasible, and *Baby and Child Care,* with its twenty- to twenty-six-page advertising supplement inserted prominently in the middle of each volume, was the only remaining paperback with ads.

This was the crowning ignominy. Dr. Spock, feeling that "Pocket Books was trading on my good name, that I wrote them a damn good book, that if the book had been no good they couldn't have made all this [extra money] out of it . . . and that they were tearing down my name and reputation," threatened to sue to force removal of the advertising. Freeman Lewis remarked mildly, "I don't see how Pocket Books can do what Ben Spock doesn't want. Pocket Books can't be fighting Ben Spock." Because of this, Dr. Spock later felt that if he "had raised hell right from the moment Pocket Books said they were going to put in advertising they would have backed down rather than make all that fuss." But by then advertising had been in the book for several years and Lewis's boss, Leon Shimkin, the president of Simon and Schuster, decided that it was too profitable for his firm to relinquish.

So Spock decided to sue, but he hadn't much of a case. When a lawyer tells his client that he has, at best, a fifty-fifty chance of winning a proposed suit and suggests that he try to settle it out of court, the client might correctly assume that the lawyer really means he'll lose miserably if the matter is ever put to a court test. Dr. Spock, however, characteristically chose to assume that he and morality would triumph over commerce and the law. He authorized his lawyers to use "every possible device to get rid of the advertising in the book," irrespective of the cost, which eventually amounted to over $40,000.

From 1962 through 1965, Cooper and colleagues protested to Pocket Books. They claimed that publishers don't have the right to insert ads into their authors' books unless the contracts specifically authorize this, and that Dr. Spock's contract did not. Spock's lawyers further argued that advertising in *Baby and Child Care* was inconsistent with public policy because it caused the public to believe that Dr. Spock endorsed the advertised products; it subjected him to the risk of violating medical ethics; and it was demeaning and degrading to Dr. Spock in particular and to the medical profession in general.

Pocket Books denied all charges, stressing that the agreement concerning the advertising had been honored by both author and publisher for six years: Dr. Spock collaborating with the advertising procedure by screening the ads, Pocket Books accommodating Spock by printing a disclaimer dissociating him from the advertising.

When arbitration attempts failed and the suit was finally settled out of court in December 1965, Pocket Books's reasoning prevailed, and they made a good bargain. The agreement stipulated that Pocket Books would remove the advertising from *Baby and Child Care* after the spring 1971 printing, provided that Dr. Spock revised *Baby and Child Care* by September 1, 1967, and by September 1968 wrote for them a book on "Facts of Life for Teen Agers." Every delay in delivering the new manuscripts would proportionately prolong the advertising period, though this penalty was later voided. The settlement was somewhat sweetened for the author by the price rise of the third edition (1968) to 95¢, and with it an increase in royalties to 10 percent (an unusually high rate for a paperback book), voluntarily offered by Lewis, with whom Dr. Spock's relations remained as trusting as if the suit had never happened. Although publishers commonly advance money to authors commensurate with their drawing power, Dr. Spock, who wrote Pocket Books's largest selling volume, got no royalty advance for the teenager book. He had received modest advances on some of his other books published by Pocket Books; the $1,000 advance from

Duell, Sloan, and Pearce on the first edition of *Baby and Child Care* came after numerous delays and considerable nagging on Spock's part. Only after twenty-five years as an author did Spock finally begin to fare much better, when in 1968 he obtained the services of Robert Lescher, a widely respected literary agent.

Dr. Spock's literary relations with parents—initially Americans, eventually the world's—were also to remain trusting and serene until the sixties, when some took offense at his views on politics and on peace.

six

BABY AND CHILD CARE: IMPACT AND REACTION

"**T**RUST yourself. You know more than you think you do. . . . Don't take too seriously all that the neighbors say. Don't be overawed by what the experts say. Don't be afraid to trust your own common sense. Bringing up your child won't be a complicated job if you take it easy, trust your own instincts, and follow the directions that your doctor gives you."

With these words, which began the first edition and set the tone for the five hundred pages that followed, Dr. Spock began the process of emancipating over fifty million American parents—and their children. He freed grandmothers from the manual his own mother swore by, Dr. Luther Emmett Holt's *The Care and Feeding of Children* (New York: D. Appleton, first edition, 1895; fourteenth edition, 1929). With the babies' best interests at heart, Holt urged that they be bowel-trained by two months and fed a liquid diet for the first year. He cautioned parents against playing with babies under six months, to avoid agitating their delicate nervous systems. Yet by the time a child was two he was strong enough to be weaned forcibly, even if he starved for a couple of days. After his will had been broken—for his own good —he'd cooperate, and there would be no further problems.

Dr. Spock freed his contemporaries from the advice offered by behavioral psychologist John B. Watson, Ph.D. in *Psychological Care of Infant and Child* (New York: Norton, 1928). From the same benign motives as Holt, Watson aimed at producing a child "happy," "free," "independent," and "original" through letting him "learn as quickly as possible to do everything for itself"; children should be treated "as though they were young adults." Said Watson, echoed soon after by the U.S. Children's Bureau's widely circulated *Infant Care*, "Let your behavior always be objective and kindly firm. Never hug and kiss them, never let them sit in your lap. If you must, kiss them once on the forehead when they say good night. Shake hands with them in the morning. Give them a pat on the head if they have made an extraordinarily good job of a difficult task."

Dr. Spock's volume simply replaced other books on child rearing popular in the thirties and forties, such as Dr. Herman Bundesen's *The Baby Manual* (originally titled *Our Babies*), which had sold over ten million copies between 1925 and 1944. Though in later editions Bundesen's advice on diet, breast feeding, and gentle treatment of children was congruent with Spock's own, there were important differences in style and substance.

Understandably. After an era of anxiety, the postwar generation wanted to love. Dr. Spock urged, "Don't be afraid to love [your baby]. . . . Every baby needs to be smiled at, talked to, played with, fondled—gently and lovingly." After the grimness and constraint of the Depression and the war years, when children were raised in a rigidly scheduled fashion reflecting the times, the new generations were ready for peace, for relaxation of the rules and freedom from regimentation. Dr. Spock advised, "You may hear people say that you have to get your baby strictly regulated in his feeding, sleeping, bowel movements, and other habits—but don't believe this. He doesn't have to be sternly trained . . . [but] will fit into your family's way of doing things sooner or later without much effort on your part." They wanted to have fun. Dr. Spock encouraged, "Be natural and comfortable, and enjoy your baby." He was saying exactly what they wanted to hear.

Because of his sensitivity to the viewpoints, emotions, and reactions of parents and children, Dr. Spock could humanize what other experts on child care made artificial, statistical, clinical. Children, for Spock, are neither dolls to be babied nor miniature adults, as they are in some other baby books. Dr. Spock acknowledges the dignity, as well as the humor, of a child's struggle to learn and to mature, and writes about it simply, with love but without sentimentality. He animates the cardboard child of other baby books, portraying typical child behavior in precise, vivid detail, often with dialogue and setting. "A baby taking his first teaspoonful of solid food is quite funny and a little pathetic," says Spock, viewing the baby as a fond parent would. "He looks puzzled and disgusted. He wrinkles up his nose and forehead." Then, subtly shifting to the infant's point of view, he continues, "You can't blame him. After all, the taste is new, the consistency is new, the spoon may be new. . . . What he can't stand is to have a whole spoonful of lumps dumped into his mouth when he's not used to it."

Often, as Dr. Spock captures the essence of intimate parent-child relationships, he appears to be inside the parent's mind—and the child's—simultaneously, unobtrusively, while still retaining his own medical, psychological, humanistic perspective. "Be quietly friendly with your baby whenever you are with him," he encourages from his role as parent advisor. "When you hug him or make noises at him, when you show him that you think he's the most wonderful baby in the world, it makes his spirit grow," Spock interprets psychologically, "just the way milk makes his bones grow." Then Spock the humanist recognizes what it's like to be a new parent with a new baby, "One trouble with being an inexperienced parent is that part of the time you take the job so seriously that you forget to enjoy it." After that the pediatrician becomes advisor again, "It's the gentle, easygoing kind of companionship that's good for him and good for you." Finally, he synthesizes the perspectives of parent, child, and pediatrician in a lyrical conclusion to the section: "It's the comfortable feeling that goes into your arms when you hold him, the fond, peaceful expression on your face when you look at him, the gentle tone in your voice."

Among the many ways that Dr. Spock identifies with the reader is by vividly talking in the reader's own terms. His sentences tend to be short, averaging under twenty words. He uses three times as many one-syllable words as multi-syllable words. His colloquial language is full of commonplace expressions, so appropriately tailored to what he is saying that they seem inevitable, rather than clichés: Compliment a young child who is "doing a good job of self-feeding . . . but don't be so enthusiastic that he smells a rat." Even Spock's invented figures of speech are still comfortable and homey: "If the adults around [a child] are undemonstrative, he dreams of comfy, understanding playmates as the hungry man dreams of chocolate bars."[1] Favorite words of Spock's are, predictably, "natural," "sensible," and "wholesome": "It's sensible for babies . . . to be in the sun for part of the time"; "The adolescent should think of [sex] as primarily wholesome and natural and beautiful." In *Baby and Child Care* (but not in his political or more moralistic writings) Dr. Spock seldom uses the common suffixes and locutions of bureaucratic prose: "-tion," "-sation," "-ize," and "-wise." His unique substitute is "-ness." Thus, in discussing toddlers' attitudes toward toilet training he says, "I think it is sensible for you to encourage the swing of the pendulum, from possessive*ness* to aversion, by emphasizing the uncomfortable*ness* of having the movement in the diaper." [Emphasis supplied.]

What Dr. Spock says, like the way he says it, is designed to help the parent build self-confidence (in contrast to Watson's indictment: *"No one today knows enough to raise a child"*). Spock suggests that parents follow their convictions, their instincts, for he attributes to parents, rightly or wrongly, universally benign motives and a standard of common sense and wholesomeness comparable to his own. If parents "naturally lean toward strictness [they] should stick to their guns and raise their children that way." On the other hand, "Parents who incline to an easygoing kind of management . . . can also raise children who are considerate and cooperative, as long as the parents are not afraid to be firm about those matters that do seem important to them."

As he is reassuring about the validity of the parents' own styles of child rearing, so is Dr. Spock reassuring though realistic about accidents and unavoidable physical problems: "More than nine out of ten of the babies who are distinctly slow in motor development turn out to have normal intelligence." As many a parent has realized at midnight when trying to thumb through *Baby and Child Care* with one hand while holding a screaming infant with the other, Dr. Spock is extraordinarily calming about the onset of alarming disease symptoms. He begins the section on convulsions by reassuring the parent: "A convulsion is a frightening thing to see in a child, but in most cases it is not dangerous in itself." (As opposed to the *Better Homes and Gardens Baby Book* which introduces the same subject with, "A convulsion is terrifying to parents, but a baby rarely, if ever, dies because of one." What is intended to be comforting is more a reminder of the potentially devastating consequences.) Then Spock gives the medical justification for his view: "Most convulsions stop in a short time, whether or not any treatment is used." After this he suggests the course of action with which most other baby books open their discussion of convulsions: "Telephone for the doctor." But then comes more reassurance: "If you cannot reach him immediately, don't worry. The convulsion is usually over anyway and the child asleep by the time the doctor can get there." Only then does Dr. Spock explain how to care for the child, and the symptoms and causes of convulsions.

Baby and Child Care is even reassuring in its omissions. Although Dr. Spock is implicitly in accord with the noted Yale researcher in child development, Arnold Gesell, in his view that child development proceeds in an inevitable pattern independent of parental influences, Spock's book contains no list of specific things a child should be able to do at a certain age, as Gesell's books and many others do. Without such a list, parents are less likely to compare their child with what they think is the norm, less likely to worry if he doesn't come up to it, less likely to boast if he surpasses it.

Like many experts, Dr. Spock makes the process of rearing a child sound a lot simpler than it really is for the inexperienced or harassed parent, not because he is intentionally deceptive, but just because he is so reassuring and so optimistic. For instance, he confidently assures parents that a great majority of babies will adapt easily to the family's life style, and "will give up the 2 a.m. feeding within a month after birth"—scant comfort to the groggy parent whose starving six-month-old has awakened her twice a night since his birth.

However, unlike many other expert theoreticians, Dr. Spock supplements his theories with very specific practical advice on how to apply them. For instance, in discussing an older child's jealousy upon the birth of a sibling, Dr. Spock theorizes, "One of the ways in which a young child tries to get over the pain of having a younger rival is to act as if he himself were no longer a child, competing in the same league with the baby, but as if he were a third parent." Instead of leaving it at that, the pediatrician then suggests ways in which parents can help such a child "to actually transform resentful feelings into cooperativeness and genuine altruism," by suggesting "how he can help them at times when it wouldn't occur to him, and by showing their real appreciation of his efforts. . . . Even a young child can fetch a bath towel, a diaper. . . . A small child almost always wants to hold the baby, and a mother is apt to hesitate for fear he may drop it. But if the child sits on the floor"—and here Spock characteristically thinks of all the details and other alternatives—"(on a carpet or blanket) or in a large stuffed chair or in the middle of a bed, there's little risk, even if the baby is dropped."

Dr. Spock's own practicality and his realistic knowledge of human behavior have made *Baby and Child Care* into a jewel of practical wisdom on thousands of matters large and small, wisdom which in its attention to minute details gives the impression of having been gained the hard way. One can only speculate on the number of thermometers which have remained intact because of the suggestion, "Shake the thermometer over a bed or couch," and the number of children with croup who have escaped being parboiled because of the doctor's foresighted directions on how to treat the ailment: "If the water runs hot, you can take the child into the bathroom and run hot water into the tub (to make steam, not to put the child in)."

Dr. Spock can anticipate contingencies, not just because he is a practical person who can view a situation from many perspectives, but also because he is concerned with the total environment in which a child lives and develops. He is particularly aware of the psychological milieu of the child and his family, sometimes within the larger context of neighborhood, school, community, or—after he entered the peace movement—of the entire world.

Dr. Spock believes his psychoanalytic perspective is his most significant contribution to advice on child rearing. During the twenties and thirties psychoanalytic theory had intrigued not only many medical people, but the intelligentsia in literature and the arts, as Eugene O'Neill's plays exemplify. But it had not permeated popular literature on child rearing until Dr. Spock first applied it in 1946[2] to such aspects of child development as common nervous symptoms, readiness for weaning, toilet training, one-year-old independence and outgoingness, toddler duties, discipline, jealousy, worries, and stuttering. Dr. Spock claims also to have introduced psychoanalytic theory to the layman in discussing various problems of thin, fat, sick, or handicapped children; and special issues involving separated parents, working mothers, and fatherless children. Today Spock still uses psychoanalytic theory much more prominently than do many other baby books which focus on the physical or mechanical aspects of a topic, rather than on the psychological.[3]

No summary of Freud can do justice to his complex theory of the nature of the human psyche, a theory which he changed drastically several times, and which a host of his followers also changed during his lifetime (much to his outrage) and have continued to modify since his death. Yet so influential are Freud's ideas on Dr. Spock's pediatric advice that it is appropriate to mention some of Freud's central themes.

Freud's developmental psychology concerns the ebb and flow of psychic energies around certain aspects of bodily functioning as the developing child interacts with others. The first year of life centers around the oral mode, in which the child literally lives through his mouth, sucks milk, and learns whether the world is nurturing or rejecting. The anal mode occupies the child from about one to three years; he learns that he has control over the musculature of his body, by which he can give (or withhold) the cooperative behavior which his parents ask of him. The child of approximately three to six lives in the phallic mode, in which he has a strong "romantic" attachment to the parent of the opposite sex, based on sexual feelings. The unattainable romantic aspect of this relationship drives the child into the latency period, a sexually quiescent state increasingly preoccupied with the abstractions taught in school and with friends of the same sex. At the onset of puberty comes a renaissance of sexuality. Inhibitions of the latency period disappear as sexual explorations and attachments outside the family eventually lead the matured adult to a marriage partner.

Counterpoint to this developmental picture is the growth in another mode of the personality. The first aspect, which Freud labeled the "id," views the young infant as a seething cauldron of desires that demand immediate gratification, ignorant and uncaring of society and its rules. Obviously this situation cannot last, and so social reality is forced on the child (such as through demands for control of bladder and bowels) and a reality-oriented problem-solving aspect of the personality emerges, the "ego." But society is more complex than mere problems to be solved; it also contains a myriad of values and biases which the child has to learn if he is to take his place in society. Freud names the "superego" as repository of such learned sanctions, values, and ideals.

Another basic theme of Freud's personality theory is the concept of psychic energy, which is largely unconscious, contained in a closed system (analogous to a steam engine). Some people transform this energy into socially valued activities such as achievement in a career or artistic creativity. In others, the energy bursts out of control and results in various forms of behavior labeled pathologic. Freud views sex and aggression as basic outlets of this energy, which are frustrated by "the harsh masters," society and the superego. The psychoanalyst or psychologist of the unconscious identifies these psychic problems and helps the client to "work them through" in hopes of making the engine run better.

With neither the condescension nor the jargon of many clinicians, Dr. Spock interprets Freudian theory for the lay reader. Occasionally he makes the theory explicit: "This romantic attachment to the parent of the opposite sex in the years between 3 and 6 is what you might call Nature's way of molding a child's feelings in preparation for his eventual life as husband and father or wife and mother. But Nature doesn't want the attachment to go so far or get so strong that it lasts through life or even through childhood. Nature expects that the child of 6 or 7 will become quite discouraged about the possibility of having the parent all to himself. The unconscious fears about the parent's supposed anger and about genital differences will turn his pleasure in dreaming about romance into an aversion. . . . The previous intense attachments to his two parents will have served their main constructive purpose and will be progressively outgrown. (Freud called this shift the resolution of the Oedipus complex.)"

From a more subtly psychoanalytic perspective Dr. Spock continually emphasizes preventive psychiatry. *On feeding*: Don't force the child to nurse or to eat or you'll take away his natural (and therefore, rightful) pleasures and cause problems. *On sleeping difficulties:* They're often "caused by romantic jealousy. The child . . . wants to get into [the parents' bed] because subconsciously he doesn't want them to be alone together." Don't let him do it. *On puberty development:* An adolescent's strong romantic feelings are first directed toward his parent of the opposite sex. As he subconsciously realizes this is not right, he works hard to steer his feelings toward someone outside the family, and often becomes quite antagonistic toward his relatives. If the parents understand this, they can help to minimize the almost inevitable family conflicts. *On the home atmosphere:* Keep it warm, responsive, stable, guided by love and discipline, which are at times identical. The mother can do this best; her place is in the home with the small child. *On parental conflict:* See a psychiatrist or counselor, try to save the marriage. If divorce comes anyway, consult a child psychiatrist to help plan what's best for the children affected.

Parents took to his advice like a famished youngster to an ice cream soda; thousands (mostly mothers) the world over sent him their compliments. Yet Dr. Spock's first fan letter came from a new father who wrote to publisher Charles Duell in October 1946: "Dr. Spock is my boy. In largely the same manner that I have previously sat down and studied manuals on the operation of the contact camera or the proper upbringing of Irish setters . . . I entered the realm of pediatrics with the good Doctor Spock as guide and mentor. I read up until 'Weaning from Bottle to Cup' and then . . . I reread passages, committing certain esoteric things to memory.

"I must explain that I am surrounded here by a) Joan b) Joan's aunt c) Joan's mother on occasion d) Joan's grandmother on her father's side e) Joan's grandmother on her mother's side f) neighbors on all sides. With the exception of Joan, who is modest and retiring, all of the above mentioned know just about everything there is to know in this world about bringing up babies. It is no concern to them that the things they know are all different. You may imagine to what depths of abysmal ignorance I was relegated almost automatically and definitely unanimously, but I had Spock.

"One day, casually, I mentioned that I was glad Jimmy didn't have thrush. Every single savant in the house would have died before they asked me what the hell thrush was. Later I confided to Joan it was a whitish discoloration in the baby's mouth, sometimes induced by milk becoming rancid there. Good old Spock.

"With that for an opening gun I pursued my campaign. I talked about baby ailments as though I had done nothing all my life except raise infants. I quoted chapter and verse as I went along, and when I was contradicted or challenged, I merely brought out Spock. Jesus Christ! His name has been used around here so often his ears must be burned to a frazzle. . . .

"I sincerely find the gent amazing. I have read him again and again, sometimes for sheer pleasure. He is acute, accurate, and worldly. . . . I don't know how he managed to get in all the little odds and ends and trivia that beset new parents, but we have not had a problem yet that Spock hasn't solved.

"Incidentally, we told our doctor that we were using Spock as a guide and he said we could find no better. . . . Spock, I love him. . . . There were a couple of times I would have jumped out of my skin if it were not for the sane, reassuring words of Spock."

From then on the trickle of mail grew to a flood over the quarter century as new parents, experienced parents, grandparents, and children themselves discovered Dr. Spock: "Our motto is, 'When in doubt, consult Dr. Spock.'" "It always seemed to me and my husband that you had written that book about our son!" "THANK YOU FOR TAKING CARE OF OUR BABY SISTER." "How I love you, your book. I named our third son Benjamin after you." "I saved my first child's life because of your book. A penny had gotten down her windpipe and I knew instantly what to do." "You must love children an awful lot to understand them so thoroughly—mentally and physically. I only wish you were my children's doctor." "When I was bringing up my children there was very little money. You just couldn't afford a Doctor. So Dr. Spock's book was the most important Book in our home." "My friends, from constant book-readers to those who usually stick to the comics, and from those who are authors themselves to those for whom English is at best a second language find your book clear and understandable." From the annual skit of psychiatrists' wives at the Menninger Clinic: "If they have neurosis and psychosis/ And a bit of halitosis:/ If they're impulsive and compulsive/ And their speech becomes repulsive. . . ./

Don't call the Doc./ Refer to Spock." And, characteristically, "A bouquet to you, Dr. Spock, from a mother who has really been through the mill. I know you'll always be there, and I feel safe."

American mothers abroad are among Dr. Spock's most fervent admirers. A missionary's wife writes: "Your book in our household is worn and well used and really came into its own when our first child was born, in an African bush delivered by an African doctor. Most of the time we have not had the help of a doctor so we have been truly grateful for the practical advice you give." She is echoed by other missionaries, nurses, military families around the world, and by Peace Corps parents (in whose lockers *Baby and Child Care* is automatically included) : "For anything less than an emergency, we are loath to make the long, long trip to the hospital, so we use your book all the time. How about a translation into Swahili?"

Within five years of its publication *Baby and Child Care* had become quintessential America, at home and abroad.

Dr. Spock is wary of prideful preoccupation with his book, and treats his authorship casually. To an interviewer he observed, "When readers said, 'I'm doing everything that you say, and I have four copies, one in the living room, one in the bedroom, one in the bathroom, one in the kitchen,' it scared me a little. Psychiatrically it isn't meant to be good to have your patient dependent on you. You help them get over whatever dependency they bring, rather than get them to buy four copies so that one can always be within arm's reach.

"I was afraid at first that children might be killed or made dangerously ill by parents misunderstanding the advice. But as the years went by I gradually found that nobody was reproaching me for having killed their children. I also became used to the fact that the book was popular, and by the time people began calling it 'The Bible' that wasn't terrifying to me anymore. [immense laughter] I didn't feel that I was defying God or acquiring too much hubris. [more laughter] I think *all* New Englanders know what hubris is whether they know the word or not—you mustn't be puffed up because you'll *catch* it if you're puffed up."

As the above letters reveal, during the fifteen years when the first Spock generation was growing up, people were so delighted with his words and his music that he became the symbol of all that was good and grandfatherly, and his book became an indispensable work on Everyman's bookshelf. Then, during the era of the war in Indochina, the first Spock generation came of age. Some reared their children more casually than Spock advised, pronounced *Baby and Child Care* "too complicated," "too cookbookery"—even "too scary" —but they bought it anyway, "for reference, like the dictionary." Many followed sedately in their parents' footsteps. But not the flamboyant ones who made the headlines: the hippies, Yippies, political radicals, draft resisters, and other student activists who because of Dr. Spock's efforts to end the war saw him as a symbol of peace, freedom, and opposition to the hypocrisy they found in many among their parents' generation.

Their behavior has led their critics, an increasing multitude, to claim that Dr. Spock is a pied piper and that his tune, like the beat and accompaniments of acid rock, has seduced American youth into a land of willful self-centeredness, irresponsibility, anarchy, treason. Dr. Norman Vincent Peale, good friend of Presidents Eisenhower and Nixon, from the pulpit castigated Dr. Spock's "permissive" child rearing advice, interpreted as "Feed 'em whenever they want, never let them cry, satisfy their every desire," and proclaimed him responsible for "the most undisciplined age in history." Liz Carpenter, Mrs. Lyndon Johnson's press secretary, called such youth "a charming group of little children who never made it through the toilet-training chapter of Dr. Spock." Vice President Spiro Agnew, too, alliteratively proclaimed that the student activists "were raised on a book by Dr. Spock and a paralyzing permissive philosophy pervades every policy they espouse."

Permissive child rearing, only rarely objected to before the onset of protests against the war in Indochina, suddenly became for many the fatal flaw in the old symbol which they had admired, and their justification for rejecting the new. For, whether they disagreed with Dr. Spock's political endorsements, his views on domestic issues, or his stand on peace in Indochina, they made the same equation: Dr. Spock = *Baby and Child Care* = Permissiveness = whatever view Spock took that his antagonist disapproved of. Some critics added to the formula = Communism or Socialism = Treason. Once they had made this equation, using Spock as a scapegoat for their own disillusionment with contemporary events, they could proudly, patriotically hate the man they had formerly loved.

Though the critics opposed Spock's expression of views contradictory to their own, they felt no inhibitions whatsoever about stating their own opinions most forthrightly. A disillusioned parent fulminated, "It would be a pleasure to have you go back to discussing infantile vomit & snot, which you are expert at. You are responsible for . . . raising the crop of nutty kids we have on our scene today. Not satisfied with that, you are leading them down a path of negativism, lawlessness, and thoughtless protest. You are like the overwhelming parent who can't let go. Can't you grow old gracefully in dignity—This country has been good to you and does not disserve [sic] your ingratitude."

Another typical correspondent stormed, "You are responsible for today's Hippies—because you preached that *children* are wiser than parents . . . . I wonder to whom you are loyal—the God-fearing Americans or the unlawful kids who are more Communist than *freedom's* children."

Dr. Spock seldom argues individually with his detractors except to defend his stand on the war. He answers his critics courteously, and offers to interviewers a predictably psychiatric explanation of why he does so: "These people have obviously taken a lot of care to write to me; it's a healthy and responsible act to write to persons you're angry with. In a sense, they want to dissuade me from what they see as a crazy course. As a psychiatrist you learn to understand and empathize with your patient's attitude, whether you share it or not. I write politely not to make the other person feel guilty. [laughter] I just say, 'I don't blame you at all,' for this will leave them less disturbed in the long run."

Yet for some years most readers opposed to Dr. Spock's views on national policy have had enough common sense to separate his politics from his pediatrics, and sales have continued fairly steadily at a million copies a year. "Give up Spock?" exclaimed one mother when asked whether Dr. Spock's peace stand would affect her use of *Baby and Child Care.* "I'd rather give up my husband!"

Yet publicly Dr. Spock has often said, "I'd be proud to be responsible for producing [today's idealistic] youth, but I don't think there is evidence that *Baby and Child Care* has played more than a very small part.

"In any case, all the recent student protests can't be caused by my book because they have been occurring in France, Spain, and Italy, where few copies are sold, and behind the Iron Curtain, where no copies are sold. And I have seen no reports of riots in Holland, Norway, Denmark, Sweden, Canada, Australia or New Zealand, where my book is as widely used as in America.

"I believe that three principal factors have evoked radicalism and revolt in youth: the depersonalization of education, caused by its rapid expansion; revulsion against the fantastically expensive and brutal destruction of Vietnam; and the inexcusable persistence of poverty and racial injustice in the richest country in the world's history. . . .

"By my standards the hippies and the radicals are thoughtful, conscientious, self-disciplined people, despite the fact that they often do things that bother conservatives, often in a manner that is further irritating. I think that most of them will outgrow their eccentricities and provocativeness in time, yet will still remain workers for peace and social justice. I believe this is our main hope for a better future."

Researchers have found that whether or not *Baby and Child Care* has changed the character of American parents and children, it reflects their changing characters. They further imply that Dr. Spock may be more responsible for these changes than he acknowledges. Cornell's child development specialist Urie Bronfenbrenner concluded that during the fifties "greater permissiveness toward the child's spontaneous desires; freer expression of affection," and gentler discipline—promoted by books such as *Baby and Child Care*—were likely to produce boys "more conforming and anxious, less enterprising and self-sufficient," and somewhat more feminine than boys of the pre-Spock generations.

But many adolescents have changed radically during the two decades since Dr. Bronfenbrenner conducted his study. The apolitical, uninvolved "quiet generation" of the fifties, subdued by McCarthy investigations and engaged in a quest for security, has been replaced by a generation oriented toward peace, student power, black power, and which marched, for a time, to the drum of a different McCarthy—though in both decades parents were using the same baby book. As University of Chicago sociologist Richard Flacks, himself one of the founders of the Students for Democratic

Society, indicates, student activists, reared as Dr. Spock recommends by parents whose life styles "emphasize intellectual, aesthetic and humanitarian concerns and de-emphasize occupational and material achievement," are self-expressive, anti-authoritarian, egalitarian, idealistic, honest, and concerned more with improving society than with acquiring money or social position. (In defending the hippies, Dr. Spock notes that these traits were emphasized by the early Christians and have traditionally been associated with the Christian ethic. In *Baby and Child Care* he says nothing at all about religion.) A social-psychological study by M. Brewster Smith, Norma Haan, and Jeanne Block of the University of California at Berkeley says, "It may be argued that the emergence of a dedicated spontaneous generation concerned with humanitarian values and personal authenticity is a triumph of Spockian philosophy and principles." Amplifying Flack's findings, these researchers see such youth as "sensitive, creative, curious, free, frank, idealistic, as well as restless, impulsive, critical, and rebellious . . . . not a bad way to be young."

Dr. Spock himself becomes indignant at the charge that he's encouraged the kind of permissiveness that is license. Nevertheless, he does admit to being permissive in the sense that he is Deweyan. Like Dewey, Spock has encouraged parents to relax their discipline, to understand their child's nature, to trust his drive to become mature and responsible, and to regard his needs as equally legitimate and important as those of grownups. From the writings of Dewey and Kilpatrick, Spock had come to believe that significant learning takes place by experiencing, feeling, exploring, practicing rather than by rote. Children learn—and learn well—through desire rather than coercion as, according to Freud, they grow to be responsible adults not by being controlled by fear of punishment, but mainly by their loving ties to their parents.

A colleague of Dr. Spock's has observed, "Because of his strict upbringing and rigorous moral sense, when Ben says 'relax' his assumption is that an awful lot of control is in the air. In a more casual background, 'relax' is interpreted quite differently." Perhaps for this reason has Dr. Spock's advice to parents to "relax" and to "trust yourself" been interpreted as a cue for greater laxity than he intended, particularly by readers of the first edition. He always meant for parents to be in control, but for them to exercise their authority rationally and flexibly rather than with arbitrary absolutism.

So, explains Dr. Spock, "when, in the early 1950s, I saw that some inexperienced parents were interpreting my advice about flexibility in feeding to mean that the baby always knows best and that the parents' job is always to follow the child's lead, I wrote a lot into the second edition of my book . . . about the need for firm parental leadership." He added a section on "Strictness or Permissiveness?" to the second and third editions and emphasized: "Strictness or permissiveness is not the real issue . . . . The real issue is what spirit the parent puts into managing the child and what attitude is engendered in the child as a result . . . . The way we avoid irritation [under normal family circumstances] . . . is by keeping our children under reasonable control and by being extra firm or sufficiently disapproving when things first threaten to go wrong. Such firmness is one aspect of parental love. Firmness, by keeping children on the right track, keeps them lovable. And they love us for keeping them out of trouble."

Whether or not he intended it that way, Dr. Spock did sound quite permissive to some people in the first edition of *Baby and Child Care*. In a book as radical in its pervasive psychiatric orientation as *Baby and Child Care* was in 1946, the radical aspects stood out, no matter how conventional the advice may have been in other respects.

In the first edition, the section on "Discipline" began with three and a half pages of suggestions on "how you handle a young child by distraction and consideration." The bulk and tone of this tended to overshadow the ensuing three-quarters of a page on the need for setting limits, particularly when the whole section was followed immediately by three pages of the author's views on "Punishment," which he said was "seldom required." Spock believed punishment generally undesirable because it might make the child "furious, defiant, and worse behaved than before"—or it might break his heart or his spirit. With uncharacteristic severity Dr. Spock warned parents against frequent punishment (as he does in later editions, too): "If you seem to be needing to punish your child frequently, something is definitely wrong in his life or you are using the wrong methods. . . . What makes your child behave well is not threats or punishment but loving you for your agreeableness and respecting your rights and his. Stay in control as a friendly leader rather than battle with him at his level." (Twenty years later clinical psychologist Haim Ginott, Ph.D., in benign manner and sympathy to children a latter-day Spock, amplified this dictum in the best-selling *Between Parent and Child,* a loving discussion of how parents can communicate and empathize with their children.)

The section on "Discipline" in the 1957 and 1968 editions is quite different in emphasis from the 1946 edition, though the fundamental Freudian orientation remains. In the later editions Dr. Spock explains that in the last half-century psychological studies have shown that, above all, children need strong parental love ("the main source of good discipline") ; children independently try to assume responsibility and to grow up; each child should be allowed to maintain his individuality—severely repressed children may become neurotic. He then applies a corrective to the parental reactions to these new theories, which he had recognized from responses to the 1946 edition of *Baby and Child Care:* "[Some parents] have often read meanings into them that went beyond what the scientists intended—for instance, that *all* children need is love; that they shouldn't be made to conform; that they should be allowed to carry out their aggressive feelings against parents and others; that whenever anything goes wrong it's the parents' fault; that when children misbehave the parents shouldn't become angry or punish them but should try to show more love. They encourage children to become demanding and disagreeable. They make children feel guilty about their excessive misbehavior. They make parents strive to be superhuman."

After explaining psychologically "how feelings of guilt in parents lead to discipline problems," Dr. Spock includes the discussion on parental firmness that appeared in the first edition, and follows it with recommendations, later adopted by Ginott, to "Let the child know that his angry feelings are normal" at the same time you're insisting on "reasonably good behavior," for parents should remain in the leadership role. Instead of rejecting physical punishment altogether, as he did earlier, by 1957 Dr. Spock was saying "it is *never* the main element in discipline—it's only a vigorous additional reminder that the parent feels strongly about what he says."

In toilet training, too, Dr. Spock has shifted emphasis but not theory (Freud, too, assumed that children need to be trained) in attempting to help parents stay in control of their children. In 1946 he had confidently assumed that without parental interference "a child will completely train himself sooner or later if no struggle has taken place." By 1957 mothers had let him know that waiting for the child to take the initiative didn't necessarily work. So he suggested another approach. When the child was between eighteen months and two years the mother could "gradually and gently" encourage him to signal his need to use the bathroom. If she persisted pleasantly, the child would be likely to catch on within several weeks—though Spock gave elaborate advice on what to do if the child resisted.

Some children—particularly of college-educated mothers—were not catching on until they were three or four, and difficulties were common. (The children of less educated mothers were often trained by two, without struggle or psychic harm.) As a result of what he had learned in the Child Rearing Study at Western Reserve (see Chapter 9), Dr. Spock attributed the educated parents' problems to the well-meant efforts of educators such as himself, who were trying to help parents get around their fear of conflicts over training. So he changed his recommendations again, advising in the 1968 edition of *Baby and Child Care* that the mother *should* begin to toilet train the child—ready or not—at eighteen months. She should persist, by means of pep talks and by sitting with him up to half an hour (instead of the ten-minute maximum in 1946) to help him concentrate on the task.

By 1968 Dr. Spock had also modified his views on aggression. In the first and second editions of *Baby and Child Care* he had explained, following Freudian theory, that aggressive feelings are natural and that causing a child to "bottle up his hostile feelings" may make him permanently hostile: "When your child at 2 bangs another over the head, or at 4 plays at shooting, or at 9 enjoys blood-and-thunder comic books, he is just passing through the necessary stages in the taming of his aggressive instincts that will make him a worth-while citizen. Let him be his age all the way" (though Spock, like other Freudians, would "never permit a child to take out physical aggression on another"). In 1957 he had added an explicit warning for the parent to curb the child's "extra aggressiveness," though he left the distinction between the normal "child who can play at hurting and killing" and the extra-aggressive child up to the parents.

By 1968 he had seen the piling up of nuclear arms and the aggressiveness of the great national powers as leading eventually to annihilation. He had heard nursery school teachers describe the increasing aggressiveness of small children who watch violence on television and had read of experiments which demonstrated that adults who have viewed brutality on film will behave more cruelly afterwards. He concluded that part of preparing children for social responsibility in an aggressive nation is to "firmly stop children's war play" or any other kind of deliberately cruel or mean play, for "when we let people grow up feeling that cruelty is all right provided they know it is make-believe, or provided they sufficiently disapprove of certain individuals or groups, or provided the cruelty is in the service of their country (whether the country is right or wrong), we make it easier for them to go berserk when the provocation comes." Parents should also "flatly forbid" violent television programs. They should stop giving war toys to children, explaining their reasons, but not forbidding the child to buy such toys for himself if he insists. With this advice Dr. Spock subordinated the recognition of aggression in Freudian theory to his own humanitarian philosophy.

Furthermore, Dr. Spock sought to modify the "child-centered psychological approach" which he had come to believe was useful but insufficient unless "backed up by a moral sense . . . of what's right and proper." He saw as too limited "the tendency of many conscientious parents to keep their eyes exclusively focused on their child, thinking about what he needs from them and from the community, instead of thinking about what the world, the neighborhood, the family will be needing from the child and then making sure that he will grow up to meet such obligations." Children should be reared to feel "that they are in this world not for their own satisfaction but primarily to serve others," for Dr. Spock the moralist now objects strongly to allowing children of any age to be excessively self-indulgent, whether through jealousy, rudeness, aggressiveness, or selfishness.

In other areas of child rearing as well, in the third edition and sometimes even in the second, Dr. Spock encouraged parental firmness that would please not only the Dr. Peales but the most strict of disciplinarians. *On children fooling around at meals:* "It's inconvenient and irritating, and it's apt to lead to feeding problems, too. I wouldn't let it go on." *On biting:* "Show [the child] clearly that you don't like it and won't let it happen." *On preadolescent sloppiness:* "You may be able to overlook some of his minor irritating ways, but you should stick to your guns in matters that are important to you." *On teenage dating:* "I believe myself . . . that it's better that younger adolescents—up to the age of 16 or 17, let's say—not have individual dates or go steady." (An engagingly old-fashioned remark which overlooks the fact that its author proposed to his future wife when she was only seventeen!) "Parents should specify . . . the hour at which their children are to come home from parties and dates, where they can and can't go. They should know and approve of the others with whom their children are going out, and who is to drive. . . ."

Those who condemn Dr. Spock's "permissiveness" are reacting essentially to the first edition of *Baby and Child Care* which was trying to help parents deal with rigid and arbitrary doctrines that no longer exist. Dr. Spock observes, "Anyone who has looked at my book knows that, far from advising instant gratification, it leans in the opposite direction. Sometimes I think I sound like an old crank." But custom dies hard, irrespective of the facts, and it is likely that Dr. Spock will ever be considered in relation to child rearing as John Dewey is to education and, for his efforts, be cursed by some conservatives as he is praised by many liberals—and by some who are not so liberal.

People in the helping professions—doctors, nurses, psychologists, social workers—generally approve of *Baby and Child Care*. Even if their orientation is not psychoanalytic they think it is a good book; if they themselves have received psychoanalytic training since 1930, they think it is a masterpiece. One doctor wrote, in nominating Dr. Spock for the 1967 C. Anderson Aldrich Award of the American Academy of Pediatrics (which he didn't receive):

"Benjamin Spock is a tradition in his own time. . . . The amazing thing to me about 'The Book' is the wealth of material relative to child development and child psychology—all stated . . . without the usual psychological and psychiatric jargon. As a textbook it is a classic in its field and internationally accepted."

Doctors also valued *Baby and Child Care* for helping parents whose increasing recognition of and reliance on the specialized expertise of physicians had undermined their self-confidence (unlike the grandparent generation which relied on its own intuition and common sense). A professor of pediatrics observes, "When *Baby and Child Care* appeared with formulas that mothers could understand, this struck a blow at the authoritarian, mysterious manner pediatricians had customarily adopted toward parents. It also freed mothers from the fear that pediatricians inflicted upon them; no longer were there 'dread diseases,' but instead, manageable problems that parents could cope with. Dr. Spock's concern with normal, healthy children, instead of with the medically bizarre and abnormal, is a welcome perspective in a country where 'pediatrics' implies 'sick children' and where medical school graduates see very few healthy children." Another pediatrician, mother of four, approves of the book's flexibility, for it "gives people the idea that there is more than one way of doing things and, by having a choice, they're more relaxed as parents."

The late Dr. William Wallace, Chairman of the Western Reserve Medical School Department of Pediatrics, complimented the book's comprehensiveness: "It covers everything that young mothers want to know and don't have any other way to get." Another university pediatrician notes a different aspect of the same matter: "I doubt whether, because of their sophisticated, specialized textbooks, most physicians have ever read *Baby and Child Care* completely except as a means of knowing what their private patients consult. Even so, it's a great convenience to busy doctors, because mothers can look up various routine matters without having to bother them." Such a use of the book results in the refrain painfully familiar to many pediatricians, "I know I didn't follow your advice, but DR. SPOCK said . . . ."

Although many medical and academic professionals praise *Baby and Child Care*, a number also have reservations about it. A few old-style pediatricians still promote advice that more recently trained doctors consider outmoded; they insist on splinting the infant's elbows to keep him from thumb-sucking, or on beginning toilet training when the baby is three months old.

Other more up-to-date doctors, although they approve of the advice in *Baby and Child Care* and concede its value, object to the fact that a medical doctor rather than a lay person wrote it. Fumes one pediatrician, his irritation mounting nearly to apoplexy, "Academic medicine puts its *all* on scientific contribution. Anybody who writes a popular book or for lay publications is cutting his throat among his medical peers. This is just like self-advertising, something that professional ethics absolutely forbids doctors to do. It's demeaning to the medical profession, too, for a doctor to write books that anybody and everybody can understand."

Other objections from doctors are either to Dr. Spock's essentially middle and upper class orientation, or to his psychology. It's regarded as either too Freudian, not Freudian enough, or out-of-date. No one faults his advice on physical medicine, on the practical, mechanical aspects of baby care, or his style; these are virtually unassailable.

If being focused on the middle and upper classes is a fault of *Baby and Child Care*, it is also a fault of medicine as traditionally practiced in the United States—as a private, doctor-patient, fee-for-service enterprise. Dr. Robert Ebert, Dean of the Harvard Medical School, said in 1969, "Medicine until now, in this century, has been a middle-class institution. You practice on poor people, but you really are going to take care of the middle class. All of medicine is essentially this way. At every level the poor come off badly. They are used for teaching purposes, they have more serious diseases, their mortality rates are higher at all ages, they have more serious psychological disorders, their medical care is fragmented and discontinuous, they are powerless in the system.[4] And yet, until recently, medicine has not considered this medicine's problem. The change that is occurring—the most important 'revolution'—is that this concern is for the first time being injected into medical schools." Only since the beginning of World War II have there been in existence comprehensive prepaid group medical insurance and facilities (such as the Kaiser plans, and Health Insurance Plan in New York City) affecting large numbers of lower and middle class patients who would otherwise rely on the emergency room for a family doctor, if they had medical care at all. Only since the early 1960s has there been in America much medical concern with the population explosion, chemical and biological warfare, the medically indigent, comprehensive national health insurance, ghetto medicine, and discrimination in medicine, among other social medical concerns.

Doctors working with lower class patients point out great discrepancies between the middle class norms implied in *Baby and Child Care* and what their patients actually do.

One pediatrician whose clientele is primarily the children of welfare mothers observes that *Baby and Child Care* is a symbol of middle class morality. "Dr. Spock," she says, "talks about the family structure he knows—upper and middle class two-parent families in which the mother can stay at home with the children while the father works. Welfare families often have only one parent. The husband, when there is one, is sometimes at home because his wife can get a better paying job than he can. Or, commonly, both parents work and leave the children with the grandmother or older siblings. Dr. Spock assumes a consistent caretaker for the child; in welfare families this sometimes simply isn't possible.

"Dr. Spock's concern," continues the pediatrician, "is whether the child has a room to himself. He assumes that each child has his own bed. But many lower class children sleep with their parents or other children, either from choice or from necessity. Only the bedwetters sleep alone—for obvious reasons. And ghetto babies don't necessarily sleep in cribs. Often there's no room for a crib— or no crib at all.

"The doctor of a welfare family has to consider sanitation, rats, roaches, lead poisoning from old peeling paint. Dr. Spock takes for granted a house in good repair, clean, and free of infestation, and therefore doesn't discuss these problems."

This doctor observes that *"Baby and Child Care* talks extensively about relations between *one* child and a parent. In fact, it's a good first child book. In the book, the parent is constantly teaching the child, telling him the rules, controlling him. The Spockian child, especially the preschooler, is influenced very little by brothers and sisters. In lower class families, a one-child household is very unusual. Children in these families learn a lot from other children, whether they're relatives or not, and proportionately less from adults.

"And they learn a lot from TV, which is on all the time, uncontrolled." The doctor explains, "A lot of the mothers of eight or ten children under ten aren't used to telling anyone what to do and use TV as a babysitter. The kids stay up late to watch it—and to see their parents, who have been working late. TV-oriented families follow the 'advice' in the medicine ads; they give aspirin for a cold because that's what the ads say to do. [Dr. Spock doesn't mention aspirin in connection with colds.] TV is nine-tenths of the uneducated family's education. But *Baby and Child Care* doesn't discuss the effects of TV on families."

A pediatrician who supervises the care of indigent patients observes, *"Baby and Child Care,* like the middle class, assumes a future and plans for it. Consequently, both focus on routine, preventive medical care and on matters of psychological development. Lower class patients, and sometimes even nouveau middle class ones, traditionally haven't been allowed much thought for the future and have no way of providing for it economically. To them, the idea of preventive medical care is foreign. Usually they don't discuss developmental or behavioral problems with the doctor, or arrange for routine checkups for their children, or provide dental care. Most of them end up on crisis medical care only; perhaps that's the only care they can get—or can afford."

A public health nurse who has spent many hours helping welfare mothers with baby care agrees that *Baby and Child Care* implies a way of child rearing quite uncommon among the "grandmother-oriented" mothers: "In middle class families Dr. Spock has replaced grandmothers—and their advice—with recommendations very different from that the grandmothers in the welfare families actually encourage. Whereas Dr. Spock suggests that weaning begin when the baby is between five and six months, these babies are on the bottle until they're two or three years old. But they're toilet trained by a year—again, quite a change from Spock. To encourage regularity, these mothers control infant BM's manually, a subject not even mentioned in *Baby and Child Care,* which discourages suppositories."

She continues, "Lower class children are fed table food from the time they're three months old, including 'pot likker,' which is excellent nutritionally, and greasy bacon, which is very hard to digest. Their diets just don't follow what Dr. Spock says young children should eat. They can't afford the more costly foods and they haven't the knowledge of inexpensive substitutes.

"These kids are highly disciplined while they're being toilet trained. The discipline is physical, and the kids fear their parents. But as they get older, unless the threat of physical punishment is constantly present, the children are likely to be out of control. These families often communicate more by physical actions than by words; Dr. Spock assumes a lot of verbal communication.

"And Dr. Spock implies a lot of cooperation within the family and among larger groups," she concludes. "In these families there's terrific competition among the children—for attention, for grades at school, for material things. A lot of these kids compete for attention at home by misbehaving."[5]

Doctors and nurses who work with such families feel that many of the mothers would be unlikely to consult *Baby and Child Care* even if it were more relevant to their way of life, for they do not have (for better or worse) the middle class reliance on and reverence for books of advice. However, that the book may not be relevant to—or read by—a particular group, however large, in no way diminishes its applicability to the groups that do use it.

The Spockian family consists of father, mother, and children, rather than a clan, kibbutz, or extended kinship group. It is a family in which parents expect and want to spend a great deal of time with their children. Dr. Spock endows the family with such conveniences as electricity, indoor plumbing, a refrigerator, telephone, television, alarm clock, frozen foods, and accessible professional medical care. This orientation toward western culture reflects the fact that Dr. Spock is an American pediatrician writing for at least moderately affluent American readers.

It is hard to tell how many of the book's translations into thirty languages reflect its relevance to other cultures and how many are essentially a tribute to its popularity in the United States. The book has been translated not only into the Germanic and Romance languages, but into Japanese (large sales in Japan are probably an index of the country's westernization), Hebrew, Vietnamese, Malayan, Burmese, and the Indian dialects of Gujerati, Hindi, Marathi, Sinhalese, Tamil, and Urdu.

Thus *Baby and Child Care* has become an ambassador abroad, a symbol of America. In many non-European countries where it was sent by the nonprofit Franklin Books, Inc., it has become more a means of informing other cultures about how Americans rear their children than a model to be followed. This is true in spite of technical and cultural adaptations to the countries in which the translations are distributed: weights and measures are converted to the metric system; native diets are substituted for American foods (the Japanese translator worried for years because she had changed "bread" to "rice" without checking with Dr. Spock). Even entire sections are eliminated; the Farsi edition omits (among other portions) the long discussion of "hospital impressions," for most Iranian babies are born at home.

One commentator on the psychology in *Baby and Child Care* is psychologist Jane Kessler, Ph.D., a child development specialist at Case Western Reserve University and author of a highly regarded textbook, *Psychopathology of Childhood* (1966) and many professional papers. She is personally fond of Dr. Spock and approves of many aspects of *Baby and Child Care,* but with reservations: "Dr. Spock is very knowledgeable about child psychology up to the age of six, and particularly good on sex identification, but from the school-age child on through late adolescence he's out-of-date, partly because he generalized a lot from his personal experiences. For instance, he sees middle childhood, six to eleven years, as a period of the secret clubs and small friendship groups of his own youth, and never considers the child's affiliation with such contemporary organizations as Scouts or YMCA's. His description of a seventeen-year-old's idealistic fantasies are of a knight-errant-on-a-white-horse type, which today are typical of a much younger person." Adds a social worker, "Nowadays, as the saying goes, Booth Tarkington's *Seventeen* would have to be retitled *Twelve* to be up-to-date, and on sex Dr. Spock is still with Tarkington."

Dr. Kessler takes issue with Dr. Spock's claim that "the more people have studied different methods of bringing up children, the more they have come to the conclusion that what good mothers and fathers instinctively feel like doing for their babies is usually best after all," and that their instinctive feelings are derived from their remembrance, however imperfect, of the way they were raised. She believes Dr. Spock is thereby encouraging parents to consider models of child rearing which are in some cases obsolete, in other cases unsound: "All kinds of parents swear by Spock. This is both good and bad—depending on what kind of parents they are. *Baby and Child Care* gives parents freedom to do what they feel is natural, and this ends up as too casual, sometimes, even if Ben didn't intend it that way."

In *Your Child Is a Person: A Psychological Approach to Parenthood Without Guilt* (Viking, 1965), psychiatrists Stella Chess and Alexander Thomas and pediatric researcher Herbert Birch (see Chapter 7 footnote) continue where Dr. Kessler left off. The authors politely but firmly take psychoanalytically oriented child guidance experts, Dr. Spock implicitly among them, to task for providing what they consider vague guidelines (such as "common sense" or the child's seeming happiness or sociability) for handling children: "How does a mother know when reasonable restraint becomes frustration, or when frustration is good or bad? How can she decide when permissiveness results not in freedom but in license?"

Chess, Thomas, and Birch characterize several common types of children according to the major personality dimensions discovered in their research: the child may be "slow to warm up," "difficult," "easy," "highly active," or "persistent, nondistractible." This is a major departure from Spock, who implicitly equates "the easy child" with the normal child. These researchers claim that if the mother predetermines a goal, such as weaning or toilet training, and adapts her method of training to fit the specific personality and reactions of her own child, she is much more likely to achieve success than if she is overly permissive, insufficiently goal-oriented, or afraid that the child will cry.

They also emphasize that as long as the baby's welfare is not jeopardized, a mother should feel free to accommodate her own temperament as well as her child's. The implications of this differ markedly from Spock's views on some (not all) subjects, for he tends to disregard parents' proclivities in such matters as encouraging mothers to breast-feed and to stay at home with their small children. (For such recommendations as these Spock is also the target of the more militant advocates of Women's Liberation, paradoxically among the most enthusiastic users of other portions of *Baby and Child Care*.) Thus Chess, Thomas, and Birch declare the working mother "Not guilty," claiming that the quality of the mother-child relationship is more important than the amount of time mother and child spend together. If the relationship is good, they say, the child will usually accommodate happily to a sitter while the mother is at work; if it isn't, the situation will probably not be improved even if she remains at home.

In the United States in the past sixty years, styles of child rearing have swung like a pendulum between flexibility and rigidity. The standard books of advice, written to reflect, effect, and modify the practices occurring at any given point in time, tend to last on into the beginning of the next major revolution. They have a life span of thirty to forty years. Does this mean that *Baby and Child Care*, now nearing its third decade of publication, is fast approaching retirement?

Yes and no. If and when Freudianism runs its course, the advice in *Baby and Child Care* concerning stages and dynamics of emotional development, and the function of the unconscious, will become outdated, unless Spock modifies it. In 1971 Dr. Spock, explaining his recent accommodation to the views of women's liberationists on these subjects, indicated, with amazing flexibility for one who has for over forty years adhered to Freud's "basic concepts of psychosexual development," that although he did not yet "find reason to recant, I acknowledge that Freud also had his prejudices like the rest of us. Perhaps after I have been educated further I will see the light differently." Even today parents can substitute for Dr. Spock's subdued Freudianism the individualized social psychology of Drs. Chess, Thomas, and Birch. *Your Child Is a Person* or other volumes on limited topics, such as Ginott's *Between Parent and Child*, may supplement *Baby and Child Care*, but they are not intended to replace it. Today, no other publication seriously rivals Dr. Spock's sound, sympathetic, comprehensive, practical advice on the medical, physical, and mechanical aspects of child care, particularly of infants. A few other baby books, such as *The Better Homes and Gardens Baby Book* and the Government's *Infant Care*, both in some respects seemingly derived from

Baby and Child Care, guide readers over the same territory, but with a much less appealing map.

Baby and Child Care has become a classic. Although a book can and does become a classic without large sales if it retains a small but sagacious readership over the years, a baby book written for a mass audience must have that mass audience in order to endure. A baby book bought by few would influence few. It would quickly become forgotten and irrelevant as it became part of the sediment of the cultural mainstream.

But *Baby and Child Care* has become a vital part of contemporary American life which Dr. Spock himself has helped to form, and to which Dr. Spock has adapted. As long as Dr. Spock (and whoever takes over the authorship after his death) can continue to accommodate the changing American parent—and child—as Spock has always been willing to do, *Baby and Child Care* will survive, in the same way a sound dictionary or other reference work survives, by continually incorporating advances in new research and ways of thought while retaining the best and most viable of the old.

seven

AT THE
MAYO CLINIC

DR. Spock began his full-time career in academic medicine in the same unorthodox, informal manner that was to characterize all of his relationships with the academic world.

Although in May 1946 Dr. Spock had returned to private practice, he was not wholly satisfied with it. To continue in New York as he had been before military service would have meant high esteem from his clientele. It would have meant a rising income and a reputable career as a practitioner and part-time teacher. But it would have meant little time for investigating pediatric and psychiatric interests beyond what he'd already done, and little time for writing. The long hours, the interrupted evenings, the weekend duty that prevailed before the Navy intervened with a forty-four-hour week had been resumed; Dr. Spock even continued to make house calls when many other doctors (as a result of the war) had stopped.

By temperament or habit, Dr. Spock seemed

incapable of allowing himself some relief by sharing the responsibilities of practice with a colleague. Characteristically, he wanted to control fully every aspect of his own work. He felt conscience-bound to attend personally to every problem of each patient, even to the mother who roused him once at 7 a.m. on a Sunday to ask why her baby had stopped liking oatmeal. His feeling of "wanting to earn every nickel that I could," ingrained in the early, relatively impecunious years of practice, meant that even though a comfortable income was now assured, to keep expenses down Dr. Spock habitually continued to do as much himself as he could.

Yet, paradoxically, he was uneasy about making too much money. He charged less than many doctors, and procrastinated about sending out bills. The world of academic medicine, with its fixed salary, regular hours, and the chance to teach and to pursue individual research interests, began to seem more and more appealing.

Jane, too, had enjoyed the Navy's regular schedule and had said, "If you ever get a chance to go into full-time academic medicine after the war, take it. But," she recalls, "I didn't expect Rochester, Minnesota. I had thought an appointment might come from Washington, Boston, Baltimore, or San Francisco, and it was hard to accept the idea of Minnesota. But once I had said, 'Sure, I'll do it,' I made myself say, 'Yes, I'll even do Minnesota.' "

The first offer came not from Minnesota, but from Detroit, in the summer of 1946. The Merrill-Palmer Institute, a center for research, training, and treatment in educational psychology, asked Dr. Spock to direct the department of child development, which would also be linked to the Department of Pediatrics at Wayne [State] University Medical School. He found the idea appealing and in a long letter to one of the directors worked out an elaborate variety of ways in which he would do this.

However, the salary, $7,000 a year, was not so appealing, and the fact that the position was half-time meant that Dr. Spock would have had to start building a private practice all over again, a laborious process still too poignantly remembered from the thirties to be welcome. Though *Baby and Child Care* had just been published, Dr. Spock had no idea whether anyone would read it, and could scarcely count on any patients as a result of its yet untested reputation. So to his partial regret, and his wife's unalloyed pleasure, he declined the offer.

In November 1946 the fates beckoned again, and Dr. Spock journeyed to Rochester, Minnesota to give lectures at the Mayo Clinic and the Rochester Child Health Project. When invited to remain permanently, he was delighted. The job seemed ideally suited to his interests in pediatrics, child psychiatry, and preventive medicine, and the salary, $15,000 plus an annual bonus of $5,000, well-suited to the Spocks' standard of living. Half of his time was to be spent as the first consultant in child psychiatry at the Mayo Clinic and as Associate Professor of Psychiatry at the Mayo Graduate School of Medicine, part of the University of Minnesota.

But it was the other half of the job which appealed particularly to Dr. Spock. He had been asked by Dr. C. Anderson Aldrich, Director of the Rochester Child Health Project (later incorporated as the Rochester Child Health Institute), supported by the Mayo Foundation, to join with other professionals to discover and provide the best physical and emotional preventive care for all the children of the city. "Andy" Aldrich, author (with Mrs. Aldrich) of *Babies Are Human Beings* and *Feeding Our Old Fashioned Children,* had become, says Dr. Spock, using words sometimes applied to himself, "the leader of a profound shift in pediatric philosophy away from arbitrariness and rigidity and the first integrator of pediatrics with preventive psychiatry." He was known fondly to generations of child specialists as "the granddaddy of modern pediatricians," and was beloved by countless friends and associates as a liberal, humane doctor, administrator, and person. Their medical and philosophical affinities had made it appropriate for Dr. Spock to send Dr. Aldrich the galleys of *Baby and Child Care* for commentary (which was highly favorable). It was just as natural for Dr. Aldrich to want Dr. Spock on his staff.

At Christmas time Dr. Spock took Jane to Rochester to see whether it would appeal to her. Ninety miles southeast of Minneapolis and St. Paul, in a saucerlike valley of the Zumbro River, amidst tidy dairy farms and cornfields, it was a city of 30,000, dominated practically, spiritually, and psychologically by medicine and the Mayo legacy.

Rochester, Minnesota was and still is a company town, synonymous with the late Mayo brothers, Dr. Will and Dr. Charlie. They had settled in the town where their father, Dr. William Mayo, had also practiced medicine. Because of their skill, their attentiveness to the patients, and their organizational genius, their practice expanded, attracted other outstanding specialists, and developed into the monolithic Mayo Clinic. They donated one-tenth of their income to civic improvement—partly for its own sake, partly to provide an attractive milieu to lure competent medical personnel to this secluded town. From 1904 until their deaths in 1939, they financed wholly or in part schools and school equipment; a public library; a civic auditorium containing an art gallery, theater, and arena; a variety of parks; an outdoor swimming pool; and improved roads.

By the time the Spocks arrived the Clinic had grown into a sprawling but highly organized network of medical specialties and sub-specialties. The more difficult, complex, obscure, or bizarre the ailment, the more likely a patient from anywhere in the country—or world—was to be sent to the Mayo Clinic. Over one-sixth of the town's population was employed directly by the Clinic or its affiliated hospitals, Saint Mary's and Rochester Methodist, not to mention additional employees of the state mental hospital located there. Nearly as many people operated the town's plethora of hotels, motels, guest homes, restaurants, and related facilities which had sprung up to accommodate Rochester's enormous transient population of over 300,000 annually. A unique pedestrian subway system was constructed to connect the Clinic with downtown hospitals, hotels, stores, and parking ramps.

Jane found Rochester more Siberian than Olympian. When the telephone operator at their hotel woke them with a cheery, "It's 7:30 a.m. and twenty-seven degrees below zero," Jane's enthusiasm was chilled at the start, and she vowed never to commit the Spocks to permanent residence by buying a house. But in the postwar housing shortage no suitable rentals were available, so the Spocks soon purchased their first house, a modest white frame colonial at 1313 Second Street, N.W. (near Dr. Aldrich's). There was barely enough room for the four Spocks, a dachshund, and their housekeeper, Bessie Quigg, whose teenage son had to rent a room from the next-door neighbors.

The Spocks trekked west on St. Patrick's Day, 1947, to what Jane thought of as the last outpost and her husband as the new frontier.

He took pleasure in "the cold and in the clean snow. Every morning I'd open the bedroom shade and look out at the white clapboard houses capped with snow. Everybody used natural gas, which meant that when the temperature got to zero, as it did most of the winter, a little plume like a white ostrich feather came out of each chimney, as in a child's drawing. Every day the sun sparkled on the snow and the snow creaked underfoot. (In New Haven or New York it might creak one day a winter.)"

Dr. Spock was more pleased with his work than ever. For the first time in his career he was able to do a great deal of intensive, organized teaching, compared to the intermittent, casual talks to medical students in New York Hospital's pediatric outpatient department.

At the Mayo Clinic he had charge of teaching child psychiatry to psychiatric and pediatric fellows (the equivalent of hospital residents) for a solid three months of their training. The fellow took a long history from the parents and then talked with the child patient. He next reported his findings to Spock, who conferred at length with the parents to bring out additional aspects of the case and make recommendations while the fellow listened. There was usually no follow-up at the Clinic, for most patients were from out of town, and prolonged treatment had to be carried out nearer home.

In his teaching Dr. Spock encouraged the integration of medical disciplines, pointing out that "Each profession dealing primarily with one aspect of the child *must* know something of the child's other aspects and his needs as a whole personality. . . . The pediatrician must know enough psychiatry to recognize psychosomatic disturbances. . . . The psychiatrist should know about infancy in practice as well as in theory." Most importantly, interdisciplinary study would give both pediatricians and psychiatrists an understanding of what is normal and how to foster it.

At the Mayo Clinic, for historical reasons, the emphasis had always been on the physical rather than on the psychological, on the diseased rather than on the normal, on research, diagnosis, and treatment rather than on preventive medicine. Consequently, Dr. Spock's emphasis on normal children and on preventive psychiatry was somewhat of an anomaly. So was the Rochester Child Health

Project, where he worked in the afternoons. The Project was begun during World War II when the Mayo Clinic, a nonprofit institution, understaffed but overcrowded, needed expensive research projects to help spend its income. The Project was committed to studying and fostering normal development in all the children of Rochester from their birth to the age of twenty-one. Dr. Spock, for his part, intended to supplement the "vague and incomplete knowledge of the pattern of normal emotional development, of what children of different temperaments need at different age periods, and of just what causes emotional disturbances," recognizing that "many of our ideas about what is normal have been derived indirectly from the study of the abnormal, which at best is an unreliable method."

The Project staff of three psychologists, two pediatricians in addition to Dr. Spock (who functioned as a preventive psychiatrist), a nutritionist, and a nursery school supervisor worked with the personnel and facilities already established in Rochester: the Mayo Clinic's maternity service; clinics for well babies and preschool children; schools; and the city health department. Dr. Spock and his fellows treated young children with problems involving such matters as eating, sleeping, anxiety, and sibling rivalry. The crucial element of expert supervision of the psychotherapy was supplied by Dr. Adelaide Johnson, formerly of the Chicago Psychoanalytic Institute, a psychoanalyst of adults and children and an extraordinarily clear and daring teacher. She had no fear of overseeing therapy carried out by quite inexperienced trainees, in the presence of a dozen other trainees, all of whom attended the twice weekly supervisory sessions together, to extend their own experience and to take advantage of Dr. Johnson's limited time available. There the emphasis was "as much on community management as on psychotherapy, as much on what might have been done earlier in prophylaxis as on treatment." Dr. Spock became convinced that the most productive way to break through the resistance of pediatric fellows to considering the emotional life of the child and family is to involve them in the therapy of a troubled child.

Dr. Spock also conducted in Rochester the kind of school conference he had participated in under Caroline Zachry's leadership at the Institute for Personality Development in New York. Spock and trainees met weekly with a public school teacher, school nurse, and principal to discuss a problem pupil. Dr. Spock helped the group to consider the underlying psychodynamics, the ways of using the curriculum and the teacher's relationship with the child to help him academically and socially, and whether additional counseling of the parents or child might be useful. Whether or not such conferences aided the teacher, they were surely educational for the fellows, who learned how differently various teachers conceive of their job, how one teacher eases an emotional problem and another accentuates it, how many ways there are to help a troubled child in addition to psychotherapy.

In 1948 Dr. Spock began a preliminary research project informally known as the "Inborn Temperament Study." The Study was based on the assumption that it was necessary to determine the importance and the nature of variations in inborn temperament in order to adequately understand normal emotional development. Dr. Spock felt that "if it could be demonstrated that temperament varies greatly and plays a significant part, in interaction with environment, in personality formation, then the need for a much greater degree of individualization in [child rearing] advice would be apparent. . . . If one child is born docile and another aggressive their parents should not be using identical methods in rearing them."

So Dr. Spock, the fellows he supervised, and other visiting physicians pored over the bassinets of the six hundred or so infants born in Rochester in 1948 and 1949, observing each baby three or four days after birth and again four days later. Each observer independently rated each baby on thirty-seven pairs of roughly opposite characteristics, such as frustratable or adaptable, lighthearted or solemn, reasonable or demanding, resourceful or ineffectual, mean or humane, vulnerable or stable, mannish or womanly, likeable or uninspiring. That many of these criteria seemed irrelevant, inappropriate, or impossible to tell from looking at a baby less than a week old wasn't wholly the point, for these same criteria were to be drawn on in assessing the child at nine and eighteen months and at various intervals during his school career, when they would be more meaningful. The crucial part of the Study was to consist of noting the more objectively determinable personality characteristics in the older infants to see whether they were indicated in the newborn period.

Though six or eight doctors observed each baby, even if their ratings coincided, there was no guarantee that their observations were objective, reliable, or meaningful, for the infants didn't have to accomplish any particular performance—they were simply watched and interpreted subjectively. Moreover, Spock was the only constant observer of any given baby at more than two of the specified intervals; the other observers were involved for a year, at most.

Another incidental aspect of the Study demonstrated the potential unreliability of such observations. The staff tried to determine a baby's sex (a possible clue to its temperament, they felt) by looking at its face. One woman fellow was accurate over 90 percent of the time, but could never explain how she knew. The shape of eyes and nose, absence of skin pigmentation, straightness of hair, flatness of forehead, had been suggested as clues, but even with these criteria the other doctors were right only between 40 and 75 percent of the time. The traditional way to find out remained the best.

Dr. Lloyd Harris, a Mayo Clinic pediatrician, Assistant Director of the Rochester Child Health Institute under Dr. Aldrich and later its Co-director, explained that preliminary comparisons of the assessments in the newborn period and at nine and eighteen months "offered no promise of significant data." That disappointment and the imminent dissolution of the Institute brought an end to the Study, without complete statistical analysis of the data or further follow-up of the children. The Study was unfruitful because it generated no publications and made no impact either on other researchers or on the general public. Nevertheless, Spock's conviction about inborn temperament remained firm, and was indeed validated by the remarkably rewarding study of children's temperament begun in 1956 at New York University School of Medicine by Dr. Alexander Thomas and others.[1]

By 1949 the regular members of the Mayo staff had long since returned from military service, inflation had set in, and money for research was becoming scarcer. The Mayo administration wanted to spend their limited research funds to investigate problems closer to the Clinic's main concerns, so they decided to decrease the budget and activities of the Child Health Institute at the very time the Institute's staff was eager to expand services and facilities.

Then, in October 1949, Dr. Aldrich died, and with him went a good deal of the Institute's spirit and purposiveness. For the remainder of 1949 and throughout 1950 and part of 1951 Dr. Spock and Dr. Harris shared the administrator's duties until the Institute was dissolved.

A major index of a researcher's prowess is the number of his publications in reputable professional journals; articles in the popular press count negatively, if at all. Because the Clinic had been criticized by the A.M.A. for self-advertisement in the earlier part of the century when the newspapers were idolizing the Mayo brothers, it had become so shy of publicity that it would hardly permit its doctors to be interviewed about new developments in medicine, let alone publish articles or books for the general public. Though his appointment at the Mayo Clinic was based mainly on the views expressed in *Baby and Child Care,* Dr. Spock feels, with some amusement, that "I couldn't have published the baby book without a lot of rumpus if I'd been on their staff then."

The Clinic did encourage scholarly publication, and by this criterion Dr. Spock's most productive years were the late 1940s, when he averaged two published scholarly articles annually, and the early 1960s, when he averaged a paper a year. Though this record is acceptable, it is not spectacular. This figure, though, does not take into account the very publications many of his peers might not consider seriously, his writings as a parent educator, speaking directly to and for parents in the mass-circulation magazines, which he began extensively in 1954, and his various books.

The papers Dr. Spock wrote and the addresses he gave to professional societies while he was at the Mayo Clinic appear to be derived more from his prewar experience as a pediatrician in private practice than from his activities at Rochester. The exception is "Teaching the Broader Aspects of Pediatrics" (*Pediatrics,* January 1950, pp. 21–23), in which Dr. Spock explained the emphasis of his teaching. He wanted to promote "the child's total development and total adjustment [through an] interest in preventive psychiatry and psychosomatic medicine" and to arouse in doctors "enthusiasm not just for diagnosing the unusual case—enthusiasm for trying to understand and solve the common, everyday problems that trouble children and parents everywhere." But his words have gone largely unheeded. Unless they're planning on a career in research, few of the most brilliant medical students enter pediatrics; they claim that it is too routine.

Dr. Spock's own writings consistently reflect his enthusiasm for the common problems. During the forties he discussed "Some *Common* Diagnostic Problems in Children: Tic, Chorea and General Restlessness (*Medical Clinics of North America,* July 1950); "The Middle-Aged Child" (*Pennsylvania Medical Journal,* July 1947), which correlates *common* phenomena of psychological and physical growth and development in children between six and the beginning of puberty; and *"Common* Behavior Disturbances in the First Two Years of Life" (*Journal of the American Medical Association,* March 20, 1948). [Emphasis supplied on "common."]

Partly because of consuming involvement with his work, partly because of the temper of the time and place, during his four years in Rochester Dr. Spock was less involved in politics and controversial public issues than at any other time since his marriage. Rochester's geographical isolation and homogeneous medical and social community were scarcely conducive to the fervid political discussions and espousals of liberal causes that moved the Spocks and their New York friends. Rochester's mood of quiet conservatism reflected the mood of the country, weary of war, frightened of communism, and eagerly receptive to the investigations conducted by Senator Joseph McCarthy and the House Un-American Activities Committee. Hundreds of otherwise inconspicuous citizens were tarred with the Communist brush and lost their jobs and career opportunities. The *cause célèbre* of the decade was the trial of Julius and Ethel Rosenberg and others for allegedly conspiring to steal United States atomic secrets. Their pleas for clemency failed, President Eisenhower ignored the pickets circling the White House, and on June 19, 1953 the Rosenbergs were executed. Yet the Spocks took up no cudgels; Dr. Spock was immersed in his work, while his wife's current cause was raising money for the local art association.

When Mike came home for Christmas vacation during his freshman year at Antioch sporting a bright red beard, his father forbade him to leave the house until he'd shaved. "Within half an hour that beard was off," Dr. Spock said in 1967. "I was worried about Mike's reception and perhaps my reputation, too. I wouldn't dare

give such an order today. I assume I'd be unconcerned about such
a mild expression of independence now, but perhaps that's because
I'm a long way from Rochester. I don't think today Mike would
have shaved it off." (In fact, when John grew a beard in Cleveland
in 1963 not a word was uttered, and he simply wore it until he got
tired of it.)

By the late 1940s and early 1950s, when *Baby and Child Care*
was already selling a million copies a year, Dr. Spock began to be
called on by various agencies of the Government when they wanted
a well-known endorser of their policies relating to children. During
President Truman's administration Dr. Spock was asked to testify
on behalf of a national child research bill (S. R. 904), but it didn't
pass. He was on the Advisory Council on Community Services of
the National Institute of Mental Health.

Spock was also appointed to the fact-finding committee of the
1950 White House Conference on Children and Youth, a meeting of
the nation's most eminent professionals on the subject, held once
each decade. Preparation for the Conference required monthly
meetings, which he enjoyed partly because they provided an opportunity to emphasize nationally his views on preventive pediatric
care, child development, and parent education. In an address to
the Conference on December 4, 1950 he stressed, among other
points, what he considered a fundamental question, "Why are so
many parents unable to enjoy their children?" Then he suggested
an approach to finding out the answer: "We know that some of the
causes are in individuals and that individual psychotherapy can be
effective in certain cases. But we have not studied the problem from
a broad public health point of view and we have not begun to
think of broad solutions. One of the investigations will be to see
what educational methods, from nursery school through college, can
do to keep alive the delight in children which is usually present in
childhood, and to bring the boy and girl to adulthood with the
feeling"—Spock's own—"that there is no more important, honorable, and soul satisfying job than having and caring for children."

A fringe benefit of membership in the Conference was the
monthly trip to Washington, D.C. At that time Jane didn't want
her husband to fly, though with his accelerated schedule in recent
years she has withdrawn her objections. Instead he took the train.
Dr. Spock explains: "It was all right to take off three days from

the Mayo Clinic to make this kind of journey because it was a professional trip and they didn't dock your vacation time, though it was a mild vacation anyway.

"In March, April, May, I would leave Rochester in a deep snow storm, arrive in Chicago where it was black and rainy and sloppy, get on a train and work and read and go to bed. I'd wake up the next morning in a lower berth, raise the shade and look out on the Virginia countryside, where the earth was red. The farmers would be out there in the steamy spring morning plowing their fields. The leaves were already green. Oh, it was like magic, to transfer from winter to a soft, moist, misty kind of a spring for one day. I loved that feeling."

He adds, "The reverse weather shift wasn't so pleasant, though there was fun going north from Chicago. There I'd get on a Burlington train that cut across Iowa to the Mississippi River, where it would sneak right along the river's edge on the Wisconsin side. I'd always sit on top, in a vistadome car, which is entirely different from looking out of a conventional train window. By being able to see ahead and out both sides you really feel you're part of the countryside. For hours there's a bluff on your right and on the left the Mississippi River with long strips of islands covered with willow trees. Those were lovely trips."

Jane felt stranded in Rochester, and much more dependent on her husband than she liked to be. Both the Spocks missed their intellectual New York friends with diversified interests. "In Rochester, at a dinner party," says Dr. Spock, "two women would be talking about canning or deep freezing. You'd sit down and try to horn into it and laugh or break it up a little but they wouldn't let you. So you'd have to sit and listen to canning for a while. We went from the fanciest level of conversation to the earthiest in that one move. Jane hated it and she took it out on the weather. She was angry at the weather all the time. Every time she went out she'd put on a fur hat and a wool scarf wrapped round and round so that just two angry eyes showed."

However, Jane gradually found a place in the community, and for the duration of John's nursery schooling she was on the nursery school board. In time she made friends with several women who "didn't talk just about sewing and baking rolls and pies," she says.

"The young medical fellows and their wives were more fun than the older doctors our age who were so involved in their specialties that they would get together at one end of the room during a dinner party and talk about medicine and hunting. So with the fellows we'd get up a party at the country club every Saturday night. Everybody would pay for his own dinner and then we'd dance for the rest of the evening. We never again danced as much as we did there."

The Spocks also enjoyed their weekends and vacations. They bought a twelve-foot aluminum skiff in which they assiduously explored the local streams and lakes, and the Mississippi and St. Croix Rivers. In spite of his gregariousness, Dr. Spock, still his mother's child, has always sought vacations in isolated, watery wildernesses of the same stern sort that his mother had imposed on him decades earlier. The Spocks spent a month each summer, 1948–50, at a state park in the Keweenaw Peninsula, a little finger protruding from Michigan's Upper Peninsula into Lake Superior, glorying in the evergreen trees, icy water, and rocky shores much like the Maine of his childhood.

The children liked it too, though as adults neither has craved rough water and wind with the same passion as his father. Mike enjoyed life in Rochester more consistently than the rest of his family. In many ways he was the model of the All-American boy, the ideal Spockian teenager, though more critical than the stereotype. He was a loving and understanding big brother to little John, who was continually irritable until he outgrew the celiac disease around five and a half. (John basked in Mike's paternalism until he was twenty. "Even when I began Harvard," John acknowledged at the age of twenty-four, "Mike was very good at explaining how things really were. He was very good as a big brother, but found it hard to be just a brother and to accept me as an independent person.")

Though Mike claims that "I've never been very outgoing or the kind of wildly energetic person my father is," he thrived on the first close friendships of his life. For the first time in his life he lived near his classmates. He got a driver's license when he was fifteen so he could see them more easily. His parents, permissive against their better judgment, forebore setting a curfew, even when he and his girlfriend skidded into an icy ditch at 3 a.m. Though his early reading disability had left him a permanently slow reader, Mike earned honor grades in Rochester High. He had a fine physique and became an excellent swimmer, winning the Minnesota backstroke championship in his junior year.

Like typical American parents, the Spocks took pride in Mike's scholastic and athletic achievement and approved of his emerging gregariousness. No different from many other fathers, Dr. Spock would have liked one or both of his sons to be a doctor, to do as he had done only better, just as he himself had surpassed his own father's progress through Yale. "But," he says, "we had that American overscrupulousness about trying not to hint to our children our ideas about their careers or spouses, though the boys knew I would have liked them to be doctors."

Indeed, for a time Mike had planned to follow his father to Yale, where swimming was important, and to become a doctor. Then, in his senior year of high school, the swimming team, expected to become state champions, failed badly because of illnesses. Soon after, Mike decided against Yale and against swimming, which Spock interprets as a reversal of Mike's impulse to compete directly with his father's college career. Instead, Mike chose academically excellent, non-athletic, ultra-liberal Antioch College in Yellow Springs, Ohio because, he says, "I found the student self-government appealing. The Antioch catalog was compelling, unlike any other college catalog I'd ever seen. It was obviously written from the students' point of view and *not* by an administrator."

His father admired Antioch for its experimental spirit, its work-study program, and the independence and thoughtfulness encouraged in the students (a remarkable contrast to Yale in the twenties). He uncomplainingly paid the bills for an undergraduate program that turned out to take nine years instead of Antioch's regulation five. Yet he couldn't help being irritated at that time by the students' appearance. Spock shudders, "Mike expressed his adolescent revolt by being terribly messy. At Antioch in the fifties, long before there were hippies, you could get away with incredible extremes of dishevelment. It used to make me almost sick at my stomach when on a visit we'd go into the cafeteria for breakfast and see the students who had just tumbled out of bed and had come in wearing tattle-tale-gray T-shirts and blue jeans; men unshaven and their faces shiny from not having been washed and their hair touseled. The girls might have put an elastic band around their pigtails but their faces seemed also to be greasy from not having been washed. And no sign of makeup. I didn't think that in any significant way this was important. Still, as a neat, organized person myself (compulsive by the standards of many), it bothered me to see people, as my mother would say, 'just letting themselves go.' " But by the late 1960's Dr. Spock had learned to suppress his intolerance of sloppy personal appearance in his admiration of students whose position on peace in Indochina and draft resistance he was currently championing. In fact, he came to accept their grooming with equanimity.

Mike was not at all upset by Antioch's sloppiness, but ran promptly into what his father describes an "an academic block." Even Dr. Spock, with his commitment to preventive psychiatry, was not able to anticipate or to prevent Mike's difficulties in college, and once they appeared, he could only provide the money for their treatment. In the May 1968 *Ladies' Home Journal* Mike explained that in "the black phase of my life. . . . I had a hard time settling down to work, switched courses, did well in some subjects, but found it excruciating to do a paper. I'd sit in front of a typewriter for three days and not move. Nowadays, they talk about an identity crisis. Then, all I knew was that I was having a [hard] time keeping up. I had once been interested in medicine, but my first co-op job as a hospital orderly made me realize that doctors spend most of their time with sick people—a thought that hadn't occurred to me before. Sick people are too self-absorbed, and I decided I preferred the well." His father's own interpretation is predictably psychoanalytic: "It was fairly soon obvious when Mike touched on chemistry or physics or similar subjects that he had the most trouble. A psychoanalyst would immediately assume that this was related to rivalry with the father."

Mike continues: "At spring vacation I told my parents about the severe studying problem. They suggested a counselor or a psychiatrist. My mother was convinced it was important. Initially, despite his sophisticated psychoanalytical training, my father felt it was a matter of my willpower—that I wasn't buckling down to study. Nevertheless, they looked for help, and discovered a psychiatrist at the University of Cincinnati. He said to me, 'Let's start talking.' I thought we'd only discuss my studying trouble, but by age eighteen I was in full-scale psychoanalysis, which lasted nine years. . . .

"It was hard for my family, especially since I had been successful in grade and high schools. I did stutter a bit—still do occasionally—but never had appeared to be a troubled child. It was only when I left the family structure that everything seemed to disintegrate. It takes a long time to wean yourself."

Less affluent parents than the Spocks, or less devout believers in psychoanalysis, might have pressed for speedier treatment, more dramatic results, or a transfer of schools. Dr. Spock claims, "Antioch was a wise school in the sense that they would make all kinds of allowances, even letting Mike take only one course a semester when his problem was at its most severe. Arguing the other way, we know from school phobias in young children, if the school and parents are so sympathetic that they drop all requirements it may make the cure take longer. At a more demanding school he might have been more scared, and this fright might have counteracted his deeper anxieties and kept him at work. Still, the work-study plan led him to museum work, for he found that museums satisfied his strong interests in building things, interior decorating, and teaching biology." (An index of Dr. Spock's satisfaction with the school was that he later became one of its fund raisers, writing the solicitation letter that went to parents.)

The Spocks had another reason to be pleased with Antioch, for there Mike met Judith TenEyck Wood, an art student a year older than himself, whom he married in 1955. Parents less accommodating might have refused to subsidize the marriage of a son in psychotherapy who had dropped out of college three times and had worked as a gas station attendant, a cabinetmaker, an advertising copyboy. But the Spocks, having great confidence in Mike's maturity, were pleased with Mike's marriage and delighted with Judy. Observes her father-in-law, "As soon as we met Judy we thought she was marvelous—she's fun, she's sensitive, she's artistic, she's witty as hell, and she's beautiful. My God, she's beautiful. She can wear any kind of clothes, gypsy or formal, and look ravishing in them. And she has been an inspiring wife and mother."

While Mike was combating challenges on the psychiatrist's couch, his father was undertaking new professional and personal challenges which were to involve far more combat than he had anticipated.

The Medical School of the University of Pittsburgh had just been offered a great deal of money by wealthy industrialists (some of whom were also trustees) who wanted to transform the University, as they were transforming the rest of the city, from a manifestation of sooty mediocrity to an establishment of the highest quality. They wanted the Department of Psychiatry to be particularly strong in psychosomatic medicine, child psychiatry, and child development, and sought illustrious faculty members to do this. Dr. Spock was without doubt the pediatrician best known to the public in the latter areas, and the ideal choice of the trustees. As funds for the Rochester Child Health Institute were terminated and its personnel obliged to seek other jobs, Dr. Spock was offered and accepted a very complicated position at the University of Pittsburgh: Professor of Child Development in the Medical School, with faculty rank in the Department of Pediatrics at Children's Hospital, in the Child Guidance Center, and in the Graduate School of Public Health.

So in June 1951 the Spocks left the clear crisp atmosphere of Rochester, Minnesota for the murkier climate of Pittsburgh, Pennsylvania.

LEFT: *Baby Benjamin Spock with mother, Mildred S. Spock, ca. 1903.* RIGHT: *Benjamin Ives Spock, father of Dr. Spock.* (James T. Evans, Jr.)

Spock home at 165 Cold Spring Street, New Haven, Connecticut, 1900–1919.

Baby Benjamin Spock on his father's shoulders, ca. 1904, at home.

LEFT: *Nannie (Mrs. Ada Stoughton) and baby Benjamin Spock at 165 Cold Spring Street, New Haven, Connecticut, ca. 1904.* RIGHT: *Benny Spock at one year.*

LEFT: *Mildred Spock with Hiddy and Benny Spock as young children.* RIGHT: *Benny Spock as a young child.*

The Spock children, l. to r., Bob, Anne, Betty, Hiddy, and Benny [Sally not yet born], in Maine for summer vacation, ca. 1914.

BELOW LEFT: *Benny Spock, schoolboy.*

ABOVE RIGHT: *Spock home at 67 Edgehill Road, New Haven, Connecticut.*

RIGHT: *Ben Spock, l., and roommate Geo Dyer, r., in 701 Harkness Quadrangle, Yale University, ca. 1924.* (George Dyer)

Yale Olympic rowing crew, practicing on the Seine before the 1924 Olympic race: l. to r., *Leonard Carpenter, Frederick Sheffield, Alfred Wilson, James Rockefeller (captain), Lester Miller, Howard Kingsbury, Benjamin Spock, and Alfred Lindley.*

RIGHT: *Ben Spock working on the Canadian Pacific Railroad in Manitoba, summer 1926, as a member of Frontier College.*

BELOW LEFT: *Jane Cheney Spock, wedding photograph, June 25, 1927.* RIGHT: *Ben Spock, wedding photograph, June 1927.*

Dr. Benjamin Spock, center, and fellow pediatric interns on rooftop of New York Nursery and Child's Hospital, ca. 1930. LEFT: Jane, baby Mike, and Ben Spock, New York, 1933. BELOW LEFT: 112 East 81st Street, New York City, Spock residence in the '30s. RIGHT: The proud father, Ben Spock, with Mike in Central Park, ca. 1934.

Mike, Nannie (Mrs. Mildred Spock), and Ben Spock on Maine coast, ca. 1940.

LEFT: *Dr. Spock, pediatrician, examining Margaret Mead's baby, Catherine Bateson, in New York.* (Gregory Bateson) RIGHT: *Lt. Cmdr. Benjamin Spock, M.D., U.S. Navy, 1944.*

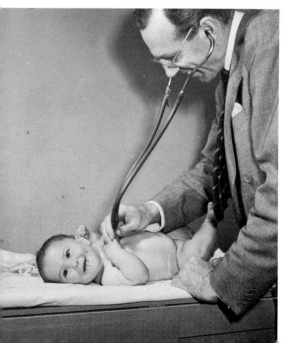 

Jane, Mike, John, and Ben Spock at home in Rochester, Minnesota, ca. 1950.

LEFT: *Dr. Spock rides again. Rochester, Minnesota, ca. 1950.* RIGHT: *Spock home, 1313 Second Street, N.W., Rochester, Minnesota.*

Dr. Spock in his office at the Mayo Clinic, Rochester, Minnesota. (Gene's Photo, Rochester, Minnesota)

Mike, Nannie (Mrs. Mildred Spock), and Judith Wood Spock at the wedding of Mike and Judy, Antioch College, Yellow Springs, Ohio, 1955.

Dr. Spock and friend in the sandbox at Arsenal Family and Children's Center, Pittsburgh, Pennsylvania, ca. 1954.

LEFT: *Of this effort at figure skating in 1961, Dr. Spock says, "Terrible form; I'm a little better now."* (Henri Cartiér-Bresson, Magnum Photos) BELOW LEFT: *Dr. Spock lecturing at Western Reserve University, 1961* (Henri Cartiér-Bresson, Magnum Photos) RIGHT: *Dr. Spock at home in Cleveland with first grandchild, Daniel Spock, 1959.* (Cowles Magazines, Inc.)

Dr. Spock in a typical conversational posture in his office at the Western Reserve University Medical School, 1959. (Cowles Magazines, Inc.)

BELOW: *Spock residence at Inglewood Drive, Cleveland Heights, Ohio, 1955–57.*

ABOVE: *Dr. Spock in 1959. He always writes at this table, on this high stool. He gave up smoking in 1962, on doctor's orders.* (Cowles Magazines, Inc.) LEFT: *Spock residence at 2220 Woodmere, Cleveland Heights, Ohio, 1957–67.*

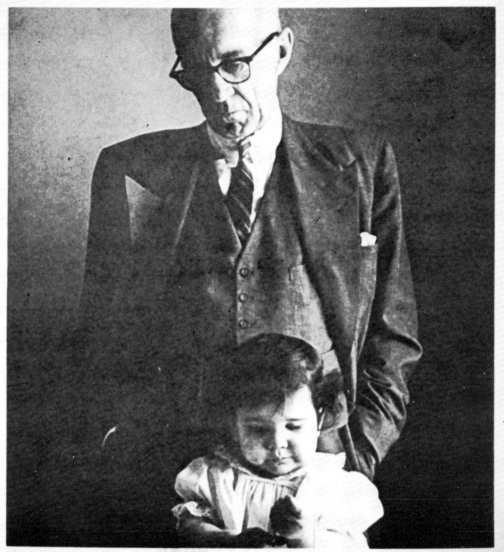

Dr. Spock is worried.

SANE advertising campaign, 1962–1966.

ABOVE: *Dr. Spock and Charlie Chaplin in procession accompanying the awarding of honorary degrees by Durham University, Durham, England, 1962.* (Newcastle Chronicle & Journal Ltd.)

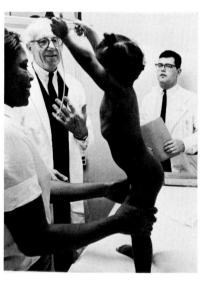

RIGHT: *Dr. Spock instructing a medical student at the Family Clinic, Western Reserve University Medical School, 1964.* (Hella Hammid for U.S. Information Agency)

BELOW: *Sargent Shriver, Vice President Hubert Humphrey, and Dr. Spock consulting on the National Advisory Council of the Office of Economic Opportunity, 1965.* (O.E.O.)

Ben and Jane Spock sailing in the Virgin Islands, ca. 1966. (Dr. and Mrs. David Goldthwait)

Dr. Spock, Chief Henry Crow Dog of the Redbud Sioux, Dr. Martin Luther King, Jr., and Msgr. Charles Rice at Spring Mobilization to End the War in Vietnam (the "Old Mobe"), New York, April 15, 1967. (Syeus Mottel)

Dr. Spock and small marcher at the UN Plaza, New York, April 15, 1967. (Syeus Mottel)

BELOW LEFT: *Professor Sidney Peck, Dr. Spock, and Jane at a peace rally in Cleveland, July 13, 1968, in support of Dr. Spock after his conviction of conspiracy to encourage draft resistance.*

BELOW: *Dr. Spock addressing a rally on Boston Common after a reversal of his conviction for conspiracy, July 11, 1969.*

Dr. Spock at Welfare Rights Organization rally, 1969. (Wide World Photos)

Judy, Susannah, Peter, Mike, and Danny Spock at home in Lincoln, Massachusetts, 1970.

John C. Spock, 1971.

Ben and Jane at home in New York, 1968. (New York Times)

eight

PITTSBURGH: PROBLEMS AND POPULARITY

THE differences between Rochester and Pittsburgh are in some ways like the differences between Dr. Spock's jobs in the respective cities. Pittsburgh, a city sixteen times Rochester's size, is trisected by the polluted Allegheny, Monongahela, and Ohio Rivers—as opposed to Rochester's sparkling Zumbro. Rochester's gently rolling terrain was a sharp contrast to greater Pittsburgh, a city sprawling grimly over the worn spine of the Allegheny foothills. Rochester's homogeneous, relatively comfortable Anglo-Saxon and Scandinavian population seemed extraordinarily problem-free in comparison with the turbulent and vital mixture of religious, racial, and ethnic groups in Pittsburgh.

Just as the Mayo tower, medicine, and money dominated Rochester, so the smoking stacks of the steel factories, steel-related industries, and steel money dominated Pittsburgh. The Mayo brothers had been integrated into Rochester from the very beginning of their careers and had always maintained its interests, while to Pittsburgh's post-Civil War industrialists the city and its mineral and human resources were there to be exploited. In 1900, for instance, Carnegie Steel alone made a profit of forty million dollars; Andrew Carnegie's salary was ten million, tax-free. In the same year the average worker earned $417. Only after the industrialists had extracted hundreds of millions of dollars from the workers in the mines and blast furnaces did they return a small fraction in the form of libraries and other public endowments. Their descendants, the Carnegies, Mellons, Scaifes, Falks, and others, demonstrated social consciences far more responsive to the city's needs and began to contribute magnificently as the twentieth century wore on. They realized that the industrial blight included in the legacy of their forbears was gradually—and literally—choking the city to death. For years during the winter the city had been blacked out by a dense pall of smog that turned noon to midnight; for years during the spring the rivers had flooded and turned the downtown "Golden Triangle" into a fetid sea. So they decided to clean it up—and at the same time, to tone it up. After World War II ended, plans were made to eliminate the floods, air and water pollution, to revamp various commercial areas, and to improve the city's intellectual and cultural life. The renaissance of the University of Pittsburgh, known at the time more for its forty-two-story skyscraper classroom building than for academic excellence, was part of that plan. And in that plan were included Dr. Henry Brosin, new director of Western Psychiatric Institute and head of Pittsburgh's Department of Psychiatry, Dr. Spock, and Dr. I. Arthur Mirsky, who was a rare and productive combination of psychoanalyst and biochemist, outstandingly successful in designing research projects that got to the heart of psychosomatic mysteries. The trio arrived July 1, 1951, welcomed by Dr. Alan Magee Scaife, president of the University's Board of Trustees, as "the finest psychiatric team in America."

Dr. Spock's salary was comfortable—$20,000 for the first year, $24,000 for each of the three remaining years of his stay. His office, with ceiling-to-waist-high leaded casement windows, was spacious, as was his refurbished red brick Georgian house at elegant 1090 Shady Avenue. His hopes were high, for Dr. Spock, a perennial optimist, always begins each new job with great enthusiasm.

His responsibilities were enormous. His aims were fourfold: to integrate the previously independent Pittsburgh Child Guidance Center into the University Medical School; to start a psychiatric inpatient service for seriously disturbed children in Western Psychiatric Institute Hospital; to provide psychiatric and teaching services at the Children's Hospital of Pittsburgh, another affiliate of the Medical School; and to develop a teaching and training program in child development, family relations, and preventive psychiatry at the Arsenal Health Center for the benefit of students and public health department practitioners of medicine, public health, nursing, psychiatry, and pediatrics. In short, he was to wear at least five hats concurrently as teacher, administrator, program planner and coordinator, and liaison between various departments, hospitals, clinics, teaching settings, and the community.

In the year prior to coming to Pittsburgh, Dr. Spock's main task was to recruit key personnel in child psychiatry, psychology, psychiatric social work, and nursery school education with the vision not only to make advances in their particular fields but to try to weave their specialties to some extent into an integrated mental health program which might become a model for other places. This visionary plan was a precursor to the current community mental health movements in which teams of workers in related health fields bring their collective knowledge to bear in solving particular problems in community settings.

Dr. Spock wanted his staff who would be members of the Division of Child Psychiatry and Child Development to have sufficient perspective to continually examine such basic questions as the relationship between the "normal" and the "abnormal" child of various temperaments and of various family backgrounds, the relationship between therapy and prevention, the most efficient and effective forms of therapy (including group therapy), and the mental health needs of the whole community. He sought a psychodynamically experienced staff who could impart their special knowledge of the deeper dynamics of the psyche to other helping professionals (schoolteachers, public health doctors and nurses, and others) who ordinarily rely on surface, "common sense" explanations of children's behavior rather than on seeking explanations in the unconscious. Thus Spock was pleased to have hired two psychoanalytically trained child psychiatrists: Dr. Doris Phillips to head the Child Guidance Center, and Dr. Joseph Cramer to develop the psychiatric consultation and teaching service at Children's Hospital. For the preventive program at Arsenal he had engaged Dr. Margaret McFarland, nursery school director; a psychologist, and a psychiatric social worker.

Gone was the established, unhurried workday of the Mayo Clinic. In its place were the problems born of newness, abrupt restructuring of the Medical School, expansion and innovation of programs. There were many people new to new jobs, as well as people accustomed to old jobs which had suddenly been altered. In addition to the problems of the old adjusting to the new was the conceptual conflict between those who believed that all the key guidance personnel should be psychoanalytically trained, and those who felt that non-analytic training was often sufficient. An institutional conflict occurred in selecting the replacement for Dr. Phillips, who married and left Pittsburgh after only a year as Director of the Child Guidance Center. By solemn agreement, nominations for the professional staff were to come from the psychiatric faculty; and if that faculty had agreed on a candidate and had presented a unified front in pressing their suggestion, a new director might have been found with a minimum of friction. Although Dr. Spock and Dr. Cramer agreed that the director should be an experienced child analyst, neither was enthusiastic about the other's choice of candidates. At one time, Dr. Brosin insisted on a woman without analytic background whose husband he wanted to employ in another area. Other nominations and counter-nominations were made but not agreed upon.

Finally the Guidance Center Board, annoyed by the delay, nominated its own candidate, a person without psychoanalytic background. The Medical School Dean, Dr. William McEllroy, sided with the Board, which contained relatives of the University's benefactors and trustees. Spock wanted to stand firm in opposition to the Board, but Cramer did not. Even now, nearly twenty years later, distrust and antagonism engendered by this conflict (and many others) still prevent the protagonists from discussing it objectively.

Other problems impeded the endeavors of Spock and Cramer to develop a psychiatric program at Children's Hospital. Any such institution needs psychiatric consultation services for the behavior problems and psychosomatic problems which keep cropping up on the wards and in the clinic; and theoretically it wants its pediatric trainees—medical students, interns, residents—to become familiar with the meaning of such difficulties.

"But in reality," says Spock, "almost any chief of a children's hospital will interpret these objectives quite differently than will the consultants from child psychiatry, for the approach of the two disciplines to the human psyche is fundamentally opposite. Psychiatrically oriented people believe that similar-seeming symptoms may have different causes and that, conversely, different symptoms may indicate the same causes. They believe it is of highest importance to recognize and understand the feelings of others (and of themselves) in order to get at the deep cause of psychological problems. But scientists—and most professors of pediatrics have achieved their high positions by being good scientists—tend to be made uncomfortable by being asked to recognize feelings. They want feelings, in themselves and in others, to be kept strictly subordinated to and controlled by reason. They are made particularly uncomfortable by psychiatrists because psychiatrists emphasize the power not only of conscious but of unconscious emotions. For the past forty years this conflict has been a basic and continuing problem for those psychiatrists whose main job in medical centers has been to teach the role of the emotions in disease and in health."

The problem was epitomized by the situation at Children's Hospital. The pediatric staff asked for numerous quick psychiatric consultations that would expedite the diagnoses and discharges of their many patients. They requested simplified teaching sessions on child psychology that would tell them how to treat such cases on their own, quickly and easily. They were chronically dissatisfied that Dr. Cramer could give them so few consultations and that Cramer and Spock spoke so lengthily about feelings instead of cures. The staff constantly demanded more consultations, more teaching sessions.

Spock felt that the pediatric staff didn't really want what they had asked for. He explains, "When I could offer the Professor of Pediatrics more of my time for teaching sessions—discussions of general topics, common behavior deviations, and problems presented by specific children in the hospital—he always backed away from making an arrangement. In February he would say, 'Let's talk about that in June.' And in September he'd suggest delaying until January.

This went on for two whole years. Yet in his annual report, disseminated far and wide, he would complain that our Division had bitterly disappointed his department. Eventually the pediatric residents themselves asked for a weekly conference and the medical students attended too." So the services were supplied, but considerable frustration persisted on both sides.

After two years of unavoidable delays, Dr. Spock was finally able to fulfill another of the obligations of his job, establishment of a children's inpatient service at Western Psychiatric Institute. Well-trained child psychiatrist and analyst Dr. Earl Loomis undertook the job and organized a devoted and tightly knit staff. He decided to focus on the study and treatment of autistic and symbiotic children, much of whose daily care was provided by graduate students enrolled in a new Master's program in Child Development. The students proved to be adaptable caretakers and were pleased with the elaborate, thorough training provided for them.

Also successful were the activities that Spock directed at the Arsenal Health Center (so named because the location had been an arsenal during the Civil War) which served the neighborhoood's predominantly Polish, Italian, and Negro population. Here the ideal of a neighborhood health center which Dr. Spock had helped to formulate in Rochester came closer to fruition. The facilities consisted of a generalized public health nursing service to cover clinics, schools, and homes; there were also clinics for chest and venereal disease, and a nursery school organized by Spock and McFarland.

Spock's aims were to have staff people from pediatrics, psychiatry, nursing, child development, and social work; students of medicine, nursing, and public health; pediatric and psychiatric residents; and special advanced students (who came from around the world) work together and learn from one another, thereby broadening and deepening their own understanding of individuals, families, groups, neighborhoods, and the multiplicity of their needs. Reciprocally, the professionals' separate skills and insights could be combined to help the patients with their problems.

In promoting these aims Dr. Spock had the enthusiastic assistance of Dr. Florence Marcus, able and humanistic Director of the Pittsburgh Maternal and Child Health Division of the city Health Department. With some difficulty Drs. Spock and Marcus were able to persuade the Health Department to allow its nurses to remain in the Arsenal district for at least a year at a time so they could get to know their families well, and to put them on general duty, dealing with all the health problems of all family members (as a general practitioner does) rather than dividing them into nursing specialties.

Drs. Marcus, Spock, and McFarland saw to it that, among other things, the primary emphasis in teaching and in health care was always on a comfortable, friendly, neighborly relationship between staff and family. The parents, with whom Dr. Spock occasionally conferred, were delighted with the services they and their children were receiving. Although they loved Spock's grandfatherly manner, they were not awed in the least by the fact that he had written *the* baby book.

But it was only after working at Arsenal for three years that Spock and his staff were able to admit, to themselves and to each other, the extent of the hostility they had encountered in coming almost as invaders to bring a somewhat unfamiliar philosophy to an established staff of nurses and pediatricians of the Health Department. The antagonism was manifested most often as an insistent, irritable demand for more teaching sessions—which were rejected or cut down on when offered—combined with a critical attitude toward the teaching provided (shades of the situation at Children's Hospital!). On one occasion an uninitiated public health nurse was heard to grumble after a staff conference conducted by Spock which the regulars had found particularly interesting, "Same old crap! Another hour wasted!"

No one felt that time was wasted when Erik Erikson, who had just recently published *Childhood and Society* (New York: Norton, 1950) with its perceptive discussion of the identity crisis and other phenomena, came to Pittsburgh for monthly conferences, as a visiting professor at Spock's behest. He divided his time among presiding at a case conference at the Child Guidance Center, discussing a child at the Arsenal Nursery School, a case conference of some mentally ill Pittsburgh working man for the adult psychiatry staff, and a staff meeting for the whole Division of Child Psychiatry and Child Development in the Spocks' living room in the evening. Dr. Spock comments, "After he had heard a case presentation he knew more about the patient than the staff members treating him, and he could make interpretations of obscure aspects of the case which usually proved, in time, to be brilliantly accurate. Erikson's intuitive insights about patients, his impressive psychoanalytic credentials (including his friendship with the Freud family), his anthropological perspective, and his independent judgment were a tonic to the entire staff even on such an infrequent basis."

But even during the times of Erikson's visits, from 8:30 a.m. to 5:30 p.m. five days a week Dr. Spock was involved in meetings, conferences, training and teaching sessions, consultations with myriads of people. All had understandably vested interests in their own specialties; some had reputations for being "difficult." There might have been fewer problems if the various institutional settings had been established for longer periods, if the approaches to patient treatment had been in agreement, or if the many new programs had been introduced in phases, rather than simultaneously.

A person fond of tackling personnel problems might have enjoyed being an insider in such a fluid environment, but that was not Dr. Spock. A person with a strong base of power, either with strong executive authority as a department chairman or institute director, or with control over a large budget, would have had the means to impose and enforce his decisions. But Dr. Spock, a coordinator rather than a director, was member of many departments and master of none.

Though Spock saw the personalities and faults of others as contributing to his difficulties in Pittsburgh, he has always claimed that the major responsibility was his own. He had taken on a kind of job guaranteed to produce endless administrative and personal problems without having had extensive practice in administration. In his relations with the child psychiatry staff he was inhibited unnecessarily by his incomplete psychiatric and psychoanalytic background from asserting an assured leadership. Moreover, by upbringing and personality he was too afraid of arousing antagonism to be able to speak bluntly with the people above or below him with whom difficulties arose. He observes, "If I'd been a bolder person then, and had argued more emphatically right from the beginning, I wouldn't have got into such trouble. For instance, Joe Cramer and Doris Phillips were determined, loud arguers and I was no match for them. I think I was too deferential because they had more psychiatric and psychoanalytic training than I. For three hours of their arguing I'd be like somebody at a tennis match, watching first one and then the other. Then at the end, when I'd be exhausted, they'd laugh and agree, 'It really wasn't that much of an issue.' "

Spock felt that Brosin was interfering increasingly and was compounding his administrative problems. When repeated direct discussions failed, they agreed to refer the conflict to the Dean. But the latter characteristically kept postponing any decision month after month for a year and a half. Finally the dispute was referred to the new Vice Chancellor for Medical Affairs, who eventually proposed that Spock become a professor without a department and without administrative authority. Spock was quite willing to relinquish his authority in the Child Guidance Center and at Western Psychiatric Institute. But to give it up at Arsenal might eventually result in a sharply reduced child development program and no opportunity to teach well-child care to medical students (which in fact proved to be exactly the case). Dr. Spock rejected the proposal and resigned.

From a personal point of view Spock felt that, in having to resign, he had to admit failure. On the other hand, he did succeed in setting up the teaching program in child psychiatry and child development in the Medical School and its related clinics, for which he had gone to Pittsburgh, and he was proud of this, particularly of the innovative program at Arsenal.

Dr. Mirsky, in lauding Spock's efforts at the University, said, "There isn't a soul in Pittsburgh who can say an evil word about Ben Spock. He had an uncanny ability to relieve people's anxieties, whether an audience of 2,000 mothers or a single close friend." But Spock's own academic productivity was impaired. In contrast to the two papers a year that he wrote during his four years at the Mayo Clinic, he wrote only two professional papers during his entire four years in Pittsburgh. The major one was an address before the International Congress of Child Psychiatry in Toronto, August 1954, on "Preventive Applications of Psychiatry." In this he praises the intuitive, spontaneous responses of loving parents to managing their own children, and identifies the troubled parents as those "who have to stop and think what they ought to do or what the experts say they ought to do. They tell us that the thought-out method,

however theoretically correct, too often fails to work, too often
leaves the parent feeling either guilty or frustrated."

However, in Pittsburgh Dr. Spock did collaborate on two other
books for parents. When Pocket Books suggested that he write a
simple text to accompany photographer Wayne Miller's sensitive
pictures of his daughter's development from birth to first birthday,
Dr. Spock agreed, if he could have some help. He proposed as a
collaborator Dr. John Reinhart, a young psychiatric resident whose
original training, like Spock's own, had been in pediatrics. They had
come to know each other at the Rochester Child Health Institute,
where Reinhart had taken a year of child development training
under Spock's supervision. Reinhart became, in some ways, a
surrogate son; as he explains, "Ben opened up whole new vistas
professionally, and treated me, my wife, and baby just like his own
family. In Rochester, when we were miles away from our own
relatives, he had us over for Christmas day. He's been one of the
most important people in my life; he may have had more influence
over me than my own father."

Spock encouraged Reinhart to come to Pittsburgh for full psychiatric training, and their friendship flourished because of the simi-
larities of their professional interests, philosophies, and styles of
child rearing. Dr. Reinhart wrote the original text of *A Baby's First
Year,* Dr. Spock modified the style, and together with Miller's
evocative pictures they produced a paean to infancy and to parenthood, with bits of advice tactfully tucked in. The accompaniment to
a picture of Mrs. Miller cradling the baby is typical: "Clean dry
pajamas, cuddling arms and cooing sounds make bedtime delicious.
The comforting thumb is already in the mouth. Baby and mother fall
into routine patterns at bedtime, which may carry over, effortlessly,
for months and years. It's worthwhile to keep such pleasant habits
going."

Of the book, published in hardcover by Duell, Sloan, and Pearce
in May 1955 and eighteen months later in paperback by Pocket
Books, Dr. Spock says, "I'm very proud of it. I love that book. It
has very moving, appealing pictures, partly because of the soulful-
ness of Mrs. Wayne Miller. But even though it's an inspired book it's
sold very few copies. It was this book which taught me that just
because my name is on a book doesn't mean it'll sell." "Very few
copies" means, in this case, about 941,000 copies during a decade in

print, quite respectable for any picture book, whose sales could scarcely be expected to equal those of a reference book such as *Baby and Child Care.*

Even more disappointing in sales was *Feeding Your Baby and Child,* the small hardcover printing published in November 1955 by Duell, Sloan, and Pearce–Little, Brown; the paperback in March 1956 by Pocket Books. During the early fifties Dr. Spock co-authored this 202-page book with Miriam E. Lowenberg, Ph.D., who had been Nutritional Supervisor at the Rochester Child Health Institute when he was there. This chatty book talks about diet, menus, mealtime atmosphere, and feeding problems; it contains forty-one pages of recipes, from peanut butter sandwiches to grape ice cream. Perhaps because Dr. Spock effectively covered many aspects of nutrition and feeding problems in *Baby and Child Care,* parents have purchased only one copy of *Feeding Your Baby and Child* for every thirty copies of the master book. Or perhaps it is because most mothers already know how to fix the simple dishes and are not inclined to prepare separate menus for their children once they've outgrown pureed baby foods.

Another reason that Dr. Spock couldn't—or didn't—do much original writing in Pittsburgh was that the stresses of his job drove him out of town as often as he could get away. He explains, "Sailing became an obsession. Every weekend in the spring and fall we would go down to Deep Creek Lake in Maryland, two and a half hours from Pittsburgh, loaded down with picnic baskets, cool-a-paks, aluminum boat, and outboard motor. The lake was beautiful, free of algae, in the mountains 2,400 feet above sea level, and we got a complete rest. John, in fourth grade, and I built an eight-foot sailing pram in the cellar. It looked big there, but in Deep Creek Lake it took us a long time to find out how to fit two people in so that we wouldn't swamp on coming about. Jane fished from the aluminum boat, I sailed, John took turns. We spent the nights in a motel, ate Saturday supper and Sunday breakfast at a hotel in Oakland, Maryland, and picnic lunches under a tree in the cow pasture near our dock—sometimes with the cows, until we put up a fence to keep them out."

They left the city for the summer, too. After spending a frustratingly inactive vacation in 1951 at crowded Rehoboth Beach, Delaware, they sought more space, and, sailing farther east, they found what they wanted at the bleak Quisset Harbor House on Cape Cod near Woods Hole, Massachusetts. Dr. Spock had finally succeeded in recapturing exactly the spartan atmosphere of his childhood summers. The rambling, angular Quisset Harbor House, of Civil War vintage, has just three bathrooms for the twenty families which share them, though each bedroom is equipped with a compensatory bowl and pitcher. A bare bulb hangs from each bedroom ceiling, illuminating the white iron bedsteads, white bedspreads and curtains. The public rooms, in which the decor runs to philodendron and paintings of boats, reinforce the stark atmosphere. Here the Spocks happily spent portions of the next fifteen consecutive summers, except in 1954. In an extraordinary understatement Dr. Spock observes, "It suits a New Englander. You don't feel suffocated by luxury. The food (on the order of pea soup, broiled fish, cabbage, potatoes, and apple pie) was relatively plain."

The year 1954 was the bleakest of all for the Spocks. They were concerned, of course, with the problems of the nation as a whole— the Korean War, the confrontations in the South over school integration, the moral and political implications of nuclear stockpiling, the Oppenheimer atomic security trial. But their major problems were personal, and more pressing than either had been willing to acknowledge after they moved to Pittsburgh.

That year there were none of the cocktail parties the Spocks had been accustomed to giving several times a year in their forty-foot living room for a hundred or so "friends, staff, interns, and medical students, at which we've tried hard to introduce everyone to everyone," as they said in their 1952 Christmas letter. That year faculty dissensions could not be banished by the harmonious monthly seminars when Erik Erikson was in town, nor the mounting strain of Dr. Spock's job alleviated by weekends at Deep Creek Lake.

By 1954 Jane had become emotionally overinvolved with her husband's problems. She explains, "When we lived in Pittsburgh I was so impatient with the fact that Ben let himself be run around that I couldn't help but show my criticalness. This didn't make for a good relationship. There were parts of the Pittsburgh time that were very difficult for both of us, very." These difficulties doubtless contributed not only to Jane's great tension and unhappiness during 1954, but to John's thinking of Pittsburgh as the difficult period of his childhood: "I was always stuck in the wrong situations, and felt uncomfortable with my classmates at the [private, well-endowed] Falk School, and with the kids in the neighborhood."

The problems in Pittsburgh also led Dr. Spock to agree to write a monthly article for the *Ladies' Home Journal.* The distinguished editorial couple Bruce and Beatrice Gould offered Spock $2,000 for each article of 1,500–2,500 words, which he accepted gladly, for the Spocks' medical expenses, including Mike's continuing analysis, amounted to nearly $11,000 that year. As he later wrote in "Should Not Physicians' Families Be Allowed the Comfort of Paying for Medical Care?" (*Pediatrics,* July 1962, pp. 109–110), "in a majority of medical situations . . . the recipient physician's family is receiving insufficient care, not through any fault of the donor [doctor] but because the recipient is so inhibited in asking for it." Spock's analytic training had convinced him of "the practical and theoretical importance of the physician paying for the analysis of himself or a member of his family"; he had generalized this to cover all areas of medical care and insisted on paying for all the care received.

Dr. Spock, the careful craftsman who always submitted manuscripts, impeccably typed in triple space, either on or ahead of schedule, found a congenial match in the gentlemanly, crisply efficient Bruce Gould. From the start their relationship was based on trust, mutual regard, punctuality, consideration—a welcome antidote to the difficult relationships Dr. Spock was enduring at Pitt.

Mr. Gould observes, "In Dr. Spock we had a very solid asset. We felt that if the American woman were to raise her children according to his precepts—which became less and less permissive—it would be a very good thing. The average mother felt that she was sitting on Dr. Spock's lap listening to advice that was extremely thoughtful and down-to-earth, expressed easily, persuasively, and in detail."

Dr. Spock reciprocates this esteem, "Bruce Gould was very thoughtful. It would never occur to most editors that an author who has been writing for their journal for a long while (ten years in this case) wants reassurance any more. Yet it was always very nice to get that occasional telegram from him saying, 'Marvelous piece.' " Two of Spock's *Journal* articles, "U.S. Versus U.S.S.R. Education" and "What Is 'Softness' in Education?" won the 1958 School Bell Award given by the national P.T.A. for the year's best articles on education. Although the Goulds preferred him to discuss child rearing, in the interests of keeping him happily within their fold they let him write on other subjects as well, and in general his efforts pleased one and all.

In the process of earning enough to pay his medical bills Dr. Spock nearly doubled his income, from $42,000 in 1953 (nearly half of which came from royalties on *Baby and Child Care*) to $74,000 in 1954, the $32,000 increment coming from the *Ladies' Home Journal* and *The American Weekly*. Between 1954 and 1967 writing for popular magazines provided between one-quarter and one-half of his income, and royalties from his books another third to half. In 1954 Dr. Spock, whether intentionally or not, was providentially shoring up a tenuous, tempestuous academic career with nonacademic sources of income—partly in case academia should fail him, partly because retirement (when writing would provide his entire income) was only fourteen years off.

Yet Dr. Spock has never tried to make money just for its own sake. He could have easily quadrupled his income by succumbing to the enticements of various commercial promoters, but medical ethics and his own scruples have combined to keep him from going on commercial lecture tours, endorsing commercial products, or engaging in any other commercial self-promotion.

He has steadfastly refused to dismember *Baby and Child Care* for daily syndication in newspapers or on radio, claiming that this would violate the book's integrity and "I couldn't give the time to edit the material myself and . . . I wouldn't let anyone else do it." The brief advice on immunizations and matters related to doctors' visits in Spock's *Baby and Child Care Medical Record* (Duell, Sloan, and Pearce, 1958) is seemingly condensed from the more lengthy discussions of the same subjects in *Baby and Child Care*. Dr. Spock had hoped that this sixty-four-page spiral-bound notebook for recording inoculations, developmental data, questions for and recommendations from the doctor would be used by mothers for notetaking during appointments with the pediatrician, but only 3,400 copies were sold over seven years.

Until 1968 Dr. Spock refused to make phonograph records, either original material or readings from *Baby and Child Care,* because he couldn't imagine a mother turning to a record for advice. When he finally capitulated, Caedmon eagerly issued *Dr. Spock Talks with New Mothers*—and promptly disappointed producers and pediatrician, for parents simply didn't buy it. Perhaps at $5.95 a copy it couldn't compete with the far more thoroughgoing *Baby and Child Care* at 95¢, or perhaps new mothers simply hadn't the equanimity to listen to it over an infant's squalls.

Dr. Spock has avoided making any commercial commitments unless he thought he could control what they foreseeably involved. It is not surprising, then, that he was wary of offers of television programs, even when they were to involve dramatizations of *Baby and Child Care.* He had agreed in 1951 to be in a March of Time film and, he explained to another promoter, "[I] was assured of all cooperation, and the people involved were intelligent and sincere. But in the editing and rewriting, which always becomes necessary, and in the absence of the author, the end results become the editor's ideas or the editor's interpretation. I know I won't change my mind again."

However, Dr. Spock did eventually take to television, but not with the affinity with which he took to live audiences—and not, at first, for pay. In 1954 he appeared on a weekly half-hour show, *Parents and Dr. Spock,* on Pittsburgh's educational station, WQED. The program usually consisted of a panel of four parents and the pediatrician, casually and spontaneously discussing common issues on child rearing or child development. The title indicates Dr. Spock's emphasis on the parents, for he saw himself on the show, as he had imagined himself at Western Psychiatric Institute, as "a sympathetic listener . . . the reconciler . . . the interpreter," the nondirective synthesizer subtly leading. He wanted the parents to do most of the talking, and felt that the ideal television presentation would "convince parents they know most of the answers." The show's directors had wanted Dr. Spock to do most of the talking, but when he protested they let him have his own way.

The next year NBC wanted and bought such a show, called simply "Doctor Spock," and ran the series of forty-five half-hour programs from September 1955 to June 1956. Its format of casual discussion was the same as the WQED show, except that sometimes there was a toddlers' play area nearby, also televised, where the children of the program panelists provided some relief from the sight of earnest grownups conversing. One of the producers says, "We had a nurse standing waiting in stocking feet, ready to grab a baby out of camera range when it screamed or spit up or worse. A sitter presided over the play area for the older kids, and suddenly the sound effects would include a loud crash of blocks, or thuds, shrieks and lamentations. Once five kids started throwing ice cream at each other, and a father went into shock."

Each program had a theme, and articulate mothers (and occasionally fathers) from a variety of backgrounds were recruited to discuss their specific experiences with the week's subject, whether "Working Mothers," "Twins," "Learning to Read," or "Now and Then—As Seen by Grandmothers." Nobel scientist Dr. Frederick Robbins discussed "Polio Vaccine"; and on "Bathing a Baby" an experienced mother taught a pregnant woman, tense with the anxiety of inexperience, how to do it in a most engaging program.

Though he found Bill Parrish, the producer, a congenial person to work with, Dr. Spock, ever the parent educator, was never oriented toward the kooky or the cute which some of Mr. Parrish's assistants tried to promote. They wanted a program on pets, but Dr. Spock infinitely preferred children. (He once chided the friend who had given John a dachshund, "The puppy's awfully cute, but when he jumps up on my lap and crushes the newspaper he's really very rude.") He finally consented to the appearance of a magnificent boxer on the program, but the dog became so excited that he raced about the studio, entangling the equipment and exasperating the cameramen, who never filmed a single picture of him. So Dr. Spock got his way—no more pets.

Spock also won the Battle of the Santa Claus Suit. His researcher for the program, effervescent Mrs. Elizabeth Cramer, recalls fondly, "Dr. Spock is a very controlled person. I think he decided in advance when he'd get mad. When the TV people asked me to suggest to him that he come onto the Christmas program in a Santa Claus suit I said, 'Don't even ask him. He won't do it.'

"They said, 'What do you mean he won't do it? Bob Hope does it. Arthur Godfrey does it. Why not Dr. Spock?' "

Mrs. Cramer continues, "Knowing his views about his dignity and about Santa Claus being frightening to children, I said, 'Don't ask him.' They asked him anyway, and got the predictable 'No,' but very politely. So they asked him again. Again, 'No,' more firmly. When they asked him a third time I could see he was ready to explode, and he thundered, 'Don't EVER ask me that AGAIN!' So they didn't." Dr. Spock would not be used.

The disagreements over the format and emphasis that had begun at WQED continued with NBC. The producers and the viewers who wrote in wanted a lot more Spock and a lot less parental chatter. Dr. Spock insisted on accentuating the parents' views, with himself acting as moderator. Spock won the battle, but after a year he lost the program because of sponsorship difficulties. The initial sponsor was bought out by another company, and the viewer ratings, although moderately successful, were insufficient to attract new sponsors.

Partly as a result of appearing on nationwide television, partly as a result of writing for the *Ladies' Home Journal* with a monthly circulation of several million, Dr. Spock came into contact with millions of parents in a much more direct, personal way than he had through the comparative anonymity of *Baby and Child Care*. Most of the mothers loved him, and he loved their warm response to his own warmth, though he later confided, "Suddenly finding that my advice was being docilely followed by most of the parents of America scared the hell out of me, at first. This had the effect of making me less and less arbitrary in my advice, though I'm by nature teacherish and dogmatic."

Letters began to pour in by the hundreds, and the flood continued until Dr. Spock became prominent in the peace movement. They were written on lined paper from children's school notebooks, on the insides of Christmas cards, on the backs of promotions for various worthy causes, on monogrammed bond, on air letter folders. Written in pencil, in pen, in typescript, they came from such places as Gary, Indiana; Wilacoochie, Georgia; Needham, Massachusetts; Houston, Texas; Tasmania, Australia; Winnipeg, Manitoba; Yamagucki Ken, Japan; Oxford, England. The letters contained pictures of children, including many of infants "reading" *Baby and Child Care;* recipes; newspaper clippings; hand-crocheted potholders; poems. They included requests for autographs, for recipes of Dr. Spock's favorite foods ("hominy grits with thick cream"), and for items to be auctioned off for charities (he usually sends an auto-graphed copy of *Baby and Child Care*).

They began: "Dear Doctor Spock," "Dear Dr. Sprock," "Dr. Spook," "Dear Doctor Ben," or sometimes, "Hello, Ben—Because your writing makes me feel that we're such old friends, I can talk to you this way. So come into my kitchen, take off your shoes, and let's chat over a cup of coffee." The letters ran to the extremes of familiarity and awe: "Dear Dr. Spock, I tell myself that it is possible to write to you but I feel that it's like writing to God or a super-natural power. If I wrote to God I'm not sure He'd read my letter, and I hope you will."

The correspondents often proceeded in this vein: "As my Doctor advised, I have read your book like a Bible. Now I have a problem. . . ." To ask advice from a stranger about one's intimate problems is to objectify the personal. Dr. Spock didn't know his correspond-ents; he wouldn't gossip about them as their families or close friends might. He wasn't around to make them take his advice. He'd never see or hear from them again—unless they wished it (5 percent wrote more than once), so they could tell him whatever they wanted without the embarrassment of subsequently encounter-ing their confessor.

They wrote in concern about medical problems: "Dear, Dear Doctor, My two year old son Henry is always sick with croup and I'm ready to have a nervous breakdown because it never disappears. Doctor Spock, if you told me to come to Pittsburgh so *you* could see him I would bring him right away—I'll do anything." They wrote in grief: "I believe in you . . . and plead that you consider these facts and provide some sort of explanation for the death of my little boy. He never complained that anything hurt, he didn't ask to sleep with me or anything. I still relive that night, not knowing how sick Tim was. . . ." They wrote with mixed emotions about the handling of children: "I am the Mother of an 18 year old Retarded Child who is lovable, good, + considerate but at times she gets nervous + throws the dishes off the table. After that she says she is sorry . . . + asks to be fed. I try to reason with her but to no avail. . . ."

They wrote in perplexity about a variety of other problems. *Discipline:* "I am a nervous wreck because of my two year old's constant screaming, rocking on furniture, banging her head. Whenever I tell her no she throws a tantrum. She bites constantly and scratches and pinches. She will not listen to me nor . . . her father." *Feeding:* "Since my 2½ year old is born she only lives on milk, orange juice and apple juice. We tried everything—she can go without milk for several days, and never any solid food." *Toileting:* "The most I could do toward movement training was to persuade him to have stools on the floor. Now at 4½ he still won't sit on any kind of toilet." *Aggressiveness:* "Our kindergartener has become a child on the defensive. He teases, tells his friend he is going to hit her. . . . He *expects* trouble, and he gets it." *Personal problems:* "I am 15 yrs. old, not married and five months pregnant. I want very much to keep my baby but even more then [sic] that I want whats best for my baby. . . . P.S. I wrote to where you worked because I don't know where you live. Give my regards to Jane your wife." *Family problems:* "Little things the children do set me off on spells of screaming and using poor language. My husband has said I nag when I complain about his inability to support his family. Then he turns to drinking. I've gotten to be a 'monster size' mother . . . over 300 pounds."

Dr. Spock customarily advised a variety of people with a variety of problems such as those above (excepting matters of physical medicine) to "consult a family social agency or a child guidance clinic." His typical replies kindly and carefully explained the reasons for his suggestion. Thus he advised the unwed mother: "The most important thing is for the mother to arrange for regular counseling with a social worker throughout pregnancy (preferably once a week) so that she can be sorting out her mixed feelings and be sure she makes her eventual decision on the basis of really knowing her own mind rather than on impulse or well-intentioned self-deception," and he told her how to obtain counseling.

His advice to seek counseling was sensible, ethical, logical, and expedient for such a psychiatrically oriented physician to give at long distance. Though counseling need not be the invariable solution —and indeed, it may not provide the hoped-for answers—it is certainly the safest remedy to suggest without direct personal knowledge of the situation.

This advice is similar to the recommendations he proffered in the *Ladies' Home Journal* columns, which were later published in two volumes. The first, *Dr. Spock Talks with Mothers* (Boston:

Houghton Mifflin, 1961; New York: Crest Books, 1964), dealt with the child's health, position in the family, behavior problems, "Attachments and Anxieties between Three and Six," "Turning to the Outside World After Six," and "The Strains of Adolescence." This book sold moderately well—52,000 hardcover copies and 380,000 paperbacks in seven years.

The following year Houghton Mifflin published a second volume, *Problems of Parents* (the paperback issued by Crest in 1965), which discussed such topics as "Easing Family Tensions," "Anxieties and Overprotection," "Divorce, Widowhood, and Remarriage," and, a harbinger of Dr. Spock's future concerns, his articles on "Prejudice," "Cold War Anxiety," and "Will Our Children Meet the World Challenge?" In six years the book sold 131,000 hardcover copies, mostly as a Literary Guild selection, and a meager 118,000 paperbacks, which the publisher attributes to its "worrisome title and unattractive cover." In 1963 *Problems of Parents* received the Child Study Association of America's "Annual Family Life Book Award for Parents," which commended "Dr. Spock's warm supportive and reassuring approach. . . . a welcome antidote to the negative critical note so often struck by many who write on the American family today."

Author and critic Paul Goodman damned the very features of *Problems of Parents* that the Child Study Association praised: "In *Problems of Parents* we are mainly dealing . . . with a highly conventional society which, bluntly, is a bad one—a venal economy, a phony culture, a meretricious standard of living, and a Cold War.

"Doctor Spock is unhappy about some of this, yet when he now reassuringly advises the parents to affirm their own 'high standards,' it comes usually to affirming prejudices, conformity, base values, and suburban isolationism. . . .

"These parents do not deserve reassurance, but a shock. In fact, their growing children are increasingly giving them the shock and are miserable themselves, but one would have little sense of this from Doctor Spock. . . .

"There is no mention of drug-taking, of serious sexual difficulties or deviations, of delinquency, of kids in jail for noble causes, of youth-unemployment, of urban poverty. Maybe it will be said that he is not writing for families like that; my guess is that . . . there are very few families that are not 'like that.'

". . . [Doctor Spock's] uniform advice for coping with problems is, astoundingly, to seek help from a psychiatrist, a child guidance clinic, a family social agency.

"This refrain, which recurs again and again, is of course the opposite of the self-reliance that inspired the baby book, and it is disastrous to reassurance. Maybe it is wise advice, but its meaning is that the adults, too, are not taken seriously.

"When the chips are down, modern life is too complicated for them; it is no use even trying to explain it to them in any mass circulation medium. But the professionals and administrators can apparently take over better. Consider the following: 'If the dread of going to school is intense and persistent, the parent should promptly get in touch with a child psychiatrist.' Maybe so; but the doctor does not equally suggest that the parent might wisely clamor at the school board. Why in such a case Doctor Spock assumes that the child is crazy is quite beyond me."

Mr. Goodman does concede the book one redeeming virtue: "By the time he gets to the end . . . Doctor Spock is also disturbed. He is strongly concerned about the bomb-testing and the threat of total destruction facing us. And in this book, as in his public life, he stands up for his own values. Suddenly his tone is entirely different. It is a responsible advocacy for what he holds to be prudent and just, with objective arguments. There is no more recourse to clinics or psychologizing about a secure structure no matter what the structure."

In spite of Goodman's criticism, Dr. Spock today still reserves his moral indignation for political matters, such as the Indochina war (on occasion joining Goodman himself on the protest platform), and for various social issues, such as poverty and racism. But for about one-third of the personal problems people write him about, he still recommends professional counseling.

Like any scrupulous physician, Dr. Spock neither prescribes for medical problems at long distance nor recommends self-medication. Yet he still places New England emphasis on self-reliance, and like Dewey encourages pragmatic solutions to many problems. To the mother whose infant's "eating and sleeping habits are completely erratic" he advises: "I'd just feed her three meals on schedule . . . and put her to bed at regular times whether she sleeps or not."

Dr. Spock also recommends self-reliance to a seventh-grader who complains: "When I was born my parents took your advice about respecting the first child's rights. As you said, they even put up a gate. Since then my sister, two years older, has treated me like someone who is going to wreck and poison her room if I so much as step foot inside it. I lend her anything which she wants to borrow but if I want to so much as borrow a pencil or a book she screams at me as if I would tear the pages out or put a time bomb in her pencil. . . . What shall I do now?" Dr. Spock's answer, typical of his letters to younger children, includes subtle support for the parents' implied preferred course of action, as well as suggestions for what the children can themselves do to remedy the situation: "If your parents hadn't protected [your sister's privacy] she would be even more jealous and touchy. Time should mellow your sister somewhat. It would help her to lose some of her insecurity if you can be careful not to compete with her or upstage her."

As children approach maturity, Dr. Spock weighs their views more heavily in arbitrating generation gap arguments, and suggests that parents do too. In judging many problems that occur when adults question or contradict the ways of their elders, Dr. Spock, grandfather though he is, usually sides with the younger generation, particularly against grandparents. When one correspondent crabs, "Since your book does not teach common sense my children are doing such outlandish things that grandma is quickly turning gray and old. . . . The baby runs around on the pavement without shoes. . . . My daughter-in-law turns a deaf ear when I give advice," Dr. Spock answers succinctly: "Keep out of the situation. . . . When a grandmother acts distressed it only makes the mother act more extremely."

Dr. Spock has a knack for brevity, and often answers a ten-page letter in a single, cogent sentence, particularly if it is from a person who writes to him frequently for therapeutic or confessional purposes. He treats every letter with dignified seriousness, whether it be the plight of a nursing mother whose breasts have become so enlarged that she can't find a brassiere that fits ("make one"), the woman who wants to know why children eat dirt ("tension"), the parent who can't decide whether to take her small children on vacation or to leave them with a sitter ("suit yourself"), or the comically expressed letter from an engaged lass who asks, "My cousin and I recently discovered we could be married in our Church, however my father says that our children will be idiots." ("The marriage of cousins has risks only if there are certain hereditary diseases (of baby or brain) in the family. These diseases are rare.") With the same concise gravity he replies to the mother whose six-year-old daughter has exceedingly hairy legs ("see a dermatologist"), to the father who seeks a medicine to retard a gangling daughter's growth ("I don't know of such a drug and wouldn't use one anyway"), and to the woman whose child won't eat properly ("It's the mother's problem, not the child's"). Dr. Spock relishes the normal, and concisely expresses a typically democratic aversion to child prodigies and toward parents who prod their children into precocity and brag to him. He replies, "Don't become preoccupied with this accomplishment."

Dr. Spock, both moralist and physician, gives sympathetic attention to problems the conventional moralist might find reprehensible. Thus he answers a guilty parent who asks whether or not to tell his child that he was conceived out of wedlock: "I'd admit it [if asked], blaming it on the intensity of love and say at the same time [to young adolescents] that I think it's wiser to wait." Similarly, to the parent who inquires, "Why would sex play be taboo?" "It's better not to give children an excessive sense of guilt or shame about sex. . . . Unless parents themselves are sexual delinquents the child will acquire taboos himself." As a general rule, the more serious the problem, the more prompt and detailed Dr. Spock's answer, the more extensive his attention to the psychological factors involved, and the more elaborate his reassurance to the parent.

Prognostic of the future, in the fifties Dr. Spock's stands on social and political issues drew a moderate amount of criticism, to which he also had to reply. His support of federal aid to education and of Adlai Stevenson for President in 1956 provoked incensed rebuttals to which he answered, "I don't agree with the letter writers who say that a professional man has no business trying to influence the public with his beliefs during a campaign, that this is a betrayal of the trust people have in him. . . . I think everyone should make politics his business, and that if he has very strong convictions about an issue and has any influence, his obligation to speak up is great." As Dr. Spock became more deeply involved in controversial issues, much more criticism was to come. But he gradually grew accustomed to it, adopting as his credo Harry Truman's dictum "If you can't stand the heat, get out of the kitchen," and such criticism ceased to bother him—much.

But the heat in the University of Pittsburgh kitchen had become more than Dr. Spock could bear, and although the floods of adoring letters from parents were gratifying, they were an insubstantial barrier against the buffetings from his turbulent superior and subordinates. Spock prepared to leave by July 1, 1955, when his contract ended, and eagerly accepted a Visiting Professorship in Child Development and Child Psychiatry at the Western Reserve University Medical School in Cleveland, Ohio. Says Dr. Mirsky, "Although Ben and Jane were two of the most popular people in the city, they left as if Ben were being pushed out of town on a rod, tarred and feathered. Ben had come with tremendous public recognition and potential. He could have had anything. But because he was so convinced by Brosin that he was a lousy administrator, his productivity and career were permanently impaired." Dr. Spock left Pittsburgh, not defiantly as many of his tempestuous colleagues had already done, but quietly, in accord with the excessive willingness to accept blame that accompanies his own chivalrous nature.

Though the Arsenal Family and Children's Center (formerly Arsenal Health Center) is still functioning, its most generous benefactors stopped giving money the year Dr. Spock left. The various training programs for medical and social work personnel were also cut back with the departure of Dr. Spock. In the largest office at Arsenal there sat unused for fifteen years an enormous mahogany desk, about five by eight feet, with a high-backed, green leather chair tailored to Dr. Spock's contours. For fifteen years no one thumbed through the professional journals that slumped limply on the nearly empty bookshelves lining the walls of Spock's former office. Such is the fate of many a project when an attractive leader departs.

nine

SEASON OF MISTS
AND MELLOW
FRUITFULNESS

BY 1955 Dr. Spock was America's most popular pediatrician. His benign countenance beamed from three million television screens, his reassuring column was delivered to seven and a half million homes every month, his baby book reposed comfortingly on ten million night tables. Had he resumed private practice, his waiting room would have been jammed with children from all over the world.

But by 1955 Dr. Spock was also a maverick in academic medicine. A number of research-oriented physicians objected to his work, and when it was rumored in Cleveland that Western Reserve University was considering appointing him to its Medical School faculty, some doctors there muttered, "He's done an excellent job in *Baby and Child Care* applying seat-of-the-pants psychiatry which all of us doctors use every day" and "No matter how bad your child is, you can look in *Baby and Child Care* and find that his behavior is perfectly normal." Or, simply, "Ben Spock in a university? What the hell, he's just a television doctor."

Professional opinions about Dr. Spock seem perpetually divided between those who value highly his intuition, common sense, and direct practical advice, and those who place little value on any medical work unless it is the result of rigorous scientific research. Dr. Douglas Bond, psychoanalyst and in 1955 Dean of the Western Reserve University School of Medicine, believed Dr. Spock to be "a more benevolent influence on young people than any living American," and had told Dr. Spock when they'd met the year before, "If you ever get restless, let me know." "I really wanted him," says Dr. Bond, "and Ben thought that being wanted was very important."

A year later, when Dr. Bond was visiting Johns Hopkins to recruit additions to Reserve's three-hundred-member medical faculty, he was paged by a phone call from Dr. Spock, who told him of the insolvable situation in Pittsburgh, said that he'd just resigned, and asked about the possibility of a job at Western Reserve. Dr. Bond, surprised, said "Come ahead," so the next day Dr. Spock flew to Cleveland to discuss the new program in medical education that had been introduced three years earlier and was already attracting international attention.

At most schools undergraduate medical education had not changed much since Spock had gone to medical school. Aware earlier of the deficiencies of the conventional system, in which the first two years of lifeless laboratory work were punctuated by frequent examinations, in 1948 Dr. Spock had written, in an unpublished manuscript, "A Pediatric View of How Undergraduate Psychiatric Education Might Better Meet the Community's Needs," "This [system] not only deprives the student of opportunity to progress in his awareness and responsiveness to broad human needs but, more important, actively encourages a desensitization of his feelings, a depersonalizing of the patient. It would appear essential that the student from the beginning of his first year be thrown in contact with patients in such ways and under such supervision that he cannot avoid an appropriate degree of emotional involvement and an opportunity to learn from it. . . ." He said that the most common danger was that the physician would preserve his technical judgment at the cost of sensitivity to the suffering and feelings of his patients. To avoid this impersonality Spock had urged classroom training in such subjects as child development, interpersonal relations, interviewing, psychodynamics—but always related to continuing clinical experience.

Two years before affiliating with Western Reserve, Dr. Spock had met with Dr. T. Hale Ham, the genial Director of Reserve's Division of Research in Medical Education. Ham had explained the details of Reserve's new system, which was putting into effect the very principles that Spock had articulated in 1948: "Doctors, nurses, social workers spent two years evaluating traditional medical education and deciding how to modify it to better accommodate the students' interests and make them better doctors. We realized that students enroll in medical school because they're interested in people and in medicine. We thought there must be some better way to keep their interest alive than the 'deathhouse philosophy' which the first day initiates the student into the dissection of the symbol of medicine's failure, the cadaver, and has him start cutting."

Continuing, Dr. Ham emphasized, "We decided to begin the student's education with the beginning of human life. Phase I, lasting thirty-four weeks, would focus on the 'Normal Biology of Man,' starting with the fertilized ovum, then proceeding to gestation and fetal growth. Within his first month of school, the student would be assigned to a patient in her third trimester of pregnancy. Through visits in the clinic and in her home, he'd get to know the expectant mother, her close relatives, and as much about her family situation as he could. He'd attend the delivery and help to bring the baby home from the hospital. Then, in the Family Clinic, the student would see the baby once a month for regular checkups, under the supervision of a pediatrician, and get to know more about the baby than any other medical person."

Dr. Spock had become more and more excited, occasionally murmuring, "Wonderful!" as Dr. Ham continued, "At the same time, the student would be attending lectures on normal infant and child behavior, development, and care. Groups of eight students would meet weekly with a preceptor to discuss in depth the lectures and their clinical experiences and problems. The first year, the student would also begin to study the body's systems—cardiovascular, respiratory, endocrine, and so on, as he dissected an infant cadaver. In his second and third year, after he understood what the healthy norm was, he'd study pathologic physiology, again through a systems approach, but this time with an adult cadaver. His last sixteen months would be concerned with clinical medicine, patient care, experience in teaching of research, and writing a thesis. The study of the body as a set of systems, rather than as a collection of separate cells, tissues, and organs, would break down the departmental barriers, oblige the faculty to cooperate, and excite the student tremendously.

"Furthermore," Dr. Ham continued, "during his first two and a half years, the student would have three half-days of free time every week—to read, study, relax, go to the clinic, or to do research at his own lab bench. This was unheard-of at most medical schools, for with the continuing increase of medical knowledge and minute specialization, the tendency has been to cram more and more into the curriculum. At Reserve the emphasis is on the individual student's active self-teaching, as a junior colleague of the faculty, rather than on his being, as in the old system, an anonymous, passive vessel into which the faculty simply poured information."

Drs. Spock and Ham emerged from this earlier meeting with tremendous rapport that was to continue over the years. Now Dr. Spock told Dr. Bond of his interest in the Phase I Clinical Science program, particularly of his enthusiasm for the Family Clinic. Dr. Bond replied, with equal enthusiasm, "Most of the rest of us get bored after a while with the normal, the healthy. You don't. I want you to come here, but I've heard you're a terrible administrator. I'll manage the administrative details if you'll just manage to come!"

So as a Visiting Professor of Child Development in the Departments of Pediatrics and Psychiatry, Dr. Spock came with a token salary of $5,000 a year, one-fourth of the faculty average. His low salary is explained partly by the fact that his appointment was "geographical full-time"—like many other medical school faculty members he was expected to earn part of his income from outside professional work, though his full-time office was geographically in the medical school. And it is partly explained by the fact that his outside earnings, primarily from his writings, were sufficiently high so that even after twelve years as a tenured professor in the Western Reserve University Medical School he was content with an annual salary of $11,500.

The tentativeness of Dr. Spock's initial appointment at Reserve is explained only partly by its suddenness. "Doctors are a bunch of bastards in many ways," snorts a Cleveland gynecologist, "and medical politics is often a lot dirtier than national politics. Nevertheless, a full-time academic appointment, especially a full professorship, is the most prestigious honor the profession can give, and it has to be based on real, hard scientific research. Ben hadn't done any of that. He got the job primarily because of his name and his book." Another Cleveland pediatrician observes, "As an individual, Ben is one of the most wonderful guys I know. I think his book is magnificent; you can't beat it anywhere. But the pediatrician who goes down in history, or who wins a Nobel Prize, is the one who tells people how to cure a rare disease, rather than how to diaper a baby. It's all right for a sociologist to educate parents, but a doctor as a parent educator has no legitimate function in a medical school." Another pediatrician, on the Reserve faculty, says, "Ben has fallen in between psychiatry and pediatrics with no real stature in either department. He's much more effective with the public than with physicians." Given such feelings, which pervaded one segment of the Cleveland medical community throughout Dr. Spock's career there, it was tactful for Spock to request and be given a Visiting Professorship for the first year, rather than the tenured appointment which came a year later.

The Spocks moved in the summer of 1955 to Cleveland, Ohio. Though relieved to be away from Pittsburgh, Jane, like many easterners, did not expect any location west of the Hudson to be the intellectual equivalent of New York, even the self-proclaimed "best location in the nation."

In some ways the city deserved that suspicion. Under three decades of lackluster mayors (dynamic Carl Stokes, the first Negro mayor of a major United States city, was not elected until the year of Spock's retirement), expanding industrialism, and a decaying core, Cleveland had earned the nickname "the mistake on the lake." Not only had Lake Erie become so polluted that it was dying, as the waste and dead fish washed up along its dingy shores testified; but also Cleveland's principal river, the Cuyahoga, was in that rare class of rivers to be declared a fire hazard. On at least one occasion it did burn, causing $60,000 damage to two bridges.

Yet Cleveland had many assets. Its people were surprisingly diverse, and of many nationalities. It was wealthy, and some of its money went to support Cleveland's points of pride: the Cleveland Orchestra, under the direction of the late Georgé Szell; the Cleveland Museum of Art, second in some areas only to New York's Metropolitan Museum; the Cleveland Browns (and Indians); and the Western Reserve University Medical School, believed by many to have the most progressive curriculum in the world.

The suburbs which ringed the city were enclaves for industrial workers, executives, and other groups segregated by income—and by race, though on Cleveland's East Side integration has proceeded with all deliberate speed in the last decade. Cleveland Heights was two status notches lower than neighboring Shaker Heights with its highest per capita income in the country in 1960 for a city of its size. Cleveland Heights was full of large old houses ranging from the tattered to the magnificent. It bordered the museum, the concert hall, and the University, and many of the personnel of these institutions lived in this tree-lined suburb. The Spocks chose to settle there, first in a rambling gray-shingled five-bedroom house at 1285 Inglewood Drive, three miles from the Medical School. Three years later they moved two miles closer, to a slightly smaller, more formal gray stucco house at 2220 Woodmere Drive, still in Cleveland Heights.

Baby and Child Care and the Spocks' own friendliness assured them of quick acceptance, and Jane made a number of friends as interested in the arts as she was. She enrolled in courses in painting and silver jewelry making at the Cleveland Institute of Art, and set to work campaigning for Adlai Stevenson. John was happy: "I can recall my extreme pleasure at leaving Pittsburgh," he said as an adult.

"Ben was pleased, too," says John. "He had gone to Pittsburgh for professional stature, but by the time we moved to Cleveland he'd changed a lot. He saw in his new job not a prestigious title, but a really enjoyable working situation." Indeed, Dr. Spock's duties were varied and just what he wanted, without the complexities or administrative problems that had plagued him in Pittsburgh. For the first time in his professional life he could relax.

As part of the Clinical Science Phase I program, in which he spent a large percentage of his time, Spock lectured to the first-year medical students five or six times a semester on such subjects as "The Management of Infant Feeding," "Attention and Spoiling," "Hospitalism and Autism," "Doctor-Patient Relationships," and "Examination of the Ear Drums." ("No one could examine an infant's ear drums with the skill and sensitivity of Ben Spock," exclaims an admiring colleague, "even after he'd been away from private practice for twenty years. He was great at getting wax out of ears gently, too.")

One or two afternoons each week Dr. Spock supervised two first- and second-year students in their roles as apprentice physicians in the Family Clinic, a series of small cubicles in an aging hospital basement. The 270 mothers who brought their children to the Clinic were usually lower-income Negroes from intact households where grandmothers or neighbors rather than Dr. Spock were relied on for child rearing advice.

As part of the Clinical Science program each student saw his patient, the infant whose birth he had observed earlier, once a month, or more often if the baby was sick. He spent an hour or two on a home visit, taking a detailed history of what had occurred during the baby's past month. Then, in the Family Clinic, he gave the infant a thorough physical and spent another forty-five minutes discussing his findings with the supervising physician, while the waiting mother tried to amuse her child. Dr. Spock usually appeared vitally interested in what each student had to say, even after he'd listened to hundreds of descriptions of infant colic, rashes, and thumb-sucking, though he was suspected of dozing during particularly droning recitations.

He questioned the students and offered suggestions on examining techniques, well-baby care, and the importance of sincere concern for the patient, the mother, and the family situation. "He never self-consciously played the role of Superdoctor in front of the students as some less secure physicians did," observes a colleague, "so they forgot about his fame because he himself never seemed aware of it." In fact, he readily admitted his lack of first-hand experience with the newer forms of treatment that had been devised since he had been in private practice. For this reason he never wrote a prescription or took the ultimate responsibility for treating the occasional sick child, but left that to his faculty colleagues—a phenomenon which would have surprised the worshipful readers of *Baby and Child Care,* had they learned of it.

After their discussion, which Spock tried to keep free of excessive technical, dehumanizing jargon, the student and the doctor rejoined the mother and child and Dr. Spock examined the baby again, partly to verify the student's accuracy, partly to give him and the mother further instruction. Dr. Spock considered the Family Clinic "the meat of the student's first year. Our students were much more human and much more comfortable in dealing with people and much more satisfying as doctors because they were aware of the patients as people. The patients loved our students, too, and if a student appeared to disagree with the supervising doctor, they'd take the student's word. The mothers were very enthusiastic about the care they received, even though it was from inexperienced students who had to refer every question to their instructor. The mothers would say, 'I was always able to reach the same doctor,' and 'I was touched when the doctor called me by name.' We didn't want the patient to call the student 'doctor' because that's sloppy in medical school. But the patients insisted, so we gave in and called the students 'doctor,' too—at least, in front of the patients."

One of Dr. Spock's former students, Dr. Edwin Roth, attributes a great deal of the satisfaction of both students and parents with Family Clinic to Dr. Spock's influence and enthusiasm: "If I had to single out one thing about medical school that I liked best, I'd say Family Clinic. Although Dr. Spock was an excellent theoretician, as a preceptor and clinical professor he focused on the practical aspects, which were very important to us as new students. We got from him a feeling of the importance of well-baby care, as well as the knowledge of how to give it."

Because instructing in the Family Clinic was very time-consuming and not nearly as medically dramatic as teaching on the sick wards, it would not have appealed to many doctors. Some faculty members recommended that it be abandoned entirely because they believed that the students were being required to play doctor before they had the knowledge and skill to do so appropriately. Dr. Spock disagreed, and his zestful support helped to give the

Family Clinic the reputability it needed at a time when it was under attack, just as his national reputation helped to attract a flood of students to Western Reserve's new program. By the time Dr. Spock's charismatic influence had worn off because of familiarity, the Clinic was securely established. It continues successfully to this day, though the students now spend only two and a half years following their family, rather than the three and a half years required initially.

Eventually Dr. Spock became chairman of the Clinical Science Phase I program. He and his committee had to determine the lecture topics, select the twelve preceptors and chair their weekly discussions, and coordinate the parts played by the various departments involved — pediatrics, obstetrics, psychiatry, internal medicine, social work, the medical school. Because, as Spock says, "the deans and department heads were exceptionally open-minded, liberal, and accommodating, and the faculty was unusually friendly and highly cooperative," his task, though time-consuming, was free of the personality conflicts and administrative strife that had prevailed in Pittsburgh.

Dr. Robert Frymier, who succeeded Dr. Spock as chairman of Clinical Science, speaks warmly of his predecessor's contributions: "Ben has a sensitivity to emerging forces, and the tendency to be out in front of the rest of us by a few years. He was the first person at Reserve to see the need for bringing the behavioral and social sciences—anthropology, sociology, psychology—into the program, which had traditionally been biologically and psychologically oriented, and the first to make the students aware of the physician's tremendous social concerns and responsibilities. As part of the program's lectures, he engaged a Negro social worker to talk about medical folklore, such as the belief among many Clinic patients that an ailing baby 'had to be wrapped up in ten blankets to get the humors out of him.' He arranged for a philosopher to discuss medical ethics, involving such matters as research on human beings, 'professional secrecy,' 'the hopeless case,' homosexuality, and euthanasia. As he became more involved in extracurricular peace and political activities, Dr. Spock included in his lectures more radical views on the physician's relation to contemporary events. His views on the constricting effects of convention, institutionalism, and the political orientation of the American Medical Association would have been heretical in another era or a more conservative school."

Dr. Frymier adds, "As chairman of Clinical Science Phase I he encouraged preceptors to make the teacher-student relationship friendly and relaxed. He suggested that preceptors call the students by their first names and invite them to their homes. His main difficulty as chairman was caused by this same fantastic respect for other people's rights and his willingness to give them the benefit of the doubt. Even if he knew a preceptor wasn't doing a good job, Ben couldn't tell him so, and he wouldn't get rid of him. Nor would he single out for reprimand a resident or house officer who, as a senior trainee, was setting a bad example for our beginning students by acting insensitively to the patients' fears and desires. Instead, even though such behavior might make Ben very angry, he'd write a gentle note to the resident's chief, asking him to mention the matter to the whole staff."

A typical note to the head of obstetrics said: "[Preceptors have noted] student distress about episodes on the delivery floor: a) An intern who was conducting a delivery ignored the student altogether. . . . 2) An anesthesiologist read a comic book which he propped against the patient's head; 3) A delivery was carried through without any member of the medical or nursing staff ever addressing the patient by name . . . . 4) [An] employee publicly scolded another patient for being pregnant illegitimately. Would you discuss this with your OB personnel?" The most explicit criticism Dr. Spock ever directed toward students was, he says, "to speak with particular vehemence to medical students who came to lectures late and with coffee, or who came to the clinics wearing the pants and shoes one should use for house and yard work."

During ten of his twelve years at Western Reserve, Dr. Spock also taught a two-semester course in "Child Management" to undergraduates. One of his purposes was to give academic recognition to his belief that "Girls and boys should be educated in schools and colleges so that they think of parenthood as the central, most important, most creative, most rewarding part of their lives as adults —not a secondary occupation." Perpetually distressed by the low esteem in which he believed many college-educated women held full-time mothering, he hoped that through his course they would learn to value the occupation of parenthood as highly as any other career for which college might prepare them. Another of his purposes was to balance the intellectual, conceptual approach of the liberal arts education with "something more real and firsthand."

Using as textbooks *Baby and Child Care* and Selma Fraiberg's *The Magic Years,* pleasant, practical, and psychological, but not very demanding reading for four hours of upper-level credit, he lectured on many of the topics common to child development and rearing that he was teaching to medical students—"Feeding," "Toilet Training," "Mother, Discipline, Stuttering," "The Oedipal Years," "Latency," "Adolescence," concluding with a single lecture on "Marriage and Maturity." An associate who shared the lecturing for seven years, Dr. Jane Kessler, observes: "It was a very practical course—humanized, slightly analyzed Gesell. No one could teach the first year of life better than Ben Spock. He knew all about feeding, weaning, sleep problems. His lecture on the Oedipal complex was truly inspired."

As in his writings, Dr. Spock in his lectures translated complex psychiatric concepts into popular terms—and acted them out, to the students' delight. Despite his towering frame, graying hair, and dark-rimmed glasses, when Dr. Spock demonstrated the delights of the thumb-sucker, the writhing contortions of the colicky three-month-old, or the rebellion of the defiant toddler, the child virtually materialized on the lecture platform. In fact, the real children who were occasionally invited for demonstration purposes —"Girl babies have high brows and wide-open eyes. Boy babies have low, slanting foreheads and slitty eyes"—were often upstaged by the lecturer, though he treated them with utmost deference— "no 'kitchy koo,' " says an observer.

When the course got into the "terrible twos" and beyond, Dr. Kessler found a number of deficiencies in Dr. Spock's presentation: "Although a very intelligent man, he was the least well-read of any parent educator. He was temperamentally a pioneer like Piaget and Freud; he started afresh every time he encountered a problem, without reviewing the literature. He deliberately avoided other people's thoughts for fear they might contaminate his own thinking, or that he might plagiarize. His lectures were autobiographically anecdotal. Perhaps this is why he attributed so many

problems in school-age boys—such as stuttering and bedwetting—
to dominating mothers, though I can think of many other causes.
It's not all one-way, either. Children can deliberately provoke
their parents, but Ben underplays this.

"This is also why," says Dr. Kessler, "even though he's the idol
of today's teenagers, his description of adolescence as a period
mostly of painful shyness and inhibition was as dated as a tintype,
and as individual. Although I could convince him of a point by
telling an anecdote, I could never make him believe the same point
by citing research. In fact, he'd either become sarcastic when someone discussed research—or he'd go to sleep, which I interpreted as
extremely aggressive and rude.

"Because of his tremendous conscience, his morality too greatly
influenced his understanding of psychology. Contrary to what he
said in *Baby and Child Care,* he really believed that masturbation
was sinful, though he acknowledged that kids did it, and he thought
parents must make their moral disapproval clear. Although I used
to argue with Ben about these things in class and out, I never said
too much that was critical because his feelings were easily hurt.
He brings out a protective feeling in his associates."

Sometimes he brings out love. His other associate lecturer in the
course, psychiatric social worker Mrs. Eleanor Weisberger, says
vehemently, "Dr. Spock is a lovely, living legend and he deserves
to be. Some impatient medical students and hotshot scientists
downgraded his discussions of child development because they said
he wasn't scientific. Somebody has to interpret science to the layman, and Ben did it fantastically well. He's a refreshing voice in
the wilderness because he trusts his feelings, and his feelings are
so right. He's *not* equivocal, *not* relativisitic. He's the kind of model
people need. He thinks people should be true, and just, and honest
—to their spouses and children and everyone else. Because of his
stature and his genuineness he could say these things and make an
impact. His was the one course in the University where the students could hear some good old-fashioned horse sense; if they
wanted sexy, Freudian stuff they didn't get it there."

If they wanted A's or B's, they did get them there. The *Student
Guide to Courses* in 1967 observed: "[This] course meets only once
a week, has such a large enrollment [300–400 undergraduates, some

grad students, and Cleveland housewives] that taking attendance is impossible, and is so simple and straightforward that one misses nothing by not attending classes and copying someone else's notes. Cheating is prevalent during tests, and any grade below A or B is the exception. The course is fun, if you can plan to be in class . . . when Spock lectures, and if you cannot, then there is the consolation that it is perhaps the easiest course in the school." The fact that Spock himself did not conduct the examinations or determine the grades did nothing to dissipate the student feeling that Spock's reputed permissiveness prevailed in the classroom.

Dr. Spock also instituted a Practicum in Child Development to accompany the Child Management course, because he believed, like Dewey, that "Concepts in education should grow out of experience. All students from high school through graduate school should be doing some practicum work with people. Otherwise they fill their heads exclusively with abstract concepts which, however true, can easily unsuit them for practical work in the field, and make them overtheoretical as parents." Students who wanted to learn firsthand about children with and without problems were placed in different children's institutions throughout Cleveland— day nurseries, hospitals, and a residential treatment center for disturbed children. For ten hours a week, the students functioned as participant-observer aides to their field work supervisors, and earned three hours of A or B if they worked with reasonable diligence. Dr. Spock himself stopped meeting with the students after he found that they always wanted him to diagnose and prescribe for their cases, for he feared that his suggestions might conflict with their supervisors' advice. Nevertheless, he was particularly satisfied that most of the students were pleased with the Practicum, and today is still delighted to have introduced a course that was among the first at giving the students the relevant experience in the real world that today's students clamor for.

With a modicum of work, a student could get ten hours of honor grades for Dr. Spock's courses, nearly half the number of hours he needed for an undergraduate major in psychology. The psychology faculty, realizing that such a lopsided course distribution didn't give their students sufficient educational breadth, in 1967, the year of Spock's retirement, substituted for "Child Management" a more rigorous course in "Child Development," and toughened up the Practicum by requiring readings, papers, and group discussions in addition to the field work.

Dr. Spock's teaching of graduate physicians has evoked the same division of attitudes as the rest of his academic endeavors, and for the same reasons. In 1957 the Department of Psychiatry initiated a residency in Child Development under the joint chairmanship of Dr. William Boaz, a child psychiatrist, and Dr. Spock. This was intended for pediatricians interested in the typical emotional development of normal children—a remarkable innovation in a field that had been customarily concerned with the atypical, ill, and disabled. Dr. Ake Mattsson, a pediatrician from Sweden who first took his residency (and later full training in child psychiatry), found impressive Dr. Spock's psychoanalytic background; his inclusion in the discussions new knowledge in ethnology, animal psychology, human development, and psychoanalysis; his personal discipline and hard work; and the fact "that he could convey the phenomena of child development—burping, the baby at the breast, and so on—time after time with such enthusiasm, humor, and outstanding clarity."

Pediatric cardiologist Jerome Liebman, on Reserve's faculty, agrees enthusiastically: "As an intern and resident I never missed one of his fascinating sessions, held around a long table in the library, over coffee and pastry. That's the way Ben wanted it. He wasn't dogmatic, and he rarely gave a conference where he stood up in front as the leader. Usually a house officer would present a problem case, on a thumb-sucker, or a two-year-old with insomnia, and Ben would take it from there, calling on his experiences over the years. His earlier ones were richer than his more recent knowledge; perhaps he learned more about children when he was in private practice. Also, at that time the greatest strides were being made in the knowledge of child development, and he was one who helped to make those great strides. The conferences were great fun."

Other former graduate students view matters differently. A typical assessment is: "When Ben got to Reserve, although he had a good knowledge of anthropology and family development, he made a lot of generalizations and cited no studies. His most valuable contribution was his approach to the prevention of problems in normal children—but if you'd heard him several times you got bored."

Although Dr. Spock's students agree that as a teacher he was humanistic, broad, Freudian, anecdotal, personal, and entertaining, there is no consensus on the quality of his teaching. Depending on his own aims and scientific and psychiatric orientation, either the student liked Dr. Spock's classes or he didn't, but he was rarely indifferent. As a teacher, and as a researcher and a spokesman on public issues, Dr. Spock is a controversial figure.

The disagreement over Dr. Spock's research project at Western Reserve, the Child Rearing Study, is fairly subdued and largely confined to the small number of people professionally familiar with it. In 1957 Dr. Spock proposed a study to determine whether some common doctrines and child rearing practices (such as those advocated in *Baby and Child Care*) were valid and effective, particularly in regard to controversial matters such as breast feeding, thumb-sucking, toilet training, and sibling rivalry. He wanted to learn more about the dynamics of the individual infant and its relationship with its parents, and about the interplay between parent and counselor. These, he claimed, were areas of investigation unexplored by psychiatry, and were dealt with superficially by pediatricians operating from a frame of reference of diluted psychoanalytic concepts derived from the treatment of older children and adults, rather than from young children. Because the sampling of families to be studied was small and atypical, Spock did not expect to obtain data adequate to make definitive generalizations about child development and child rearing. He did hope, however, to conduct an intensive explorative investigation, which might be highly insightful in the manner of Freud or Piaget, who had obtained remarkable results from thorough analyses of small, atypical samples. His Study received $30,000 from the [W. T.] Grant Foundation annually from September 1958 to June 1964 to pursue this exploration.

Yet Spock's staff, eleven top-level faculty members from the Departments of Psychiatry and Pediatrics at Western Reserve, were not in clear agreement about what they were supposed to be studying. One investigator says, "We wanted to see what good pediatric

counseling might be able to accomplish with normal families."
Another disagrees, "This was a naturalistic, phenomenological
study. The absence of a control group didn't matter because we
weren't trying to study the effects of counseling." A third is uncertain, "No family was left in its naïve, unwashed state. Were we
studying intervention? Or just normal child rearing?"

Their simple methodology was as casual and ambiguous as their
interpretation of the Study's purposes. The parents in the twenty-
one families who volunteered for the Study were largely college-
educated, professional, white (one Negro family), Christian (three
Jewish families). Upon entering the Study in 1959 and 1960 they
were expecting their first child, and eventually had a total of
thirty-five children. One or both parents (usually the mother) met
twice a month for six years with an assigned staff member to
discuss common matters of child rearing and management, family
dynamics, and physical and emotional problems of parents and
children—the same matters which might be considered on routine
visits to an understanding pediatrician.

The discussions were unstructured; there was no uniform collection of data. The staff kept whatever records of these sessions
they wanted to in whatever way they chose, and resisted Dr. Spock's
sporadic attempts to standardize some of the topics and the procedures. Thus reliable generalizations or statistical analyses were
impossible. The principal records were transcripts—eventually a
filing cabinet full—of the weekly two-hour staff conferences, at
which one or two staff members presented material about their
children's development and problems, and the rest commented on
it. There were also occasional, but random, notes taken by observers of the Saturday morning play period for the three-to-five-
year-olds while their mothers attended a group session.

In addition to directing the Study and gently trying to coordinate the counselors' activities, Dr. Spock himself advised two
families (including the only one with twins) much in the same
manner that he advised the readers of *Baby and Child Care* and
kept a casual eye on the weekly play session. On occasion he himself
even tried the children's activities. After wistfully watching the
moppets paint on half a sheet of paper, fold it, and then unfold it
to observe the mirror images resembling colorful Rorschach ink-
blot figures, Dr. Spock hesitantly asked Mildred Hathaway, the

teacher in charge, if he could try one. When she said "Certainly,"
he delightedly compressed his six-foot frame into a chair designed
for a three-foot child, pulled back his French cuffs, painted his
picture along with the rest, and carefully spread it out to dry. At
the end of the session, when the children collected their papers,
Dr. Spock was observed meticulously folding his and tucking it
inside his coat pocket to take home to Jane.

Drs. Grete Bibring and Sybille Escalona, summoned by Spock
as consultants, thought the research design too simple and too
casual to produce much usable information, and their assessment
is borne out by one of the experienced researchers on the staff:
"Team research usually involves a lot of friction among the researchers, for each wants to upstage the others and publish first
under his own name. Often the director wants his name on everything. But not Ben. He really wanted each of us counselors to do
our own thing, whatever that thing was. He would encourage us
to write it up, and not want any of the credit. The rest of us were
too hidebound by the conventional rules of research to use such
an unstructured situation fruitfully. Ben was as permissive and
as anti-intellectual in his research with us as in his advice to parents, and we, like permissively raised children, weren't mature
enough to take advantage of the opportunities." Indeed, nine of
the staff members have published only seven papers altogether over
twelve years, though the conference transcripts remain available
for further investigation. Adds the researcher, "Maybe senior
people shouldn't have been chosen as counselors; they're too rigid
in their ways because they think they know it all. Ben changed
the most. Many of the others went in as missionaries to convert
Ben Spock."

Spock himself, along with insightful child therapist Mary E.
Bergen, M.S.W., invested the most in the Study and learned the
most from it. Between them they published nine papers, in addition to observations incorporated in *Baby and Child Care* and
in articles in women's magazines.

Dr. Spock was most pleased with his paper, "The Striving for
Autonomy and Regressive Object Relationships" (*The Psychoanalytic Study of the Child*, XVIII, 1963). There he offers a single
explanation for several seemingly disparate phenomena of infancy
that had persistently baffled pediatricians before the Study. At

about six months some babies, particularly when under stress or fatigued, become intensely dependent on comforting objects (such as a soft toy, blanket, or bottle), or on comforting behavior (such as thumb-sucking or rhythmic motions). Spock reasons that by five or six months an infant begins to sense his separateness from his mother and has a powerful urge to become more independent of her envelopment and control; he wants to sit upright in her lap for feedings and to hold his own bottle. But at times of regression he needs again the total security she gave him. The soft material to stroke; the bottle, thumb, or pacifier to suck; rhythmic movements, enable him to re-create this pleasure and security without surrendering his new independence. Many doctors have been impressed with Spock's contribution to psychodynamic theory, previously thought by Freud's disciples to be relatively complete.

One of the Study's major values, to Dr. Spock and consequently to the users of *Baby and Child Care,* was that in most major areas of child rearing except toilet training, the parents' experiences appeared to corroborate very well the advice Dr. Spock had been giving. He learned he was indeed in tune with the mothers who read his book and that they were in tune with him (in case he hadn't already been convinced by the reams of letters still pouring in). Their children did develop along the lines he had predicted. The Study gave him additional material on breast feeding (thirty-one of the babies were breast-fed for at least two months). It also led him and Miss Bergen to new views on toilet training, which they discussed in "Parents' Fear of Conflict in Toilet Training" (*Pediatrics* 34:1, July 1964), and which Spock incorporated into the 1968 revision of *Baby and Child Care* (see Chapter 6, p. 138).

Importantly and surprisingly, the Study gave the counselors reassurance on one point of worry: parents were not as in awe of child rearing experts as Spock's mail from mothers had led him to believe. In fact, they were healthily independent. Miss Bergen, one of the staff who felt it appropriate to counsel, observes, "We had a little fantasy that we'd have more success in influencing the parents than we did. We didn't want to alter their preferred ways of raising their children, but we did think they'd take our advice about specific problems. However, that's not the way it worked. Perhaps the parents resisted because they were afraid they'd be dominated by the professional group."

She continues, "What actually happened was much healthier. The parents put us counselors in the background, the way grandparents may have been in the past, as people to turn to if things got too rough. But until problems arose, the parents would ask for advice but reserved the right to consider it, to use it if they chose, to ignore it if they preferred, or to let us know we hadn't given the right answer. This is quite different from the clinical situation most of us were used to, where people come in quite desperate about a problem they've been trying to cope with for a long time. These parents feel helpless and are willing to go along with the therapist's suggestions. But the normal mothers felt their first job was to establish the fact that the baby was theirs, and they were not interested in interference. However, probably the most important function of counseling in normal personality development is not to prevent problems from arising, but to keep them from being overwhelming. I think it's safe to say that we did accomplish this."

Perhaps because the parents were so independent, perhaps because the counselors tried not to be assertive—or because they were ineffective in some instances—the children in the Study had just as many problems as any other children. Although the counselors felt that the difficulties were "probably milder and of shorter duration" than they might have been in an uncounseled population, the children experienced, in particular, problems related to feeding, separation from parents, and toileting (one child was still wetting the bed at twelve years in spite of all the psychiatric and pediatric ingenuity expended on his case for nine of those years). And, though the parents had received at least two years of counseling before their second and subsequent children were born, the difficulties of these children were similar to those of the firstborn, say several of the counselors, though Spock disputes this. Yet most of the parents were enthusiastic about the Study; they appreciated the availability of expert counsel, they felt they were helping the staff to learn, and their children loved the play session.

The individual counselors, too, were pleased, for they felt that they had gained extraordinary sensitivity to the problems of normal and nearly normal children, which many of them (being professionally familiar primarily with the abnormal) hadn't recognized before. They became aware of the child's physical development in relation to his emotional maturity and family situation and believe this awareness has enhanced their ability as therapists. Spock felt they had collected information on all of the aspects of child rearing they had set out to study, supplemented by serendipitous findings. As these insights were conveyed not only in clinical practice but through publication in professional and popular journals and the 1968 edition of *Baby and Child Care,* Dr. Spock's vision of enabling professionals and parents to nurture sound minds in sound bodies came closer to reality.

ten

THE VISION AND
THE REALITY

A vision and a dream pervaded the early 1960s: President John Kennedy's vision of the New Frontier; Dr. Martin Luther King, Jr.'s dream of racial equality and brotherhood. The dream and the vision, both partial aspects of the Great American Dream, reflected upon each other and gave new hopes and perspectives to Americans young and old, black and white, urban and rural, educated and unschooled. They were exhibited in the idealism of the Peace Corps and VISTA volunteers; in the weary footsteps and exultant voices of those who "overcame" in Birmingham and Selma, Alabama; in the glimpses of outer space transmitted by America's orbiting astronauts. With the country effectively at peace, ample federal money seemed available to finance many manifestations of the ideals: the Job Corps, Head Start, the National Council on the Arts; funds were abundant for medical, scientific, and technological research projects and graduate education. Employment was high, interest rates were low. The 1961 defense budget exceeded $43.2 billion ($14 billion higher by 1964) ; the $65 million worth of equipment and $2,000 military "advisors" sent to South Vietnam that year were scarcely noticed. Yet even the high military spending and the Bay of Pigs fiasco (redeemed by Kennedy's masterful negotiation of the removal of Soviet missiles from Cuba in 1963) failed to quell the enthusiasm of the millions who shared the vision and the dream.

The apathetic generation of the fifties had awakened to the challenges of the sixties—a heightening of consciousness expressed in Dr. Spock's own life and in his writings in popular magazines. In 1967 Dr. Spock explained his shift in perspective: "I've gradually become more radical, not from becoming more aggressive, but from seeing things more simply, in moral terms, in terms of the unifying force of brotherhood. There's a kind of serenity and clarity that comes from getting beyond some of the smaller issues and seeing the larger ones." It is somewhat ironic though perhaps inevitable in light of the strong influence of Spock's parents that someone who had fought against a moralistic viewpoint throughout adolescence and early adulthood had come to a moralistic view of the world's problems.

Thus in the *Ladies' Home Journal,* for instance, he had written on "Anxiety and the Cold War," "It seems self-defeating to resume nuclear testing while we are still ahead of the Russians," and had suggested various means of rapprochement with the Russian and Chinese people and governments. In another article he had rebutted an army psychiatrist's indictment of American youth as soft. Spock claimed that they were fundamentally wholesome and morally vigorous, in spite of the very poor morale among captured American troops during the Korean War.

By 1962 the Goulds had retired as editors of the *Journal,* and platoons of new offensive and defensive editors charged in and out of the tottering Curtis publishing empire, strewing columnists in their wake. The new management found Spock "much too left-wing," and when they fired Robert Anderson, Spock's editor, the pediatrician decided to switch to *Redbook.* He saw the editor, Robert Stein, as "serious, humorous, diffident, determined, idealistic, liberal, down-to-earth" and sympathetic to his views. Nevertheless, both Stein and his successor, Sey Chassler, much preferred Spock to avoid social issues and write monthly articles on the care of infants and young children. Because *Redbook* is aimed at a young adult readership, they didn't even want him to discuss adolescence very often.

Spock's impatience with always sticking to early childhood had obvious causes. He had written a book of over five hundred pages on that age period, and then one hundred fifty magazine articles, so, with the exception of the half dozen articles based on the Child Rearing Study, it was often difficult for him to think up a new topic or angle. Important in the motivation of any author is the wish to write about the themes that are currently on his mind, and to convey his own insights into them. For Spock after 1962 these themes were, increasingly, the danger of nuclear annihilation; the Vietnam war; such domestic issues as racism and poverty; the awakening of youth to an awareness of the existing wrongs, and their readiness to work for change through militant action or through life style. In contrast, thumb-sucking and toilet training seemed tame subjects. However, *Redbook's* editors would accept an occasional article on one of Spock's current interests if its relation to child rearing was made evident, and he particularly enjoyed writing such pieces.

It was almost inevitable, then, that Spock, frustrated in his attempts to express fully his views on various social or political issues in magazine columns, would elaborate on them in a book. So in 1964 he began *Decent and Indecent: Our Personal and Political Behavior*. This book, Spock's spiritual autobiography, is the distillation of a lifetime of his varied thoughts on the problems of modern western man, Americans in particular. He thinks that man has lost his belief in himself and his sense of direction because the concepts of evolution, of psychology, and of sociology have undermined the authority of religion and man's identification with God. They have induced man to belittle himself, to conceive of himself as merely an animal divisible into a number of mechanical parts and drives. Spock believes that Freud's concepts of emotional development in childhood, particularly the adoration and overidealization of the parents in the preschool years, subsequently repressed and sublimated into intellectual interests and lifetime ideals, show that man's aspirations and spirituality are as real as his blood chemistry. Man must believe in himself and be inspired by brotherly love or he will be destroyed by the aggressive and paranoid aspects of his nature. On the basis of these views he discusses the issues and problems in the book's five sections: "Where Does Idealism Come From?" "Problems of Sex and Sex Role," "Aggression and Hostility," "The Psychology of Political Attitudes," and "Education for What?" His solutions are idealistic, moralistic, simple (some critics have said "simplistic").

For instance, he explains that war is fostered by man's crude territoriality and greed for power but also by "the way the male fear of appearing weak gets played out between leader and people." The national leader (such as President Lyndon Johnson) feels that "he must try to overawe the enemy leaders, convince his most skeptical followers that he will guard them and advance their interests, leave no room for his political opponents at home to call him soft." Thus the leader exempts himself "from the ordinary rules of decency which apply to relations between individuals," and the war he wages intensifies and spreads. Spock comments, "I feel that this do-or-die, my-country-right-or-wrong kind of patriotism is not merely out of place in a nuclear armed world, it is criminal egotism on a monstrous scale. The world won't be safe until people of all countries recognize it for what it is and, instead of cheering the leader who talks that way, impeach him."

He had expressed somewhat similar views in *Dr. Spock on Vietnam* (published by Dell Books in 1968. See below, pp. 276-281). In *Redbook* columns and in other essays he had discussed other topics. that he treats in *Decent and Indecent*: discrimination (we must overcome); the value of loving child rearing (enormous); the young who turn to beards, bare feet, peaceful political protests, and communal living to express their dissatisfaction with conventional society (most are sensible, kindly, idealistic).

Given the familiarity of his subjects and the firmness of his opinions, it should have been easy for Dr. Spock to write *Decent and Indecent*. Yet the composition of this book proved more difficult than any other writing he'd ever attempted. Unlike *Baby and Child Care*, this was not a book to be dictated out of the fullness of his professional expertise after a routinely busy day to a patient wife at the typewriter. Nor was it a book like *Caring for Your Disabled Child* (see below, pp. 231-232) on which a collaborator could do much of the research and initial writing. This was a cry from the heart of a public citizen, a cry of outrage, of sadness, and yet of hope—a cry that had to be carefully controlled lest it create antagonism rather than a climate of like-minded opinion. The subjects were controversial; they seemed somewhat fragmented, except for the overarching moral dimension; and unlike *Baby and Child Care,* there was little practical advice to be offered.

Spock wrote and rewrote in bits and batches; at home, still at the high stool and draftsman's table; on planes, in between speaking engagements; aboard his 23-foot sloop *Turtle* every morning in the summer before his sense of duty would allow him the indulgence of a daily sail in Maine waters. By the end of 1966 he had completed a draft, still in fragments, which his increasing concern for the opinions of young people led him to circulate among fourteen college students (as well as others), the first time he had sought student advice on a manuscript. Despite some disagreement, he was grateful that "none thought it foolish." During the next two years the fourth, fifth, and final drafts laboriously emerged, with greater coherence and a topical organization, more epigrams, less anger, and more of Spock's characteristic gentleness (though with little of his geniality). McCall Books published it early in 1970.

The book was widely received; it became a selection of the Literary Guild and affiliated book clubs and sold over 30,000 copies during its first year of publication. Compared to Spock's other writings, this book produced an unusual amount of controversy.

Many reviews were favorable: "a courageous and provocative book with a wealth of ideas, observations and conclusions on almost every page"; "full of insights, of lofty sentiments, and of righteous indignation which most of us can share"; "often controversial, thoroughly engaging, thoroughly human." Some unfavorable reviews objected to the volume's "untested logic" and "simplistic history": "In case anyone hasn't heard, 'imperialism in foreign policy and oppression at home are leading our country into deeper and deeper trouble'"; they found disconcertingly unspecific such solutions as "Our 'overintellectualized' educational system must offer 'courses linked to real life situations in order to be meaningful.'"

But, favorable or unfavorable, the reviewers almost to a man were outraged at Spock's sanctions against obscenity, which he himself has labeled "reactionary" and "conservative." He acknowledges the bases on which civil libertarians object to censorship and to obscenity laws: interpretations of obscenity are relative, "there's no proof that obscenity ever depraved anyone," parents, not laws, should protect their children. Nevertheless, he argues that even defenders of civil liberties and other sophisticates who refuse to be shocked "agree that there are certain acts—excretory or amatory, for instance—that they might consider offensive if carried out or crudely depicted in public." (Spock's argument was later cited by a Manhattan Criminal Court judge who found the cast and production staff of *Che!* guilty of obscenity on just those grounds.) Spock claims, "I would now join a majority, if such developed, in favor of new laws which would determine guilt simply on the basis of judges' and juries' sense of shock and revulsion." Geoffrey Wolff of *Newsweek* epitomizes the columnists' shock and revulsion at this view: "That we would be happier were there [no obscenity] is also manifest. But for Spock to have written the sentence above is astonishing. In 1968 . . . a judge and jury found Spock's methods of opposing the Vietnam war shocking, and he was found guilty of a crime. Would he now surrender other forms of expression to the mercies of the same court of law?" Nevertheless, Spock remains tranquil about his "unstylish" views, and is not about to modify them.

But being against obscenity is far less threatening to individuals than is his imputed appearance of misogyny, and he is much less tranquil about the irate reaction of Women's Liberation groups to his opinions on "Problems of Sex and Sex Role." The original published version of *Decent and Indecent* contained a lengthy opposition to unisex and to women "acting more and more like men," predicated on the view "that men and women are quite different in temperament and needs and that the feminists' effort to deny this is increasing the rivalry between the sexes and impairing the pleasure of both—but particularly of women." To demonstrate this, following Freud's emphasis on biology, Dr. Spock cited greater innate female compliance, passivity, nonaggressiveness, absence of hostility, and aptitude for "understanding and helping people and creating beauty." Because of these characteristics and because most women could be expected to spend between fifteen and twenty-five years raising children, the physician claimed that "it would be fairer to them if they were [educated] . . . in such a spirit that they would enjoy, feel proud of, and be fascinated by child-rearing rather than frustrated by it. Then they would be less inclined to be rivalrous with their husbands and other men."

Such opinions incensed Women's Lib, which plays down biology and psychology as it emphasizes individual self-determination. New Women, a New York Lib group, claimed that Spock warped "a human being into the stereotyped 'female role.'" They issued a broadside against *Decent and Indecent*, campaigned to remove his "sexist books" from bookstores (with apparently little effect), and threatened to write their own manual of child care and to sue him for "defamation of female character." Other Women's Lib student groups have interrupted Spock's antiwar speeches on college campuses to attack his views on women. At a lecture to raise funds for the defense of the Minnesota Eight, for instance, young women with grim faces read and chanted offensive sections of *Decent and Indecent* ("They machine-gunned me for twenty minutes," Spock notes wryly) and then marched out without waiting for Spock's rebuttal, which he felt obliged to deliver even though it made his speech on peace anticlimactic. "How ingenuous I was initially in such situations, thinking I could be reasonable and charming," he observes. "That got me nowhere. This is a transference phenomenon, a life and death matter representing real, grim hatred of father or brother. It must be devastating for their parents."

Glamorous journalist Gloria Steinem at the organizational meeting of the National Women's Political Caucus, in 1971, castigated Spock as "the symbol of repression which Freud and other male supremacists have been," and the pediatrician bowed his head humbly. Ti-Grace Atkinson, angry young spokeswoman for the Liberation movement, confronted Dr. Spock on David Frost's TV talk show, a summary of his offensive views clenched in her angry hand. She insisted on dominating both male speakers, who seldom got to finish a sentence, and explained that she tried to avoid being in the same room with any man in her social or occupational life. Her views and behavior drew snickers from the audience, though Dr. Spock himself later reacted with the typical sympathy that is part of his well-bred nature but which Women's Lib would probably consider offensive male patronization: "If she were my patient I'd feel very sorry for her. But it's unfair to expect me to have been the first women's liberator when I wrote *Baby and Child Care.*" It is ironic that the liberator of the American child, darling of the American mother for two decades, should have come to this.

Dr. Spock feels that he learned much from his numerous confrontations with Women's Lib. He freely admits "my elitism, my male chauvinism"—as he told the *New York Times,* "unconsciously, what male isn't?"—and believes this perspective governed his assumption that women will continue to take a greater share of the care of young children. He now believes that he was "insensitive and tactless to bring up the topics of inborn temperament and of teaching girls to revere child rearing at a time when women are struggling to overcome prejudice." To make amends and to clarify his views, Dr. Spock has reorganized the chapter on "Problems of Sex and Sex Role," and shifted its emphasis. He sympathizes with women's resentment "at the exploitation of themselves as characterless sexual objects," with women's desires for equal job opportunities and equal pay. He concedes the utility of good nursery schools for children over three. Yet because Dr. Spock believes that the personalities of children under three are highly sensitive and highly malleable, the focus of his discussion of the actual or desired roles of parents is centered on his conception of young children's needs. He believes that children under three should be cared for during at least two-thirds of their waking hours by parents, grandparents, or other loving, close relatives. He encourages men as well as women to take pride in domesticity, and expresses the hope "that we never come to the day when it is assumed that an outside job is an obligation (aside from financial necessity), or is more creative or gives greater fulfillment than the care of children and the home."

Dr. Spock has tactfully restated his views on the differences between men and women—in the middle of the chapter rather than at the beginning. He has deleted the statements most offensive to women, such as those quoted above (pp. 216-217) and such remarks as "Women are usually more patient in working at unexciting, repetitive tasks." Elsewhere he has ameliorated the language, substituting "agreeableness" for "passivity" in "Women on the average have more agreeableness in the inborn core of their personality." These changes make the revision seem to dwell much more emphatically on the qualities of men, such as "restlessness, tenseness, and combative aggressiveness," than the earlier version appeared to. The rest of Spock's views in the chapter, on marital problems, "Depersonalization of Sex in Adolescence," the naturalness of sexual inhibition, and obscenity, remain unchanged. And although in retirement Dr. Spock does the dishes, it is Jane who plans the meals and cooks the food, superbly.

During the years when he was writing and revising *Decent and Indecent,* Dr. Spock was also writing the book of advice for teenagers which he had promised Simon and Schuster as his concession to their agreement to remove the advertising from *Baby and Child Care.* This book was relatively easy to write, partly because Spock was discussing some of the same subjects in *Decent and Indecent,* and partly because he has always known what to say to "the shy kid who needs reassurance—the kind of kid that I myself was." Writing a book of extremely conservative advice for elitist youth—of educated, middle or upper class background— may seem an incongruity in the physician who was to be convicted for radical antiwar protests, yet there is no incongruity at all. Spock thrives in the balanced tension between the conservative and radical elements in his personality, both of which are derived from his ever present moralistic idealism. *A Teenager's Guide to Life and Love* (1970) aims, in fact, "to explain the relationship of human idealism, creativity and spirituality to the inhibition and sublimation (modification) of sexuality in childhood" and to show how these relationships bear on various attitudes toward sexuality held by diverse young people and adults.

Dr. Spock himself has claimed that his advice is so reactionary that it's *avant garde.* Many of his precepts are certainly wholesomely old-fashioned: Romantic love is "a love for a person of the opposite sex which is spiritual, tender, and idealistic as well as physical." If asked for guidelines by teenagers he would suggest avoiding individual dates under the age of sixteen; "It's sensible for a teenager not to go beyond kissing and embracing the person he loves until there is some kind of commitment to marriage," which should preferably wait until the couple have known each other for two years. He disapproves of "deliberate dinginess and messiness" in dress, "heavy seductiveness," and teenage use of tobacco, alcohol, and marijuana. He advocates daily showers, deodorants, politeness, and doing chores without being reminded. And, at the risk of antagonizing Women's Lib again, he takes the very position on temperamental differences and relations between the sexes that he did in the controversial first edition of *Decent and Indecent*: "My prime concern is that, back at the childhood stage, parents and schools not encourage girls to be competitive with males if that is going to make them dissatisfied with raising children, their most creative job in adulthood, whether or not they go to work too." (He expects to have to revise this to make it congruent with the revisions in *Decent and Indecent*.)

Yet while these views are likely to ally him with the parent and grandparent generations, on some other matters Dr. Spock is more conspicuously on the side of the young. He is neutral about masturbation, though he suggests that a boy who is uncomfortable because of petting with long periods of erection without orgasm allow himself to have an orgasm at such times. It can be done inconspicuously, Spock reassures. He is very cautious about marriage between people of different racial, religious, or ethnic backgrounds: "it takes super-human love and maturity to make it succeed." He more firmly sanctions "the arrangement" if the young people, twenty or older, living together are "responsible, thoughtful, studious types who have gotten to know each other well and developed a genuine affection before setting up joint housekeeping."

The book is written in the same friendly, direct, uncondescending, conversational style as *Baby and Child Care*. Much of the advice is equally practical: "Practice once a day being disarmingly pleasant to one person. . . . it's a valuable skill for anyone, whatever his views or purpose." Some of it is theoretical: "Romance and sex are matters of emotions and ideals, not of reasons." Reviews were favorable: "Dr. Spock hits every major problem that worries . . . young people"; "Spock displays . . . the courage to be conventional in an unconventional age"; "extremely useful." That 25,000 hardcover copies (at $4.95) were sold during its first six months of publication indicates a public receptive to this old-fashioned conservatism; whether this is a receptivity by parents or by teenagers themselves remains to be seen. The prospect of a new, wholesome, conventional (however idealistic) Spock generation in the offing might pacify the critics of Spock's alleged "permissiveness."

Dr. Spock's reasonable, nonauthoritarian tone in the *Teenager's Guide* typifies the attitude he tried to maintain in rearing John, though John himself thinks of his father as stern. At the age of twenty-four John, a lanky six feet four inches with his mother's wavy brown hair and soulful expression and—at that time—his father's slightly dandified dress (for a time in the late sixties John favored sideburns, a tight-fitting, Edwardian style suit with vest, wide tie, and boots), described his childhood: "I had the advantage of being the second only child, because my parents were a little more able to let me exist as an independent person with some of my own outlooks than they were with Mike, and made a little less effort to try to control what kind of a child I was, though they saw to it that I led a wholesome life. I was certainly never a guinea pig for Ben's theories on child rearing, and I can't remember any major conflicts with my parents when I was growing up. I wasn't spanked much, just isolated. I seldom disobeyed, not from fear of punishment, but because I had a 'guilty button' and kept myself pretty much in line."

John elaborated, "There was a very strong underlying assumption of family unity with a superficial blaséness about declarations of love and togetherness. We were a stiff family, and were never particularly warm with one another, though I really do love my mother." (Jane has kept for over twenty years a valentine John made her as a schoolboy, inscribed "I love you Jane C. Spock.") John continued, "I've always had an underlying fear of Ben as a very strict person, even though I admire and respect him. He's such a strong, dominating person that it was easy to confuse myself into feeling that Ben is the *whole* family, whereas in reality he's just my father. I can never remember wanting to be around my parents and being refused or put off; Ma was usually home when I was, and Ben made a point of spending a lot of time with me in the evenings.

"In our family," says John, "it was very clear that there was a right way to do things—that is, the way Spocks did them." All through Hawken (a private elementary school in Cleveland) and University School (private tenth and eleventh grades), John lived at home and did things the family's way, which delighted his parents and pleased him, too, though he, like Mike, was less gregarious than his parents would have wished.

As a youngster John had none of his brother's difficulties in choosing a career and in studying for it. Throughout childhood he was forever designing cars and boats, and even before he entered college he had firmly settled on a career in architecture. Whereas Mike manifested his indecision and rebellion in personal messiness, John's sureness of purpose and harmony with his parents were reflected in an orderly existence. He chose a college, Harvard, that at the time mirrored his orderly, highly intellectual life style.

But he had his own style of rebellion, at that time very subdued. John grins, "In the past anything Ben recommended I read I automatically decided not to look at. Everything he said about Yale made it seem like Harvard was the place to go. I made crew my senior year at Westminster School [in London, an ancient school affiliated with Westminster Abbey] and really hated it. I knew I wouldn't be interested in a secret society, for I had begun to look down on the kind of people with whom Ben had found his first acceptance."

John was, perhaps, unaware of the profound changes in his father's thinking on the subject: "When my sons were adolescents I didn't mention my senior society, the way my father earnestly did, and if the subject of my rowing came up, once in a couple of years, I talked of the amusing aspects. God knows these had both been enormously important to me, in youth, in a primitive way, but I had largely (not entirely) outgrown them. Looking back I can see I was an insecure and excessively ambitious person, quite ready to conform in any way to make the grade, and I'm not proud of it. In a way, my antiwar and other radical positions represent a final rejection of my adolescent values.

"Of course, there has also been a profound change in the ideals and ambitions of the young. I realized after John was in graduate school that I had never heard him say whether he had been asked to join a club at Harvard, and I had forgotten to ask. I'm sure my own father was watching my chances of election almost as hard as I was."

To gain a degree of financial independence, John got a job soon after arriving at Harvard, folding copies of the *Crimson* every morning at five. The health aspects distressed Jane immensely ("He looked like a ghost") and after six months she finally convinced him to stop.

But by then John didn't need to demonstrate his independence by folding newspapers. In 1963, at nineteen, he and Kendall March, a petite, raven-haired drama student at Sarah Lawrence and daughter of a Boston physician, fell in love. John found her "dynamic, on the ball. She knows what she thinks and fights for it." They were married a year later, during Christmas vacation of their junior years, in Harvard Memorial Church, with Mike and Judy as attendants and their sons Danny and Peter, then five and three, as dignified ringbearers. Both sets of parents were happy to give their blessings—and financial support—because they thought that both the young people were mature, knew their own minds very well, and were good students.

Kendall had to commute from Bronxville, New York to Cambridge for long weekends that academic year, but was allowed to earn her senior year credits at Brandeis University. As the couple went on to graduate school, John in architecture at Harvard, Kendall in drama at Brandeis, their disparate schedules intensified the increasing divergences in their friendships and interests. Kendall's rehearsals often ran from dinnertime through the evening. John worked later than that, and lost forty pounds (from two hundred) because he thought he was too fat. They separated after two years of marriage.

Ben and Jane characteristically carried to the extreme their effort to refrain from the slightest interference—even any negative or positive criticism—of their sons' lives after marriage. In fact, since his sons came of age Ben has gone out of his way to avoid interference in their lives in any form. The Spocks and their sons treat one another with great courtesy, though of late, physical reserve has been supplanted by father-son bear hugs, as a result of family therapy sessions in which both sons complained of their father's physical reserve in their childhood. They talk together as mature adults, and respect their rights to disagree—politely.

There is not much temptation to interfere with Mike's stable and satisfying life. He relishes his job as Director of the visually and intellectually appealing Boston Children's Museum, where youngsters can participate in the exhibits, from crawling through tunnels to flushing a bisected toilet to petting live animals. His aim is to "bring kids together with three-dimensional materials in such a way that real communication occurs between the child and the object. Museums often represent dead circuses to kids—

all the life has been sucked out of them. Who likes going to a circus without the band, the crack of a whip, the smell of a menagerie? We want to make the exhibits live again." The success of his aim is indicated by the Museum's widely expanding and innovative programs and a sixfold increase in its annual budget (to $300,000) since he took over in 1962. From there he commutes (in an old car) to a contemporary house in the woods in nearby Lincoln, a casual and warm haven for himself and Judy, two lively sons (born in 1959 and 1961), a daughter (born in 1967), a shaggy dog, and two cats that sleep on the tabletops.

There might be more inclination to advise John, who in his late twenties is in many ways a quintessential member of the first Spock generation. A soft-spoken idealist, now with long, carefully combed hair and sometimes with a full beard, John found his four years at Harvard's School of Architecture more and more disenchanting as he developed a progressively stronger social conscience. He has currently rejected a number of aspects of conventional life in addition to his marriage: materialism (he wears jeans and has few possessions); a career as an architect (which he now defines as "sitting in an office for a fee paid by institutions that perpetuate what makes them run the easiest, rather than helping the people they're supposed to serve"). Only gradually, with the aid of a therapist twice a week for the past three years, has he become more certain of what to substitute for what he has rejected: communal living to dissipate his loneliness; work with his hands as a builder. He wants to try at least one summer in rural, natural Vermont instead of congested Boston. Whether his search for stability will end there remains to be seen; it is the quest of the sensitive, the thoughtful youth who are often his father's referents in *Decent and Indecent* and other writings.

Though Spock has frequently restrained himself from interfering with the lives of his children (as with those he supervised professionally), he is under no self-restraints when sailing. He only partially jests when he says, "Though I pretend to be preoccupied with children and peace, I'm really thinking about sailing a lot of the time, especially when things are tense." He basks in the isolation a boat provides; he relishes each opportunity to prove over and over again that he can master the wind and the waves; he is exhilarated at being close to mild—or more threatening —danger, and in overcoming it.

According to a number of sailing companions, Dr. Spock sometimes keeps on sailing in weather that makes other intrepid salts stay by the fireside. Jane laments, "He's a mad, mad sailor." But Dr. Spock gently shrugs off Jane's distress that the *Turtle* was dismasted three times at sea, and that he and John nearly drowned near Copenhagen on a trip to Europe in 1962, when their rented catboat capsized in a squall. (They were picked up by an old man in a skiff after they had been clinging for an hour and a quarter to a small part of the bow, all that protruded above the icy water.)

Echoing Jane's lament is Ben's sister Hiddy, in her sixties, a kindly, Thoreau-like, self-reliant philosopher who for several years has run an immaculate oceanside farm in remote East Sullivan, Maine. Like her brother who sometimes rises before dawn to sail, she rises at 4 a.m. in the summers to translate anthroposophical treatises from the German before attending to her biodynamic garden, where she grows all her own food and food for the livestock, prizeworthy goats and chickens. "You'll never have a sick chicken if you feed it earthworms," she says firmly, and raises her own worms, too, in dirt-filled troughs she built herself. She advocates organic farming partly from philosophical reasons, partly because she had recognized the dangers of pollution and other problems attendant on chemical fertilizers and insecticides twenty years before the Government banned DDT and ecological issues began to plague the national conscience. Anticipating her brother's lawsuits on moral grounds, in 1957 she and others conducted a costly lawsuit to prevent tree spraying in Nassau County, Long Island, and lost. Though he was asked to appear as a witness for the prosecution, Dr. Spock declined; today he might have accepted.

One day, as storm clouds lowered, Ben, Jane, and John sailed into the cove on Frenchman's Bay where Hiddy lives and invited her and her partner to go for a sail. Two other boats tacked into the harbor, their skippers calling, "Don't go out, it's getting rough." "But we got into the boat anyway," remarks Hiddy. "Ben snorted and said he wasn't going to take us for a ferry ride, but for some real sailing. On we sailed. As the wind gusted, the choppy waves lapped higher, thunder boomed in the distance, and Ben's spirits mounted. Ours didn't. We now realized the meaning of the saying 'There's no fool like a sailor,' and we were scared. But we were just as frightened of Ben as of the weather, for we'd heard how angry he could get when people criticized his sailing. As the wind blew harder and the rain came, we just had to speak up. 'We've taken a vote,' we said, 'and we want to turn around.'

"Ben didn't say a word," Hiddy observes lovingly. "He took down the sail and turned on the motor. We chug-chugged into the harbor, he let us out, didn't even say good-by, and sailed off."

When the Spocks moved to Cleveland they had looked forward to weekend sailing on Lake Erie, Cleveland's big bathtub, but found it disappointing. Dr. Spock explains, "After fifteen minutes on the choppy water John, then eleven, would turn green and whine, 'I don't feel good. When are we going in?' I'd snarl, 'Listen, we've been waiting all week to get out here and I'm not going to turn back just because you're seasick.' Then we'd sail a while longer, and as we watched him, John would gradually turn greener. I'd feel sorry for him and we'd return to the harbor." Spock accounts for John's seasickness psychiatrically, "He wasn't feeling too good about life generally then—partly because of his age and partly because of the move."

Dr. Spock adds, "We also found two-thirds of the pleasure gone because there was no place to sail to. Lake Erie has an absolutely flat, straight, sandy shore that stretches from Sandusky to Ashtabula and Buffalo. The beach is gray and dirty, with a shack every fifty feet. There's no scenery, there's no harbor, there's no swimming, there's no destination."

So they gave up Lake Erie, and eventually found Pymatuning Lake, an eighteen-mile-long man-made sliver wedged between Ohio and Pennsylvania. For the next ten years they were among the first to put their boat in in the spring, and the last to take it out in November. The lake was more scenic, with attractive islands and coves, and still large enough for sporty sailing, which satisfied Spock. It had a fair number of fish, which satisfied Jane. And it was calmer, which satisfied John, who often sailed by himself—for a time, even with a broken leg in a cast—or with his own friends in an eight-foot pram, one of the three boats he and his father built. John observed as an adult, "I really enjoy boat building. I thought I liked to sail, too, but when I don't do it I find that I don't miss it."

Jane learned to enjoy sailing more than John. Now, despite a skin sensitivity to the sun which is so severe that on the water she must wear a wide-brimmed hat, heavy veil, gloves, and protective cosmetics, Jane has taught and disciplined herself to the point that unassisted she can take the boat out of a crowded harbor. Her husband beams, "She's really a good sailor and a good sport."

She was also a good sport about caring for her mother-in-law. Jane says, "As she got very old and sick, I was available and went to take care of her, including escorting her from New Haven to Florida and back by train. I was definitely the best person to do this because I could manage her and nobody else could."

The magnitude of Jane's solicitude toward her mother-in-law, especially as Mrs. Spock became increasingly infirm, is clear when one reads Dr. Spock's description of his mother in her eighty-sixth year. He wrote to Mrs. Spock's physician in 1962: "She has alienated her few surviving old friends with her rudeness. . . . She soon becomes critical and disagreeable to the part-time help she has. She dismisses them or they walk out. . . .

"To tell a nurse or companion that Mother shouldn't be held responsible for what she says would not give enough protection to their feelings. Her criticalness is perceptive. Her tongue is sharp. She has no qualms about her rudeness or ruthlessness. You know that she means what she says and you know that she means you. Her scorn is not easy to shrug off. Her disagreeableness has been much less than usual during this present illness. [stroke] That is the reason her children have been glad to visit her.

"If she were at home and in charge of herself she would refuse any treatment that did not appeal to her. A year ago in the summer she had a respiratory-cardiac illness and my wife Jane and I were with her for seven weeks, trying to take care of her. She was 90% uncooperative. The 10% of cooperation was only in situations where we had an absolute upper hand. ('No back rubbing until you take a bath.' . . .) She cannot tolerate anyone controlling her to the slightest extent.

"When she says 'I want to get home [from the hospital] where no one can boss me and I can be in charge of my life,' she means, 'Where I won't do a thing if I suspect someone wants me to do it and where I can treat people just the way I feel like treating them.'

"The only time of the year she has been happy in the past few years has been in the two inns in Florida in winter. She generally behaves well and is amusing with people who are only acquaintances. (It is with relatives, good friends, servants, and tenants that she is dominating and rude.)"

So for the last three years of her life Mrs. Spock, no longer able to walk, was cared for in a nursing home. She gradually became a relatively docile, though peppery, patient with a private nurse in constant attendance. The irony of her dependent position must have been painful to a woman so habitually dominating, but she bore it with surprisingly good grace and incisive wit. She made peace with her family, and they responded with increasing mellowness toward her. She delighted in the many gifts her children sent her, particularly the silver birch planted outside her window by Hiddy and Betty. In January 1968 she died tranquilly at the age of ninety-two, transformed, say her daughters, with the beautiful features of her youth miraculously restored.

In Cleveland the Spocks' winter recreation was somewhat more circumscribed than sailing, though no less energetic. They were accepted as members of The Cleveland Skating Club, and by the time that they realized that the Club discriminated against Jews and Negroes, Spock had become such a devotee of ice dancing and so delighted with the exercise and the Club's convenient location that he decided against resigning in protest. As partial excuses he said that he doubted that resignation would embarrass this particular Club in the slightest, and that he was acting publicly to discourage discrimination through his magazine articles and television programs such as *The Victims*.

At the age of fifty-four Dr. Spock began to learn to dance on skates. He took lessons for ten years from the Club's petite blonde professionals, Mrs. Sue Scherer, young enough to be his daughter, and Mrs. Claire Staples, young enough to be his granddaughter. Mrs. Scherer says, "It's harder for long-legged people to skate, especially around turns, than for people who have solid legs and are built closer to the ice. But his height didn't deter Dr. Spock in the least. He wasn't afraid of falling, and he fell a lot—on his head at least twice a week. He'd always laugh and get up and try again.

He had a good stroke and could really push around that rink with abandon. Over the years he learned to do every one of the compulsory dances in the U.S. Figure Skating rule book, from the pre-silvers, to the silvers, to the pre-golds, to the gold medal dances."

Mrs. Staples observes, "He was exceptionally good, though when I'd tell him that he wouldn't believe me. But if I said, 'Dr. Spock, you stink,' he'd laugh, though I could tell he thought I meant it. You can't criticize most men."

A number of the Club's more timid ladies felt that Dr. Spock's style had more flamboyance than finesse and refused to dance with him. But even the women who wouldn't dance brought their friends to lunch at the rinkside dining room so they could watch the baby doctor in action. However, as he became more prominent in politics, his value to the Skating Club as a celebrity and entertainer declined. In 1968, after he retired, he visited the Club once again to skate, and was ostentatiously snubbed by several members. He has never had occasion to go back.

He was snubbed, too, by some medical colleagues who were angered by his advocacy of Medicare in 1963 and 1964. (The American Medical Association contributed over seven million dollars to the campaigns of candidates pledged to vote against Medicare.) In an AFL-CIO circular supporting Medicare, Dr. Spock cited with disapproval the A.M.A.'s past objections to earlier health and welfare proposals, such as: "extension of Social Security benefits to [persons] permanently and totally disabled at age 50, to elimination of the means test in the crippled children's program, to voluntary health insurance plans, and to Federal grants for maternal and child welfare programs. Some doctors even opposed the Red Cross blood bank on the grounds that *it* would lead to socialism!" As recently as 1967, A.M.A. President Milford O. Rouse carried on the Association's conservative tradition, claiming: "We [of the A.M.A.] are faced with the concept of health care as a right rather than a privilege. Several major steps have already been taken by the federal government in providing health and medical care for large segments of the population. Other steps have been proposed—these we must continue to oppose.

"What is our philosophy?" Rouse answered, "It is the faith in private enterprise. We can, therefore, concentrate our attention on the single obligation to protect the American way of life. That way can be described in one word: Capitalism."

Typical of many physicians with full-time academic appointments, Dr. Spock objected strongly to this entrepreneurial philosophy. During 1963, as a member of the Physicians' Committee for Health Care for the Aged Through Social Security, he had through public statements and financial contributions promoted President Kennedy's Medicare plan. After Kennedy's assassination Dr. Spock testified in favor of the bill, pointing out the financial hardships on the entire family that a few weeks' hospitalization could cause; claiming that without hospitalization insurance low income groups put off seeking medical care, with tragic effects; and concluded that hospital insurance for the aged could best be paid for through Social Security deductions, as a "practical way to cover these people who would be least able to secure it for themselves. This method involves no charity or means test [as did the Kerr-Mills Act, which *ex post facto* the A.M.A. grudgingly approved as the lesser of two evils]. It would leave people their dignity and their sense of security."

Dr. Spock's advocacy of this bill was at that time the climax of his involvement in national politics. He became adroit at answering hostile letters from doctors throughout the country (particularly in the Far West and Southwest) who disapproved of his views. One group wrote: "You are destroying the esteemed image we have of you and anyway what special interest would you as a pediatrician have in a bill for the aged?" Another doctor saw high medical fees as a source of pride to patients who could boast over the bridge table, "My hysterectomy cost $1,800." Another's remark was typical: "My practice is a consequence of eleven to twelve hours daily, sometimes six or seven days a week, and while it is true that I am amply repaid for such dedication, this dedication is one of personal motivation and control. This cannot possibly exist under any social system."

To these arguments Dr. Spock replied, ". . . half the aged have incomes under $1,200 and are hospitalized twice as much as the rest of the population; half the aged cannot possibly afford ordinary hospitalization insurance." And even more emphatically he said, "To me this [A.M.A. attitude] is hysterical and self-centered and ignoble. Sickness was not invented for the benefit of physicians nor is it their private property."

To what extent Dr. Spock's support of Medicare influenced the passage of the bill is impossible to determine. At the very least his outspokenness helped to make audible the minority medical opinion that might otherwise have been drowned out by the angry roar from the A.M.A.

Throughout the fifties and sixties Dr. Spock had also taken a stand on fluoridation, both as chairman of the Committee to Protect Our Children's Teeth, Inc. and as a private citizen—and this time he was on the side not only of the American Dental Association, but of the American Medical Association as well. Over Bruce Gould's initial objections (subsequently withdrawn), Dr. Spock inserted a paragraph promoting fluoridated water into an article in the *Ladies' Home Journal* in 1955. At the request of local fluoridation committees, he wrote letters to the newspapers of cities and towns throughout North America where fluoridation was on the ballot, saying, "As a pediatrician interested in preventing ill health, I am enthusiastically in favor of water fluoridation. . . . Committees of impartial experts of the A.M.A., the A.D.A. . . . thoroughly evaluated all the extensive research and evidence regarding fluoridation and only then recommended it as valuable and safe. These recommendations are not casually made. . . . To know that fluoridation has this professional endorsement should reassure citizens who have been in doubt."

Dr. Spock's endorsement didn't reassure every doubting citizen. Some said fluoridation was a Communist plot to poison the water supply. Others feared it would turn their teeth black or make their bones radioactive. But, for his efforts, in 1965 the Society of Public Health Educators awarded Dr. Spock a citation "for outstanding contributions to the Health Education of the Public," and in the same year he received a plaque from the U.S. Public Health Service "In recognition [of] his continued and invaluable efforts in advancing the dental health of children."

At about the same time Dr. Spock also made a major contribution to the Association for the Aid of Crippled Children (at the Association's insistence) by donating his services in collaboration with widely published health educator Marion O. Lerrigo, Ph.D., on a book, *Caring for Your Disabled Child* (Macmillan, 1965). Dr.

Lerrigo did the research and wrote the first draft; in 1963 and 1964 Dr. Spock rewrote it three times—though the collaborators never met in person until after the book was completed!

Caring for Your Disabled Child contains sympathetic, practical, knowledgeable but not technical discussions of how the family can help a mentally or physically handicapped child to live as normal and healthy a life as possible, at home, at school, at work, at play. The authors are aware of the psychological, as well as physical, problems that may occur within the family as the result of a given child's handicap, and approach them with realistic sensitivity:

"Help your child work hard to make the most of the abilities he has and those he can develop. That will give you both enough to do without straining after the impossible.

"Enjoy your child for what he is. It's unfair to yourself and him to keep thinking of what he might have been."

Drs. Spock and Lerrigo also provide helpful suggestions on how to use, care for, and accommodate within a conventional household therapeutic equipment such as braces, crutches, wheelchairs, and artificial limbs. Throughout, they maintain a tone of realistic optimism: "Some parents and children hate the thought of braces. But braces may make it possible for a child to go to school, to play ball, to travel around with his friends, help him to develop a better looking body and a better looking walk, deliver him from jerky, futile motions and help him learn coordination—not today or tomorrow, or next week, but eventually. . . . The doctor prescribes braces only if he believes they will help the child, so the prescription is good news."

The book was favorably received by professional rehabilitation groups and parents and has been adopted as a textbook in some college courses in physical therapy and nursing.

In 1962 Dr. Spock was awarded an honorary Doctor of Science degree by Durham University, in Durham, England, and, accompanied by Jane, attended the ceremonies along with the other degree recipients, P.M.S. Blackett, eminent English physicist and disarmament advocate; W. H. Auden, the poet; Frederick Ashton, the choreographer; and Charlie Chaplin.

The Spocks enjoyed dining in medieval Durham Castle and found awe-inspiring the services in the dark Norman cathedral, damp even in June with the chill of nine centuries, as the choir sang and the organ pealed. The townspeople turned out to see the ceremonial procession of scarlet-robed academics, hoping particularly for a glimpse of Durham's favorite expatriate, Chaplin, who at the age of seventy-three was nervously awaiting word of the birth of his ninth child in Switzerland. Because the parade was supposed to be dignified, Chaplin began by responding to the crowd's excited shouts, "There's Charlie! There he is!" with a discreet flutter of his hand. But gradually he became as uninhibited as the spectators and waved back, moderately at first, then harder and harder. As he was on the way to receive his degree, Chaplin did a little heels-up dance reminiscent of his performance in *The Gold Rush* and the crowd went wild.

In comparison, the ceremonies in 1965 when Dr. Spock received honorary degrees from the University of Hartford and, to his delight, from Yale were conventional. However, there was dissension behind the scenes, as perhaps there always is in such cases, for anyone prominent enough to merit an honor is also sufficiently prominent enough to have aroused resentment. Some members of the Yale Medical School faculty resented the fact that Dr. Spock, not prominent in medical research, was being honored for his popular accomplishment of having been, as the degree citation read, "the grandmother of a generation, concerned not only with the children of the world, but with the world in which they lived." But the desires of Dr. Spock's friends among the Yale faculty and alumni prevailed.

However, Yale did not love him in 1968 as it did in 1965, and President Kingman Brewster moved to dissociate the university from one of its most controversial alumni. The *Yale Alumni Magazine* elected to publish its initial alumni profile on Dr. Spock just at the conclusion of his trial for conspiracy to aid draft resistance. Upon learning, "somewhat accidentally," of the profile's impending publication, Dr. Brewster explained, "I strongly urged its cancellation or postponement, lest it be interpreted as some kind of Yale bias in favor of Dr. Spock's current position. . . . With the galaxy of nationally prominent public activists [among the alumni] from Harriman to Lindsay it seemed to me just an open invitation to suspicion of ideological promotionalism to single out Spock. . . ." The article was removed, and its author, Mrs. Rita Berkson, resigned from the magazine's staff in protest, but Dr. Spock himself remained unflappable. Yet a year later Dr. Brewster too had become an outspoken critic of the war, and for some alumni (and later Vice President Agnew) even more controversial than Dr. Spock.

In 1960 John Kennedy's vision of the New Frontier strongly attracted Dr. Spock, along with millions of others, as he campaigned in a hard-fought election against Richard Nixon. Spock wrote an Australian mother curious about American politics: "I met [Kennedy] twice. During his campaign in 1960 I was asked by campaign headquarters to go to Youngstown [Ohio] to be photographed shaking hands with him as he stepped out of his plane. Inside the plane he said, 'My wife is a fan of yours,' and my wife Jane said 'We're fans of yours.' But he forgot to shake hands for the photographers as we emerged from the plane. I backed down 15 steps of the ramp, at each step half-extending my hand, but he kept waving to the cheering crowd all the way down.

"Jane, my 16-year-old son John, and I rode in a reporters' bus in a parade to town and were finally pushed past 100 individual policemen to the hotel suite where [Kennedy] was changing his shirt before the speech to 10,000 people in the square below. Only half a dozen people were in the sitting room, including Governor DiSalle [Ohio]. . . . Kennedy chatted with us again, but again forgot the photograph, so I reminded him. He spoke the word, and two photographers appeared before you could rub a lamp. Kennedy was more large, robust, handsome, engaging than his pictures showed—a really impressive person.

"After the speech, from the marquee over the hotel entrance, as he was pushing his way through a mass of the local politicians and their wives in the hotel corridor, a woman with a face expressing deep infatuation tried to close in on him. Two photographers raised their cameras, but Kennedy coolly straight-armed her away. Her embarrassed husband growled at her, 'What the hell did you think you were doing?'

"Since that photograph was apparently never used, I was asked to come to Washington to do a bit of TV film with Mrs. Kennedy in their small Georgetown house. The interior was beautifully furnished, mostly French, but the double living room was full of cameras and cables. When Mrs. Kennedy came down, the producer said, 'You just talk and I'll start rolling.' We protested violently that we had to decide what to talk about. He gave us five minutes, and away we went. It was stiff the first time, but better the second. By this time, I wanted to keep on talking because Mrs. Kennedy was such a responsive and feminine interviewer who would make a man want to do anything for her, no matter how arduous; but the producer, who had other interviews to do, had to push me out."

In May 1963, amidst speculation that Dr. Spock was about to be appointed White House pediatrician, the Spocks were invited, with 180 others, to dinner at the White House for the Grand Duchess Charlotte of Luxembourg. Jane bought a new dress for the occasion, a dusty pink formal with a bouffant skirt: Dr. Spock wore his tails; but to save money they stayed overnight in Washington with the children of a friend and arrived at the dinner, amidst the chauffeured limousines, in a borrowed Volkswagen.

To Joyce Hartman, his interested editor at Houghton Mifflin, Dr. Spock described the evening: "Jackie wore a rough taffeta in lavender that Jane said was ingeniously concealing [of her pregnancy].... Every woman was in a long dress and every man in tails except for Shriver. The reception was stiff. Kennedy said, 'Hello, Doctor.' Jackie looked me right in the eye and said, 'So we meet again!' It seemed very personal at the moment. Dinner was, by contrast, very relaxed, at tables of 10. The only trouble was that I failed to chew my roast beef fine enough and it stuck in my gullet for 20 minutes while tears streamed down my face and I debated whether to make a dash for the door and a bathroom. Everybody pocketed his place card, menu, matches. The musicale was as God-awful as all musicales, only worse because Basil Rathbone recited Shakespearean sonnets between numbers in a quivering syrupy manner. Afterwards the Kennedys mingled for half an hour and I seemed to be involved in a reception of my own with a half dozen ladies of the press, all young, beautiful, long-gowned, each of whom wanted to know, 'Is this a consultation?' and 'What is your opinion on 5 Caesareans?' No comment. I also received the Udalls, the Whizzer Whites, the Ambassador to Luxembourg, and various Luxembourgers, all of whom use you know which book. Others at the dinner included Helen Hayes, Rex Harrison, the Steinbecks, Steichens...."

In October of the same year, President Kennedy singled out Dr. Spock for an additional honor—special ambassador to the inauguration of Argentine President Arturo Illia, himself a physician. Dr.

Spock recalls the trip, his first and only diplomatic mission, with the same mixture of small-boy glee, enthusiasm, and realism that he felt at the Presidential dinner, though this time he didn't choke: "We left Washington on a typically cool, crisp autumn morning by Presidential jet. We found Surinam (Dutch Guiana) 95 degrees, and when we arrived in Buenos Aires it was a cold, rainy spring evening.

"Our four days were occupied with official ceremonies, including the presentation of credentials, the laying of the wreath at the tomb of Argentine hero José San Martin, a magnificent military parade, and an American Embassy steer roast, a gala performance of the ballet at the national theatre. . . .

"Life has been full of embassy assistants to run errands for us, a couple . . . to escort us everywhere in a car constantly at our disposal, invitations all on cardboard with a Gold Coat of Arms of the U.S. or Argentina, motorcycle police escorts with screaming sirens whenever we attended the official functions, military attachés from all the armies of the world, in dress uniforms covered with gold braid, and with gold epaulettes . . . diplomats with huge star-bursts on their chests or medals hung round their necks, wives dressed and coifed to the limit. . . .

"However, we spent a lot of time just standing around waiting. For example, our delegation arrived at the palace for the official reception at noon and we weren't able to greet the President until 2:30 p.m. We were fortified by a thin sandwich and a glass of champagne.

"There was also lots of hard work: a meeting with the pediatric and clinical psychiatry staff of the British Hospital, being a visiting lecturer in the class of a professor of psychology in the University, a visit to the Dental School, a talk to the residents and staff of the University Children's Hospital. I was very impressed with the awareness of Argentine physicians and dentists of the psychological needs of children."

In general, however, despite the intricacies of domestic and foreign diplomacy, the Spocks' personal life during their twelve years in Cleveland was much less complicated than it had been anywhere else they'd lived, and much more enjoyable than any place except New York. Jane coped with her anxieties about her husband's increasing political involvement by becoming active in politics too—in the Cuyahoga County Democratic Women's Club, and on the national board of Americans for Democratic Action. Occasionally she'd talk with a psychiatrist, certainly a relief of the tensions that beset the wife of any controversial public figure. It's never easy to accept with aplomb the fact that one's spouse is receiving hate letters, obscene phone calls, and threats of murder, even if he himself shrugs them off with airy imperturbability, saying, "If somebody really has murder planned, he's not going to call up the victim first."

As Spock had gained reassurance through his achievements as professor, author, and peace advocate, he relaxed more at home. He and Jane enjoyed the concerts of the Cleveland Orchestra—and adjacent seat-holders enjoyed Spock's enthusiastic 'Bravos' and standing ovations, even when he was the only one standing. He became more sensitive to his wife's wishes; he was considerate of her desires on vacations, sailing, and social engagements; he gave her advance warning before bringing home dinner guests; and acceded to her wishes for a gold and geranium living room after thirty-one years of his preferred grays, greens, beiges—and was delighted with the effect.

Yet Spock had also come to enjoy the dignified aspects of big-time politics. He relished the icing on the political cake and, romantic that he is, assumed that everything underneath would be as sweet as the superficial layer. Cleveland friends thought of entering his name in the Ohio senatorial race, but he never liked the idea, partly because he believed that he'd have to spend most of his time on constituents' problems and could devote only a small fraction of his efforts to causes particularly meaningful to him. Dr. Marvin Rosenberg, politically active community organizer as well as the father of Dr. Spock's twin patients in the Child Rearing Study, theorizes, "Dr. Spock is healthily narcissistic. He enjoys publicity and is comfortable about his notoriety. Although he doesn't grandstand it, he is not inappropriately modest. But, much as he likes being in the papers, if he had run for the Senate it might have destroyed him as an individual. He has a basically non-conspiratorial view of how public affairs are run; he's so trusting and optimistic he doesn't recognize the sinister side of politics. So he couldn't anticipate the viciousness of a political campaign and what he'd have been subjected to. Because he would never have compromised his principles or his behavior, he'd have been only a symbolic martyred candidate for a cause."

This aspect of Dr. Spock's personality is as controversial as much of the rest of his life and work. Case Western Reserve sociology professor Sidney Peck, one of the organizers of both the old and new Mobilizations Against the War in Vietnam and close personal friend of the Spocks, disagrees: "The general stereotype of Ben is that he is politically naïve and that political sophisticates can run rings around him. This is fallacious. Ben is not a political ideologue, but he is a good and very careful listener. His psychiatric training has made him quite sharp to committee sessions and to personalities in conflict. Ben has his own private way of assessing a political situation. His political analyses are impressive; he's much sharper in this area than some people give him credit for."

There is some truth to both sides of the argument. Dr. Spock, with this mixture of naïveté and acumen, innocence and information, had almost unintentionally attained as much power, popularity, and prestige as a doctor possibly could have in this country. Yet Dr. Spock recognized that a serious national and international problem was mounting, and prepared to contribute—and to sacrifice if necessary—the entire force of his reputation and esteem to a cause, to his vision and his dream.

eleven

PEACE AND POLITICS

THE cause was peace. By the end of 1970 U.S. participation in the Indochina war was entering its seventeenth year, with over 45,000 Americans killed and ten times that number wounded. Significant events of 1970 had signaled the public disaffection with the war. Across the nation colleges closed or suspended classes to protest the Cambodian "incursion" and the subsequent killing of four Kent State students during antiwar protests. Congress passed a resolution intended to prohibit the United States from sending ground troops to still other Cambodias. In 1970 alone more than 89,000 troops deserted from the U.S. armed services. Given this climate of opinion, with more and more people wanting out—from Wall Street businessmen to Black Panthers to the staffs and supporters of over fifty GI underground newspapers—it is difficult to remember that even as recently as 1967 the climate of opinion was quite different. A Gallup poll of January 1971 revealed doves 73 percent, hawks 26 percent; in 1967 the doves ranked 55 percent, hawks 31 percent. Yet two years earlier, in 1965, the figures had been reversed—hawks 52 percent, doves 26 percent.

In 1965, the year after the Tonkin Gulf resolution permitted the President to undertake "all necessary steps including the use of armed forces" to assist threatened SEATO member nations, the vast electorate assumed that with a few more million dollars and a few more thousand men Lyndon Johnson could end the war once and for all. In 1962, only the most idealistic or politically astute and watchful were even aware that President Kennedy had committed 11,000 "military advisors"—a paltry figure by later standards—to "assist" the corrupt but pro-United States Diem regime in its fight against the Viet Cong. To have protested Kennedy's action then, or the deaths of the fifty-one American servicemen killed in Vietnam in 1962, would have been considered unnecessary, unpatriotic. By 1970 President Nixon was claiming that his "Silent Majority" held the same attitude toward contemporary protesters. But yesterday's radical is today's moderate; yesterday's Jeremiah, today's voice of reason. Dr. Spock's moral outrage against the Indochina war did not change from the moment he first opposed it in 1963. His milieu did.

At no time, either before joining the peace movement or after becoming one of its most prominent spokesmen and symbols, has Dr. Spock been a pacifist. He explains, "I thought we ought to get into the war against Hitler long before we actually did. I supported the NATO alliance and the Marshall Plan as defenses against what I took to be Stalin's expansionism. In 1950 I agreed that the United States, as part of the United Nations police action, should go to the aid of South Korea when it was invaded by North Korea, though I think differently today." But the Indochina war was different in Spock's eyes, and he was at a different stage in his life and able to respond to such a political and moral problem with far more time and independence than he had before been able to.

For the first three years after its founding in 1957 by Norman Thomas, pacifist A. J. Muste, and *Saturday Review* editor Norman Cousins, the small, intellectual National Committee for a Sane Nuclear Policy had consistently condemned United States foreign and armament policies in its efforts to stop nuclear testing. SANE had first invited Dr. Spock's sponsorship shortly after it was founded, and he declined. When SANE asked him again in 1960, its officers were seeking reputability, for they were about to expel some of their members for taking the Fifth Amendment before Senator Thomas Dodd's Internal Security Subcommittee. The well-spoken Dr. Spock epitomized liberal respectability and would have appealed to just the sort of moderate liberals that SANE was hoping to attract. So inoffensive was Spock that even as late as 1966 he was named in *New York Times* columnist Russell Baker's quasi-serious "Inducing a State of Sneerlessness" as one of the "ten American phenomena that even the most highly-paid curmudgeon would not have the courage to dip in acid."

But Dr. Spock said "No," replying with the type of letter that he had used, with variations, to avoid lending his name and influence to a multitude of causes, from the Planned Parenthood League, to Integrated Education, Inc., to No War Toys, to the Emergency Civil Liberties National Council. To SANE he wrote: "I am in agreement with [your] policy. . . . But when I was first asked to participate in its work a couple of years ago I declined on the following basis: I have no expert knowledge at all about the relationship between radiation and health. . . . If I were to take any official part in the work of the Committee I think that many parents would assume 1) that I was, to some degree, an expert and 2) that as an expert I was alarmed by the present dangers of irradiation.

"To put it another way: I have tried as parent educator to be non-alarmish, and I want to save my influence to use in areas in which I feel I have competence. 3) To put it a third way: I'm always under pressure to participate actively or nominally in many children's causes. I have to limit myself strictly. I join the cause only if it is clear to me that it is one that will make appreciable use of my knowledge and experience.

"As you can see from my protesting I feel ashamed to turn you down, but I have to. I hope you . . . will forgive me."

Two years later SANE asked again. Again, on January 17, 1962, he proffered his customary refusal. But in the next month a number of events caused Dr. Spock to change his mind. Unitarian minister Homer Jack, then SANE's director, replied to his refusal with a quotation from Philipp Frank's biography of Albert Einstein: "Einstein realized that the great fame that he had acquired placed a great responsibility upon him. He considered that it would be egotistic and conceited if he simply accepted the fact of his recognition and continued to work on his research. He saw that the world was full of suffering and he thought he knew some causes. He also saw that there were many people who pointed out these causes but were not heeded because they were not prominent figures. Einstein realized that . . . . he could command public attention and he was not afraid, if necessary, to stake his reputation . . . [and to accept the fact] that many of his political opponents would also become his scientific opponents."

Mrs. Dagmar Wilson, the vivaciously determined organizer of Women Strike for Peace, claims for her organization part of the credit for Dr. Spock's conversion: "We broke the paper curtain. Our first Women Strike demonstration at the White House, in January '62, to support a test ban treaty, put women's news on the front pages for the first time since the suffragette movement. The sight of us out there on that cold, snowy day touched President Kennedy, who sent out coffee to warm us. Hearing about it touched Dr. Spock; he told us later that he decided if a group of mothers, with our gay anger, could picket for peace, he could do it too."

Marvin and Janet Rosenberg, members of Cleveland SANE, claim some influence too. About this time they asked Dr. Spock, their counselor in the Child Rearing Study, whether they should switch their twins from whole milk, likely to be contaminated by fallout, to safer powdered milk. Dr. Spock, previously unaware of the problem, studied the matter, concluded that it was appalling for children to have to live in a world where even the best pediatric care couldn't protect them from fallout or other nuclear disaster, and decided to do something about it.

Dr. Spock acknowledges these influences but says that the moment of truth came in February 1962 when he listened to President Kennedy's words as he resumed nuclear testing. "For a long time," says Dr. Spock, "I'd been on the—I hate to say hawkish—strong armament side. In his 1960 campaign Kennedy said he thought that Eisenhower and his Secretary of the Treasury George Humphrey had economized so much that there was a missile gap, as well as a complete lack of preparation for an ordinary non-nuclear war. I was convinced. But then after Kennedy's election it turned out that there was no missile gap—we were well ahead of the Soviet Union.

"There had been an informal agreement between the United States and the Soviet Union to refrain from testing, which the Soviets publicly broke in the fall of '61, because they were way behind us in the development of nuclear arms. Kennedy first tried to persuade them to stop, and they wouldn't.

"Then in February 1962 President Kennedy announced that he'd gone into the matter of nuclear testing with his advisors at great depth. They had assured him that we were well ahead of the Soviet Union in every respect; however, if we didn't resume testing, conceivably someday the Russians might catch up to us. I didn't argue with Kennedy's political position. I think he *did* have to resume testing, or he might have been impeached. But the illogic of it suddenly struck me. Obviously you can't decline to test if you're behind. But Kennedy said that even though we're well *ahead* we've got to test. In other words, there's *nothing* to stop the testing, [with increasing earnestness] there's *nothing* to stop the accumulation unless the people rise up and demand it. I also suddenly realized that it wasn't just a question of whether the United States and the Soviet Union could trust each other enough to agree to stop testing and arming, but of all the countries of the world wanting nuclear arms and adding to them as fast as they could possibly afford it. Then it's only a matter of time before the world blows up."

So, on February 28, 1962, he accepted SANE's invitation to become a national sponsor. He had eminent company. There were international sponsors Pablo Casals, Gunnar Myrdal, Francois Mauriac, Lord Bertrand Russell, and Albert Schweitzer; and national sponsors Harry Belafonte, Helen Gahagan Douglas, Ray Bradbury, Dr. Martin Luther King, Jr., Walter Reuther, David Riesman, Louis Untermeyer, among others.

More often than not, the role of a national sponsor of any organization is purely symbolic if he himself has become a symbol. His name adds luster to a letterhead, visibility to an obscurity, prestige to a promotion or fund-raising. But characteristically, once Spock has made a choice, whether of job, spouse, recreation, writing, he pursues it with the devotion of a lover and the zeal of a messiah.

SANE wasted no time in publicizing his acceptance. William Bernbach, SANE board member and partner in Doyle, Dane, Bernbach, offered his advertising agency's services to place a full-page ad in the *New York Times* to proclaim Dr. Spock's views. Laughs Spock, "This was quite an opportunity when they said, 'You can have a whole page of the *New York Times* to give a message to the world.' I felt that I had to establish relatively unassailable reasons for becoming a peace person and for persuading others to do so, too. For I could already anticipate being challenged all over the place by the press and the public.

"So for a month I wrote incessantly to clarify my own views— anytime that I wasn't doing something else that was absolutely obligatory. I wrote and destroyed and wrote and destroyed and wrote and destroyed. Finally I ended up with a 4,000-word statement that I thought was pretty good; I jokingly called it 'The Manifesto.' Then I asked Doyle, Dane, Bernbach, 'How many words are you going to use for this ad?' and they said, 'Well, less than 400.'

"Having spent a month on this, it was like an abortion to destroy the thing I had just created, by reducing it to ten percent of its size. Then I took the 400 words to the agency and talked with a young executive who very politely suggested that I leave out half of it, the parts in which I was arguing with an imaginary adversary. He said such a reader would immediately dismiss everything else I'd said because of the parts he disagreed with. In retrospect I think he was very wise, but the further cut nearly killed me at the time. The result was an almost purely moral statement."

Then came the problem of a photograph to accompany the text. "The photographer," says Dr. Spock, "took at least 4,000 pictures in two hours. The child in the picture was one year old, a very restless age. But she was extraordinarily patient, for she sat on an examining table playing with my watch chain all that time. I had written in my appointment book that somebody was coming, but I'd forgotten what it was about, and that day I was wearing a very old double-breasted suit with out-of-style peaked lapels. It wasn't even very well pressed. Afterward I apologized for the suit, but Doyle, Dane, Bernbach thought it was good, for it gave a slightly country-doctor touch."

On April 16, 1962, the country doctor appeared in the *New York Times* advertisement illustrating what was to be one of SANE's themes for the next several years, "Dr. Spock Is Worried." The poster-sized picture showed an elderly, bespectacled, balding (the photograph was cropped to cut off his hair) man with a Gandhiesque face, sunken and sorrowing, looking down at a little girl innocently intent on the object in her hands. (It was such a surprising contrast to Dr. Spock's real life appearance of youthfully animated cheerfulness that Jane hid the original poster behind the living room couch and refused to look at it.)

In seven short paragraphs Dr. Spock announced: "I *am* worried. Not so much about the effect of past tests but at the prospect of endless future ones. As the tests multiply, so will the damage to children—here and around the world.

"Who gives us this right?

"Some citizens would leave all the thinking to the government. They forget the catastrophic blunders that governments have made throughout history.

"There are others who think that superior armaments will solve the problem. They scorn those who believe in the strength of a just cause. They have forgotten that a frail idealist in a loin cloth compelled the British to back out of India.

"There are dangers in any course. I would rather we took small risks today if there is hope of lessening the enormous risks which lie ahead.

"And if I am to be destroyed through some miscalculation I would prefer to be destroyed while we are showing leadership in the search for a cooperative world than while sitting in an illusory fortress blaming our opponents for the lack of a solution.

"In a moral issue, I believe that every citizen has not only the right but the responsibility to make his own feelings known and felt."

SANE's staff was delighted to nurture this moralistic image of the man who was to become their most vivid proselytizer. Says Donald Keys, for four years SANE's executive director, "The most beautiful thing about Ben was his magnificent moral indignation. We were creating for him a public image of the sober, considered, powerful moral commentator, buttressed by access to every aspect of American life and a wealth of resources. All Ben had to do was to stand there and absorb it."

During the time of his apprenticeship in politics Dr. Spock was willing to do this. He explains, "I came to realize that if you're going to try to lead people you also have to let them tell you what kind of leader they need and to let those characteristics come to the fore.

It was clear from people's response to *Baby and Child Care* that they valued the benign side of me rather than the pediatric reformer, so I fell more and more into that role. The reaction to the SANE advertisement suggested I could probably help the peace movement more by being the benign person rather than the cantankerous one—at least, most of the time."

In regard to his awareness of his public image in general Dr. Spock says, "I really don't think of myself as a public person until somebody recognizes me. I feel like a private citizen. This is lucky, because it would be an awful strain to be as self-conscious about being an author or a peace person as I've been about other things in the past, for instance, to be walking down the street wondering what people were thinking and whether I was making the right impression."

Jane disagrees and complains, "Every time we walk down the street someone recognizes Ben, so we have to be careful. We can't look cross or have an argument in public. But I treat Ben like an ordinary person. I'm the only one in the world who speaks frankly to Ben, because I'm not in awe of him."

"Even so," adds Dr. Spock, "my first two years in the peace movement were very painful as I was trying to find out what I needed to know to be able to reply to the questions and challenges, especially from hostile interviewers and hostile audiences. For a while I used to worry every time I had a press conference. I couldn't wait to read the paper to see if they quoted me right or whether I'd said something disastrous, but from habituation I've become fatalistic about that. It's rare to be quoted with complete accuracy, so I don't worry unless I'm put in a very bad light. Trying to get a press conference for an unpopular cause like disarmament is just a business; you have to be somewhat satisfied to get any publicity at all."

To promote its views, SANE occasionally took to the streets, not with tumultuous demonstrations, but with quiet, placard-carrying marches which on special occasions attracted a few thousand participants, but routinely involved only a faithful few hundred. In 1962 the Cleveland SANE chapter of a hundred active members (in a city of a million), invigorated by Dr. Spock's adherence to their cause, invited him to join their symbolic Easter walk down

Cleveland's principal street to Public Square. He agreed, and with mixed emotions beneath a smiling facade and his wife on one arm, he participated in his first peace march. In "The Professional Man's Muzzle," published in the *American Journal of Orthopsychiatry* in January 1965, Dr. Spock describes his experience:

"I suspect that a majority of the professional and business people who have marched or picketed for some cause such as a nuclear test ban or integration would confess, as I do, that though they were very glad they did it, they found the experience to be personally painful and embarrassing. . . .

"In a civil demonstration one usually is shuffling along without style or rhythm. . . . One feels like a two-legged squirrel in a public cage. Even in the situation where there is no threat of violent reaction, one is acutely conscious of being in the minority. A few of the onlookers make crude remarks, but these aren't too painful because one can dismiss them as senseless.

"Quite disconcerting, though, is the reaction of the majority of passers-by. They look at the signs and the marchers with a baffled expression, as if they had never heard of the issue. This gives the demonstrator a nightmarish sense of being on the wrong planet. He feels shorn of purpose and dignity. Hardest to take are the people who smile contemptuously and shake their heads, or the reporters who ask cynical questions as if they thought a collection of stuffed-shirts had been caught in a vice raid. These condescending ones don't specify just what their criticism is, so the demonstrator can't rebut. Their scorn gets right through to his own conscience and stirs up his *own* doubts. He wonders, not about the cause he's upholding, but about whether he has gone off half-cocked, for instance, or is hurting the dignity of the organization which employs him and trusts him, or is perhaps just an exhibitionist."

He continues, explaining why he feels that doctors, particularly psychiatrists, should publicly defend just causes: "We are the ones who know how irrational discrimination is. We know that it is cruel and disfiguring to its victims. We know that it warps the thinking of each new generation of discriminators. We know that it corrupts the souls of those who disapprove but fail to lend their weight. . . ."

Dr. Spock's solution is to suggest what he himself does: to write articles and letters to the editors of professional and popular magazines, to speak, to picket. "If more of us were willing to be bold," he concludes, "then boldness would become more respectable."

Though obsessed with his cause, Dr. Spock tried hard not to bother or embarrass colleagues who he knew were unsympathetic to his views. But as he saw less of some of them, he and Jane began to find many new friends among the "peace people." The first such friends were from SANE, which has typically attracted white, middle-aged to elderly, middle income, respectably bourgeois liberals. Typical SANE members are earnest, highly principled and highly committed, and articulate; some are extremely argumentative, though always on firm principle. But they didn't argue with Dr. Spock, at least not for his first five years as SANE's principal speechmaker, fund raiser, and, from 1963 to 1967, national co-chairman with Harvard historian H. Stuart Hughes, grandson of Supreme Court Chief Justice Charles Evans Hughes.

They listened. And before this audience Dr. Spock was publicly worried. Before the escalation of the war in Vietnam in 1965 he talked on "The Cold War—Trauma or Challenge?" "What Are the Real Dangers of the Cold War?" "The Cold War and Children," and "Raising Our Children in a Cold War Age." He always emphasized the effects of the Cold War on children, especially the emotional hazards, feeling that with this approach he was granted more credibility: "Recent studies show that American children are being made increasingly anxious by the Cold War. Between a quarter and a half of them . . . expect nuclear attack. Young ones worry most about being poisoned by fallout, about being separated from their parents in a disaster, about the maiming or death of their families and themselves. Adolescents speak with some bitterness about the uncertainty of their futures, about the possibility of their giving birth to deformed children, about the futility of working too hard at school. Children have also been infected with an unhealthy suspiciousness. When a 5th grade class, for example, was looking at a picture of the Russian countryside, which showed a tree-lined road, and one child asked what the trees were for, others quickly suggested, 'So that people won't know what's going on beyond the road' and 'It's to make work for the [political] prisoners.' "

His solutions sounded simpler than their implications. With your children minimize fear by minimizing alarm. Try to understand and urge communication with Communist nations to build mutual trust, ease political tension, and progress toward universal disarmament. Join peace groups. March. Write legislators. Work to solve chronic unemployment, racial injustice, urban blight. Imbue children with generosity of spirit, for "Our hope is our children. Children . . . aren't afraid of bold ideas. They can respond to a cause with great idealism." Dr. Spock encouraged, "Don't be intimidated. The worst fault, I think, is to feel indignant but to do nothing about it. That is a self-indulgence, a form of self-pity, that does no good for the world and corrupts the soul. . . . Only action counts."

Dr. Spock gave such addresses to SANE locals and other groups ranging from several hundred to several thousand, throughout the Northeast, along the West Coast, and in Chicago, St. Louis, and Cleveland. He earned between $200 and $1,000 for SANE with each speech, and netted the organization over $15,000 a year. He paid his own expenses on speaking tours, which added up to $4,000 in a busy year; if reimbursed, he donated that money to SANE too.

His activity inspired audiences, but his early speeches were not so inspiring, for the relaxed, warm good humor that pervaded his talks on child rearing had been replaced by tense moral indignation. In the early sixties he carefully threaded his way through the maze of literature on disarmament, radiation, world government, and areas of world stress, more ready to learn than to teach. As his knowledge grew (gained mostly from the *New York Times, I. F. Stone's Weekly, The New Republic, Marshall Windmiller Reports, Bulletin of Atomic Scientists, Nuclear Information, War/Peace Report,* and piles of pamphlets) so did his assurance, though he has never claimed political or military expertise beyond what any layman could glean from reading the same sources.

Then the Dr. Spock people had hoped to see appeared again on the lecture platform. His honesty was still there, so was his absolutist morality, but he was again able to laugh at himself, able to find humor in the most serious of situations without undervaluing their gravity. He could even see the humor in the sniping of William Buckley's conservative *National Review,* which published "The Spockery of Dr. Quack" as a commentary on his speeches for SANE:

> I do not love thee, Dr. Spock.
> The thing is this: I've got a block
> Against the sort of seedy hat tricks
> You're sneaking into pediatrics.

Let a mother ask you why
Her kid is nervous—*you* reply
She's stuffed the moppet's head with rot
About a Communistic plot
And if she only had a brain
She'd run right out and go in SANE.
Well, Mom, let me say beware
Of all this bogus baby care,
And don't let Benjy muddle you.
You know more than you think you do.

Dr. Spock was busy. In addition to his varied professional activities at Western Reserve and his monthly magazine articles and other writing chores, he was accelerating his public activities for peace to the level of a political campaign. The speaking tours for SANE were hectic. Dr. Spock explains: "The local committeemen get excited and see a chance of squeezing some more value out of you, so they ask, 'How about having lunch with a dozen rich people who might make a significant contribution?' Well, you wouldn't mind having lunch with them and saying a few words, but then you've got to think of some words you're not going to use at the big meeting if you don't like to repeat yourself.

"Here's a peace group that's been desperate to get on radio or TV for a year and they can't insert themselves for five minutes because no commentator is interested in peace. But if you've got Spock there in the flesh, all of a sudden the radio and TV stations are interested in interviewing him. Maybe they'd ask questions about child care, but they would be willing to throw in one or two like 'By the way, what are you in town for?' and then I'd get in a fast little speech about peace.

"The pressure can be terrific, especially in a place like Los Angeles. I was there once for two days and was literally rushed from one station to another, to a luncheon, to a press interview, to a fund-raising cocktail party, to a reception after the big speech. I'd still be in one studio talking to an interviewer on the air and the person who had me in tow would be gesticulating through the control window [Spock mimes and grimaces] mouthing, 'Hurry up! We've got to go! It's almost time for the other program!' I'd start to get up from the table and the interviewer would say, 'Doctor, can I ask you just one more question? What general bit of advice would you have for American parents?' These situations used to get me quite tensed up."

Early in 1964 when Dr. Spock was testifying in Washington before the House Ways and Means Committee for Medicare, the tension culminated in what was diagnosed as auricular flutter, a functional heart disorder. He had left Cleveland early in the morning, arrived at the hearing room by 10 a.m., but had to wait to testify until 5:45 p.m. Meanwhile, TV and radio interviewers were continually summoning him to the corridor for interviews, particularly disconcerting because crowds of sightseers would stop to watch. During lunch with three hundred Golden Agers from New York who had also come to lobby, he received a request to call a local number which turned out to be a radio newsman who said, "I want to ask you some questions and the tape is running."

This unexpected interview in a phone booth proved to be the final straw, and Dr. Spock's pulse jumped to a beat of 240 a minute, accompanied by slight breathlessness and weakness. He had experienced similar symptoms a number of times since becoming involved in politics, but they had disappeared in an hour or two. This time they didn't. After Dr. Spock gave the interview, finished his lunch, testified at the hearing, and returned to Cleveland, he had to be kept in the hospital for four days before his heart was finally induced to calm down. His doctor sternly restricted him to one out-of-town trip a month and only one event a day when he was traveling, and Spock was sufficiently impressed to stick to this schedule for half a year. As a result, among the invitations he had to refuse was Ambassador Chester Bowles's request that he consult and lecture in India for several months as a good-will ambassador under the American Specialists Program for the State Department.

But after six months had passed free of symptoms, Dr. Spock gradually stepped up his pace, and since then has been busier than ever, with no trace of auricular flutter or other medical problem except, in 1971, a recurrence of his back strain, from hours of plane riding. He explains cheerfully, "Some fundamental shift has happened inside. I seem to be no longer afraid of being caught without an answer or afraid of being attacked for my position. I'm actually enjoying this political life more than any previous phase of my career. I almost never get nervous."

Though Dr. Spock had slowed in 1964 from a tornado to merely a gentle whirlwind, he became more deeply involved in politics. As a spokesman for the peace movement he felt obligated to participate in a Presidential campaign in which the candidates took opposite positions on peace and war. Along with Buckminster Fuller, General James Gavin, Drs. Michael DeBakey and Paul Dudley White, and other eminent scientists, Dr. Spock accepted an invitation to work for Scientists and Engineers for Johnson-Humphrey. Judging from their brochures, Scientists and Engineers, like many liberal groups in the '64 campaign, seemed more eager to demonstrate the unfitness of Senator Barry Goldwater, an avowed hawk, for the Presidency than to show the suitability of President Johnson. They spent most of their efforts damning Goldwater with his own remarks: "The child has no right to an education. In most cases the children will get along very well without it"; "Sometimes I think this country would be better off if we could just saw off the Eastern Seaboard and let it float out to sea"; and "Extremism in the defense of liberty is no vice."

Dr. Spock's rebuttal on national television of these remarks drew fire from a number of Goldwater supporters, mostly Texans and Californians. One fumed, "Fallout-Schmallout! I guess you would rather treat children dominated by the Red Flag rather than children under the Stars & Stripes. Nuclear-test-ban:-Bah! Are you not intelligent enough to comprehend that since the Russians think they can win, *they will push* the button?

"However, they don't want war—they want to subvert us with Pacifism and then we will fall . . . without a shot being fired! Can't you fuzzy-thinking people realize that Peace is *guaranteed* by strength? A pox on you!"

And a parent who returned to Dr. Spock a well-thumbed copy of *Baby and Child Care* with "Traitor" scrawled across it argued, "In view of the fact that you could make such 'wild, irresponsible statements' about Senator Goldwater . . . I feel that there is no alternative but to discontinue buying your books on child care— that is, if you were not misquoted by the reptile press. My 4½ year old daughter will get along fine without parental advice from you."

To all his critics (no one wrote to praise his advocacy of Johnson) Dr. Spock politely but firmly reiterated his position, as he had done earlier in response to attacks on his support of Stevenson. Encouraged by President Johnson's programs of domestic legislation, particularly in civil rights and health care, and impressed by his contention that "We are not about to send American boys nine or ten thousand miles from home to do what Asian boys ought to be doing for themselves," Dr. Spock spoke out for Johnson often and emphatically, on radio, TV, and in the newspapers. The most widely received was a half-hour television discussion in which Spock and such science advisors to Presidents and the Pentagon as Harvard chemistry professor Dr. George Kistiakowsky and M.I.T. Dean of Science Dr. Jerome Wiesner took turns blasting Goldwater. President Johnson is said to have been so pleased that he watched it three times.

Two days after Johnson's victory, Dr. Spock recalls, "The President himself called my office at Western Reserve. The secretaries were flustered, and dashed up and down the hall looking for me, thinking he was about to offer me the Secretaryship of Health, Education, and Welfare." But Dr. Spock was in Hartford, Connecticut, visiting his sister Betty and his mother, when the phone rang. "I happened to answer it," he says, "just being useful, and was startled to hear a friendly drawl say, 'This is Lyndon Johnson. Is Dr. Spock there?' I said, 'This is he.' And he said, 'I want to *thank* you [Spock's accent adopts overtones of a Texas drawl], I want to *thank* you for what you did during the campaign. I'm deeply appreciative.' And then he said, in this humble voice [Spock sounds humble], 'I *hope* I will be worthy of your trust.' I was so embarrassed to have the President of the United States hoping to be worthy of *my* trust that I cried, 'Oh, President Johnson, I'm *sure* you will,' little knowing that within three months he would have betrayed me and the millions of other Americans who voted for him because he said he was the peace candidate."

A month after the election the Spocks were again invited to dinner at the White House. With typical Johnsonian eclecticism, the guest list included not only the most prominent Scientists and Engineers for Johnson-Humphrey, but Mayor Daley of Chicago, DAR President-General Mrs. Robert Duncan, Metropolitan Opera Manager Rudolph Bing, and TV cowboy star Dan Blocker. The guest of honor was British Prime Minister Harold Wilson. At the reception an interviewer asked Dr. Spock his opinion of the proposed Multilateral Nuclear Force, a fleet of surface naval vessels armed with nuclear weapons and manned by crews from the NATO powers and West Germany. Dr. Spock had tried in vain two weeks earlier to tell President Johnson personally of his opposition, and he announced to the reporter, "I would get out and picket the White House tonight against MLF if it was necessary."

Within four months Dr. Spock was in fact picketing the White House, on a SANE-organized rally to promote general, complete, inspected universal disarmament (one of SANE's prime goals after a limited nuclear test ban treaty had been concluded in 1963).

Both as SANE co-chairman and as a citizen, Dr. Spock had hoped that President Johnson would fulfill his campaign promises of August and September 1964 when he said in separate speeches, "[The South Vietnamese] ask us to take reckless action which might risk the lives of millions and engulf much of Asia and certainly threaten the peace of the entire world. Moreover, such action would offer no solution at all to the real problem of Viet-Nam." "So we are not going north and we are not going south; we are going to continue to try to get them to save their own freedom with their own men, with our leadership and officer direction [20,000 men at the time of Johnson's election] and such equipment as we can furnish them."

But by February 1965 General Khanh, "neutral" toward the United States, had overthrown the pro-western South Vietnamese Premier Huong. President Johnson, refusing to discuss a negotiated settlement, had announced that he would resist aggression from the north and make American aid "more effective." The Viet Cong had raided American barracks at Pleiku and American jets had retaliated by beginning a restrained aerial bombardment of North Vietnam. Escalation had begun, in spite of UN Secretary General U Thant's repeated appeals for negotiation, and by the end of 1965 there were 170,000 American troops in Vietnam.

As the trend of events became clear, Dr. Spock's worry became mingled with astonishment and outrage at what he believed was President Johnson's betrayal of those who had voted for him as a peace candidate. The day after the State Department revealed that the United States was supplying South Vietnam with a "non-lethal gas which disables temporarily," on March 23, 1965, Dr. Spock communicated his assessment of the situation to President Johnson in a letter that turned out to be prophetic: "I am particularly dis-

mayed that the State and Defense Departments base our South
Vietnam policy on two assumptions which are denied in large part
by history and impartial observers: that we are there to preserve
the freedom of the people and that our lack of success is due primarily to interference from North Vietnam.

"I and many other people—in America and in friendly nations—
would summarize the situation as follows:

> Secretary Dulles in 1956 encouraged Diem to refuse to allow the elec-
> tion specified by the Geneva Agreement of 1954, in which it was
> expected by everyone that the South Vietnamese would vote by a large
> majority in favor of joining North Vietnam. (In my opinion Mr. Dulles
> was not defending freedom.)

> The Viet Cong, according to non-governmental observers, is still getting
> plenty of reinforcements and arms from Saigon deserters, and could
> continue the war indefinitely if aid from the North were cut off.

> There is little likelihood that the Viet Cong and the North Vietnamese,
> who believe their cause is the just one . . . and who defeated a large
> French army, will desist because of the demand of a foreign country.

"I believe that our present policy is militarily foolhardy, morally
wrong, and detrimental to our country's cause in its rivalry with
Communism."

President Johnson's reply led Spock to conclude that Johnson
was committing himself irrevocably to what seemed a brutal, per-
fidious, and disastrous policy. But he ingenuously assumed that
Hubert Humphrey, whose judgment and decency he had come to
respect in efforts to promote civil rights and to end poverty, would
first use all his influence to change the President's mind and, failing that, might even break with him publicly. So he wrote a long,
heart-to-heart letter to Humphrey, similar to that to Johnson, very
supportive of what he assumed the Vice President's independent
and rebellious views would be.

As a more politically sophisticated observer might have expected,
Humphrey's reply supported the President:

"We are not in Viet-Nam because of any imperialistic notions,
and no one in a position of major responsibility—civilian or military—has any illusions about the dangers we face. We are in South
Viet-Nam to help that country repel aggression from its northern
neighbor. . . .

"We have neither yielded to aggression nor precipitated war. President Johnson's prudent and firm policies are designed to preserve the freedom of South Viet-Nam without risking undue U.S. military involvement."

Spock was still outraged over this reply when he explained in 1971, "To hear these rantings coming from Humphrey was somehow more horrifying, more nightmarish, than hearing them from Johnson."

However, on November 27, 1965, Vice President Humphrey received a delegation from a SANE-organized "March on Washington for Peace in Vietnam," including Mrs. Martin Luther King, Jr., Norman Thomas, and Dr. Spock. Before meeting with the Vice President, Dr. Spock addressed the marchers, estimated at between 15,000 and 35,000. He affirmed their patriotism and said, "Patriotism surely does not consist in cheering your country on when you believe it is heading in a fatally wrong direction."

He pointed out that "Repeatedly our top military men have warned against the folly of our becoming involved in a land war in Asia—which is just where we find ourselves today. Though we had no lasting success against the Viet Cong forces of approximately 50,000 men, we are now provoking a North Vietnamese army of 400,000 and challenging the millions of Chinese soldiers behind them. None of our allies is willing to give us more than token assistance and our European allies disapprove so strongly that they won't even make a gesture."

Dr. Spock concluded, ironically prophetic of events that were to occur in the next six years, uttering sentiments which would have struck many, had they listened, as utterly at variance with the American myth of its military invincibility on foreign shores: "So we see our country blundering deeper and deeper into a war which it cannot possibly win, a war which will bring first tens of thousands of casualties and ultimately hundreds of thousands of American casualties, a war which never was in the best interests of our country, most certainly a war which is incompatible with the ideals of our country as we understand them, a war that has earned us the scorn of people everywhere."

The Vice President listened politely and discussed with Dr. Spock and the delegation the matter of stopping the bombing, but it was apparent that the rapport was gone which the two had enjoyed only a year before, when the Vice President-elect had written to Dr. Spock, "What a delight it was to see both of you at the White House on Monday evening. . . . Mrs. Humphrey and I enjoyed our brief visit. We only hope that we can have the privilege of seeing you often."

By late 1965 the Administration was treating the antiwar views of Dr. Spock, called sardonically by *Time* "The Great Pacifier," no differently from those of any other outspoken, antagonistic citizen. However, until the winter of '65 President Johnson or his staff had invited Dr. Spock to participate in various meetings of national significance—the White House Conference on International Cooperation, the White House Conference on Education—and to be a member of the National Advisory Council to the Office of Economic Opportunity. As an OEO advisor, Dr. Spock met several times yearly with fellow advisors, including John Kenneth Galbraith, Archbishop Lucy of San Antonio, Urban League president Whitney Young, *Ebony* publisher John H. Johnson, and the wife of Defense Secretary Robert McNamara. Together the group reviewed the work of the OEO and made suggestions, considering particularly its efforts to improve the status of various minority groups in America, and its Youth Corps and Job Corps programs. In one of the many OEO reorganizations, the Advisory Council was disbanded in the winter of 1965. Dr. Spock was not included among its reconstituted membership, nor did the Johnson administration ever again seek his advice. Spock assumes this was a deliberate ostracism, for an administration rarely appoints public critics.

In the interests of peace, Dr. Spock was also becoming more deeply involved in political activities only tangentially related to SANE—campaigning in the '66 primaries in fifteen states through assorted media and personal appearances for peace candidates for national and local offices. A few of them won, notably Senator Stephen Young (D.) from Ohio. Most of them lost, such as Chicago's Clark Kissinger whose city council campaign slogan snarled, "If a machine short changes you, KICK IT!"

In Cleveland Dr. Spock offered his services to liberal Congressional candidate Jack Day—"I'd be willing to go out on the sound truck if I'm not too much of a liability because of extreme antiwar views." On Day's behalf, pied-piper-like he led a parade of children sporting campaign buttons and balloons around a suburban shopping center. For Day, Spock spent his sixty-third birthday distributing literature door-to-door. Though Jane admired Day, she was irritated with her husband and the campaign manager for this non-specialized use of so many of her husband's hours of work and felt that his unique influence might have been employed much more effectively.

As a campaigner, Dr. Spock would ring the doorbell, introduce himself, and recite a short speech on Day's political virtues: "He is fighting for fresh air, for clean water, for more funds for education . . . and a safer world. He is opposed to all wars." His reception was varied. One homeowner thundered, "I've done without your advice all my life and I'll do without it now!" and ordered Spock off the premises. Women were happier to see him, and one suburbanite, on learning who he was, hugged him and invited him in for a cup of coffee and a chat about child rearing. He accepted. But Day lost anyway.

In 1965 Dr. Spock also began to attend the weekly meetings of the University Circle Teach-In Committee, a group of antiwar Case and Western Reserve faculty and graduate students. Here he became friends with sociology professor Sidney Peck, a fortyish, sweet-faced, soulful-eyed radical who uttered the doves' militant language in accents of love. For the next two years Dr. Peck's politics were to be the radical rabbit running before Dr. Spock's greyhound liberalism.

In the fall of '66 the Teach-In Committee organized the second of several marathon teach-ins against the war, in which Dr. Spock participated. It was followed by an all-night vigil at Cleveland's Public Square (Dr. Spock went home to bed), and continued the next day by speeches, including Spock's. Then the group marched to an induction center to invade it and to distribute anti-draft leaflets to spectators and inductees alike. Dr. Spock declined to participate in this march, for at that time, he says, "I didn't feel I had any business in forcing my way into somebody else's property." So he stayed inside the law, for the time being.

At the same time Dr. Spock was continuing to protest the war in more conventional ways as SANE's major spokesman. During the academic year of '65–66 he spent a great deal of time either on the road or on the phone for SANE. (One skeptical long-distance operator demurred at placing a person-to-person call from Dr. Spock to Marlon Brando on location in Tahiti. "You gotta be kidding," she kept saying, until the pediatrician himself convinced her.) Because of this new emphasis, he contemplated retiring from teaching a year ahead of mandatory retirement at sixty-five to devote a third of his time to SANE and peace, a third to sailing, and the other third to writing. He was finding the efforts of peace groups to stop the war as challenging as he had previously found the new medical curriculum at Western Reserve (and as he had before that found his pediatric practice) ; as his commitment to peace increased, his responsibilities in teaching and research diminished proportionately. The refusal of a number of wealthy patrons to contribute money to the Medical School as long as that "dirty Red traitor" remained on the faculty made Spock feel that his continued presence might embarrass the University, though the Dean himself, Dr. Douglas Bond, remained unperturbed, recommending only that when faculty members spoke publicly on issues unrelated to their professional fields they clearly did so as private citizens.

As the war continued to escalate, to 380,000 American troops in Vietnam at the end of 1966 and costs of two billion dollars a month, Dr. Spock's commitment to end it intensified in ever more radical ways. He did decide to retire in June '67, just after his sixty-fourth birthday. He would return to Western Reserve at intervals to lecture to the Phase I students and to follow up on the Child Rearing Study. But, much to Jane's regret, he declined offers to join the faculties of some respected eastern medical schools, on his own terms. Such an affiliation, Jane felt, would lend him respectability when he needed it, and it would help to keep his medical knowledge current—essential in continued revisions of *Baby and Child Care*. He decided to have his office in New York, headquarters of many peace organizations, and Jane gracefully acquiesced, despite her wish to move to Boston where their sons were. So they moved to a one-bedroom apartment on

East 83rd Street, although their legal residence was to be a boat in the Virgin Islands, where they would spend the largest amount of their time.

So Dr. Spock spent the spring of '67 completing his duties at Case Western Reserve (Western Reserve University had just merged with adjacent Case Institute of Technology); trying to dovetail plans for peace strategy with SANE, the Teach-In Committee, and Dr. Martin Luther King, Jr.; and selling his house to a black physician and thereby integrating his neighborhood—with no fuss—and buying instead the *Carapace* for sailing in the Virgin Islands. In contrast to the Spocks' subdued departure from Pittsburgh twelve years earlier, their leavetaking in Cleveland was filled with testaments not only to the pediatrician's influence in child care and peace, but to the Spocks' enormous personal popularity; there were farewell breakfasts, luncheons, cocktail parties, and a public testimonial dinner attended by nine hundred well-wishers from medical organizations, peace groups, and the community in general. The nature of Dr. Spock's immense influence would change radically as he left Cleveland, but in ways unanticipated by either himself or the peace movement.

twelve |

RETIREMENT AND RADICALISM

Iɴ the fall of 1966, as Dr. Spock was preparing through his impending retirement for major changes in his life, the peace movement as a whole was also undergoing profound changes—that is, if a movement running the left-wing gamut from the 'Maoist' Progressive Labor Party, to the Students for a Democratic Society (then moving from radical to revolutionary tactics), to the leftist Young Socialist Alliance, to the politely bluestocking Women's International League for Peace and Freedom, to the somber Clergy and Laymen Concerned About the War in Vietnam, can ever be considered as a whole.

By this time the Johnson administration had transformed the internal struggle in Vietnam into a war largely directed and fought by Americans against the Viet Cong and the North Vietnamese. In November 1966 SANE summarized the situation: "The Ky regime's attempt to hold elections in September 1966 in the Saigon-controlled areas did nothing to change the reality of rule by a military junta. Under ground rules established by those in power, 'Communists' and 'neutralists' were forbidden to run for office. Those who did not vote were considered enemies of the regime and threatened with the loss of rice and the right to travel. Most of those who voted had little idea of what they were doing."

Despite President Johnson's professed willingness to negotiate a settlement, the American offers of peace talks were hedged with so many qualifications and conditions that they were never held. Hanoi repeatedly refused to negotiate under a bombing *pause*, rather than under a complete *cessation* of bombing, claiming that to do so would be equivalent to talking with a loaded gun on the conference table.

As the credibility gap widened, peace group incredibility hardened. The Johnson administration repeatedly refused to discuss its policies with members of the peace movement. Public policy took little heed of the pleas of the conservative segment of the left wing, which petitioned for "Negotiation Now." An immediate cease-fire was not to be considered, despite the efforts of a few sympathetic Senators.

As the Administration became more intransigent, the peace movement became more desperate—and more radical. The conventional means of communication between the people and their Government—letters, petitions, newspaper ads, speeches, rallies— appeared to have little visible effect. Consequently many of the peace groups sought more unconventional means to make their point that the war must end. Their more moderate members feared these measures would lead to violence; the most radical hoped they would do just that.

One such means was a peace and protest march, conventional enough in mode, unconventional in its anticipated mammoth size, called the Spring Mobilization to End the War in Vietnam. After the march the name of the continuing organization was changed to "National Mobilization Committee," the "Mobe"; in '69 it was changed again to the "New Mobilization Committee," "New Mobe"; in '70 renamed the "National Coalition Against War, Racism and Repression"; and in 1971 "firmly" labeled "Peoples Coalition for Peace and Justice"—not to be confused with the separate New Democratic Coalition, the National Peace Action Coalition, or the

Peoples Party (see Appendix). The march was to be held April 15, 1967 in New York at the UN Plaza and in San Francisco, United Nations birthplace. Though youth were to predominate in the march itself, its organizers were on the far side of the generation gap: A. J. Muste (82); Dagmar Wilson (defended by Dr. Spock during a HUAC investigation of Women Strike); Sid Peck; and Dave Dellinger, career pacifist, editor of *Liberation,* and later one of the Chicago Seven. Its aims were to "Tell it like it is to the world [through] the largest gathering in opposition to the war in the history of the American peace movement. . . . It will urge moral and political support for all young men of conscience who refuse to be drafted and to soldiers who refuse to fight an unjust war. It will assert the right of the people to make their own peaceful settlement when the Establishment is hell-bent on a military solution. It will assert that the American people reject the concept of the United States as the policeman of the world."

The Mobilization hoped to involve 150 antiwar groups ranging from the near right to the far left, and embracing a multitude of diverse and unrelated causes, from Red power to black power to Puerto Rican power to flower power, from the Catholic Peace Fellowship to World War II Veterans Against the War, to the National Conference for New Politics. A few of these groups, such as the Youth International Party (Yippies), were composed of precisely the bearded, barefooted (even in winter), turned-on, tuned-out contingents that SANE had always kept at fastidious arm's length.

In fact, in February 1966, Dr. Spock as SANE co-chairman had supported the action of the SANE board in dissociating the organization from a Fifth Avenue peace march that Muste was organizing. He explained, in a letter to Muste, that SANE wanted to "discreetly and tactfully avoid identification with distinctly provocative and radical appearing elements or demonstrations in the peace movement . . . because extreme positions effectively scare the moderates away. . . ." But at the same time he deplored in-fighting, unintentionally prophesying what was to occur in SANE itself within a year because of his own political coming-of-age: "Backbiting and in-fighting and doctrinal disputes have always been the curse of liberal organizations and are particularly inappropriate in the peace movement which has such a pathetically small number of adherents anyway. . . . I think it's better in a pinch to be embarrassed by the behavior of a fellow organization than to . . . split a group open."

So in June 1966 when plans for the Mobe were still nebulous and Sid Peck asked Dr. Spock to help organize it, the physician said "No." Dr. Spock explained later, with some amusement, "My visible personality, my image of gentleness, disingenuousness, and non-authoritarianism sometimes encourages people to try to control me. Sid Peck, whom I admire and trust, tried on a couple of occasions. I told Sid in June '66, 'You can use my name to the extent that you convince the SANE staff that it won't hurt SANE.' Sid never did convince them. But by August he was trying to list me as a sort of sponsor for the organizing meeting. I remember blowing up when talking to him from a phone booth in Southwest Harbor, Maine, where I was cruising. I didn't want to appear responsible for the Mobilization in any way since the SANE board might well refuse to participate, and I felt then that my first loyalty was to SANE. It would certainly be worse to pull out than not to join in the first place."

However, three months later Dr. Spock became disaffected with what he perceived as an excessively conservative and critical attitude of many SANE board members and staff toward other peace groups. He decided to bridge the chasm he saw between SANE and organizations composed of young activists; to accept co-chairmanship of the April 15, 1967 march; to be listed as a fund raiser for the radical, eclectic National Conference for New Politics [NCNP]; and to urge SANE to follow his new direction.

Some members of the SANE board agreed with Spock and wanted to give the SANE locals, generally more progressive than the national board, more voice in national SANE policy, alliance with other peace groups, and participation in the Mobe. SANE's executive director, Donald Keys, and others opposed such "ecumenical promiscuity" and wanted to stick to the "undecided American Middle" and moderation. Norman Cousins explains, "Some of the [Mobe's] leaders had black racist tendencies streaked with violence. Some were Viet Cong supporters. Some were opposed to negotiations. We couldn't control what those people would say or do, and we didn't want SANE to be taxed with ideas that most of us didn't share."

Dr. Spock, who often personalizes the theoretical and the abstract, angrily provided in 1967 a personalistic, psychological interpretation of SANE's opposition to his actions: "In some new situations I give people such as Don Keys the impression that I'm not only gentle, hesitant, but that I'm quite incapable of dealing with the world. I was certainly that way, and very cautious, when getting into the peace movement.

"But I understand a lot about the components and conflicts of the peace movement now. I once told the SANE board, 'If you want a leader, here I am. That's what you chose me to be, and I know what I'm doing.' It was very easy for me to see that SANE couldn't go on slapping in the face other organizations in the peace movement. SANE is scorned by many peace people around the country for being such a holier-than-thou, condescending, social climbing organization." Contradicting what he had written the year before to Muste, Spock speaking for himself now rather than for SANE said, "I now believe in leaning in the direction of recruiting more militant people into the peace movement rather than worrying over scaring off the timid ones. . . . I believe in going in with other groups as long as their aims are roughly those of SANE; I believe in solidarity."

Dr. Spock added, "It was perfectly clear in some of the strained discussions that Don's feelings were badly hurt. It was not just that he didn't approve of NCNP and the Mobilization. It was that I graduated from asking his advice about every move and usually taking it to deciding things on my own. But Don and some of the Board were afraid that I'd get off their reservation and might involve SANE in all kinds of trouble."

To the last point Keys acquiesces, with mild resignation: "I experienced Ben as a tremendously humane Yankee righteous person who could not tolerate injustice, who identified with youth but made this identification with political uncriticalness. We were all aware of the danger of Ben's isolating himself, and feared that he would become the messianic leader of the forlorn and the radically irrelevant left, thereby losing much of the credit and influence he had established as the leader of SANE."

Month after month SANE's national board meetings erupted with narcissistic scrutinizings. Constructive business was suspended for the airing of innuendoes and invectives, charges and countercharges, proposals and counterproposals, with Dr. Spock as the focal—and most vocal—point of the controversy.

By February 1967 the board had reached a compromise which, like many compromises, satisfied no one affected by it. By this time Dr. Martin Luther King, Jr., Nobel Peace Prize winner, acknowledging the intimate connection between peace, civil rights, and black welfare, had added his enormous prestige to the Mobe by agreeing to be its principal speaker. Nevertheless, the SANE board, Dr. Spock and others notwithstanding, decided not to endorse it. However, SANE would allow its members to participate as individuals; it could scarcely do otherwise without being repressive—an illiberal position for a peace organization.

So as an individual Dr. Spock participated as one of the Mobilization's most notable members. Though it involved other activities, the Mobe focused on a gigantic peace march and rally April 15, 1967—timed to attract college students during their spring vacation.

The Mobilizers, between 125,000 and 500,000 strong, depending on which of the widely varying newspaper estimates one accepts, over half of them under thirty, chanted ("Hey, hey, L.B.J., how many kids have you killed today?") and sang ("This land is your land . . .") as they surged with decorum down the thirty blocks from Central Park to the United Nations Plaza. Arm in arm Dr. King, Dr. Spock, and Jane led the march, flanked by Harry Belafonte, Supreme Court Justice William Douglas's wife Cathy, labor priest Msgr. Charles Rice of Pittsburgh, Sioux Chief Henry Crow Dog, and representatives of various peace groups, cordoned off from the following throng by Dr. King's funereally garbed bodyguards. The marchers came from the East Coast and the Midwest. (Half as many westerners congregated in San Francisco; southerners appeared to have stayed home, except for a contingent from Atlanta.) They traveled by foot, crutch, wheelchair, and baby carriage. Many wore business suits. Others wore work clothes and old military surplus with the insignias ripped off, the uniforms of the militantly peaceful; tricorn hats proclaiming "U.S.A. in 1776 —Viet Nam in 1967. Stop the War Now"; academic robes, ponchos, saris, dashikis, miniskirts, leather jackets; and sunglasses everywhere, in spite of the overcast skies. They wore signs on strings around their necks because sticks had been forbidden for fear of violence, though this turned out to be the first of the great non-violent peace marches during the Indochina war. Most of the placards lacked the grace and good humor of those who bore them: "I Don't Give a Damn for Uncle Sam," "Children Are Not Born to Burn," "No Vietnamese Ever Called Me Nigger," "Forced Democracy is Hypocrisy; Bring the Troops Home," "No Puerto Ricans in Viet Nam." The few hecklers' signs were wittier: "Draft Stokely," and "Dr. Spock Smokes Bananas." Cooed one matron, "If he smokes bananas, I'll smoke 'em too."

Folksingers Tom Paxton, Phil Ochs, Pete Seeger, and Peter, Paul, and Mary, who arrived spectacularly by helicopter, entertained the front ranks for an hour while waiting for the rear contingents to catch up ("We were waist deep in the Big Muddy, and the Big Fool said to push on"). Dr. Spock then briefly emphasized the Mobilization's inclusiveness: "*All* Americans who are opposed to the war [have been invited], people of all ages, people of all shades of political opinion"; and the marchers' patriotism: "Many of those Americans who strongly back Lyndon Johnson's war policy . . . assume that we ignore our country's peril and the fate of our fighting men. This is *not* true. We oppose this war because we believe this war is damaging to our country in every way."

Dr. King's speech, the focus of the afternoon and of the hundreds of reporters assembled, accentuated America's "untenable position morally and politically. We are left standing before the world glutted with wealth and power but morally constricted and impoverished. We are engaged in a war that seeks to turn the clock of history back and perpetuate white colonialism. . . .

"One of the greatest casualties of the war in Vietnam is the Great Society. . . . shot down on the battlefield of Vietnam. . . . It is estimated that we spend $322,000 for each enemy we kill, while we spend in the so-called war on poverty in America only about $53 for each person classified as 'poor.' And much of that $53 goes for salaries of people who are not poor."

In an impassioned climax Dr. King urged, "Let us save our national honor—STOP THE BOMBING. Let us save American lives and Vietnamese lives—STOP THE BOMBING. Let us take

a single instantaneous step to the peace table—STOP THE BOMB-
ING. . . . Let our voices ring out across the land to say the American
people are not vainglorious conquerors—STOP THE BOMBING."

In a democratic movement everybody has a voice. So for four
hours other speakers continued to sympathize with the plight of
Vietnam ("When you're being raped you don't want negotiation,
you want immediate withdrawal"), to attack the "imperialistic,
militaristic" United States establishment, and to urge "massive
social, economic and political reconstruction of the United States."
The morning's promising spring turned wintry as the speakers
earnestly droned on, all but incomprehensible through the distor-
tions of the loudspeakers that lined the two-mile parade route. The
devout audience, under 25 percent black, remained, momentarily
electrified by Stokely Carmichael, SNCC leader, whose differences
with Dr. King over black power and black racism were for the
moment subordinated to unity for a common cause. Carmichael
exploded: "There is a higher law than the law of Racist McNamara; there is a higher law than the law of the fool Dean Rusk;
there is a higher law than the law of the buffoon Lyndon Baines
Johnson." But though Carmichael's revolutionary implications
were there, he didn't spell them out.

After he had finished, the rhetoric was more subdued and so
were the marchers, grateful for the warmth of being jammed
together. And the march ended with neither bang nor whimper but
downpour, dispersing all to the nearby coffee shops and subways
with the same good cheer as if their side had just won a predictably
easy football victory.

But victory was not theirs. The Mobilization appears to have
influenced U.S. policymakers more in prospect than in retrospect.
In a speech to the League of Jewish Women the week before the
march, Vice President Humphrey, with tears in his eyes, had lamented, "America needs to tell the world of the lives it is saving.
We need to be known as a nation of peacemakers, not just peace
marchers."

As a result of the Mobe—and of the independent pleas of UN Sec-
cretary General U Thant and Pope Paul VI to stop the bombing—
the bombing did not stop, the fighting did not cease. In fact, in the
week immediately following the Mobe, and for many weeks there-

after, the war continued to intensify. In the month beginning April 20, 1967, U.S. planes battered Haiphong and other North Vietnamese targets that had previously been immune from attack: airfields, railways, power plants (which produced 90 percent of North Vietnam's electricity), an oil depot, an ammunition dump, various industries. Senator George McGovern led the Senate attack on this "new level of escalation . . . [which] has brought us one step closer to World War III involving the limitless legions of China backed by the enormous firepower of Soviet Russia." Within a month, the total tonnage of bombs dropped on North Vietnam exceeded a million, more than we dropped on Germany during World War II. Within nine months American troops in South Vietnam had increased to 500,000, with 100,000 more in Thailand and at sea off the Vietnamese coast. American casualties in 1967 exceeded the total of all the previous years of the war: dead, 9,353; wounded, 99,742.

Within a week after the Mobe, General William C. Westmoreland, commander of U.S. forces in South Vietnam, had flown back to the States to address the Senate and other groups—a trip scarcely casual or coincidental. Typically, before a meeting of the Associated Press on April 24, Westmoreland claimed that "American fighting men in South Vietnam were dismayed, and so am I, by recent unpatriotic acts here at home." These encourage the enemy to believe "he can win politically that which he cannot accomplish militarily," and make him "determined to continue his aggression from the North."

So the heat was on the home folks to show their opposition to the protesters, and the specific rebuttal came on May 13, as 50–70,000 flag-waving marchers, many of them union members, off-duty policemen, and veterans, paraded down Fifth Avenue in a hastily planned march to "Support Our Boys in Viet Nam." The marchers emphasized "Escalate, Don't Capitulate," "Burn Hanoi, Not Our Flag," "My Country Right or Wrong," "Down With the Reds," in clearly belligerent ways, attacking with shouts and fists bystanders who urged the war's end.

About the time of the Loyalty Day Parade, the Mobilization sponsors went to Washington to follow up their April demands by petitioning the President. At the White House gate the group waited for the President to allow them to come in and confer. When the futility of their mission became apparent, Dr. Spock gave a Presidential aide a copy of his familiar antiwar speech. As he was departing, an egg thrown by the anti anti-Vietnam war White Power Committee, which had gathered nearby to heckle, hit him on the right temple. Jane, ever by her husband's side on major peace missions, was horrified, more at the thought of what the weapon might have been than at the affront to her husband's dignity. Spock himself was torn between maintaining his decorum and discovering what had hit him. Curiosity won, and he found an eggshell perched atop his ear. To his amused disgust, the omnipresent reporters found his First (and Only, at this writing) Egging much more interesting than his speech or his purpose.

Minority groups of any sort are Lilliputians in a world of giants; they gain visibility and heart from the strength of numbers. One of the Mobilization's most important effects was the new vitality it gave to the peace movement itself—not just to the marchers, but to the organizations and causes they represented. It gave heart, for instance, to the promoters of Drs. King and Spock as third-party candidates for President and Vice President in 1968. Dr. King had repeatedly declined to run. He claimed that his major role and effectiveness was as a non-political civil rights leader, though those favoring him thought he might be drafted. Dr. Spock saw such a campaign as a further means to educate the voters about his views on the war, and told a reporter in July 1967, "While I don't picture myself as a political type, I'd be proud to be Dr. King's Vice Presidential running mate. I'd run for dog catcher if I thought it would end the war in Vietnam [though he later hesitated to run on the more extreme platform of Eldridge Cleaver or of Dick Gregory, whose election he eventually supported]. I'll do everything but kiss babies. I'll shake hands with small children and admire babies." His announcement depressed his wife: "He'll have another heart attack with all that running around. He's driving himself too hard." But it inspired a Stanford physician, Dr. Richard White, to begin a personal crusade and newsletter to promote the candidates; it got him on the ballot in Pennsylvania and Virginia; it prompted a scattering of King-Spock buttons and bumper stickers; and it delighted humorists.

They forbore jousting at Dr. King, for his distinguished civil rights accomplishments and his race precluded humor in a year when ethnic jokes were out anyway. But WASP Dr. Spock was fair game. Even after he had become an outspoken advocate of peace, cartoons referring only to Dr. Spock's pediatrics had been benign. In *Family Circle*, April 1965, Shirvanian sketched two ladies drinking coffee. At their feet a toddler played with blocks and a large dog lay reading *Dr. Spock*. The hostess proudly remarked of the dog, "She's wonderful with children." *This Week Magazine* of March 14, 1965 featured a glum father driving off in a car crammed with exuberant children, to the mother's reminder, "Dr. Spock is in the glove compartment."

Even when pediatrics and peace were mixed, cartoon treatment was initially mild. Fischetti in the *Washington Post* of April 16, 1965 depicted a park full of screaming, teasing, unruly children, with one harassed mother saying to another: "I appreciate his concern about Viet-Nam but I hate to see Dr. Spock let up for a minute on the mess at home." (Beneath a notice at Case Western Reserve that Dr. Spock would lecture on Vietnam one wag penciled, "And the week after, General Maxwell Taylor will speak on toilet training.") In a similar vein is a cartoon showing a hairy young child, holding a picket sign which reads "The Draft Is a No-No," saying to his horrified parents, "You used to quote Dr. Spock— Why can't I?" A more sarcastic commentary came from Yale folk-singer Tony Dolan when he entertained conservative audiences with:

> Join the S.D.S. and learn to love the Communists;
> Now Dr. Spock is with them,
> And that I'm gladly for.
> No other protest movement
> Needs a baby doctor more.

When it came to the Presidency, the humorists sided with Dr. Spock's ninety-year-old mother, who exclaimed, "Why, Benny, you're not qualified." *Time* magazine, whose caustic flippancy had long been anathema to the doctor, smirked, "There must have been a gap of at least ten seconds between Pediatrician . . . Spock's announcement of his possible presidential candidacy and the beginning of the jokes—like how he would turn the Pentagon into the Triangle and replace the rifle with a burp gun." And later in 1967, after President Johnson's first grandchild was born, a cartoon depicted an anxious Johnson on the phone explaining, "No, no, Dr. Spock. I didn't call about your views on Viet Nam!" A more sardonic cartoon, "A Candidate is Born—The 'Spock-for-president' movement is still in its infancy," showed a diapered, hairy-legged, grotesquely adult Dr. Spock hunched in a neonatal pose in a baby carriage festooned with signs: "Spock's Our Baby!" "Take a Walk with Spock—Out of Vietnam!!" "C'mon! The push is on!!"

Along with many others, Dr. Spock had become convinced that there were no fundamental differences between Democratic and Republican foreign policies, and that the only hope for peace in Vietnam was through a strong showing in the '68 elections of a third party committed to peace. Idealist though he is, Dr. Spock didn't believe a third party could win right away, whether or not he was their nominee, but he hoped they could shout so emphatically in the political wilderness that the more powerful parties would be obliged to listen.

He thought that such a party might be sponsored by the National Conference for New Politics, which imaginative Arthur Waskow of the Institute for Policy Studies in Washington, D.C., among others, had begun in 1965. The following spring, NCNP solicited funds over the names of Dr. Spock and the Reverend William Sloane Coffin, Jr. to promote peace candidates who were running as living referenda on the war. They lost.

NCNP decided to try again and to hold a fall conference of 500 activists at Chicago's staidly grandiose Palmer House. Because the firmest of NCNP's many amorphous principles was "non-exclusionism," the original number eventually swelled to 2,000 delegates and 2,000 observers from the 125 organizations which had participated in the Mobe and 75 others. SANE came this time. So did the Communists, in some ways the most conservative group present; droves of young radical community organizers; and a hippie claiming to be from the "Apolitical Freaks of San Francisco" who unsuccessfully tried to disrobe at a press conference. (The hotel employee who booked the conference was allegedly sacked for admitting such a motley crew.)

White delegates outnumbered black three to one. Under a system of weighted voting intended to insure the ultimate in democratic representation of each organization present, white votes outnumbered black six to one. The blacks felt themselves the vanguard of the new radicalism and wanted more power. To get it they employed a tactic which won their battle but which nearly wrecked the conference and helped in the end to destroy the NCNP.

They ominously boycotted preconvention sessions and the first day's meeting of the convention proper while they held their own secret Black Caucus. On the second day they sent to the plenary session a thirteen-point platform and demanded adoption within three hours—or a boycott of the rest of the convention, too. Some of the demands teased: "Make the conference slogan not peace and freedom but freedom and peace." Some tantalized: "Support all the resolutions of the recent Newark Black Power Conference" (nobody, including the blacks, recalled exactly what these were). Some taunted: "We strongly suggest that white civilizing committees be established immediately in all white communities to civilize and humanize the savage and beast-like character that runs rampant throughout America, as exemplified by [the] George Lincoln Rockwells and Lyndon Baines Johnsons." Others, demands to set policy, seemed like attempts to test limits: "Condemn the imperialistic Zionist war; this condemnation does not imply anti-semitism." And, most importantly for the convention, give blacks 50 percent representation on all committees and in all voting.

These incendiary demands ignited the assembly. With a cry of *"Goyim* do not understand Zionism," a Jewish delegate stomped out, followed by other delegates who later returned, only to leave again in protest. Others said that to accept the black platform intact would be the worst sort of white racism. But the blacks said the thirteen points were a test of the whites' "social barometer." One white delegate exclaimed passionately, "I'm not going to quibble over words while Negroes are dying in the streets of Newark and Detroit." Dr. Spock himself remarked with characteristic mildness, "I'm not angry. Most whites have no awareness of black desperation. Blacks think of themselves backed into a corner facing savage repression, as they literally have been for centuries. They feel that black power is their only salvation, because they can't count on white people. They see the United States destroying a colored people in Vietnam. In the Middle East they identify with the Arabs because the Arabs are the underdogs and because the U.S. government is predominantly pro-Israel."

As Walter Goodman of the *New York Times* reported, "The walls of the Palmer House began to drip with guilt" (a view Dr. Spock emphatically rejects). "The 13 points were accepted by a 3–1 majority. . . . Having come together in a convention pledged to 'reflect your goals, your programs and your plans . . . through the process of participatory democracy,' the new Jacobins acclaimed their compliance with an ultimatum." They then agreed by a 2 to 1 majority to give the blacks equal voting power, whereupon, says Goodman, "A woman . . . sadly burned her delegation card, good now for 15 worthless votes. 'This is the old politics, not the new politics,' she said, and went home."

The reconstituted convention then got down to its chief policy issue, whether or not to conduct a national third-party campaign in '68. The community organizers' sentiments, buttressed by black votes, prevailed by a very small majority and the convention voted against a national Presidential campaign because of lack of manpower and money. It would expend its effort locally, on such campaigns as those of the sixty candidates of the Mississippi Freedom Democratic Party, and on community organizing between elections. Thus ended the King-Spock Presidential ticket.

The rest of NCNP's efforts were to be strictly local, too. In addressing the convention, Dr. Spock's emphasis on local control sounded as if it might as readily appeal in some respects to the Birchite right as to the radical left: "I believe that the white and integrated neighborhoods of our cities—as well as the black ones—should find ways to achieve the greatest possible degree of self-government, in regard to the schools, the police, health and hospitals, sanitation, zoning, the rehabilitation of housing and new housing, so that the people who live and work will be able to control their environment and facilities, and, equally important, will have a feeling of responsibility for doing so. For part of the deterioration and disorganization of our cities comes from the feeling of the residents that their votes and their wishes count for nothing in the hugeness of the metropolis."

In this populist vein the NCNP agreed to help recruit college students into community organization projects, to try to organize urban unions on a residential rather than an occupational basis, to work for neighborhood control of schools and police. They went on record as favoring immediate withdrawal from Vietnam, ending the draft, and reinstating Adam Clayton Powell in Congress, and in a rare spirit of compromise they bypassed a resolution that would have triggered a debate over nonviolence.

They elected as co-chairmen James Rollins, a young black organizer from St. Louis, and Dr. Spock. Spock was their most prominent and least controversial white member, and one of the few financial contributors remaining after the angry walkouts over the anti-Israel resolution. He had to choose between SANE and NCNP, for even his friends in SANE felt he could not be co-chairman of two organizations with such conflicting policies and principles. He had no hesitation in choosing NCNP, he explains, "because of its broad spectrum of viewpoints, its greater radicalism and militancy, its larger black segment, its emphasis on nonelectoral as well as electoral political activity, its skepticism toward the two old parties as constituted." But he made a point of remaining on the SANE board to avoid any appearance of attacking it and to indicate his belief that it had a valuable function in stirring moderate liberals to political and educational antiwar activity.

After the NCNP convention, Dr. Spock began a speaking tour to raise money for his new stepchild, in much the same manner that he had once worked for SANE. Only this time the magic wasn't there and neither was the money. Dr. Spock, still as personally attractive as ever, was too patrician to be a soul brother of the black poor and represented too great a compromise to the middle class, moneyed liberals who could not forgive black anti-semitism. So, for the first time in Dr. Spock's life, people stayed away in droves from his speeches. Dr. Spock "loaned" NCNP as much money as he could, but with other contributions dwindling, the organization continued to sink under the weight of radicalism, black power, and "honkie subservience" that it had heaped upon itself during the convention. It never even raised enough money to mail out a wide appeal for funds, and was quietly buried in a pauper's field before the spring primaries in 1968. Yet Spock still continues to hope that a political and social alliance of black and white can be formed.

Dr. Spock's new cause agitated the tempest already brewing in SANE's teapot. The conflict in SANE was to be resolved by an unprecedented election of a new board, half by the national membership, half by the old board. Before it was held several conservatives eliminated themselves by resignation. Donald Keys resigned his directorship in disgust, for he felt that SANE had not dealt forthrightly with the issues of Spock and of collaboration with radicals. The election removed several of the militants in both the conservative and liberal factions and added some noncontroversial newcomers. Stuart Hughes remained chairman; Sanford Gottlieb, SANE's Washington representative, became executive director. An executive committee, without Spock, supervised operations from month to month; the full board met only quarterly. Tensions cooled, and, despite its change of spots, SANE remained the same old leopard underneath.

Though still listed on SANE's letterhead as a national committee member, Dr. Spock had little influence on SANE policy. He was a sponsor of such diverse organizations as the Medical Committee for Human Rights (concerned with promoting a variety of social action medical projects), the Women's International League for Peace and Freedom, New York's radical Freedom and Peace Party, and Resist (over-draft-age supporters of draft resistance). Although he contributed money and an occasional press release or speech to these organizations, his membership did not entail the consuming activity he had expended on SANE or NCNP. With the NCNP moribund, for a brief time Keys's prophecy that Spock would become a political isolate, a "messianic leader of the forlorn and radically irrelevant left," seemed on the verge of fulfillment.

To be sure, he was working on two books that would explain some of his political views. But one, *Dr. Spock on Vietnam*, wasn't to be published until March 1968, and the other, *Decent and Indecent*, would not appear until 1970.

To describe the conception and birth of *Dr. Spock on Vietnam* is to answer a question frequently put to Spock by hostile interviewers, "Doctor, how can a man of your—uh—reputation associate with the people in these radical organizations? Don't you think you're being used?" At this the Doctor groans "No!" and then relaxes. "They're not using ME in the sense that I don't know what I and they are up to. I'm using THEM as much as they are using me to get across what all of us want to say!" Certainly *Ramparts* was exploiting Spock's name when it took a full-page ad in the *New*

York Times to publicize his very brief introduction to a long article by William Pepper on the napalmed "Children of Vietnam." *Ramparts* misrepresented him in "Dr. Spock says, 'A million children have been killed or wounded or burned . . .' " for Spock was quoting Pepper.

But this didn't disturb Spock too much. He is receptive to nearly all efforts to publicize his opposition to the Indochina war. He eagerly cooperates with magazines, from *Life* to the now-defunct *Fact*, and with newspapers, which range from the *London Times* to small-town dailies to campus publications to a junior high paper in Greenwich Village whose reporters, their teeth in braces, interviewed him for an hour. He willingly appears on talk shows, from Les Crane to William Buckley to local radio stations of various political stripes.

So, with only slightly greater hesitation, he agreed to collaborate on a book on Vietnam with Mitchell Zimmerman, out of City University of New York, SNCC, the New Left, and Princeton (M.A. in political science, 1967)—a most peaceful member of the Spock generation. Zimmerman wanted to write for a mass audience a radical analysis and critique of the war then confined to Vietnam. But he surmised that unless he could affix a famous name to the book it would go the forgotten way of many another political tract, if it got published at all. So, after preliminary correspondence, he appeared at Spock's office door, with knapsack, dusty clothes, and longish hair, to discuss the idea. Spock was at first lukewarm, pointing out that the weakness of the antiwar movement was not due to lack of books—there were dozens by then—but to the fact that "people who were potential converts unconsciously avoided reading them for fear they might feel obliged to join the then unpopular minority." But he was persuaded by Zimmerman's sincerity and judgment: "He's modern youth at its most impressive; thoughtful, idealistic, quiet-spoken, a warm and wise person."

In what Dr. Spock characterizes as "an efficient and pleasant collaboration," much like the process of composing *A Baby's First Year* and *Caring for Your Disabled Child,* his colleague structured the book and produced the first draft. Then Spock revised it. He altered the contents in places, on the basis of his lecture experience, simplified the style, deleted the analogies to the American Revolution which he felt weakened the emphasis, and carefully removed three-quarters of the outrage for, he says, "If an author is too indignant, it relieves the reader of feeling any indignation on his own."

Zimmerman adds, "I don't believe it would be possible to find a single paragraph in the book which represents the unaltered work of one or the other of us. I did the great bulk of the work on the book (nearly full time for the better part of a year), but the significance of Ben's contribution (not even considering his name) is disproportionate to the amount of time he put into it. Certainly Dell never would have considered the book if it hadn't been Ben's. Some sort of split on the royalties would have been fair, so I count the arrangement [Zimmerman gets all the royalties] as Ben's generosity. Of course, neither of us was particularly concerned about the money. I don't think a word was said about it between us until the book had been months underway."

Dr. Spock on Vietnam is in some ways like Dr. Spock on babies, a clear, simple, forceful, and thoughtful exposition of a series of problems and questions, though with far more references to outside authorities and with fewer practical solutions than *Baby and Child Care* contains.

The authors have written a brief history of the United States involvement in Vietnam up to 1968, combined with criticisms of our reasons (explicit and imputed) for being there and suggestions on how to get out. They explain that we got involved in Vietnam, among other reasons, because as President Eisenhower admitted, we wanted to control the tin and tungsten from that part of the world. They then discuss the Geneva Agreement of 1954, which called for the temporary partitioning of Vietnam ("to allow the French and the Vietnamese aristocrats who fought on their side to settle their affairs and get out if they wished") and for free elections in 1956. They claim that "If the Geneva Agreement had been respected . . . Vietnam would be a single country at peace, united according to the will of its people as expressed in a free election in 1956." Instead, the U.S. installed cruel, corrupt puppet ruler Ngo Dinh Diem, a Vietnamese aristocrat whom our Government had found living temporarily in Ossining, New York.

The eventual result was a rebellion in the South, provoked by "excessive rents, unemployment, inflation, the cancellation of national and local elections, the favoritism, the wholesale jailings and torture." Buddhists, Socialists, liberals, Communists, nationalists, and village leaders, persecuted by Diem, banded together to overthrow him. In December 1960 they established the National Liberation Front of South Vietnam (NLF) which intended, among other things, to reduce rents, redistribute land, wipe out illiteracy, and to be politically neutral. Diem called them "Viet Cong" (meaning Vietnamese Communists), though most of them weren't Communist. They had the support of most of the South Vietnamese people, to the extent that by 1964, a year after Diem was finally deposed, "the 34,000 full-time and 80,000 part-time soldiers of the NLF were able nearly to destroy a Saigon force three times their size." So in 1964, as in 1954, the United States had to decide whether American troops should be used to prevent defeat of a government favorable to its interests. Lyndon Johnson's answer was yes, and he increased American troop strength from 14,000 in 1963 to a half million in 1968.

Spock and Zimmerman refute the argument "If we lose Vietnam to the Communists, our children will have to fight them on our own shores," claiming that the Communist world is not a monolithic power bloc but a loose conglomerate of nations with independent, often divergent, policies and interests. On similar grounds they dismiss the domino theory. They argue strongly for non-negotiated withdrawal of American troops from Vietnam: "What is there to negotiate about or to compromise on? . . . [The Vietnamese] cannot offer to stop bombing our cities if we stop bombing theirs." If we don't withdraw, we're likely to be drawn into a devastating nuclear war with China or Russia.

The authors use historical and documentary evidence to combat various "myths" which argue against withdrawal, among them:

Myth 1: We must remain to fulfill our commitment to the South Vietnamese. (Our commitment involves economic aid and consultations as provided for by the SEATO treaty, not military men and materials.)

Myth 2: To withdraw would be to abandon the South Vietnamese to a form of government they don't want. (Election results and mass collaboration with the NLF reveal Vietnamese approval of the Viet Cong.)

Myth 4: "An American withdrawal would encourage Red Chinese expansionism." (No, but continued American involvement might, by driving the hard-pressed North Vietnamese to seek aid from China, whom they strongly distrust.)

Myth 7: If we withdraw we will lose face. (On this the authors take a typically Spockian position: "What is important is not what other people think but whether the decision is a good one or a bad one on its own merits." We are losing far more prestige and influence abroad by remaining in the war.)

Spock and Zimmerman humanize the Pentagon's computerized body counts and depersonalized reports of "pacified villages" to show the devastating effect of the war on a land and a people, on civilians as well as soldiers, on women and children as well as men. (This was later corroborated by the estimate of the U.S. Senate Subcommittee on Refugees that by the end of 1969 over 300,000 South Vietnamese civilians had been killed, and accentuated by the terrifying testimony during the trial of Lt. William Calley and others for the alleged murder of over 100 civilians—"mostly women, children, and old men" at My Lai on March 16, 1968. As a song of the U.S. skytroopers puts it:

> Napalm sticks to kids, napalm sticks to kids,
> When'll those damn gooks ever learn?
> We shoot the sick, the young, the lame,
> We do our best to kill and maim,
> Because the 'kills' all count the same,
> Napalm sticks to kids.

The authors soberly conclude with ways in which citizens can help end the war: petition congressmen, boycott domestic products of war manufacturers, distribute antiwar literature, join peace groups, engage in discussions and "orderly legal protest demonstrations," and either resist the draft or encourage draft resistance—"even though it subjects us to the same legal penalties."

At the time it first appeared in the spring of 1968, *Dr. Spock on Vietnam* was a concise (94-page) summation of the radical, doveish interpretation of the war. (The essence of the hawks' stamp-out-communism-at-any-price counterargument remains General Curtis LeMay's boast in 1965, "We can bomb them into the Stone Age.") Eighteen months after publication the book still spoke for the doves.

But because there was so many more who not only belived as Spock and Zimmerman did but who were willing to act on their beliefs, it began to approach the mainstream of contemporary thought.

The book was not widely reviewed, and prompted only a few letters to Spock, mostly favorable. About 80,000 paperbacks were sold in its first year. Indicative of the interest of foreign readers, an Italian translation was published immediately, with Swedish and Dutch versions not far behind.

The book had not been published when on January 5, 1968 the Government indicted Dr. Spock and four others for conspiring to aid, abet, and counsel American youths to resist the draft and to defy the Selective Service Act. Dr. Spock was again being used, this time by the U.S. Government, as the most prominent symbol of the antiwar movement. His political relevance was again assured.

thirteen

DR. SPOCK, CONSPIRATOR FOR PEACE

DR. Spock learned of his indictment in a way that still seems thoroughly comical to him. He says, "Just before we left New York for two weeks of sailing in the Virgin Islands, I went to Pocket Books to make some last-minute revisions in the third edition of *Baby and Child Care*. I had in my pocket the unused half of a round-trip ticket to Philadelphia, where I'd been speaking a month or two before. I'd been given a ride home by Viveca Lindfors and her husband who were at the same meeting—a *marvelous* improvement over riding the train. But my frugal upbringing said I mustn't let the statute of limitations expire on the ticket, so I walked from Pocket Books, at Rockefeller Center, to Penn Station. It was hardly worthwhile because I only got $2.43—I had expected something more like $6.

"I had promised to call Jane so she'd know when to put supper on, so I called her from the station about six. She answered the phone with a tense 'Where are you? Do you know you've been indicted?' 'No,' I said, surprised, and she went on, 'Don't talk to any-one. The lobby of the apartment house is full of reporters.' "

Dr. Spock continues, "I was taken by surprise, but not until I'd hung up did I begin to wonder who told Jane that I shouldn't say anything to anyone. I didn't like the idea of dodging past the press saying 'No comment,' because I was sure that what I had been doing for peace was right and I didn't want to seem to be running away.

"So I kept trying to telephone Jane again to find out who told her I shouldn't talk. I was coming home by subway, the way I always travel when I can. I tried to call her from the Seventh Avenue sub-way and the line was busy. I went up to Times Square and tried again—still busy. I went across on the shuttle to Grand Central, called from there—busy again.

"As I got onto the Lexington Avenue subway the man standing next to me was reading a *New York Post* with a headline in four-inch letters, 'SPOCK INDICTED.' I tried to peek over his shoulder to see what it said but I couldn't read the rest. I wanted to tell him, 'That's me, buddy. Do you mind if I see what it says?' But I didn't think he'd believe me. When I got off at 86th Street I tried to call once more, but everybody else was trying to get through. So I steeled myself, and decided that as I came through the lobby I'd say to the waiting reporters, 'I'll be back in just a minute, gentlemen, after I've said hello to my wife.' I walked into the lobby—and no-body was there but the doorman. They'd all left. That was quite an anticlimax.

"But Jane was still excited. All the press services and television networks had been on the line. A wise friend had called to recom-mend Leonard Boudin as the lawyer to get. I didn't know him, but I knew of his brilliant reputation for defending people in trouble over left-wing causes. When I reached him he laughed—he's a very low-pressure sort of person—and said, 'I *thought* somebody would be calling me this evening.'

"I told him I'd like him to defend me, but the only thing I needed to know at the moment was how important it was not to say any-thing. He answered, 'Ordinarily you find out what the charge is first, before you go around talking. But in a case like this if you're determined to be aboveboard I don't see any great harm in it.' I was very much relieved that I didn't have to run away. So I asked my secretary to call the reporters and tell them I'd talk with them that night.

"By 8:30 the whole apartment—it has only a large living room and one bedroom—was jammed. I was sitting on the couch and the space near me was filled with radio and television sound men lying on the floor, holding up a forest of mikes. Beyond them were the cameramen and the reporters. The main difficulty with such a large press conference is that every time you pause when you're talking six questions are shouted at you all at once. Several reporters, because of hostility or a desire for drama, kept asking, 'You *are* guilty, aren't you?' and I kept parrying by saying, 'No, the war is illegal and we're using these means to try to end it.' "

The indictment, when finally delivered prosaically the next day by U.S. mail, specified clearly what "these means" were. The Federal Government charged that Dr. Spock, Yale chaplain William Sloane Coffin, Jr., Harvard graduate student Michael Ferber, novelist and travel writer Mitchell Goodman, and political scientist Marcus Raskin "did unlawfully, wilfully and knowingly combine, conspire, confederate, and agree together and with each other, and with diverse other persons, some known and others unknown to the Grand Jury, to commit offenses against the United States." (Ferber, working on a Ph.D. in English, found the language awkward and redundant, graded it C—, and commented in the margin, "You should see me." They did.) The defendants were said to have violated the Universal Military Training and Service Act, 50 U.S. Court of Appeals 462 (a), by sponsoring a nationwide program of draft resistance, including "the interruption of the induction process at induction centers throughout the United States; the public counselling of Selective Service registrants to resist the draft, to refuse to serve in the armed forces of the United States, to surrender their valid Selective Service notices of classification and registration certificates. . . ."

To promote this program, charged the Government, four of the defendants, Ferber excluded (along with 2,500 others) signed "A Call to Resist Illegitimate Authority." Spock was an original signer of this document, published in October 1967 in the *New Republic* and the *New York Review of Books,* and of its covering letter, which were widely circulated in academic communities during the fall of 1967 to obtain faculty support for draft resisters. Its signers, among them authors Norman Mailer, Robert Lowell, and Susan Sontag; sculptor Alexander Calder; and Nobel prizewinners Linus Pauling and Albert Szent-Gyorgyi, claimed that the Vietnam war was *unconstitutional* because it was never declared by Congress. It was *illegal,* they said, because the United States violated the UN Charter which "specifically obligates the United States to refrain from force or the threat of force in international relations" and to submit insolvable international disputes to the Security Council. They labeled the war *immoral* as defined by the Geneva Conventions of 1949 and the Geneva Accords of 1954 because American troops aided in the destruction of food, crops, livestock, villages, and civilians. The signers supported selective conscientious objection to *unjust* wars. Claiming that "every free man has a legal right and a moral duty to exert every effort to end this war . . . and to encourage others to do the same," they prepared to back, with funds for bail or legal defense, people who refused induction or who, once inducted, refused to go to Vietnam or who, once in Vietnam, refused to obey "specific illegal and immoral orders."

Attached to the Call was a lawyer's opinion—Leonard Boudin's— that signers should be aware that they subjected themselves to five years in prison and a $10,000 fine. Apropos of his signing both the document and the cover letter, in 1971 Dr. Spock said, "I thought I ought to, on principle, and also because my children were grown and I was financially independent. Yet I felt some caution, too. I delayed for a while and talked with Jane. But when, like a realistic woman, she asked whether I thought there was any chance of my being prosecuted, I said, 'They wouldn't be so foolish as to try to put a well-known old person like me in jail!' Though not quite convinced, she saw that I wanted to sign so she said 'Go ahead.'

"At the time I signed and right up until the trial I assumed that I was protected by the Nuremberg principle, by which American, British, and French judges condemned to death Germans and Japanese for war crimes and crimes against humanity. When those accused protested that they were only obeying orders, our judges declared that that was no excuse; they were obligated to disobey such orders.

"I told Jane that even if I were jailed I'd get a chance to do a lot of reading and writing, and she said, 'But they'd make you a shoemaker or something like that.' Anyway, I can make the best of any situation. I'd have found something interesting to do. I love to make models. I wouldn't have fasted.

"I felt then that it was the right thing to do, but that we older people who had more resources, more visibility, should have been doing it long before. I still feel it was the right thing to do, morally and tactically, and that the Government was foolish to prosecute."

Offered also as proof of the alleged conspiracy was evidence that some or all of the five participated in several Illegal Actions. The first of these was a press conference on October 2, 1967 at the New York Hilton in which Spock, Coffin, Raskin, Goodman, and unnamed others spoke to publicize both the "Call to Resist" and draft resistance demonstrations planned around the country for "Stop the Draft Week," October 16–22. The speeches, which lasted less than an hour altogether, were supplemented by antiwar leaflets—assiduously collected by the FBI agents who mingled among the reporters. That was the first time Spock, Raskin, and Goodman had ever encountered one another—and then only for the briefest of introductions. It was the second time Spock and Coffin had met, again momentarily.

The second Illegal Action was a service of dedication to the Resistance Movement on October 16, 1967 in Boston's Arlington Street Church, historic bastion of a century and a quarter of liberal and radical causes. The Government charged that the Reverend Coffin and Ferber, by their antiwar sermons, had encouraged prospective draftees to turn in their draft cards or burn them (over Unitarian founder William Ellery Channing's candlestick).

The third Illegal Action, charged the Government, occurred on October 20 when the five defendants, along with several hundred draft-age members of the Resistance and many older sympathizers, gathered in front of the Justice Department to encourage resistance against the Selective Service System. The Government charged that there Ferber deposited in a briefcase, already containing draft cards collected from all over the U.S., a bundle of draft cards gathered at the Arlington Street Church ceremony on October 16.

Mitch Goodman spoke. So did Dr. Spock. Raskin turned in his draft card—4-F. Newsreel cameras ground away; the ubiquitous FBI agents took notes. Coffin's speech in particular was considered a direct violation of the Selective Service Act: "We hereby publicly counsel these young men to continue in their refusal to serve in the armed forces as long as the war in Vietnam continues, and we pledge ourselves to aid and abet them in all the ways we can. This means that if they are now arrested for failing to comply with a law that violates their consciences, we too must be arrested, for in the sight of that law we are now as guilty as they. . . . And in accepting the legal punishment we are, in fact, supporting, not subverting, the legal order."

Then, charged the Government, Coffin, Spock, Goodman, Raskin and "other co-conspirators" entered the Department of Justice [by appointment] to deliver to the Attorney General "a fabricoid [misspelled, noted Ferber] briefcase containing approximately 185 registration certificates and 172 notices of classification together with other materials"—the net tangible evidence of the week's protest.

With his customary good humor, Dr. Spock describes the confrontation: "Police were all around the huge bronze door of the handsome building, and opened it only a crack while they checked the credentials of each of the twelve people, half youths, half older people, and then we squeezed through, one by one. As we walked, escorted, down the corridors, different office doors would be opened a crack and secretaries and deputy assistants would peek out timidly at us as we went by, with their little scared mouse eyes sparkling. It was fun for a mild person like me to feel like a lion on the loose.

"In the Andretta Room," says Spock, "we met Deputy Assistant Attorney General John McDonough sitting at the end of a long table, a very decent fellow. He was trying to be cordial, statesmanlike, but he looked rather uncomfortable as he shook hands with us solemnly, and I felt a little sorry for him. He said, 'Gentlemen, what can I do for you?' and one by one we got up and denounced the war, Lyndon Johnson, the Justice Department, and the draft. At first we were hesitant and mild, but our individual indignations increased as we heard each other speak, and by the end we were denouncing everybody in ringing tones. I ended my speech by saying [Spock growls] that I wished he would tell the Attorney General himself [Ramsey Clark] that it had not escaped our notice that he did not have the courage to meet with us himself.

"As we got up to go, Coffin left the briefcase on the table, so

McDonough had to ask, 'Am I being tendered something?' Coffin offered him the briefcase full of draft cards, which McDonough had to refuse, primly saying that he was not authorized to accept anything. The cards should, he advised, be submitted to the registrants' local draft boards. Coffin tried again, 'You are herewith tenderly being tendered some hundreds of draft cards and supporting statements.' Again McDonough refused. In a formal and obviously strained manner he read us the draft law and emphasized the penalties for violations, but we left the case there anyway and departed after shaking hands with him."

As they emerged, Jane Spock was addressing the women protesters, saying, "Don't hold your husbands or boyfriends back when they have to do something that's right," while inside, McDonough was turning over the briefcase to the two FBI agents who had been providentially stationed behind the door to an adjoining room. (Said trial Judge Ford, "They're always outside the door." Later he clarified, crustily, "They're needed outside some doors.") Coffin told the small group that still remained outside, "We came here for a moral, legal confrontation. If our Government cannot accept such confrontation, it cannot have much conviction of its own morality. Then it must accept the responsibility for less responsible, less violent demonstrations."

For reasons unspecified, the Government did not choose to charge the five with violating the law through their participation in the tumultuous March on the Pentagon the following day, October 21. The slogan of the 55–100,000 protesters, "From Dissent to Resistance," clearly spelled out their militance, which had been increasing since the Spring Mobilization.

But Dr. Spock's deportment, amidst the beads, buttons, and banners, was moderate and modest, as usual. Before the reflecting pool he gave his basic antiwar speech: "We, the protesters . . . may help to save our country [from this disastrous war] if we can persuade enough of our fellow citizens to think and vote as we do." While some Yippies were attempting to levitate the Pentagon and exorcise the "pentacle of power . . . perverted" by chanting "Out, demons, out!" the rest of the demonstrators were content merely to converge on the Pentagon as a symbol of protest. Ben and Jane were with a small group walking quietly toward the building when, as

Spock explains, "A line of troops marched toward us and as we sat down, through and past us. We stood up and moved farther toward the Pentagon. A second line of troops marched toward us. We sat down. They kicked us as they marched into us. Most of us jumped up except three who were kicked a little more, then lifted into a paddy wagon. The rest of us were easily and ignominiously pushed backwards, up against the first line of troops which had halted, and we stayed penned in for about an hour, until a grinning captain came up and let us go. We trudged back to Washington."

The Spocks got off easily in comparison with many of the other demonstrators, Norman Mailer's Armies of the Night, on whom soldiers and federal marshals inflicted MACE, teargas, incarceration for hours in airless paddy wagons, and beatings such as those described by student activist Dotson Rader: "Every once in a while someone in front would be pushed too close to a marshal (and the Federal marshals, in terms of my experience, are beyond doubt the cruelest of police) and he would bring his club down and the person would scream and the young troops near would wince involuntarily . . . and the poor bastard [would] be dragged away by the marshals, his head being clubbed as he neared the police vans."

Another Illegal Action dwelt on during the trial was the demonstration to symbolically close Whitehall Street Induction Center in lower Manhattan on December 5, 1967 during "Stop the Draft Week." As conceived by David McReynolds, slim young leader of the pacifist War Resisters' League, demonstrators would show their disapproval of the war and the draft by sitting on the courthouse-like steps on the Center's four sides, though they would not harass or hinder the inductees as they reported at 6 a.m. McReynolds, the police department, and Mayor Lindsay (who later caused a furor by characterizing the Indochina war as "unproductive, unwanted, endless, bottomless and sideless") worked out the plans well in advance. The police were to allow protesters intending to be civilly disobedient through the barricades at prearranged spots to sit down momentarily before being arrested and taken to jail.

Though it began in dreary dark at 5 a.m., in Spock's view the demonstration itself was nearly as amiable as the planning session. Protest creates incongruous associations. On one side of the police barrier: Dr. Spock, muffled in his heaviest overcoat; Mitch Goodman, casually academic; beat poet Allen Ginsberg, bearded and balding; 2,500 demonstrators of draft age; reporters, cameramen, FBI agents, and the director of the New York Civil Liberties Union. On the other side: a phalanx of 2,000 policemen. The demonstrators milled about idly, waiting for word from police which would allow them to climb over or under the barriers and sit on the steps.

Dr. Spock explains, "I was pushed by the crowd up against the police barriers, just sawhorse things. All the press were right there crouching all around me, pushing about a dozen microphones in my face. While I was waiting for instructions to go ahead they kept asking me embarrassing questions like, 'What are you going to do now, Doctor?' Since I didn't really know, I thought it was best not to answer. Then they'd ask, 'How are you feeling, Doctor? Doctor, are you feeling trepidation?'

"Ten, twenty, thirty minutes went by, so I finally decided, this is *intolerable* just standing here. Maybe Dave McReynolds has been arrested and no orders will ever come through. So I decided to go ahead anyway. I suddenly dropped to my hands and knees [crouches] and tried to go under the barrier and between the police legs. But the police *immediately* closed ranks, so that I was against a solid phalanx of their shins. I had to admit defeat and stand up a little bit disheveled. And of course all twelve mikes were in my face, 'Doctor, what were you trying to *do*?'

"I moved sideways about ten paces to where I thought the police were spaced a little thinner. When they didn't seem to be noticing I dropped down again to my knees [crouches again], but the ranks closed. I did that three times. Then I saw a place where there was a police barrier with a little cross step on it and I thought, 'If I step up on it just right I could leap on top of the barrier and maybe go over.' So, like a high jumper getting ready for a race I *picked* my spot, moved in. But when I suddenly leaped, *immediately* the police stuck up their arms [demonstrates] and there I was swaying on top of the barrier holding onto the policemen's cuffs trying to keep from falling backward. Again the television people asked, 'Doctor, what are you trying to do?'

"Just as if in a dream, the ranks of the police opened up and there was Chief Inspector Garelik. But by this time I felt so frustrated and bereft of my dignity that my tone of voice became that of a small child who was promised a lollipop and didn't get it. I whined reproachfully, *'I want to commit civil disobedience!'* He indicated, in a soft-spoken voice, not wanting to connive too openly with a potential lawbreaker, that if I would go down to the corner of the barricade I would find an opening there.

"I went there, got through the barrier and the policemen, up to the steps, and sat down, followed by others. Immediately Inspector Fink said, 'One, two, three, four, five, six, seven, eight'—they did everything in batches of eight—'you're under arrest.' So we obediently got up and marched into the paddy wagon and were trundled off to the Tombs. There we spent a long day being fingerprinted, being frisked over every inch of our bodies, being moved from pen to pen. They even took away our pencils. [laughter]

"Unexpectedly we got a sort of *filial* feeling for our own police officer. You'd be in a pen of twenty-four people for a while—three groups. Then Group A's policeman would come to move them to another pen. By this time—we were arrested at six in the morning and didn't get out until three in the afternoon—the policeman had learned the names of his group and would say, 'Charlie, Pete, Harry,' and they would spring up with happy looks on their faces. He'd unlock the door and lead them away while the other two groups would feel deserted. Then *our* policeman would come along and we'd all jump up with happy expressions just like children in nursery school.

"I made very good friends," says the former prisoner. "Every once in a while since, in demonstrations and at talks, I run into somebody who looks familiar and he says, 'Remember me? I was in the Tombs.' And you welcome him like a long lost college classmate. You have this feeling of having shared a really significant experience."

Of the subsequent "Stop the Draft Week" activities Dr. Spock recalls good-naturedly, "I didn't expect to go back. I thought I'd done my duty, lost enough dignity. But there was so much police brutality later in the week that I was asked to go to a press conference in the Mayor's office to complain. There we were interviewed on television. With one more day's demonstration to go, one of the questions asked me was, 'Doctor, are you going to be in the demonstration?' so I had to say, 'I *certainly* am.' So I had to go in again on Friday, when I had made an appointment to talk with the FBI. I asked Jane—I had to leave again at four-thirty in the morning because the demonstration began at five—'At nine would you call the FBI and tell them I'm terribly sorry, but something interfered.' She called and told them I had to be in another demonstration, and they said [Spock assumes a sinister, smug tone], 'Yes, we knew that already.' "

"So they came around a couple of days later, two very gentlemanly fellows who had asked for an appointment 'to discuss my peace activities.' A lawyer told me that I didn't have to cooperate but I didn't like the implication that I had anything to conceal. I said, 'Come along. I've been trying to tell the President and Secretaries of State and Defense about my views and they don't pay any attention.' Of course that was very ingenuous of me. Never trust the FBI if you are opposed to Government policy; they are unscrupulous. They knew what I didn't know, that I was about to be indicted, and they wanted to hang something on me. When I didn't incriminate myself, they made up statements to incriminate me, couched in pompous language, to the effect that my main purpose was to disrupt the functioning of the Selective Service System and the 'levying of troops.' Even in Whitehall Street I didn't think of the demonstration as disrupting the Selective Service System but as calling attention to the evil of the war and the draft."

Spock talked freely for an hour and a half, hardly giving the interrogator a chance to ask questions. During the trial the FBI intimated in sinister tones that he had talked far too freely as he laughed and said, "Telling you men what I'm going to tell you I will be hanging myself and I may wind up in jail." Dr. Spock admits to having said this but claims it was merely a pleasantry, "a way of poking fun at the FBI's narrow patriotism."

Of such stuff is a conspiracy made, said the Government—a petition, a press conference, a church service, a public assembly, and a private meeting with an officer of the Justice Department. But why prosecute these particular five (and why five?), upstanding men all, for this particular crime at this particular moment?

Reasons are not difficult to find. In the spring of 1967, as both the war and protests against the war continued to escalate, the House Armed Services Committee wondered why the protesters hadn't been prosecuted for violating the draft laws. Representative L. Mendel Rivers (D., S.C.—whose campaign slogan is "Rivers Delivers"—military training camps, defense installations, and war plants, bringing billions in welcome wealth to the folks back home) put the question to Assistant Attorney General Fred M. Vinson.

Vinson replied mildly that the protesters' rights to freedom of speech were guaranteed by the First Amendment, and only if their speech was a "clear and present danger" to the country could they be prosecuted. The Justice Department thought they were within the law.

This view drew fire from Representative F. Edward Hébert of Louisiana, who snapped, "Let's forget the First Amendment. I know that will be the refuge of the Supreme Court. . . . But at least the effort can be made . . . to eliminate this rat-infested area."

The interrogation continued, Vinson sticking to the Constitution, the Committee sticking to its guns.

Later on, the Committee had a much pleasanter meeting with Lieutenant General Lewis B. Hershey, then director of the Selective Service System, whose philosophy of the draft Mike Ferber characterized as, "Every time he opens his mouth he gets another couple of hundred draft cards." General Hershey suggested to the Committee that the Armed Forces might profitably "go out and hunt" reluctant youths and draft them immediately, rather than turn their cases over to civilian courts.

General Hershey's suggestion was not acted upon until the events of the October protest week proved too much for him to bear. On October 26, 1967 he fired off a letter to each of the 4,081 draft boards around the country advising that, "Deferments are only given when they serve the National interest. It is obvious that any action that violates the Military Selective Service Act or the Regulations, or the related processes cannot be in the National interest. It follows that those who violate them should be denied deferment in the National interest. It also follows that illegal activity which interferes with recruiting or causes refusal of duty in the military or naval forces could not by any stretch of the imagination be construed as being in support of the National interest."

This would apply not only to the customarily eligible group under twenty-six, but to all registrants thirty-five and under, including 4-Fs. If General Hershey's directive were followed, it would in effect make each local draft board the prosecutor, judge, and enforcer of the fate it deemed suitable for anyone in its district considered "not in the national interest"—seminary students (specifically exempt by law), demonstrators at Dow Chemical, Yippies —even a paraplegic was summoned for a physical in Oakland. That was one way to deal with protesters.

Another way to deal with critics of the war might have been to end the war, or at least to de-escalate it. Indeed, five months after General Hershey's letter to the draft boards, concomitant with announcing his intention not to run for another term as President, Lyndon Johnson proclaimed a bombing halt in North Vietnam and initiated the Paris peace talks. If a "talk" involves a meaningful dialogue, the "talks" scarcely existed at all. The tempo was set during the first year as representatives jousted once a week, through formal statements, about whether or not representatives of various factions—the NLF, the Saigon government, the U.S.—should sit at the conference table, and if so, how the seating should be arranged. After that robust beginning, the discussion slowed down.

But, dialogue or no, the existence of the diplomats assembled in Paris and the withdrawal of Johnson from the Presidential race had a disconcerting effect on the peace movement, even though the weekly body count remained high. Other than to rally around Presidential aspirants Eugene McCarthy or Robert Kennedy, the peace people didn't know what to do. They could scarcely stage demonstrations if the peace talks were in earnest. There was no point in continuing to denounce a lame duck President. So they muted their voices.

Yet another way to silence the critics, particularly those who could slip through the draft boards' nets, and to save face for General Hershey, was to prosecute them. On December 9, 1967, a special unit in the Criminal Division of the Justice Department, directed by John Van de Kamp, was formed to deal with violations of the Selective Service law. It started to work on the Spock case immediately. To silence a few protesters through prosecution might be to silence the rest.

The Government, which can choose whether or not to prosecute law violators, and which ones to prosecute, selected carefully from among the many thousands of war critics. To have prosecuted only obscure persons might have resulted in their convictions, but few would have noticed; who today can tell much about the Oakland Seven, the Minnesota Eight, the Beaver Fifty-Five? Fewer still would have been deterred. To have prosecuted Mayor Lindsay or the New York police force for cooperating with the Whitehall demonstrators would have attracted considerable attention. But it would have been foolish—or would it?

To provide an effective deterrent, to show the general populace that it was doing its job, and to find enough recorded evidence of the activities of the accused, the Government had to prosecute— and convict—the most prominent peace people it could find. To provide an effective deterrent the Government had to prosecute peace people with otherwise impeccable credentials, esteemed not only by citizens of like mind, but by the public. To provide an encompassing deterrent, the Government had to prosecute people representative of major segments of opposition to the war in Indochina, for in their fall would fall peaceniks all.

So it chose to prosecute Dr. Spock, 64, a household word, symbol of grandfatherly benevolence, involved in protest because of his humanitarian feelings. As he testified during the trial, "What's the use of parents and pediatricians trying to bring up children to be healthy and happy if they are to get killed in such an unconscionable war? . . . I believed we were destroying a country that had never done us any harm, . . . carrying out a totally outrageous and abominable thing against our heritage."

So it chose to prosecute the Reverend William Sloane Coffin, Jr., 43, representative of the liberal clergy and eastern aristocracy (son of the president of the Fifth Avenue firm, W. & J. Sloane, also president of the Metropolitan Museum of Art's board of trustees). From 1945 to 1947 Coffin had been a liaison officer to the Russian army, where he performed his first act of civil disobedience by quietly neglecting to return Russian deserters to their army, where they would have been summarily shot. He later spent three years in the CIA before being ordained a Presbyterian minister. As his personal and religious convictions led him to protest discrimination (in civil rights demonstrations in the sixties he was jailed three times), they also led him to protest the war in Indochina and to encourage draft resistance. As he proclaimed at the October 2 press conference: "Synagogues and churches at their best have always been a sanctuary for conscience. . . . Now, if there are going to be arrests, then let these arrests be made in the churches and the synagogues, that this country can see that the nation is now engaged in actions which are in violation of individual conscience. . . . "

So the Government chose to prosecute Marcus Raskin, 33, trained in law, whose research as a legislative assistant to some liberal congressmen eventually led to his becoming a disarmament advisor to President Kennedy in 1961. As he studied U.S. involvement in Vietnam he grew disillusioned by American manipulation of small nations and, with two others in the Kennedy administration, left to form the Institute for Policy Studies, an independent research organization in Washington (described by *Esquire* as "The Rand Corporation of the Left") concerned with foreign affairs, education, urban problems, economics. Raskin objected to the war on legal grounds, testifying (among other things) that the war was unconstitutional because it had not been declared by Congress, and "because the manner in which it was being conducted was a violation of our obligation under the United Nations Charter and the Geneva Conventions of 1949." (However, some of Raskin's friends speculated that the Government may have indicted him by mistake, confusing him, as did Deputy Assistant Attorney General McDonough in otherwise detailed and accurate trial testimony, with Arthur Waskow, Raskin's far more fiery colleague. "Waskow" and "Raskin" sound similar if pronounced rapidly; many of the witnesses at the trial, including FBI agents, were none too accurate on proper names. For instance, MIT professor Noam Chomsky was called variously "Neil Komsky," "Noel Kimsky," "Norman Comstock," and, Judge Ford's contribution, "Karatsky.")

Also indicted was Mitchell Goodman, 44. He was educated at Harvard, served as a lieutenant in the artillery during World War II, and in 1947 married British poet Denise Levertov. He had spent the next eighteen years quietly apolitical, writing, teaching, lecturing in New York, Maine, and California. But with the escalation of the war in 1965 he had come to view the war as destructive of constitutional democracy and the draft laws as discriminatory against the blacks and the poor. He made his views known through writing, petitioning, and peaceful protests; he organized a Fifth Avenue parade of World War II veterans carrying a coffin "with a very simple sign on it that just said the number of casualties in the war." And, between May and October of 1967 he spent countless hours, phone calls, visits trying to organize and coordinate resistance activities among professors, writers, and other intellectuals.

As a prime example of a draft-age young man, the Government could have prosecuted flamboyant Buffalo undergraduate John Sanna, who figured prominently in the draft card turn-in and meeting with Justice Department officials, bobbing about in a straw boater bedecked with poppies and protest buttons. Or it could have prosecuted the insouciant, bereted, bearded black cat Dickie Harris, likewise a participant in the Justice Department confrontation. But instead it prosecuted, as the only draft-eligible defendant, Michael Ferber, 23, who as a Phi Beta Kappa at Swathmore and a Woodrow Wilson Fellow in English at Harvard was among the most respectable and intellectually outstanding of all the young idealists protesting an unjust war. Ferber had applied for conscientious objector draft status as a lifelong Unitarian, but his plea failed and he joined the Resistance as a means of expressing his disgust with both the "whole rotten, absurd, illogical Selective Service system" and with the war. He has claimed to "rock with Spock's flock," but his ever-present idealism is all his own. It was paramount in his sermon at the Arlington Street Church ceremony on October 16 (which later received the Unitarian Church's award for the best sermon given within the year by one of its members), "A Time to Say No." There he said "No" to the Government's policies in Vietnam and encouraged resisters to say "Yes" to "working to help anyone and everyone to find ways of avoiding the draft, to help disrupt the workings of the draft until the war is over. . . . [L]et our Yes be the loudest No our government ever heard."

These, then, were the defendants, intellectually, socially, professionally respectable and respected, not a beard or sandal in the lot (though Coffin grew sideburns during the trial). Each had come to protest the war from his own frame of reference, his own state of mind. The Government had found its big fish to fry.

But why charge the five with *conspiracy* "to counsel, aid, and abet diverse Selective Service registrants to . . . neglect, fail, refuse and evade service in the armed forces of the United States"? Why not simply charge each with counseling or otherwise encouraging draft resistance? The Government didn't because it couldn't. No one, not even a single individual, testified during the entire four weeks of the trial that he had refused induction—or even burned a draft card—with the encouragement of any of the defendants. General Hershey himself—and who should know better than he?—said elsewhere that neither the defendants nor the demonstrations had deterred or prevented enlistments or inductions; in fact, in his estimation the armed forces had an oversupply of men.

Shortly after the indictment Dr. Spock explained his views on draft resistance to an audience of students: "None of the five actually believe in persuading anybody to resist the draft, and none of us ever tried to. I for psychiatric reasons, Coffin for religious reasons, others for just common sense reasons, know that you don't *persuade* somebody to make such a serious decision. A person can only do it himself. During the whole three years [1965–68] of escalation I've only discussed the subject with two medical students. I told both of them they were foolish to resist and that I thought they could do more for world peace by other means. If they got sent to jail for five years, or just convicted, they might never be able to get a license to practice medicine."

Dr. Spock continued, in 1968, "I believe that draft resistance will probably have more effect in ending the war than any other method, as it did in the French-Algerian War, and I believe that other methods should be persisted in, too, including political activity. Nevertheless, I think it would be *very* wrong for *any* young man to be persuaded by me or to be persuaded by a classmate or to be persuaded by what he'd read. At a time like this it's very easy for people with a conscience to get the feeling that they are under *obligation* to resist the draft just because somebody does something. I'd advise you to weigh all the factors that are involved. Conscientious objection should be pushed as far as it can. For some people it's better to go to Canada. If a person does decide for himself to resist the draft, it's very important that he should do it through an organization so that each individual's resistance will be exploited in the sense of encouraging other people. The point of nearly a thousand people turning in their draft cards in the fall [of '67] was to encourage 10,000 to follow. The news of the 10,000 may encourage 100,000. Then you really make it damn difficult for the Government to carry on a war."

There were other reasons for the conspiracy charge. Judge Learned Hand called conspiracy doctrine "the darling of the modern prosecutor's nursery," and with good reason. "Conspiracy" is itself a nebulous concept, and its very vagueness allows the prosecution more legal leeway than would a concept capable of more precise definition. It has been defined as "A combination of two or more persons, by concerted action, to accomplish an unlawful purpose, or some purpose not itself unlawful by unlawful means." Or, as prosecuting attorney John Wall explained during the Spock trial, conspiracy is, simply, "an agreement to disobey the law"—but the agreement must be one that incites men to action; it cannot be merely theoretical. It may be formal or informal, explicit or implicit. The agreement, if not stated directly in words, can be merely "a meeting of the minds." Often then, a conspiracy case such as the Spock trial may hinge on whether or not an agreement, however tacit, can be proven; Justice Jackson said, "A conspiracy often is proved by evidence that is admissible only upon assumption that conspiracy existed."

"Conspiracy" commonly connotes a political plot for a coup d'etat, or gangsters furtively meeting to plan some clandestine skullduggery—murder, bank robbery, hijacking. But, says the law, the agreement is the essence of the crime and may be proved circumstantially. The conspirators need not have met. Nor do they even have to know one another, either beforehand or during the continuation of the plan. They do not have to be fully knowledgeable of the plan or actions involved, as long as they are of "like mind" with regard to either the means or the ends. Conspirators may have very little communication with one another. These characteristics are common in antitrust violations, where prices of goods or commodities sold by various companies mysteriously rise to the identical level on the same day.

According to the law, conspiratorial acts do not have to be secret—or even illegal—if the method used to perpetrate them is unlawful. Conspirators do not even have to succeed in order to be found guilty; plotters can be indicted for attempting homicide even if they have not actually committed murder. Conspirators can be convicted on circumstantial evidence alone, even though the overt acts themselves may not entail illegality. Furthermore—and in the Spock trial this proved to be very important—all conspirators are held responsible for the acts of their co-conspirators. For example, a conspiracy to rob a bank might involve several persons not doing the actual robbing. One man might tie up the watchman, another might be a lookout, another might drive the getaway car, another might hide the stolen money. If one of the actors commits murder, even though this is beyond the original plan, all the conspirators might well be equally chargeable.

In the Spock trial, Spock and the other four defendants were charged with conspiracy to violate the Selective Service Act along with "diverse other persons, *some known and others unknown* to the Grand Jury" [author's emphasis]. This meant that if another trial jury were to find that other nondefendants in the Spock trial were also conspirators (and there were many nondefendants who figured prominently as signers to the Call to Resist and in the public meetings), their conduct could be attributed to the defendants. When defense lawyers asked the Government to identify the "co-conspirators," they were told to look at the faces on the TV films of the protest activities. Consequently, during the trial, Judge Ford allowed the prosecution to show movies of fiery speeches and draft card burnings by nondefendants, and in general to present evidence which would make the jury aware of protest activities by nondefendants about the country—all of which might at some time be chargeable to the five on trial.

In like vein, when defense lawyers asked the names of the "diverse Selective Service registrants" that the accused had allegedly counseled, prosecutor Wall referred them to the U.S. Census Bureau. Because the defendants' activites had been so thoroughly publicized by the press and TV, one could infer, said Wall, that every draft-eligible man from eighteen to thirty-six had been counseled."

Legal reporter John MacKenzie of the *Washington Post* pointed out that the conspiracy charge was "put to a use that has been paralleled by few cases but is most reminiscent of the abortive draft 'conspiracy' case against the German-American Bund during World War II." That case, in effect, put the entire Bund on trial because it had ordered its members to refuse to serve in the U.S.

military forces in protest against the Selective Training and Service Act of 1940. The Bund contended that the Act discriminated against its members with respect to eventual civilian reemployment. Similarly, the Spock trial provided an amorphous legal cover to put the entire antiwar movement on trial.

Wall defended the concept of a conspiracy charge and its application to the Spock case because, he said, collaboration magnifies the risk to society. A conspiracy promotes greater strength of purpose, efficiency, and specialization of its individual members, thereby making the group a greater menace than each person in it would be if he operated independently. Pursuing a hard law and order line, Wall argued that failure to prosecute would encourage not only the violation of the Selective Service Act, but anarchy: "If there is a disagreement on policy, even on morality, as long as we can go to the polling booth and vote, I submit that is the proper way to do things, if we are not going to have *anarchy*."

In deciding to prosecute a case, the Government has certain built-in advantages. It can choose the charge. Its prosecutors meet with the grand jury without defense counsel present. Because grand juries tend to rubber-stamp the charges drawn by the prosecution, they generally return the indictments automatically. Indictment carries to the popular mind the presupposition of guilt, despite the legal precept that every man is innocent until proven guilty. Thus in a political prosecution such as the Spock case, the Government can often count on the attendant publicity to arouse a great deal of popular sentiment for its side—more than enough to counteract the objections of the opposition, whose disagreement is often interpreted by Government supporters as evidence of un-Americanism, Communist sympathy, treason, or other forms of disloyalty.

Such popular prejudgment was revealed by the Cleveland reporter's question to Dr. Spock: "You did do these things, didn't you? And therefore you're guilty." Spock: "I said, 'I did these things but I'm not guilty.' And that made him so mad he just glared at me and dropped the microphone as if he had convicted me but I had refused to take it." Similar bias was revealed when longshoremen, in March 1968, refused to load Dr. Spock's new boat, a 35-foot ketch, onto a freighter that would take it from New York to the

Virgin Islands. They wouldn't handle the property of a traitor, they said. (Spock had to hire people with different views to truck the boat to South Carolina and sail it to the Virgin Islands from there.)

Unlike other criminal prosecutions, which must be tried in the district where the crime was committed, the Government has the choice of where to conduct a conspiracy trial, if the actions in question occurred in more than one federal judicial district. The Spock case could have been tried in either New York, Washington, or Boston. Since the trial was implicitly concerned with resistance to what the defendants considered an unjust governmental policy in Vietnam, it appears ironic that the Government chose to prosecute in Boston, which two centuries ago was the center of resistance to the British government's colonial policies, and a century ago was one of the headquarters of the abolition movement.

Why Boston? Partly because the Government was eager to get on with the case. The crowded court dockets in New York and Washington would surely have meant more delay than in Boston, where Judge Ford repeatedly refused to grant continuances. Partly because the international press corps stationed in Washington might have given the case greater publicity around the world, especially in countries unsympathetic to American participation in the war in Indochina. The *London Times* sent a reporter anyway. And Russian poet Yevgeny Yevtushenko, a perceptive critic of his own society, composed "Monologue of Dr. Spock." In it he contended that the United States, unmistakably analogous to Russia, was run by quacks who were themselves ill and should be put on trial for murder, and concluded, speaking as he assumed Spock would:

> I love America. But differently
> From those who 'love' but spit on our people.
> To be a patriot in our country
> Means to carry the label 'antipatriot.'

Boston may also have been chosen because so much of the populace, from which the jury was drawn, seemed solidly to support the Government's view. Their opinions of the defendants' guilt ran the gamut from A to B (though the reporting in the *Boston Globe* was extraordinarily sensitive to the issues in the case, and most understanding of the defendants). One improper Bostonian hollered at Spock shortly after the assassination of Robert Kennedy, which occurred in mid-trial, "You killed our Bobby as sure as if you'd pulled the trigger yourself, you bastard."

In Boston, too, a federal judge markedly sympathetic to the Government's point of view could be found. Judge Francis J. W. Ford, 85, emerged from semi-retirement to preside. Judge Ford had been a tough, effective federal prosecutor from 1933 to 1938, an experience which, some say, left him noticeably receptive to the prosecutor's point of view. In 1938 Franklin Roosevelt appointed him to the lifetime position of Judge of the U.S. District Court of Massachusetts. Over the years he had run a tight court and earned a reputation for fairness and an ability to confine proceedings to the issues. His decisions were rarely overturned in appellate court. Yet, observes University of Michigan law professor Joseph L. Sax, who attended the entire trial, "another judge could have found a dozen cogent reasons, all supported by precedent and good legal logic, to have dismissed the indictment before the trial ever began. . . ." Not Francis Ford, who ruled out the crucial issues in the pretrial hearings.

The trial would be a case, not a cause.

fourteen

THE TRIAL

O N May 20, 1968, began the trial of the U.S.
vs. Coffin, Ferber, Goodman, Raskin, and
Spock, who soon came to be known as the "Boston
Five." Their case was signaled throughout the
city by the neon signs on one of Boston's most
venerable financial institutions, the Boston Five
Cent Savings Bank. Day and night across the
street from the courthouse shone "The Boston
Five" in red letters. It shines there still.

The gray stone Federal Court House and Post
Office sits amidst the mixture of old and new that
characterizes the city which arrogantly calls itself
"the Hub of the Universe." It is within easy
walking distance of aristocratic Beacon Hill,
where buildings and residents have colonial ties.
Nearby is the Arlington Street Church, whose
Tiffany stained glass windows provided a quaint
art nouveau backdrop for radical religious services
(including the one which figured prominently in
the trial) and where draft resisters who sought
sanctuary during the trial were eventually

dragged out by the police, amidst violence. On the other side, near Boston Harbor, site of the Boston Tea Party, a mammoth complex of government buildings has erupted out of the rubble that only a few years ago was Scollay Square, Boston's red-light district known to sailors from Hong Kong to Halifax.

But from the five tall windows in the small, high-ceilinged yellow courtroom three, floor twelve, none of this was visible. Only the sky could be seen, and throughout the trial it was soddenly, sullenly gray—except when the sun came out dazzlingly as Wall finished his closing argument.

With the rest of the world shut out, the microcosm within the courtroom assumed universal proportions and the drama unfolded, but very slowly, according to the ritualized minuet of legal custom. At ten each weekday morning for a month, all rose as Judge Ford strode briskly in and diminutive Charlie Noonan, court crier, intoned in a Boston twang the centuries-old invitation: "All those having business before the court may now draw near and be heard —God save the United States and *this* honorable Court." Judge Ford seated himself at the bench, beneath a mural map of the United States inscribed with "Justice is the Guarantee of Liberty" and the names of his prominent predecessors, including Judges Holmes, Brandeis, and Frankfurter. Thus the proceedings began.

There was the drama of prosecuting attorney John Wall, at 36 himself scarcely beyond draft age, his experience as a paratrooper evident in his soldierly bearing and military haircut. He proved an impressive spokesman for the Government: intelligent, forceful but not belligerent (except during a few clashes with Goodman), and articulate—intoning with sonorous clarity everything from charges against the defendants to addresses on letters in evidence. There was the dramatically courteous manner of Coffin's sleekly self-assured advocate, James St. Clair, who spoke with ringing confidence as he peered quizzically over his Benjamin Franklin style glasses, in contrast to the nondramatic astringency of Raskin's counsel, Calvin Bartlett, at one time a prosecutor on the Massachusetts Crime Commission. There was the elegant arrogance of Spock's attorney, Leonard Boudin, internationally known for work in constitutional law, and fresh from defending Julian Bond in a victorious appeal to the Supreme Court to be seated by the Georgia legislature (which had refused to admit Bond because of his pacifistic objections to the war in Indochina, objections presumably intensified because of his race). There was the drama of the humble demeanor of Ferber's lawyer, experienced civil rights defender William Homans, Jr., whose hulking six-feet-four-inch frame led the spectator to expect brimstone rather than the benignity which appeared.

There was the dramatic understatement of Goodman's counsel, Edward Barshak, whose quiet strength contrasted with his client's sometimes explosive forcefulness. Barshak argued impressively that despite the fifteen volumes of words that constituted the trial transcript, the fundamental fact of the case was scarcely in the testimony at all—the war in Indochina, which in the fall of '67 was "tearing apart the American people," and which created the climate for the case. There was drama in the continuous nonspeaking presence of Telford Taylor, on Raskin's behalf. Former Brigadier General Taylor, a law professor at Columbia, had been the U.S. Chief Counsel at the Nuremberg War Crimes tribunal; his appearance served as a visible reminder of the Nuremberg argument, which he later explicated in *Nuremberg and Vietnam: An American Tragedy* (Quadrangle Books, Chicago: 1970).

There was drama in the humors displayed by the portly Judge. He alternated between abrupt gruffness (usually reserved for the defendants) and puckish wit; when one attorney asked if the Judge wanted to have a particular answer repeated he shot out, "Nothing gets by me but the wind, and I swallow half of that." He alternated between zealous concentration and casual inattention, whether from boredom or drowsiness was hard to tell. Though he ruled out "facial demonstrations" in the courtroom, the Judge's own face was most demonstrative. Sometimes his glaring glasses appeared to have no eyes behind them, yet when the shaggier Resistance kids entered the courtroom the Judge's disapproving eyes seemed as big as saucers.

There was drama, too, in the crowded courtroom audience. Facing the Judge sat a semicircle of attorneys and their clerks, always abustle with activity at large tables. To the Judge's immediate right, the witness stand—a comfortable black leather chair with wooden arms and a microphone in front of it. Directly before the witness stand was the court stenographer's small desk, occupied alternately by a graying wraith of a middle-aged man and a voluptuous blonde, each frantically transcribing a verbatim report of the proceedings.

To the Judge's extreme right, next to the wall, was the jury box, occupied by the least dramatic-appearing persons in the entire court-room, but on whose decision the ultimate drama would be resolved. The twelve jurors and three alternates, all white, all men, mostly middle-aged, were technicians, salesmen, and small businessmen. ("I wanted mothers, beards, and eggheads!" lamented one of the defense lawyers.) Five had completed high school, six had some college, one had a college degree. Sequestered after courtroom hours in the fading gentility of the once-fashionable Parker House, the jurors seemed to have absorbed some of the drabness of both their quarters and the weather, and appeared impassively resigned to the proceedings. (After the trial, one juror movingly confessed in a newspaper article his extreme sympathy for the defendants and their point of view, in spite of the fact that he felt obliged to find all but Raskin guilty because of the Judge's charge; two jurors ex-pressed similar sentiments to trial interpreter Jessica Mitford.)

Much more visibly engrossed were the defendants, seated just behind the attorneys, though unlike the trial of the Chicago Seven, soon to follow, the drama was more in their legal situation than in their persons or actions in the courtroom. Tidily dressed and clean-shaven each day, from a row of black leather chairs they watched the drama with animated good humor, nonchalant (Dr. Spock sometimes dozed after lunch) except for Raskin, who ap-peared perpetually tense.

Small dramas occurred daily among the spectators, reminders that the real drama of life was going on outside the courtroom. In the first two rows sat the defendants' relatives, forced into uncom-fortable erectness by the courtroom's benches like church pews. The wives, pretty and petite, wore chic attire, patterned stockings, and lustrous makeup which masked the irritable apprehension that understandably began to appear beneath their deeply ingrained good manners as the trial ground on. Jane Spock was a faithful attend-ant. Vowing, "If Ben is convicted I'll go to Leavenworth and get a job clerking in the dime store so I can be near him," she sat primly, deeply tanned from a two-week cruise in the Virgin Islands. But she grew more tense each day, and after Mayor Lindsay had fin-ished testifying on Spock's behalf he sat with her briefly, and she appeared grateful for his presence.

Only Ferber had no wife (he married in 1970), though he was attended by a miniskirted lass just over from England for the event.

She was taken in protective tow by Ferber's diminutive mother lest she get shoved off the family bench by wives jockeying for favored positions. No one would have dared to shove Coffin's mother, an aristocratic and gracious matron in daily attendance. The defendants' children appeared intermittently. Raskin's dewey-faced son and daughter were scarcely old enough to comprehend the charges, but so dreadfully upset at the prospect of their father in jail that their parents bought them an "indictment dog," a poodle, to cheer them up. Coffin's ten-year-old daughter and two younger sons behaved with continental courtesy and poise; Amy thoroughly charmed Dr. Spock by curtsying to him. Goodman's son Nik, eighteen, himself a leader in the peace movement, observed, "I'm one of the few people of my generation who can respect his parents." John, Mike, and Judy Spock appeared with the ebullient Spock grandsons, whom Jane alternately amused and restrained. The prosecution would indeed have profound effects on others in addition to the defendants.

Mirrored in the other spectators was the magnitude of the prosecution. A number of men in uniform were present, including a Marine Pfc., hand in a traction cast and just ten days back from Vietnam, who was quietly scornful of the resisters. An aged black Jehovah's Witness preached antiwar sermons during court recesses while gushy ladies in cartwheel hats sought Dr. Spock's autograph. A Boston dowager in navy and lace beamed, "I'm just here because I'm a busybody." Large numbers of housewives (some with children) came and went, as did long-haired students sporting the omega of the New England Resistance.

As one heard the arguments and became aware of the arguments that were not used, the far-reaching legal implications of the case were thrown into sharp relief. The most significant unspoken arguments concerned the war in Indochina, on whose legality and conduct the defendants had hoped for a "moral and legal confrontation" in the courts. The pretrial motions of Dr. Spock's lawyers were designed to secure a dismissal of the charges or at least to get affirmative rulings which would then provide the guidelines for the trial to follow. Dr. Spock's pretrial brief paralleled much of the "Call to Resist." The Vietnam war is illegal, argued Boudin. It is therefore no crime, according to the Nuremberg defense, to advise potential draftees to refuse to break international law by participating in an illegal war and committing war crimes such as killing civilians and destroying villages. Boudin offered to supply depositions from twenty-five witnesses around the world who would testify to the war crimes committed in Vietnam by the United States.

Defense lawyers also argued that even if their clients' conception of the war's illegality was wrong, their beliefs could be found reasonable and in good faith. An acquittal on these grounds might have been forthcoming, for in spite of the principle that "ignorance of the law is no excuse," good faith intention is usually regarded as being inconsistent with criminal culpability. It is a basic rule of criminal law that to convict, the prosecution must prove criminal or deliberate intent. (Traffic violations and certain other offenses are exceptions.) Thus if Spock and his co-defendants were benignly motivated, even if their understanding of the law was in error, they should be acquitted.

In reply, the Government argued that the defendants had "no standing to raise the 'legality' of the Vietnam conflict" and reasoned that the Nuremberg defense was irrelevant to the charge of counseling draft resistance. After all, a registrant was not criminally liable, even under Nuremberg, for cooperating with the draft laws during wartime. Thus he had "no legal justification for refusing to do so." Besides, even if he went into the army he would not inevitably commit a war crime. The alleged good faith intention of the defendants was also brushed aside. If the registrant who refused induction was guilty of law violation, "one who conspires to counsel, aid and abet such refusal is in no better position."

A month before the trial began, Judge Ford ruled in favor of the Government. The Nuremberg defense claims were "not justiciable"; the legality of the draft and the war were not relevant to the case and could not be argued, even to show the defendants' good faith beliefs. Was a landmark case to be obscured in judicial fog?

During the trial itself Wall emphasized that the defendants had openly defied and challenged the Government to provide "a moral confrontation" through indicting them. However, because the war in Indochina had been decreed irrelevant, the "confrontation" turned out to be over the seemingly irrelevant issue of conspiracy— a matter in which none of the five, totally surprised by the charge

—would admit complicity. But because the Government had to stretch so far to make a conspiracy charge appear plausible, much of the evidence presented was not about conspiracy at all but about defiance of the draft law by the defendants and countless others.

The prosecution strategy was not to characterize the defendants as traitors or smear them as unpatriotic, but rather to present them as well-intentioned and sincere. Their crime, claimed Wall, came from stepping beyond protest to action, from trying to change the law to undermining it by inducing defiance of it.

In order to demonstrate the existence of such inducement, the prosecution created an immense antiwar montage of film clips, television and newspaper interviews, and reports by FBI agents to produce the first criminal case in American history in which the Government's side was based almost entirely upon selectively edited mass media reports of public political events. For instance, newsreel photographers had filmed fifty minutes of the most sensational parts of the three-hour service at Arlington Street Church on October 16. Wall drastically edited this to fifteen minutes and showed the result to the jury. In Wall's version, the Reverend Coffin, dressed in clerical robes, was shown sounding like the very model of a modern major radical, and keeping radical company as long-haired youths and anonymous hands consigned alleged draft cards to a flaming candle. Other prominent eastern clergymen, not on trial, were also shown, but Ferber, not newsworthy at the time, was scarcely photographed. To compensate for Ferber's absence from the film, Wall re-created his presence by reading "A Time to Say No." Though it seemed incongruous for the prosecutor to utter in such ringing tones the very view he was opposing, with every moving sentence Ferber grew in stature.

The Government indicated its extreme confidence that the jury would of course be hostile to the defendants' motives and intentions by encouraging much testimony that would enhance the impressiveness of the Boston Five in the eyes of any but their most antagonistic opponents. Thus the prosecution emphasized Ferber's speech. Thus it called in the FBI to describe Dr. Spock's "very cordial and gracious reception" of the agents as they questioned him. Thus the Government prompted Deputy Assistant Attorney General McDonough's elaborate testimony of the defendants' "articulate and moderate" conduct at the Justice Department on October 20. The prosecution encouraged McDonough to recount the defendants' assertions while there that the war and the draft laws were unconstitutional and that their conduct was well within the free speech guarantee of the First Amendment.

Convincing though the prosecution's ambiguous evidence concerning the defendants' behavior may have been to supporters of either side, its most compelling line of argument on its own behalf was to point out the apparently enormous discrepancy between the defendants' allegedly modest goals and their vehement antagonism to the war. It seemed incredible, said the Government, that the five who felt so strongly about the need to defy the draft and the war machine wouldn't try to persuade anyone else of their opinions. It seemed incredible that their personal prestige and their participation in resistance activities influenced only the already committed, the only ones whom the defendants (except Spock) acknowledged supporting. Said the Government, whether or not they actually counseled draft resistance, their influential participation was a form of encouragement to the fence-sitters.

To many of the peace flock who would have preferred the doves to flutter directly into the Government's face, the defendants' meager claims seemed an equivocation. But not even the peace people felt that a confrontation over the charge of conspiracy would have been meaningful. So perhaps moderation in the courtroom was the better part of defense.

Whether the multitude of stellar character witnesses that the defense lawyers paraded through the trial aided their clients or the prosecution is difficult to tell. Among the notables were New York Mayor Lindsay and Senator Stephen Young of Ohio, both of whom Judge Ford treated with exceptional severity; Dr. Robert Ebert, Dean of the Harvard Medical School; James Dixon, president of Antioch College; Paul Moore, Episcopal Suffragan Bishop of Washington and Fellow of the Yale Corporation; Jerome Wiesner, MIT Provost; and Benjamin B. Cohen, one of the drafters of the UN Charter. Though Judge Ford usually restricted their testimony to a one-word definition of the defendant's reputation, "Just good, bad or indifferent, please, or whatnot . . . no further speeches," he did allow them to present their own impressive professional credentials. The sum total of such distinguished character witnesses, seldom seen in criminal court, accentuated the defendants' respectability and responsibility while it tended to undermine the prosecution's claim that on trial were men of extraordinarily radical thought and intention. On the other hand, the very prominence of the company the five kept might also have reinforced the jury's impression of the defendants' own high level of prestige, professional competence—and power to influence others, for good or for evil.

While the prosecution emphasized inducement, the defense stressed the absence of conspiracy. Yes, certainly the five, who before the indictment had met only casually if at all, agreed in their opposition to the war. However, said attorney Homans, there is a great deal of difference between *being* in agreement with other people and in *having* an agreement with them, which is the essence of a criminal conspiracy.

And they had no agreement, said advocate Boudin, terming the trial "The Case of the Missing Agreement." He declared that the "Call to Resist" was the only concrete evidence that the Government had produced to substantiate its claim of a conspiracy. However, he said, "The Call" was not a pronouncement of conspiracy but a sober, noninflammatory public statement of belief and of moral and financial support for draft resisters. It was a political manifesto signed by thousands of eminent Americans; to indict only five from among so many signified a political prosecution. He quoted Edmund Burke, " 'It looks to me narrow and pedantic to apply the ordinary ideas of criminal justice to this great public contest. I do not know the method of drawing up an indictment against a whole people.' " In the appeal brief he added, "It was through impermissible inferences drawn from parallelism that the Government sought to tie together separately planned and disparate activities. To find or hold that all of these nationwide activities were one single conspiracy and that the defendants were involved in that vast, single conspiracy is to impute far too much to the defendants and far too little to the pluralistic nationwide opposition to the war."

In addition, the defense devoted considerable effort to demonstrating the legality of the defendants' conduct. They realized that a defense on moral or conscientious grounds would carry little legal weight; none of the five was a total pacifist; none was a member of a traditionally pacifistic religious group. They knew they could not raise the question of the legality of the war and of the Selective Service law as a basis for defending the legality of their own beliefs. (Though to pique the jury's curiosity about what they were not being allowed to hear, the defense introduced a number of witnesses with expert knowledge of the Vietnam war—a *Life* magazine photographer, an expert in international law, an authority on biochemical warfare. The judge never let them testify, but their presence signaled the cataclysm beyond the courtroom.)

The defendants believed that their actions were protected under the First Amendment guarantees of freedom of speech, assembly, and petition for the redress of grievances. Therefore, they argued, their speeches, press conferences, meetings, and written statements were well within their constitutional rights. Their actions were not admissions of guilt, but attempts to promote a test case through challenges to statutes and Government activities they believed to be illegal. They sought not to defy the law, but a forum to protest it. Thus the turning-in of draft cards (only twenty-seven were valid 1-A classifications, a meager harvest for such an elaborate prosecution) was a form of "symbolic speech." Yet actions and speeches, however innocent they may be individually, often take on criminal implications if considered in light of the doctrine of conspiracy, as Judge Ford repeatedly emphasized.

Each of the defendants testified at length on his own behalf. Though all were articulate and lucid, Coffin and Raskin had problems. Ferber and Goodman came off well. Dr. Spock was superb.

In spite of his hip vocabulary and profound religious sincerity, the Reverend Coffin's ingrained aristocratic manner showed to his disadvantage on the witness stand. For instance, after Coffin had explained his views on the relation of conscientious behavior to the law at some length Judge Ford asked, "Are you saying that you believe if a man believes a law to be bad, he is free to violate it?" Coffin's reply, "No, sir, that is not what I am saying. Not that simple," and his imperious tone left the impression that he considered the question simple-minded—an impression not likely to endear him to those jurors who may have found a humbler demeanor more appealing.

Moreover, much of his testimony seemed equivocal. This may perhaps be attributed to his lawyer's influence rather than to Coffin's own desires (each defendant had elaborate rehearsals of his testimony in private sessions with his lawyer). From the prosecution the jury had already heard Coffin's impassioned speeches at the October 2 press conference, the Arlington Street Church, and the Justice Department, in which he expressed such sentiments as, "Now, once again let it be very clear that the further mockery of American justice is not to be made. Those who are arrested for violating the law which violates their conscience, [if] they are arrested, then we, too, must be arrested for aiding and abetting them." Yet when given a chance to speak for himself in court, Coffin claimed that his pastoral role forbade him to counsel, aid, or abet youths in breaking the law by resisting the draft or in other ways.

Coffin also appeared to be playing games with the prosecution when he testified that he did not believe that turning in draft cards to the Attorney General would hinder the draft "because turning in a draft card speeded up a man's induction and in no way impeded his induction; I knew [that a man would lose] his 2-S deferment and become a 1-A delinquent if the government chose to use this occasion to change his classification." It is difficult to imagine that the jury would believe that Coffin was really on General Hershey's side after all, trying to help him hustle draft resisters into the service. As one of the appeal judges remarked, "We do not think of Coffin as one to run with the hare and hold with the hounds."

Raskin, modest and nervous, seemed quite different. During the first hours of his testimony these qualities, along with his maturely reasoned objections to the war in Indochina buttressed by his professional expertise, created the impression of a strikingly brilliant person moved to action by a combination of intellectual and humanitarian beliefs. He testified movingly, for example, "that there were as many as two million refugees in Vietnam in 1966 with projections of three million by 1967"; that the war was destroying an entire culture; that families were forcibly torn apart, with some children taken from their parents and others sent to resettlement camps, similar to concentration camps.

But Wall subjected Raskin to a day and a half of cross-examination, twice as long as his interrogation of the other defendants, with devastating results. Wall obliged Raskin to go over and over and over the same events in minute detail. Such reiterated testimony is bound to evoke minor inconsistencies; Raskin's certainly did. These trivial variations, which Wall pounced on with gusto, weakened the earlier demonstration of Raskin's superlative competence and veracity. Likewise, Wall's repetitive questioning obliged Raskin to deny repeatedly knowledge of or participation in many of the antiwar activities under scrutiny in the trial. Probably he wasn't involved (his very absence of involvement may have been why Wall pressed him so hard), but to be forced to continually dissociate himself from them made Raskin appear to be denying too much, to be trying to push all the responsibilities—and the penalties—onto his co-defendants. This impression was intensified by Wall's sarcastic refrain in his closing argument, "And this intellectual, this great thinker, claims he didn't know anything about anything," reiterated until Raskin's wife fled the courtroom in tears.

Perhaps because Ferber was the youngest and presumably (though not actually) more defenseless than the other four, Wall was far gentler with him than with any of the other defendants except Spock. Ferber's somber testimony about his selective conscientious objection to the war and his activities in the Resistance movement came across as sincere, consistent, and credible.

So did Goodman's. His demeanor was far more open than many observers of the trial would have predicted, given his "conspiratorial" appearance as, said one spectator, "precisely the sort of person who would be ready to put a bomb in a shopping bag." And he was far less inflammatory than was his radical plan to disrupt the Oakland Induction Center by sending in bogus inductees who would chain themselves to the building. In his colorful testimony the genesis of the "Call to Resist" and the Whitehall demonstration came to life as pathetically disorganized. "We were," he said, "very inefficient, rank amateurs," and hardly the people to plot a nationwide conspiracy. His strong feelings about the war came through effectively, emphatically without bombast, in contrast to Coffin's seeming detachment. However, Goodman, too, got his comeuppance from Wall, who used intermittent sarcasm to telling advantage. In a discussion of the First Amendment Wall taunted Goodman, "All the time you were saying, 'Kids, you're putting yourself on the line and I'm on the line with you,' but really you felt you'd be protected by the First Amendment while the kids might go to jail." Goodman's answer, "I saw myself as taking a limited risk," tarnished the lustrous picture of selfless idealism he had just painted.

Fortunately for the significance of the trial as a political and ideological forum, however limited, the defendants testified alphabetically, and Dr. Spock, for many the focal point of the prosecution, spoke last. The courtroom, usually decorous after the Judge had once cleared the spectators for applauding one of his rare concessions to the defense, was unnaturally quiet during the day and a half of Spock's testimony. Even the Judge and the prosecutor treated Spock with much greater deference than they had shown to the others on the witness stand. Perhaps the better part of prudence was the tacit acknowledgment that the jury might venerate Spock as a national institution. Or perhaps Ford and Wall figured that Spock's own complete candor would work to his disadvantage in court as it had six months earlier when he had talked so freely to the FBI.

At any rate, he was allowed to testify in far more ample detail than any of the others about the UN Charter, Geneva Accords, and Nuremberg proceedings on which he based his beliefs about the illegality and misconduct of the war in Indochina. As he spoke, the picture which earlier witnesses had already sketched emerged in full detail, of Dr. Spock's independent recognition of the problems in Vietnam and his gradually increasing personal commitment to end the war in ways acceptable to his own rigorous code of morality and ethics. From his early involvement in SANE, Dr. Spock told the court, he increased his efforts for peace by campaigning for Lyndon Johnson, writing letters, and marching and speaking as often as his professional duties would permit. In the last five months of 1967, to publicize the cause he lent his name and presence to seventy-seven public meetings or demonstrations against the war. The four the Government prosecuted him for were no different from the rest in intent or substance.

Yet the prosecution may have got the kind of answers it was seeking when Spock readily admitted to having told Women Strike for Peace that "Getting 500,000 men home from Vietnam justifies us in civil disobedience"; "I am in favor of civil disobedience right up to the hilt"; and that draft card burners "are the real heroes."

Many exchanges revealed Wall's endeavor to trap Spock in the depths of his own commitment. Thus Wall inquired, with regard to the statement in the "Call to Resist" that encouraged adults to organize to support draft resisters directly, "Did that refer also to men who had not gotten up the courage to take active steps in draft resistance?"

Spock: That's correct, in my view, my feeling. . . . I want to encourage them to take active steps, yes.

Wall: And you also wanted to reach the young men who were evading the issue, who just didn't want to think about it?

Spock: Correct.

Wall: To make them think about it and see the light, as you saw it?

Spock: Yes, if they could see the light as I saw it.

Wall: Yes, sir. Well, those are acts of persuasion, don't you consider them in your own mind, acts of persuasion?

Spock: In a very—in the sense of public education and encouragement.

Self-incriminating though such testimony may have been, it movingly conveyed Dr. Spock's profound sincerity, and he usually managed to have the last, patient word: "I *hope* that many men will refuse to be inducted and I *hope* that many men will conclude that the war is illegal and will refuse to obey orders, but that is not the same as [saying] 'I think they should, or that I urged them to.'"

In his closing argument Wall paid Spock a rare compliment, "If he goes down in this case, he goes down like a man, with dignity, worthy of respect." Yet as he continued, Wall turned the double-edged sword: "Sincerity can't be a defense. It can't be. Beliefs cannot be accepted as justification for conduct in violation of the duly passed law of the land. To permit that justification would be to say that whatever a person says his beliefs are is superior to the law of the land and would permit an objector to be a law unto himself. *Anarchy!*"

At last, after seventeen days and over 3,000 pages of testimony, all the evidence had been presented, and subjected to microscopic examination and cross-examination by both sides. All the witnesses had been called—except the one who didn't exist—someone, anyone, who would admit to having been counseled by any one of the five to resist the draft. The attorneys had proffered their closing argu-

ments, eloquent summaries of their clients' cases, eloquent mar-
shalings of reasons for acquittal or conviction. Boudin had the last
word for the defense, a sober one chilling in its implications. He
said, quietly, "This is indeed a historical case which will go down, I
think, in Anglo-American jurisprudence as an important case involving the fundamental liberties of the people in a period of national tension. In this country the findings of fact as to guilt are
in the hands of the jury, persons to whom we entrust the liberties
of our fellow citizens. This is particularly important, historically
and today, as a barrier to an overzealous prosecution, a prosecution
of political opponents of the government which is prosecuting."

Wall's argument responded to this, interpreting the case, once
again, not as a matter of civil liberties at all, but of law and order
vs. anarchy: "Free speech is not an issue in this case. If you were
to convict any of these defendants for talking about Johnson, talking about the generals, talking about Vietnam, you'd be doing a
terrible injustice to them, to yourselves, and to this country and the
institutions under which we live. . . . You may disagree with the
defendants, but by God, you are not entitled to convict them because
you disagree with their political or moral or philosophical beliefs.
. . . I submit to you, gentlemen of the jury, that these defendants
and any person in the country can attack the law from every platform in America, but cannot under the guise of free speech nullify
it by disobedience to its express provisions. . . . "

Then came the Judge's charge to the jury. The charge, the last
words the jurors hear before they withdraw to deliberate the fate
of the accused, is one of the most important parts of the trial. It
is particularly significant in a case such as the Spock trial where
no one disputes the facts and where no particularly revealing argument or evidence has been offered during the testimony. In instructing the jury the judge literally lays down the law. The aim generally
is to make the abstruse and complex legal propositions sufficiently
clear and simple so that the jurors can relate the applicable points
of law to the facts of the case before them.

Judge Ford's charge supported the prosecutor's theme of law
and order. He said that beliefs and motives alone, however sincere,
however laudable, are "never a defense where the act committed is
an intentional violation of the law—a crime. . . ." He emphasized

the assumptions of the conspiracy doctrine: "For two or more persons to conspire . . . to commit a breach of the criminal law of the United States is an offense of grave character which strikes a blow at the very existence of law and order. . . ." He observed that First Amendment rights are not absolute: "Ideas may be communicated by conduct, and words may at times be keys of persuasion and triggers of action dependent on the circumstances and setting under which they are made." He said that the morality, legality, or constitutionality of the Vietnam war or the draft laws was not on trial, nor was the right to protest these. The sole issue for the jury to decide was "whether the defendants conspired among themselves and with diverse other persons mentioned but not named in the indictment, to commit violation of the draft law."

Judge Ford then gave the jury a most surprising instruction, one the defense felt was outrageous. He told them if they found the defendants guilty of conspiracy, to "make and return special written and unanimous answers" to each of ten "Special Findings"; guilt on any one finding was enough for conviction. The "Special Findings," which, Ford told the jury, "will help to inform you as to the issues involved in this case" (though the often-reiterated issues were scarcely obscure), consisted of such questions as: "Does the jury find beyond a reasonable doubt that the defendants unlawfully, knowingly, and wilfully conspired, confederated, or agreed together and with each other and with diverse other persons to counsel Selective Service registrants to unlawfully, wilfully, and knowingly neglect, fail, refuse, or evade service in the armed forces of the United States and all other duties required of registrants under the Military Selective Service Act of 1967 and the rules, regulations, and directions duly made pursuant to said Act? Answer 'Yes' or 'No.' " And so on, down through the charges in the indictment.

Special Findings are frequently used in civil cases, with the defendant's consent, to protect his interest by helping the jury to recognize separate aspects of complicated questions on which it must render a verdict. But criminal trials require of the jury only a single decision—guilt or innocence of the crime charged. Special Findings in criminal cases are virtually unheard-of, for they work mightily against the interests of the accused. These particular Findings were submitted to the jury without the defendants' consent and over strenuous objections from their lawyers. As they argued on appeal, these Special Findings "had an immediately prejudicial effect because they treated the defendants collectively, *i.e.,* they did not differentiate among them or name them individually. This had the effect of assuming the existence of the conspiracy and of relieving the jury of its duty to treat each defendant separately in every aspect of it deliberations." Because the jury must be unanimous on so many different points, Special Findings tend to induce the jury to compromise; indeed, Judge Ford acknowledged beforehand that the Findings might help to insure a verdict of guilty. Most important, by binding the jury to the judge's inclinations, obliging them to make public the grounds on which they reached their verdict, the Findings undermine the guarantee of an independent jury fundamental to the concept of trail by jury. For a jury, claimed the defense, must be able "to render a judgment 'against the importunities of judges and despite prevailing hysteria and prejudices.' "

The Judge's prejudice was not manifested only in his charge to the jury. Throughout the trial his hostility to the defense and his sympathy for the prosecution were apparent to observers from publications of as varied political views as *Ramparts, Esquire,* the *Washington Post,* and the *National Review.*

Not all of the bias shows in the seventeen volumes of cold court records, but some of it does. The Judge allowed the prosecution to introduce a great deal of evidence of doubtful admissibility, such as that pertaining to the Oakland Induction Center disturbances, the Whitehall demonstration, a speech by Ferber in April '68 designated by Wall as indicative of Ferber's state of mind in October '67, and so on. Though the Judge eventually ordered the jury to disregard most of such evidence, it seems doubtful that the cumulative effect of so much so often could be eradicated, or even sorted out from the consideration of relevant matters.

Nor could the cumulative effect of Judge Ford's continual irascible proddings to the defense—"Get on," "Go forward "—be erased. He frequently interrupted defense counsel, but only rarely the prosecution, with a variety of adverse observations and rulings about points of law. For instance, during the defense openings Judge Ford advised the jury that opening statements were not in evidence, questioned the lawyers' statements of fact and the probable admissibility of various topics, forbade references to other matters ruled inadmissible. He reminded the jury to keep an open mind and await his ruling on the law—doing so with references to "the conspiracy" or "this conspiracy"—though that was the very issue the jury was to decide. In contrast, he did not interrupt the Government's very long opening at all, even when Wall referred to nondefendant Noam Chomsky, present among the spectators, as "not sitting at the bar as a defendant *today*."

Judicial prejudice was apparent, too, out of earshot of the jury. In his chambers as early as the third day of the trial, Judge Ford remarked to the attorneys, "There is prima facie evidence of a conspiracy here beyond peradventure of a doubt," a conclusion which he (in theory) should not have reached until all the evidence was in and the arguments were concluded. Near the trial's end the Judge predicted to counsel, "There will be one verdict and that will be guilty on the conspiracy count." That he later altered the record to read "guilty or not guilty" did not remove the revelation of his actual belief. Nevertheless, prejudice can prove a paradoxical advantage to the accused. A prejudiced judge may go out of his way to maneuver a conviction, but in so doing he may provide far better grounds for an appeal than a judge scrupulously solicitous of the rights of the defendant.

Yet the Spock case presents an issue more fundamental and far reaching in political prosecutions than even the nature of judicial prejudice. In "Conscience and Anarchy: The Prosecution of War Resisters" (*Yale Review,* June 1968), Professor Joseph Sax raises the possibility that in political prosecutions where the issues are either of lesser import (such as trespass) "or are largely symbolic in their nature and usually at the periphery of free speech; or urge passive resistance as a means to press for changes in the law," the jury might be encouraged to nullify the law by acquitting the defendants "despite the contrary instructions of a judge, and thereby to repudiate both an unjust application of the law and an unjust governmental policy. . . ." This procedure had precedent in seditious libel cases in eighteenth-century England, though a critic of this view, Yale law professor Joseph W. Bishop, says that "it precisely describes the state of mind of a Mississippi jury when it acquits a Ku Kluxer charged with murdering a civil rights worker."

Although in their concluding remarks the Judge and the prosecutor emphasized why the jury should not recognize the right to civil disobedience to oppose an allegedly illegal war, the defense attorneys never raised Sax's argument. If this jury sensed the possibility of acting independently of the Judge's instructions it was certainly not apparent in their decision. On June 14, after seven hours of deliberation, the jury found all the defendants except Raskin guilty of conspiring to aid and abet draft registrants to refuse service in the armed forces, and of conspiring to interfere with the administration of the draft, though not guilty of counseling relinquishment of draft cards. Why Raskin was acquitted is unclear since juries in criminal trials are prohibited from specifying the reasons for their verdicts.

The Government had made its point.

fifteen

TOWARD FREEDOM AND BEYOND

THE four seemed no more conspirators after the verdict was announced than they had ten minutes—or ten years—earlier. Raskin, the only defendant acquitted, was the only one who appeared both stunned and saddened. He said in a stricken voice, "I feel good for myself and very, very bad for the others," before being hurried away by his lawyers. Goodman stormed out, angrily exclaiming, "The Vietnam war is an overwhelming atrocity. . . . A man has to live by his conscience," but the others convicted reacted calmly to the jury's verdict. Dr. Spock remained as matter-of-fact as ever, "My main defense was that I believed a citizen should work against a war he considers contrary to international law. The court has decided differently. I will continue to press my case."

Jane kissed him—once for his benefit (and hers), then several times for the photographers. After that, the principals in the case (except for Coffin, Wall, and Judge Ford) adjourned to the Parker House for drinking (the Spocks are moderate social drinkers) and dancing. A few spectators began to clap when the Spocks launched youthfully into a waltz. Before they had finished, the entire roomful of bar patrons—conventioneers, vacationers, traveling salesmen—were on their feet vigorously applauding for the convicted conspirator.

Their reaction was in keeping with the mail that Dr. Spock was deluged with for about eighteen months after being indicted—as many letters on peace in a month as he used to get in a year, four to one in favor of his views. (Lately the mail has tapered off somewhat, but the ratio remains the same.) Three-quarters of his critics are men, many are members of the medical establishment. The doctors favor biological explanations of Spock's politics. Some say he's senile: "You are an old man. Your arteries are becoming arteriosclerotic. You have lost touch with modern scientific medicine. . . . You can't even talk the language of a first year medical student. This deeply wounds your ego. You are tortured by your loss of attention formerly given you so you must do SOMETHING to recoup your vanishing prestige as a 'great doctor.' So you turn to flag waving groups which . . . sponsor Communist causes. Why don't you offer public apologies to your country which has treated you so bountifully?" Other doctors castigate Spock for being preadolescent: "No wonder your book on pediatrics was so good, because you are still living as a child and not as a responsible adult. YOU MAKE ME SICK AT THE STOMACH!"

Many veterans also find Spock's views particularly outrageous. One of the more polite correspondents writes: "You should live and work for a while in a Communist country to see those bastards in action. This would cure you. You look so naive and silly marching around with the kooks." Critical mothers and grandmothers use similar arguments but milder language even as they threaten "into the fire with my dog-eared copy of *Dr. Spock.*" "Having lived . . . according to the Gospel of St. Spock I'm shook. The shock of seeing you, of all people, marching on our own Capital denouncing the war in Vietnam is brutal and still unbelievable. . . . You have no right to present yourself to the millions of people who have leaned on you all these years as *just* a citizen. You are NOT just a citizen, you are the great Dr. Spock the ANSWERER, the HEALER, the STEADY HAND when young hearts leap with fright at the cry of PAIN from their beloved child, the RE-TREAD for grandparents. . . ."

Dr. Spock replies, to Red baiters: "I'm not a Communist and don't like communism." To veterans: "I too would gladly serve in a war which I believed helped my country. I too served in World War II." To nearly everyone he tries to enhance the authority of his position by citing other responsible persons and publications of like mind: "But Generals Gavin, Ridgeway, Shoup, have all declared that this is a mistaken war." Or, "There are a dozen Senators, several times as many Representatives, the *New York Times,* the *St. Louis Post-Dispatch,* Walter Lippmann, thousands of university professors [who share my views]." He concludes with the arguments he had continued to pepper Lyndon Johnson with during his entire term of office. Whether or not Dr. Spock's reasoned replies open the way for a dialogue or merely close off a monologue is hard to say; he has never convinced any of the antagonists who have written to him more than once.

Though Spock is seldom made despondent by criticism he is always buoyed by praise. Fortunately for his morale, most of his correspondents recognize a natural harmony between his views on babies and on bombs, and applaud his stand on the war: "Thank you for my four Spock babies and for your continuing dedication to life." "Dr. Spock to me is America's sanest voice not only as a wise and literate pediatrician but as an exponent of sanity in the matter of our foreign policy." "Many Americans are in your debt—because you had the courage to stand up and say what *we* feel in our hearts. In your concern for humanity you truly embody the highest ideals of your honored profession." And a prospective draftee urged, "Please never relax your efforts, Dr. Spock. After all, it was you who helped bring most of us into this world and I'm afraid a large part of the responsibility for seeing to it that there's a world for us to inhabit has also fallen on your shoulders."

Since Dr. Spock has no need to debate people who agree with him, he confines his replies to such brief acknowledgments as, "I was moved by your good letter. Every voice raised against this pointless and horrible war helps."

As the mail poured in, the Spocks ducked out to the Virgin Islands for a respite from the close confinement of the trial. Permission for the trip was granted readily by the Judge; otherwise Spock, like the others convicted, would have been confined to the continental United States, in itself a lenient restriction and an index of the convicts' probity.

In the Virgin Islands they lived on the *Carapace,* still so new that Ben, like a proud parent, beamingly showed color photographs of it during the trial recesses to interested onlookers. As usual when on the boat, their only contact with the other world was the St. Thomas news at 7:30 a.m. They deliberately have no ship-to-shore radio, which has the obvious advantages of isolation and privacy, but which prohibits immediate communication. (Ben, cruising incommunicado when his mother died in January '68 at the age of ninety-two, was unaware of her death until after the funeral.) The boat is otherwise completely equipped, and has been described by a delighted passenger as "a perfectionist's passion, well-designed with a hand-rubbed teak interior," every item in its own place. "Ben even had the food supply so well organized," says another guest, "that he could reach into the bilge and pull it out in exactly the order of the menus planned for the next two weeks."

As usual, in the mornings Jane read or painted while Ben wrote. In the afternoons they sailed, swam, and snorkeled "at least an hour a day," says Dr. Spock. "It's not very difficult to get used to the mask and the breathing tube. Then you can enter an undersea fairyland, with gorgeous coral, fish, and seaweed like ostrich plumes, partly cocoa-colored, partly violet, partly gray, and an intense peacock blue." They anchored in quiet coves for the night; Ben knows well the waters and the spots of exceptional beauty in a uniformly lush and scenic terrain. They ate dinner aboard, read by lantern light until late evening, and sometimes prepared for bed with a moonlight swim in the tranquil waters.

Then back to the familiar Boston courtroom, a world almost as unreal as the Virgin Islands, for the sentencing on July 10, 1968. Judge Ford had the last official word, for the moment. He forcefully emphasized the views of the many who opt for law and order, regardless of what the law is or how the order is maintained: "The government in essence has charged in this case what amounts to rebellion against the law, and the defendants have been found guilty of intentional and willful violation of the law. . . .

"Rebellion against the law is in the nature of treason. The law deserves our obedience. It alone can reconcile the jarring interests of all and blend into one harmonious union the discordant materials of which society is composed.

"It is important in a government such as ours that the laws be enforced, not only for the maintenance of our government but also for the protection of each one of us in our security and our safety.

"High and low, the intellectual as well as all others, must be deterred from violation of the law. . . . Where law and order stops, obviously anarchy begins. . . .

"It would be preposterous to sentence young men to jail for violation of the Selective Service Act and allow those who, as the jury found, conspired to incite Selective Service registrants to take action to violate the law and who, it is reasonable to conclude, were instrumental in inciting them to do so, to escape under the guise of free speech."

Then he sentenced Coffin, Ferber, Goodman, and Spock to two (of a maximum five) years in prison. All were fined $5,000 except Ferber, who at $1,000 was "grateful for the student discount." They left the courtroom on token $1,000 bail, pending the appeal to a higher court.

Hand in hand with Jane, the broadly smiling Dr. Spock led a procession of 300 supporters to a press conference sponsored by the Civil Liberties Legal Defense Fund (no relation to the American Civil Liberties Union). There he announced, "We agree that the law must be obeyed. But I'm still not convinced that I broke any law or was in a conspiracy. The Vietnam war is totally abominable and illegal, and I'll continue to oppose it by talking and engaging in peace and political activities. I feel a free soul and if I'm in jail I'll still feel a free soul." Suddenly, as if realizing the full import of what he was saying, he lost the calm geniality that seems perpetually his, his voice cracked with emotion, and he fairly shouted, "I say to the American people, *wake up!* Get out and do something before it's too late! Do something NOW!"

More in disgust than in anger the Reverend Coffin commented on the trial, epitomizing the views of many of the courtroom spectators, peace people, and civil libertarians: "[It] was dismal, dreary, and above all, demeaning. It was unworthy of the best in America.

"It was demeaning in the first place to the government. . . . Instead of confronting the real issues [the war's legality, the draft laws, and the First Amendment guarantees], it availed itself of the sweeping provisions and paranoid logic of an outdated conspiracy law.

"Naturally it was demeaning to us to find ourselves held to account for what we did not do, and few I imagine are the frustrations comparable to those of having to argue a big case in a small way."

Yet whether or not the Government had played its game by the spirit of the law (or of the peace people), it had played by the letter, and it had won. For all practical purposes, in the popular mind those five, even Raskin, who were remembered would be branded criminals, anti-patriots. Even if the convictions were reversed, the procedure would be likely to take a year or more, so the convictions would have a long time to sink in. An appeal, being old news, would receive much less publicity than the original trial.

But publicity, once generated, is self-feeding, and the public and the press could have made the case a *cause célèbre*. They had done so during the twenties in the Sacco-Vanzetti case, and even two decades later as the McCarthy investigations were beginning to cast a pall on political dissent. But they didn't. Maybe not enough people cared. Maybe not enough believed it was really happening. Later, as more sensational trials were conducted—the Chicago Seven, the Catonsville Nine, the Black Panthers, Angela Davis— trial of the Boston Five would seem in comparison a model of gentlemanly and legalistic decorum, hardly capable of competing for the public interest with its flamboyant successors.

An appeal has much less overt drama than even the dullest of courtroom trials, another reason for slight public interest unless the case has unusual popular appeal. Before a three-man tribunal the attorneys for both sides present a one-half to one hour oral summary of their positions and file their written reviews of the trial itself. Then they wait, indefinitely (though cases are often decided within four months), to learn of the judges' decision. The loser has the option of a final recourse, an appeal to the Supreme Court, if that Court agrees to take the case—a choice normally within its discretion. If the case is not appealed to the Supreme Court, then the decision of the appellate court is final. Either the conviction stands, or the defendants go free, or are ordered for retrial if an error has been discovered in judicial procedure. In the latter case, the prosecution may or may not choose to try the case again.

Even if the defendants are freed, they must still pay their legal costs. A person seeking to make a case of a cause must be prepared to sacrifice to principle his economic security as well as his reputation. The trial and appeal cost the Boston Five well over a quarter of a million dollars. The trial cost Dr. Spock alone $40,000 in legal fees and $12,000 in lawyers' expenses; the appeal added another $20,000 in fees and $5,000 in expenses. Said Spock ten months after being indicted, "I consider this bill very reasonable in view of the incredible amount of legal attention necessary to do a thorough job in such a case. Leonard Boudin has given his main attention to my case since January 5th [1968]. He and his partner Victor Rabinowitz, a partner of a Boston firm [Allan R. Rosenberg], three other young lawyers and two secretaries were busy from 8:00 a.m. to midnight throughout the four weeks of the trial. (I know because I was often with them.)"

One-fourth of the legal fee was supplied by contributions from peace groups and other well-wishers. All but $20,000 of the remainder was raised though an appeal organized by Marie Runyon, a devoted friend from SANE days and a professional fund raiser for a variety of radical causes.

On January 7, 1969 the appeal was filed before Chief Judge Bailey Aldrich of the U.S. First Circuit Court of Appeals and Judges Edward M. McEntee and Frank M. Coffin (no relation to defendant Coffin). Six months later, a year and a day after the sentencing, came the decision. Judges Aldrich and McEntee ruled that by submitting Special Findings to the jury, Judge Ford committed a "prejudical error" and the verdicts would be set aside. Spock and Ferber were freed. Goodman and Coffin were ordered retried. (On October 22, 1970 the Government dropped the charges against these two, claiming that with the elimination of Spock and Ferber the remaining evidence and testimony did not warrant retrial.) Although he agreed with his colleagues that the Special Findings were in error, Judge Coffin would have acquitted all the defendants.

The majority opinion held that the Government had not violated

the defendants' First Amendment rights by prosecuting them. They
had legally expressed opposition to the war, but their suggested
means of ending it "encompassed both legal and illegal activity
without any clear indication, initially, as to who intended what."
The Court denied that conspiracy must be secret: "Openness does
not immunize an agreement. . . . A group of vigilantes agreeing
in the town square to solicit cohorts to call out a lynch mob would
not be absolved because their agreement was open." A conspiracy
indictment is justifiable because "to wait for the substantive
offense may be to wait too long. Congress has the right to prefer
registrants to felons."

Was there an agreement? asked the Court. Yes, in the "Call to
Resist," despite the defendants' claims, for "it could not occur
without parents or active participants in a joint undertaking."
Spock, Coffin, and Goodman were implicated. But was their purpose
illegal? Partly, said the Court. "The Call" had a double aspect,
to denounce Government policy and to encourage resistance to the
Selective Service Act.

Was there a specifically illegal intent? Yes, on the parts of
Coffin and Goodman. Their actions and speeches directly encouraged
civil disobedience in the form of draft resistance. No, in Spock's
case, for his speech simply condemned the war and the draft and
didn't counsel. "The mere fact . . . that he hoped the frequent
stating of his views might give young men 'courage to take active
steps in draft resistance' . . . is a natural consequence of vigorous
speech" and is protected under the First Amendment. So were
his actions, which "contributed nothing" to the turning-in of draft
cards. Spock should be freed.

So should Ferber, for though he assisted in the collection and
burning of draft cards, his "Time to Say No" sermon did not counsel
draft resistance or the surrender of draft cards. He was not a
part of the conspiracy charged because he signed neither the "Call
to Resist" nor the cover letter and did not attend the October 2
press conference.

However, ruled the Court, the lower court verdicts must be set
aside and a new trial ordered for Goodman and Coffin (whom there
would have been sufficient evidence to convict, in a properly run
trial) because Judge Ford's submission of Special Findings to the
jury was clearly prejudicial: "In a criminal case a court may not
order the jury to return a verdict of guilty, no matter how over-

whelming the evidence of guilt." The basic reason? "Put simply," agreed the Court with the defense attorneys, "the right to be tried by a jury of one's peers finally exacted from the king would be meaningless if the king's judges could call the turn. . . . A juror, wishing to acquit, may be formally catechized. By a progression of questions each of which seems to require an answer unfavorable to the defendant, a reluctant juror may be led to vote for a conviction" which he might otherwise have resisted. "The jury, as the conscience of the community, must be permitted to look at more than logic."

There it was, free on a technicality, exactly the sort of decision the four didn't want (though they were glad to be free), for it still skirted the fundamental issues in the case.

Dissenting Judge Coffin, who looked to logic and beyond, agreed with the defendants. To many critics of both the prosecution itself and the majority decision of the Court of Appeals, Judge Coffin's arguments strike at the heart not only of the Spock case but of all prosecutions in which the club of conspiracy is poised over the freedoms of speech, assembly, and petition guaranteed in the First Amendment. Judge Coffin's strategy was to "first identify the hazards to individual freedom of expression and association," then to consider "whether society can adequately protect its security in less constraining ways" than by applying the conspiracy doctrine.

He supported the defense argument that the defendants' actions and speeches, all public, were evidence not of a conspiracy but of a common concern: "We face here something quite different from an indictment for an overt promotion of a specific event for an overriding illegal purpose. Here we confront a 'conspiracy' where (1) the effort was completely public; (2) the issues were all in the public domain; (3) the group was ill-defined, shifting, with many affiliations; (4) the purposes in the 'agreement' are both legal and illegal; and (5) the need for additional evidence to inculpate . . . is recognized." This is the first time, said Judge Coffin, that conspiracy doctrine has been applied in such circumstances, and it dangerously extends that doctrine. The majority decision did not guarantee to prevent hazards to individual rights which might subsequently result, and it failed to show why the most restrictive charge—conspiracy—was essential.

The criteria established by Judges Aldrich and McEntee for

determining whether a signer of "The Call" was a conspirator have repressive implications, said Judge Coffin. "To say that prior or subsequent ambiguous statements change the color of the litmus is to say that while one exercise of First Amendment rights is protected, two are not." To say that committing an illegal act (such as encouraging the turning-in of a draft card) renders the original agreement illegal "is to say simply that the subsequent commission of one crime becomes suddenly the commission of two crimes." To say that if a legal act is performed to promote an illegal action advocated in "The Call" it "renders retrospectively conspiratorial the earlier protected ambiguous advocacy is to say that two rights make a wrong. For example, were the janitor of Arlington Church to have signed the 'Call' and subsequently to have volunteered his services to tidy the pews for the turn-in, he would have metamorphosed into a conspirator."

Judge Coffin condemned this "delayed fuse approach" to determining conspiratorial guilt in the signing of such manifestos as "The Call," for it would have, he said, "a pronounced chilling effect —indeed that of a sub-zero blast—on all kinds of efforts to sway public opinion."

"We should be slow to grant grudgingly today what may become license tomorrow," said Judge Coffin, claiming that the conspiracy doctrine under which the defendants were tried was vague, overly broad, and inapplicable to their case because of First Amendment guarantees. They could have been tried under a less restrictive alternative for their separate substantive offenses, or for a "narrow, discrete conspiracy" which would have served the Government's interest equally well. The Court should examine "the utility of the rifle before resort is had to the shotgun."

Judge Coffin also explained that the Court made no clear distinction on the basis of the evidence as to why it freed Spock and Ferber and yet ordered Coffin and Goodman retried. Consistent application of its reasoning should have led it to uphold the convictions of Spock and Ferber as well. Acquitting them, he said, "is the product of its own generosity rather than the inevitable result of its rationale. Were this only a disagreement over the application of legal principles, perhaps there would not be so much cause for concern. But this is a landmark case and no one, I take it, supposes that this will be the last attempt by the Government to use the conspiracy weapon. The Government has cast a wide net and caught only two fish. My objection is not that more were not caught but that the Government can try again on another day in another court and the court's rationale provides no meaningful basis for predicting who will find themselves within the net. Finally, there is the greater danger that the casting of the net has scared away many whom the Government has no right to catch."

Thus Judge Coffin raised the fundamental issue of whether or not such a political trial should be held at all. Have the defendants and others like them the right not to be tried for dissent? If their dissent falls within the First Amendment guarantees, implied the Judge, they indeed have that right.

And if it doesn't? In "On Not Prosecuting Civil Disobedience" (*New York Review of Books,* June 6, 1968) Yale law professor Ronald Dworkin offers an answer: "In the United States prosecutors have discretion whether to enforce criminal laws in particular cases. . . . There are, at least *prima facie,* some good reasons for not prosecuting those who disobey the draft laws out of conscience. One is the obvious reason that they act out of better motives than those who break the law out of greed or a desire to subvert the government. Another is the practical reason that our society suffers a loss if it punishes a group that includes—as the group of draft dissenters does—some of its most thoughtful and loyal citizens."

Indeed constitutional mechanisms exist for ensuring independence (such as the Boston Five exercised) without anarchy, in part through the Bill of Rights, in part through the separation of executive, legislative, and judicial powers. They exist if imposed and enforced by the three branches of the Government according to the spirit of the Supreme Law of the Land. But the letter of the law, like the letter of the Bible, can be invoked at will or whim of the prosecutor. The climate of opinion may well determine which letter of which law is invoked at which time.

Today, as the voices of dissent grow louder, the voices that would quell them grow louder too. They imply that the penetrating protests of those who would end the war drown out the unspoken but fervent acceptance by the Silent Majority of the conduct of the war in Southeast Asia as it spreads from Vietnam to Cambodia to Laos and. . . . They imply that news analyses favorable to the dissenters' point of view may require policing of the mass media. They impugn the loyalty, the intellect, even the masculinity of the "effete snobs" among the critics, termed by Vice President Agnew "the Spock-marked generation."

Other evidence disputes the view that dissent is being promoted by underage rabble rousers and outside agitators. Sweden and Canada harbor increasing numbers of American deserters, estimated at over 354,000 between 1967 and 1971; draft dodgers; and resisters, estimated in Canada in 1971 at between 40,000 and 70,000. Even the U.S. armed services (except the Marines) seemed in a short-lived experiment in 1971 to be admitting some of the amenities of civilian life (such as go-go girls and beer on base and a relaxation of petty rules of military discipline) in an effort to make the GI's more willing to participate in a war labeled by one high-ranking American officer in Saigon as "a poison in the veins of the U.S. Army." Growing military antipathy toward the war is revealed by sharp racial tensions and a severe decline in morale and discipline. One evidence of this is the estimate of General Creighton W. Abrams, commander of U.S. forces in Vietnam, that 65,000 GI's were involved in drug abuse in 1970 (about 20 percent of troop strength), though another Defense Department official estimates the military drug users at 50-56 percent, double the 1968 percentage.

So, with their beliefs confirmed that the war is tearing apart not only the country but the military, dissenters and commentators on dissent continue to rely on their constitutional guarantees. Though prosecutions for various forms of expression of dissent continue, from wearing black armbands in school, to publishing radical newspapers, to destroying military or draft board property, to symbolically or actually protesting military orders, dissent does not appear to have been forced underground. On the contrary, dissenters seem to take heart from one another's efforts—and prosecutions.

Dr. Spock, neither martyr nor precedent setter as a result of his trial, has given dissenters much heart and support. Called by Judge Coffin "a man of great public visibility," visibility enhanced rather than diminished by the trial, he continues to exercise his First Amendment guarantees as an elder statesman of the peace movement. Through the power of his speeches, writings, and personal presence he continues to work to end the Indochina war.

For the Civil Liberties Legal Defense Fund Dr. Spock barnstorms the country on the alternate months when he is not sailing. The CLLDF, formed in response to the indictment of the Boston Five, is an organization designed to raise money to defend what it claims are "the political prisoners of the Administration's War against Dissent"—conscientious draft resisters, the Chicago Seven, the D[ow] C[hemical] Nine, military dissenters against the war.

His speeches in 1969, '70, and '71 have been on "Dissent and Social Change." Dr. Spock typically discusses the legal aspects of dissent and the history and utility of civil disobedience. He makes it clear that dissent is a matter of individual conscience and that he is "opposed to violence on principle," including disrupting classes, throwing rocks, taunting police, and carrying obscene signs. For, he says, such violence brutalizes perpetrator, victim, and cause. But is dissent necessary? "You're damn right," he tells his audiences. "We have a country that could be heaven on earth, but instead it has unnecessary poverty, discrimination against the blacks and the poor, and the continuous possibility of nuclear warfare. If you agree, find the form of dissent that suits you and stick to it. If not, that's your choice."

Though their theme is similar to those speeches which provoked the indictment, the audiences have become much larger (ranging from 1,000 to 2,500) and much more enthusiastic. Dr. Spock observes, "In some ways the whole episode—indictment and trial—has been marvelous. It's given me new friends and a whole new lease on life. I'm reaching more people and they're paying more attention to what I say as a peace person. Typically I now get two standing ovations for the same speech for which I used to get none. University groups pay $1,000 or $2,000 to the Civil Liberties Legal Defense Fund for talks for which middle-aged peace groups used to pay $500. University administrations consider me controversial enough to be interesting, but not too dangerous. Young people opposed to war call me 'beautiful.'

"But my mother taught me there was nothing more deteriorating to character than too much adulation. I hear her saying, 'Benny, this is not good for you. . . .' "

That Dr. Spock has had an enormous influence on the young and on their parents, not only through his advice in *Baby and Child Care* but as their confederate in the peace movement, is undeniable.

But when the Indochina war ends, as even a war of attrition eventually must, or when the United States extricates itself from the Far East, what then? Will Dr. Spock, ever the activist, be content to have no cause except the cause of children? Will he be content to retire with his wife to an existence of sailing and snorkeling in the Virgin Islands, writing an occasional tract on child care for diversion? It seems unlikely. When asked directly about his future plans, he smiles broadly, "Oh, there'll be something to do." Indeed there is; as this goes to press he is running for President (see Appendix). Dr. Spock has said, "Everything that is wrong about the world is caused by a lack of moral conviction and moral initiative," and for the moralist there is always evil in the universe to be combated.

The moralistic Dr. Spock refuses to accede to former Supreme Court Justice Abe Fortas's cynical assertion that "Most of our people recognize war as a savage inevitability in a world which is still far from being universally civilized." For the gentle Dr. Spock, war is savage. For the idealistic Dr. Spock, war is not inevitable, as his speeches and actions of the past decade have indicated. The articulate Dr. Spock will continue to raise his voice in the wilderness of United States foreign policy as long as he is convinced that his country is engaged anywhere in military operations offensive both in the political and moral senses. But he has also begun to speak out more vociferously about what he considers evils at home too—racial injustice, second-rate education and medical care for most, pollution, overpopulation, repressive aspects of the Government (such as the FBI, and the House Internal Security Subcommittee that blacklisted him in 1970).

He is likely to be listened to, for Dr. Spock's dual reputation in pediatrics and peace is recognized by countless millions the world over. However, not everyone is aware of both facets. A teenage girl, already a veteran of a number of Spock-led peace marches, noticed a copy of *Baby and Child Care* in the home of a friend who had recently become a mother. "Oh," asked the girl in awe, "is that really by *the* Dr. Spock? How is he on babies?"

He is on babies, as on adults, a man for all seasons, who has weathered them with strength and grace.

APPENDIX

O N November 27, 1971, Dr. Spock became the stand-in candidate for President on the Peoples Party. He had been "convinced," he says, "since 1966 that a new political movement must be built, to the left of the Democratic Party but not as doctrinaire as the Socialist Workers Party or the Progressive Labor Party or the Communist Party." This resulted in his efforts on behalf of the National Conference for New Politics in 1966 and 1967, and his support of the Peace and Freedom Party in 1968.

In that year, at Marcus Raskin's invitation, he also joined the national committee of the New Party, which had been started at the 1968 Democratic convention in futile hopes that Eugene McCarthy would be their nominee. In 1969 the New Party, chaired by Dick Gregory and Antioch College president James Dixon, consisted of small groups in such cities as Dayton, Tucson, Seattle, and Miami, before which Dr. Spock spoke. Internal disagreements caused two changes of national leadership within a year, and at a convention in Tucson in June 1970, author and critic Gore Vidal and Spock were named honorary co-chairmen. Although they had no executive power they subsidized the party's Washington office.

As a result of three conventions in March, July, and November 1971, over 200 delegates from various political groups and parties, such as the New Party, the Peace and Freedom Party, and the Independent New Mexican Party, agreed on a platform and a new name, first "The Coalition," later the "Peoples Party." At the November 1971 convention in Dallas, the delegates proposed a slate of stand-in candidates for national office, subject to change in the event that desired nominees such as Eugene McCarthy or Fred Harris might defect from the Democratic Party by mid-1972 and would agree to support the Peoples Party platform.

Nicholas Johnson, Federal Communications Commission director, Ralph Nader, and others refused the nomination. Spock himself was not eager to run, explaining that he was "too old and not particularly credible in the American pattern." He would have preferred a nominee such as Shirley Chisholm, "who has the ideological advantages for us of being black, poor, and a woman. . . . But the convention wouldn't nominate a current Democrat. And the people whom I best know and respect in the Peoples Party, disheartened at the prospect of an unknown candidate, begged me to run. Since I agreed with them about the unknown, I reluctantly gave in. I'll keep on doing what I've been doing for five years—making speeches. . . ." Julius Hobson, a black educator and sociologist from Washington, D.C., was slated as Spock's running mate, and cabinet selections included Gore Vidal for Secretary of State; Sidney Lens, Chicago labor leader and peace activist, for Secretary of Labor; David Schoenbrun, lecturer and former CBS correspondent, for Secretary of Communication; and Richard Falk, Professor of International Law at Princeton, for Secretary of Humanities.

The Peoples Party platform in November 1971 stressed a decentralized power structure in government at all levels. True to its name, the Party believed that the people themselves, minority communities in particular, should have the greatest possible control over neighborhood police, welfare, zoning, housing, transportation, community courts with citizen judges, and schools—parents, teachers, and students, too, should be on local school boards. Workers and consumers should control the industries, in "hiring management, organizing production, and determining the kinds, quality and amounts of goods produced." The Party envisioned the federal government largely as the dispenser of funds (some derived from a graduated income tax) for: a guaranteed family allowance of $6,500 for four people; child care centers for preschool, elementary, and high school youth; free medical care, including access to birth control and abortion, to all; nonprofit hospitals, convalescent homes, and drug companies. The Party maintained that the federal government should withdraw military aid and troops from all other countries; it should initiate unilateral nuclear disarmament, and domestic agricultural policies to aid the small farmer.

The Peoples Party pledged to fight discrimination against women, minorities, homosexuals, ex-convicts, senior citizens, and youth in employment, education, the law, and other aspects of community life. It would therefore eliminate I.Q. scores, amount of schooling, or maximum age as criteria for employment; promote repeal of sexually discriminatory state laws concerning jury service, property rights, and sexual relations; encourage community support of alternate or "free" schools and flexible curricula adapted to students from varied backgrounds and to the "needs of real life," designed to foster not middle class conformist bureaucrats but "the growth of the individual in awareness of the environment, of mankind's potentialities and of the self."

The Peoples Party advocated a variety of legal reforms, primarily to make the judicial and correctional systems nondiscriminatory and less punitive. It would eliminate capital punishment, preventive detention, domestic spying, wire tapping, and undercover agents; and it would repeal laws against "victimless crimes" involving sex, pornography, alcohol, and possession and sale of marijuana. It would promote rehabilitative rather than punitive correctional institutions.

Typical of the platforms of parties of all political hues, the Peoples Party offered a blend of vision and revision with few specific suggestions for implementation; typical of radical or reform parties, the Peoples Party promised much more for the minority groups, the disadvantaged, the victims of discrimination, than for the establishment. Lacking in funds and wide leadership and support, the Peoples Party expected that with Spock as a candidate it might claim 5 percent of the popular vote, but that if it could run a prominent, experienced political leader it might attract as much as 15 percent of the vote and thereby be a significant influence in the outcome of the 1972 election. The value of minority parties often lies not in the votes they receive in any given election, but in the fact that they generate and publicize controversial or innovative ideas which may later become political orthodoxy. Thus for the Peoples Party, typical of every party, hope of influence if not of victory sprang eternal.

FOOTNOTES

Foreword

[1] (p. xv) *How Literary Biographers Use Their Subjects' Works: A Study of Biographical Method, 1865–1962* (University of Michigan, 1963).

[2] (p. xviii) For what turned out to be three years to completing the research and writing. An additional year of rewriting was accomplished while I was again teaching.

Chapter 5

[1] (p. 110) Other consultants for the first edition of *Baby and Child Care* were: pediatricians C. Anderson Aldrich, M.D., Clement B. P. Cobb, M.D., Frederick C. Hunt, M.D., Milton I. Levine, M.D., Samuel Z. Levine, M.D., Carl Smith, M.D., and Myron E. Wegman, M.D.; psychiatrist Marion Stranahan, M.D.; surgeon William Heroy, M.D.; ophthalmologist Gordon M. Bruce, M.D.; orthopedic surgeon John R. Cobb, M.D.; toxicologist Harry Gold, M.D.; urologist Hamden C. Moody, M.D.; educators Barbara Biber, Ph.D., Mary S. Fisher, Ph.D., and Jessie Stanton; dietitian Betty N. Richmond; adoptions expert Sophie van S. Theis, A.B., L.H.D.; nurse Velma Davies, R.N. Except for Jane Spock and Dr. Milton Levine, the consultants for the second edition (1957) were different: pediatricians David Friedman, M.D., Donald Jackson, M.D., John Kaster, M.D., John Kennell, M.D., John Montgomery, M.D., Charles O'Regan,

M.D., Samuel Spector, M.D., and William Wallace, M.D.; child psychiatrists Abram Blau, M.D., Marian Putnam, M.D., and John Reinhart, M.D.; toxicologist Irving Sunshine, M.D.; surgeon Edwin Gerrish, M.D.; child therapist Mary Hamm Flummerfelt. Consultants for the third edition (1968) not already cited above include pediatrician Lewis Fraad, M.D.; surgeon Ralph De Palma, M.D.; ophthalmologists Edwin Eigner, M.D., and Hiram Hardesty, M.D.

Chapter 6

[1] (p. 124) All of these characteristics combine to make a style that is hard to translate faithfully. Foreign translations usually keep the words relevant to their own cultures, but miss the music. Typical is the Farsi edition, translated by Princess Asharf Pahlavi, sister of the Shah of Iran, as *Mother and Child*, in 1955 (Persian year 1344). Dr. Spock begins: "Trust yourself. You know more than you think you do. Soon you're going to have a baby. Maybe you have him already. You're happy and excited, but if you haven't had much experience, you wonder whether you are going to know how to do a good job." Princess Pahlavi begins: "Trust yourself. Surely you know more than you think about having a baby." She soon undercuts these reassuring words with the worrisome, "Someday you will have a baby, and maybe now you have a child. Although this will be a cause of your happiness, maybe not having any experience about this will be a cause of your worry and whether you would be able to do your duty as you should." The translator emphasizes the very things Dr. Spock so carefully plays down: duty, worry, inexperience.

In other instances, the customary formality of all written Farsi and significant differences between Iranian and American cultures make impossible a translation of either matter or manner. In discussing a "Sensible Diet" Dr. Spock says: "A serious-minded mother who has the mistaken idea that vitamins are the whole show and that starches are inferior, serves her child carrot salad and grapefruit for supper. The poor fellow can't get enough calories out of that to satisfy a rabbit. A plump mother from a plump family is ashamed of her child's scrawniness, serves him only rich foods. These depress his appetite further." The translator interprets: "The mother who thinks vitamins are the most important ingredients in food and so for this reason gives less of starches to her child, except for slowing down his growth won't get any results. And also the mother who is unhappy because of her child's thinness and wants to make him gain weight by giving him fats and starches will cause him to undereat."

Grapefruit isn't eaten in Iran; carrots are seldom served, so they are rightly omitted in the Farsi. Though the formal language of the translation could not accommodate the idiomatic "the whole show," or the casual minimization, "[not] enough calories to satisfy a rabbit," it could have re-created the "serious-minded mother," her plump counterpart, and their pathetic offspring. Instead, generalizations about abstractions have killed off Spock's living, breathing family, the way they get along together, and the author's attitude toward them.

2 (p. 127) Dr. Margaret A. Ribble's *The Rights of Infants: Early Psychological Needs and Their Satisfaction* (New York: Columbia University Press, 1943) is a psychoanalytically oriented predecessor to the aspects of infant psychology discussed in *Baby and Child Care,* and fully compatible with Dr. Spock's views in 1946. Dr. Ribble claimed that infants have a right to develop their instincts fully. They are entitled, she said, to a full measure of tender loving care, for on "the primary relationship between the child and the mother . . . the child's future emotional and social relations are based." From this approach she discussed sucking, sleeping, eliminating, life rhythms and artificial schedules, the gratifying (as opposed to the thwarting) of babies, early emotional development, and the father's role. Although the 110-page book was required reading for Barnard College freshmen in the mid-1940's, and was intended for parents—at least, for educated ones—it never sold widely to the general public. Dr. Spock says he found that the book's emphasis on the deep needs of infants, without folksy specifics, made the conscientious, intellectual kind of mother who bought it worry about whether she had the qualities and understanding to meet her baby's needs.

3 (p. 127) The book on child development most compatible with Dr. Spock's is psychotherapist Selma H. Fraiberg's *The Magic Years: Understanding and Handling the Problems of Early Childhood* (New York: Scribner's, 1959). Although not as widely known as Spock's, it is highly esteemed by parents and professionals, including Spock himself. Employing with sane and witty articulateness the psychoanalytic knowledge of ego development, Dr. Fraiberg tries to "give insight into the mental life of the pre-school child and derive principles of child-rearing from the facts of development as well as the expectations of our culture." From this perspective she discusses subjects such as toilet training, separation anxiety, fears, the Oedipus complex, sex education, discipline, and "The Acquisition of Moral Values."

4 (p. 142) In "Medical Students: Healers Become Activists" (*Saturday Review,* August 16, 1969), Michael G. Michaelson reports: "The life expectancy of Negroes in 1965 was seven years less than that of whites. The non-white child under five years has a death rate twice that of the white child. Between the ages of thirty-five and forty-four, non-

whites have a death rate 150 percent higher than whites; between forty-five and fifty-four, 94 percent; between fifty-five and sixty-four, 72 percent. Non-white maternal mortality was twice the white rate before World War II; since the war it has risen to four times the white rate. The infant mortality rate of Negro children in Mississippi or the northern city slum is comparable to that of Ecuador; nationally it is better—nearly as good as Costa Rica's" (p. 54).

[5] (p. 145) The above observations about class differences in child rearing, which often imply race differences as well, are verified by the studies of Allison Davis and Robert Havighurst, "Social Class and Color Differences in Child-Rearing," *American Sociological Review*, 1946, XI, pp. 698–710; Ann and John Fischer, "The New Englanders of Orchard Town, U.S.A.," in *Six Cultures: Studies of Child Rearing*, ed. Beatrice B. Whiting (New York: John Wiley, 1963), pp. 871–1010; and in Leigh Minturn and William W. Lambert, *Mothers of Six Cultures: Antecedents of Child Rearing* (New York: John Wiley, 1964). See also Joanne Dann, "Wanted: A Dr. Spock for Black Mothers," *New York Times Magazine*, April 18, 1971, pp. 78–80, 87–88.

Chapter 7

[1] (p. 157) The potential fruitfulness of the Inborn Temperament Study is demonstrated by the still-continuing research begun in 1956 by psychiatrists Alexander Thomas and Stella Chess, and pediatrician Herbert Birch. Its central aims, as reported by the researchers in *Temperament and Behavior Disorders in Children* (New York University Press, 1968), are identical with Dr. Spock's study: to define objectively temperamental characteristics in children and to delineate "the contributions which such characteristics made to both normal and aberrant behavioral development." Both studies were longitudinal, considering the temperaments of a given group of children from birth through adolescence.

But there were some significant differences. The Thomas study carefully selected children from a homogeneous sociocultural and economic group of parents so as to avoid attributing to temperament characteristics which were really environmental. (See *Behavioral Individuality in Early Childhood* [New York University Press, 1963.]) The Spock study drew on Rochester's entire population, assuredly somewhat homogeneous in being white and largely Protestant, but quite varied in education, cultural level, and income. Thus even if its data had been more thoroughly analyzed, the analysis could not have easily discriminated between innate temperamental differences and the effects of varied environments.

Dr. Spock's research suited his own temperament in being flexible and informal about methodology, which meant (among other things) that the study as he conducted it would have been impossible to replicate; consequently, its findings could not have been validated. Some of the information Spock's study obtained from the mothers about "Stability," "Warmth," "Tension," "Drive," "Cruelty," and general personality when the babies were nine and eighteen months old was objective: "Hours of night sleep," "Did he ever have a playpen?" Much more of it depended on subjective answers in which facts were confused with interpretations: "Does he like to get hold of the spoon?" "Is he cautious when you hand him something new?" "Easy or difficult to manage?" "Demandingness from mother?"

Although the Thomas study asked the mothers (all of whom used *Baby and Child Care*) of the 136 children they studied similar questions about many of the same aspects of the children's development that Dr. Spock studied, they took pains not only to objectify the answers, but to make sure that the answers of each parent were directly comparable. Thus when Thomas's interviewers asked the mothers, "What did the baby do the first time he was given vitamin drops?" they were not content with the simple—and subjective—answer, "He loved it" or "He couldn't stand it" which would have been acceptable in the Spock study. The Thomas study probed and prodded until it obtained objective and therefore measurable answers: "Did the baby let it dribble out or did he swallow it? Did he lick his lips? Did he smile or have any other facial expression? Did he whine or cry? Did he turn his head toward or away from the dropper or spoon? Did he open or close his mouth at the approach of the dropper or spoon? Was any difference in response observed by changing the type or form of preparation used, or by using an admixture with another food?"

As a cross-check on the parents' observations, twenty-three children were randomly selected from the total population of Thomas's study and within two weeks of the parental interview were observed directly by two independent observers, each of whom was unaware of the data obtained either from the other or from the parents. The ratings turned out to be uniformly congruent. Except for the initial ratings of the newborns, no such cross-checks existed in the Spock study and would not have been possible because of Spock's chance and transient personnel. The Thomas study had constant observers, thereby assuring some constancy of rating.

The Spock study was not pursued long enough, and the data were insufficiently analyzed to make further comparisons of method. However, what might have been discovered in Rochester, given a more stringent research design, more money, and more time, is demonstrated in some of Thomas's conclusions. Dr. Thomas and colleagues eventually arrived inductively at nine common categories of manifestations of inborn temperament which were sufficiently variable to permit comparison among individuals: activity level, rhythmicity, approach or withdrawal (to any new stimulus—food, people, procedures, etc.), adaptability, intensity of reactions, threshold of responsiveness (does a mild or an intense stimulus have to be applied to evoke a response from the child?), quality of mood (pleasant vs. unpleasant, friendly vs. unfriendly behavior, etc.), distractibility, and attention span and persistence. On the basis of these characteristics, the researchers have concluded (among other things) that "[Because] each child has an individual pattern of primary reactivity, identifiable in early infancy and persistent through later periods of life . . . there can be no universally valid set of rules that will work equally well for all children everywhere. . . . When parents learn that their role in the shaping of their child is not an omnipotent one, guilt feelings may lessen, hostility and pressures may tend to disappear, and positive restructuring of the parent-child interaction can become possible."

The Thomas study has proven fruitful in many dimensions. The researchers have written one book, *Your Child Is a Person* (see Chapter 6, pp. 147–148) to convey their conclusions to parents, and several other books and numerous articles to communicate their findings and methodology to behavioral scientists and people in the various helping professions.

INDEX